Speaking of Flowers

Speaking of Flowers

STUDENT
MOVEMENTS
AND THE
MAKING AND
REMEMBERING
OF 1968
IN MILITARY
BRAZIL

Victoria Langland

DUKE UNIVERSITY PRESS

Durham and London 2013

© 2013 Duke University Press

All rights reserved

Printed in the United States

of America on acid-free paper ∞

Typeset in Quadraat by

Keystone Typesetting, Inc.

Library of Congress Cataloging-in-Publication Data

Langland, Victoria.

Speaking of flowers : student movements and the making and

remembering of 1968 in military Brazil / Victoria Langland.

pages cm

Includes bibliographical references and index.

ISBN 978-0-8223-5298-3 (cloth : alk. paper)

ISBN 978-0-8223-5312-6 (pbk. : alk. paper)

1. Student movements—Brazil—History.

2. Nineteen sixty-eight, A.D.

3. Collective memory—Brazil. I. Title.

LA558.7.L36 2013

378.1′9810981—dc23

2013004650

FOR NICO

Contents

Acknowledgments

Offering formal thanks to the many people and institutions who have assisted me in this project over the years is my own small act of commemoration: a celebration of others' immense generosity, and, by extension, a reflection on this book's long history. I am thrilled to have the opportunity to do so.

Some of the questions that first motivated this project emerged in discussions with my fellow graduate students seeking to organize a union at Yale. As we inquired into the history of graduate students' interactions with the university, it became apparent that there was no organic student memory of our collective past, even of relatively recent events, since students by definition regularly graduate or move on to other pursuits, and we realized that this pattern led us to constantly renegotiate previously hard-earned rights. Our fierce debates within the union about the best methods for organizing others and institutionalizing a kind of student memory sparked my original interest in the mechanisms and uses of cross-generational student memory. My curiosity deepened during an exploratory research trip to Rio de Janeiro in 1998, the thirtieth anniversary of the student protests of 1968 and a moment when the university students I met were deeply concerned about both remembering the student movement past and drawing connections to its present. As I joined them in an all-night meeting to plan the reenactment of a famous protest march of 1968, I witnessed them taking great pains to both learn and divulge the history of this event and the military regime under which it took place and to tie it to the ongoing strike at numerous federal universities. It was then that I began to consider seriously the special constraints and importance of student memory under conditions of dictatorship, censorship, and strict limits on civic action and soon thereafter embarked on this book.

These two early sources and scenarios of inspiration—the Yale campus and a lively gathering of Brazilian activists—point to two critical centers of support for me and this project: the team of scholars who mentored me through graduate school and helped me write a doctoral dissertation on this topic, and the many figures in Brazil who made this research possible. At Yale I was privileged to receive the incomparable guidance and warm friendship of Gil Joseph and Stuart Schwartz, who together offered the perfect blend of constructive criticism, brilliant insight, and unflagging encouragement that allowed me to undertake and complete this project. I also benefited enormously from the famously detailed comments of Jean-Christophe Agnew, the instruction (both inside and outside the seminar room) of Emilia Viotti da Costa, Glenda Gilmore, and Nancy Cott, and the exuberant creativity of Seth Fein. And I am forever grateful to the late, much-beloved Patricia Pessar, who often chimed in with her own sage words of advice or encouragement whenever I called on Gil at some sticky moment. Her ability to blend fierce intellectual mettle and deep personal warmth always made her a welcome presence. Finally, I benefited enormously from having brilliant fellow graduate students (who have now gone on to become brilliant colleagues at other institutions), who read my work, shared their own with me, and generally made me a better student and scholar. Thank you, Nara Milanich, Amy Rasmussen, Mark Overmyer-Velazquez, Amy Chazkel, Andrea Becksvoort, and many more too numerous to mention here.

In Brazil I never ceased to be amazed at the kindness and expertise of the archivists who helped me hunt down a wide variety of materials and then earnestly welcomed me each day as I spent weeks and sometimes months hunkered over papers at my assigned desk. Special thanks go to the team at the Arquivo Público do Estado do Rio de Janeiro, who helped me tirelessly on this project for a very extended period only to read one day in the *Jornal do Brasil* that I had decided to jettison it all and write instead about the hijacking of city bus no. 174. Their dismayed faces the day they showed me this totally erroneous story—the product of two overly inventive journalists I spoke to while photographing the improvised memorial at the hijacking site—demonstrated more than anything else how invested they had rightfully become in "my" research project, and how much all of us who do archival work owe to professionals like them. At the Arquivo Nacional in Rio, Sátiro Nunes and Marcelo Siqueira deserve particular mention: Sátiro for his astounding knowledge of the breadth and depth of the archives and his legendary ability to remember the face, name, and project of every researcher who has ever crossed his path, and Marcelo for his detailed understanding of the military period and the student movement's role during it. I also want to thank the skilled archivists at the Arquivo Público do Estado de São Paulo, the Arquivo Edgard Leurenroth, and the Centro de Pesquisas e Documentação Histórica of the Fundação Getúlio Vargas. Professor Maria Paula Araújo and her colleagues at Universidade Federal do Rio de Janeiro kindly let me access their collection at the Laboratorio de Estudo do Tempo Presente, while Angélica Müller and the helpful staff at the Projeto Memória do Movimento Estudantil allowed me to peruse their collection even before it was officially opened. Any richness in my sources is owed entirely to these individuals and the institutions for whom they work as well as to the generous and at times courageous figures who collected and then donated their materials in the first place and to those who demanded and continue to demand that official documents be released to the public. I hope the remaining military and government files on this period become publicly available soon.

Others in Brazil have offered me their intellects, experiences, and friendships over the years, making this book progressively better and my journeys to Brazil feel more like homecomings. Daniel Aarão Reis Filho and Maria Paula Araujo saw promise in me and in this project from its inception, when I was still an unsteady graduate student unsure of how to proceed. I am grateful for their early and sustained support and especially for Paula's easy, all-embracing friendship. Since then I have benefited enormously from the wisdom and collegiality of Carlos Fico, João Roberto Martins Filho, Marcelo Ridenti, Alessandra Carvalho, Samarone Lima, Samantha Viz Quadrat, Antônio Sérgio Alfredo Guimarães, Nadya Araujo Guimarães, Lucileide Cardoso, Luiz Nova, and Ligia Mefano. I am also deeply appreciative of the many people who allowed me to interview them for this book, interviews that sometimes took place over several days and that demonstrated real generosity of time and attention on their parts. Throughout the many years during which this book took shape Simone Dubeux Berardo Carneiro da Cunha has been my most beloved Rio sister, to whose Laranjeiras home and rede I always return for long talks and jointly cooked claypot meals. Her many contributions to this book, from the acquisition of books and photos to the offering of keen anthropological insights, are too numerous to mention. Patricia Pinho and Gilson Chagas have similarly taken me in when I most needed refuge and family in Salvador, have helpfully discussed my work with me numerous times, and now continue to offer their insights and solidarity from New York.

Crossing the boundaries between the United States and Brazil is the rich cohort of Brasilianistas, as U.S. American scholars who work on Brazil are called, whom I have encountered on both sides of the border at conferences, archives, and seminars and who have improved this book enormously with their suggestions and insights. James Green has been a real gift in this regard, someone who embraced me as a valued colleague with something to contribute long before I had any idea what I was doing. He has graciously invited me to join him on numerous panels and projects and, most laboriously, has commented on my work multiple times, always offering his wonderful blend of critique and countenance. Tom Holloway very generously read the entire manuscript more than once, and I am grateful for his keen eye, his ceaseless intellectual energy, and his many donations of archival and bibliographic materials. Paulina Alberto, Dain Borges, and Jan French read selections of this work and offered me invaluable feedback, while Jeffrey Lesser, unsolicited, shared relevant extracts from his own research. Sueann Caulfield, Brodie Fischer, John French, Bryan Pitts, and Daryle Williams have given me helpful comments at various presentations of my work, while Daryle, along with Barbara Weinstein, organized a provocative conference on the Brazilian military dictatorship that helped shape some of my early ideas and put me in touch with others who think about this period. Chris Dunn, Ken Serbin, Benjamin Cowan, Colin Snider, and Natan Zeichner have sat on numerous conference and symposia panels with me, and both their comments on my work and the examples they set in their own exciting research have helped me enormously in thinking about the 1960s and 1970s in Brazil.

The other major group who was fundamental to the early shaping of this project—many of whom have remained close friends and vital contributors to my thinking ever since—is the participants of the Social Science Research Council's program on Memories of Repression in the Southern Cone. While I cannot mention every one of the numerous people who made this pathbreaking program so exhilarating, I want to single out Elizabeth Jelin, the program director, for the model she has unknowingly provided me of a truly globalized public intellectual, an inspired and passionate critic, and a warm, loyal friend. I will be forever grateful to her. Ludmila da Silva Catela, the much-missed Carlos Ivan Degregori, Claudia

Feld, Eric Hershberg, Susana Kaufman, Rebecca Lichtenfeld, Aldo Marchesi, Ponciano del Pino, Steve Stern, and Peter Winn became especially important figures both in the making of this book and in my life thanks to this program.

The final direction of this book took shape at several institutions, each one indelibly marked for me by the colleagues and friends who helped to further it along. My colleagues at the University of California, Davis have all been incredibly supportive. I want to offer special thanks to Chuck Walker and Andres Resendez for being real compañeros in Latin American history, to Lorena Oropeza for insightful comments on one painfully long chapter, to Michael Lazzara for eloquent conversations about memory work, to Cathy Kudlick for acting as my official (and unofficial) mentor par excellence, to the mentors/colleagues/friends of the Program in Cross-Cultural Women's and gender History, and to the many bright undergraduate and graduate students who have made me rethink my ideas and my presentation of them. During an idyllic semester at the University of Notre Dame I was privileged to learn from the faculty and fellows of the Kellogg Institute for International Studies, and I am particularly grateful to Jaime Pensado for his careful reading of one of this book's chapters and to Erika Doss for her critical humor and acute insights on U.S. memorials. The Center for Latin American and Caribbean Studies at the University of Michigan welcomed me with open arms during a leave from UC Davis, and Rebecca Scott, Sueann Caulfield, Paulina Alberto, Jesse Hoffnung-Garskof, and Elizabeth Martins offered me a real intellectual community and home there. At Princeton University the faculty and staff of the Princeton Institute for International Studies, the Department of History, and the Program in Latin American Studies gave me the chance to research, write, think, and teach at this incredibly dynamic university. I want to thank Jeremy Adelman, Miguel Centeno, and Deborah Yashar for that privilege and especially to express my gratitude for Jeremy's frequent guidance that year and beyond. I am still nostalgic for the gifted colleagues and dear friends from Lafayette College and want to thank Josh Sanborn, Paul Barclay, and Arnie Offner for their early and earnest support of my work.

I could never have funded my graduate training, my research in Brazil, or the writing of this book without the generous financial support and implied scholarly approval I received from various institutions, their donors, and granting committees: the Andrew W. Mellon, Richard J. Franke and

Robert M. Leylan fellowships at Yale University; the International Dissertation Research Fellowship and Memories of Repression in the Southern Cone Fellowship from the Social Science Research Council; the Fulbright–Hays Program; the Princeton Institute for International and Regional Studies at Princeton University; the Kellogg Institute for International Studies at Notre Dame University; and the University of California, Davis, especially the UC Davis Hellman Fellowship.

Nor could I have completed the writing of this book without the editorial and emotional guidance of many, many people who helped me along the way. My East Coast writing group of Amy Chazkel, Mark Overmyer-Velazquez, Jay Garcia, Fiona Vernal, and Michael Cohen assisted in the arduous process of crafting the first draft, while my West Coast writing group (a.k.a. "the Surplussers") of Grace Wang, Leigh Raiford, Robin Hayes, Susette Min, Nadia Ellis, and the bicoastal Michael Cohen pushed me to transform that version into something much better than I could have ever written on my own. Then the excellent guidance of Valerie Millholland, Susan Albury, Gisela Fosado and of the two extremely helpful anonymous readers at Duke University Press resulted in this final version. Any remaining errors and gaps are, of course, entirely my own.

Finally, I could never have found such consistent joy and delight in the normally solitary process of writing of a book were it not for the affection, support, and welcomed distractions of my growing family. My parents' and sister's ceaseless championing of me inspired me to prove them right, while the love extended to me unconditionally by my parents- and siblings-in-law ironically made me want to deserve such a gift. Ada and Vera provided much-needed company at all hours of the day and night and in all conceivable writing locations and positions across Canada and the United States. But Cal arrived in our lives as I was finishing this book, already her humor, exuberance, and ceaselessly sunny spirit have made me happier when at my desk and not, reminding me of why I want to write something of significance and why I want to stop reediting my prose, put away the computer, and go play. While Theo's birth as this book was going to press meant that he did not have to suffer as many writing-related absences as his sister, his appearance has nonetheless reanimated me and given me added incentives to make sure this is something he will want to read one day. Most important of all, Nico has been my teammate, partner, and best friend in this and every other project. He has read and edited every word of this book, discussed each crazy and not-so-crazy idea I've had about it, and delivered countless offerings of moral and edible support to my desk at all hours of the day and night. More fundamentally, he shares my need to explore, explain, and engage with the world around us, and in the process he makes my little place in it infinitely better.

Acronyms

AI	Ato Institucional (Institutional Act)
AIB	Ação Integralista Brasileira (Brazilian Integralist Action)
ALN	Ação Libertadora Nacional (National Liberating Action)
ANL	Aliança Nacional Libertadora (National Liberating Alliance)
AP	Ação Popular (Popular Action)
APML	Ação Popular Marxista-Leninista (Marxist-Leninist Popular Action)
ARENA	Aliança de Renovação Nacional (Alliance for National Renovation)
CA	Centro Acadêmico (Academic Center)
CACO	Centro Acadêmico Cândido de Oliveira (Cândido de Oliveira Academic Center)
CAMDE	Campanha da Mulher pela Democracia (Women's Campaign for Democracy)
CCC	Comando de Caça aos Comunistas (Communist Hunting Command)
CIE	Confédération International des Étudiants (International Confederation of Students)
CPC	Centro Popular de Cultura (Popular Culture Center)
DA	Diretório Acadêmico (Academic Directorate)
DCE	Diretório Central dos Estudantes (Central Student Directorate)
DI	Dissidências (Dissidents)
DNE	Diretório Nacional de Estudantes (National Student Directorate)
DOI-CODI	Destacamento de Operações-Centros de Operações de Defesa Interna (Information Operations Detachment-Internal Defense Operations Centers)
DOPS	Departamento de Ordem Política e Social (Department of Political and Social Order)
ESG	Escola Superior de Guerra (Higher War College)

FEUB	Federação dos Estudantes Universitários de Brasília (Federation of University Students of Brasilia)
FUEC	Frente Unida dos Estudantes do Calabouço (United Front of Calabouço Students)
IBAD	Instituto Brasileiro de Ação Democrática (Brazilian Institute of Democratic Action)
IPÊS	Instituto de Pesquisas e Estudos Sociais (Institute of Social Research and Study)
IPM	Inquérito Policial Militar (Military Police Inquiry)
IUS	International Union of Students
JUC	Juventude Universitária Católica (Catholic University Youth)
MAC	Movimento Anti-Comunista (Anti-Communist Movement)
MDB	Movimento Democrático Brasileiro (Brazilian Democratic Movement)
MEC	Ministério de Educação e Cultura (Ministry of Education and Culture)
MR-8	Movimento Revolucionário 8 Outubro (Revolutionary Movement of October 8)
PCB	Partido Comunista Brasileiro (Brazilian Communist Party)
PCBR	Partido Comunista Brasileiro Revolucionário (Revolutionary Brazilian Communist Party)
PCdoB	Partido Comunista do Brasil (Communist Party of Brazil)
POLOP	Organização Revolucionária Marxista-Política Operária (Revolutionary Organization of the Marxist-Workers Line)
PSB	Partido Socialista Brasileiro (Brazilian Socialist Party)
PSD	Partido Social Democrático (Social Democratic Party)
PUC	Pontifícia Universidade Católica (Pontifical Catholic University)
SNI	Serviço Nacional de Informações (National Information Service)
UDN	União Democrática Nacional (Democratic National Union)
UEE	União Estadual de Estudantes (State Union of Students)
UFF	Universidade Fluminense Federal (Federal Fluminense University)
UFRJ	Universidade Federal do Rio de Janeiro (Federal University of Rio de Janeiro)
UME	União Metropolitana de Estudantes (Metropolitan Union of Students)
UnB	Universidade de Brasilia (University of Brasilia)
UNE	União Nacional dos Estudantes (National Union of Students)
UNICAMP	Universidade Estadual de Campinas (State University of Campinas)
USAID	United States Agency for International Development
USNSA	United States National Student Association
USP	Universidade de São Paulo (São Paulo University)

Caminhando e cantando e seguindo a canção
Somos todos iguais braços dados ou não
Nas escolas, nas ruas, campos, construções
Caminhando e cantando e seguindo a canção

Vem, vamos embora que esperar não é saber
Quem sabe faz a hora não espera acontecer . . .

[Walking and singing and following the song
We are all equal, arm-in-arm or not
In the schools, streets, fields, buildings,
Walking and singing and following the song

Come, let's go, waiting is not knowing
Those who know make history, they don't wait for it to happen . . .]

MAKING AND REMEMBERING 1968 IN MILITARY BRAZIL

In 1968 the song known as "Pra não dizer que não falei das flores" (So they don't say I never spoke of flowers) by the singer and songwriter Geraldo Vandré enjoyed immense popularity among university students and other young people. Its rhythmical and lyrical invocations of street marches, encapsulated by its official title "Caminhando" (Walking), made this poignant protest song resonate especially powerfully in that moment, four years after military officers and their civilian allies had deposed the democratically chosen president and inaugurated what would become twenty-one years of military rule (1964–85). As student demonstrations against the military government led to national discussions about the legitimacy of the current regime, the role of student activism, and the meanings of police and opposition violence, the song touched a nerve—both in its fans and in its detractors. In September 1968, at the finals of the Third International Song Festival, for example, large groups of young supporters bearing laudatory banners and placards came out specifically to cheer for the song. When the jury nonetheless denied the piece first prize, the youthful crowd vociferously protested the perceived foul play and pointed to the inclusion of Donatelo Griecco, chief of the Cultural Division of Itamaraty (the Brazilian foreign relations department) on the jury as evidence of military interference. He in fact later publicly commented that the piece was "a dangerous left-wing song."[1] Another military official, Octávio Costa, became so incensed by Vandré's composition that he felt compelled to respond to it by writing a literary analysis of its lyrics for the Rio de Janeiro newspaper the *Jornal do Brasil*. Costa claimed to speak for the whole military class, including "the immense majority of anonymous functionaries," when he later told interviewers that they had all found the composition profoundly irritating.[2] If young people's enthusiasm for the song in 1968 was no secret, neither was the extreme displeasure it provoked among military officials.

One particularly provocative section of the lyrics that observers often pointed to as the source of the military's displeasure described soldiers as unreasonably following deleterious orders: "In the barracks they are taught an old lesson/To die for the fatherland and live without reason." Certainly this kind of criticism of the armed forces aggravated some military officials. But what made "Caminhando" resonate so deeply was how the song as a whole—and students' uses of it—encapsulated the ethos of 1968, a year in which massive student street protests at home and abroad, fierce debates about militancy and violence, and students' disruption of gender norms all roused military concern. With its steady marching rhythm, smoothly repetitive rhymes, and refrain of "walking and singing and following the song," "Caminhando" became a regular musical presence at the many massive street protests of 1968. As students organized a series of record-breaking public demonstrations throughout the year, many in response to police violence against them, they exposed and broadened growing opposition to the military government. As they did so, they sang "Caminhando" repeatedly: at street marches and during occupations of university buildings; at university assemblies and at funerals for assassinated colleagues; and at a disastrous student union gathering in October when the police raided their secret meeting site and arrested them by the hundreds. Marching single file across the muddy fields to the police buses waiting to take them to jail, students broke out into song, alternating between "Caminhando" and a decidedly apolitical ditty about picking up girls in a Volkswagen bug. Before year's end "Caminhando" had become the quintessential demonstration song of 1968, accompanying student protests across the country and leading some, like the journalist and cultural critic Nelson Motta, to complain that it had been sung excessively. In his end-of-the-year list of the hip and square in Brazilian culture he placed "Caminhando" firmly in the square category, suggesting that students had drained the piece of its coolness through overuse.[3]

Students sang "Caminhando" at their street protests notwithstanding the fact that, after conjuring up visions of such demonstrations, the song goes on to critique them. Referring to "indecisive chains" marching in the streets, it ridicules the idea of making flowers "their strongest chorus" and believing in "flowers defeating canons." As the scholar of Brazilian music Christopher Dunn has written, "Symbolic protest marches and 'flower power' were useless in the face of armed forces. . . . Vandré was calling for armed resistance."[4] In this respect Vandré's song was but one voice in a much larger polemic in 1968 about the growing violence of the state perpetrated against heretofore protected groups like university students and about the legitimacy of using violence to oppose it. Within the student movement, students debated how best to respond to increasing police repression, from soliciting public support in condemning the violent acts against them to responding to the police in kind. Meanwhile other groups pondered the theoretical and tactical benefits of violence, in particular the so-called clandestine lefts, that is, the various covert leftist political organizations that emerged in this period with the aim of shepherding Brazil toward socialism, sometimes via armed struggle, and that multiplied so vastly and engaged in such fierce ideological and strategic disputes with one another that they are best referred to in the plural.[5] Notwithstanding the important connections between the aboveground student movement encapsulated in organizations like the União Nacional dos Estudantes (UNE, National Union of Students) and the underground associations of the left, they were distinct groups. Some students, including most of the student movement leadership, participated in both the student movement and one or more of the clandestine lefts, and rivalries for student leadership positions often mirrored deep internal leftist divisions. Nonetheless, the two spheres cannot be conflated, as the great majority of students who engaged in the protest demonstrations and other student movement activities had no direct ties to the clandestine lefts.

That students sang Vandré's call to arms during peaceful protest marches reveals not a willed ignorance of the song's message but their collective ambivalence regarding the appeal of the clandestine lefts and armed struggle. To assume that the song's immense popularity meant that young listeners had abandoned all hope for flower-power protest marches would be wrong. Just a few days after the song festival in September, when seven contingents of police shock troops amassed outside the Federal University of Rio de Janeiro (UFRJ), a young female student stepped forward to offer them a single yellow rose. Duly photographed by the many journalists attending the event, the flower came with a small note reading, "Make love, not war." One policeman at the scene jokingly shouted, "Be careful, it could explode!" but the officer in charge accepted the offering with a smile.

In case anyone missed the connection with Vandré's song, one student representative told reporters the young woman had extended the gift on their collective behalf "so they don't say we never thought of flowers." He continued, "This is not a reconciliation, but just a small prank [brincadeira] with didactic meaning. If they invade the faculties, they'll be received with rocks and paving stones as usual."[6] Rather than rejecting the symbolic power of flowers, students reconfigured the metaphor to suggest their own meaning. When student–state conflicts turned deadly, flowers, particularly funereal flowers, were harnessed for an altogether different significance.

If the song invoked both the street protests and debates about violence that permeated Brazil in 1968, it also pointed to gendered contests that marked that year. In many ways students challenged existing definitions of appropriate gender behavior, especially concerning women's participation in political organization and acts of violence and young people's experimentation with premarital heterosexual sex. In other ways, however, they reinforced established gender norms, as student assertions of militancy rested on masculinist and heteronormative assumptions. Hence the song's labeling of military men as irrational (who "live without reason") was both a pointed and a gendered insult: it destabilized the association between rationality and masculinity that has long permeated constructions of modernity, and it paralleled the ways in which students repeatedly cast police and soldiers as barbarous, unthinking "gorillas." Equally provocative, perhaps, are the verses that precede this insult, as they paint a devastating image of impotent masculinity: "There are armed soldiers, loved or not / Almost all lost, weapons in their hands." In its place, the song proposes "a new lesson," learned and taught by those with "history in our hands" and "with loves on our mind and flowers on the ground." In this suggested new order, the metaphor of flowers not only reinforces the rejection of a flower-power path to change, but also conjures up a vision of conquered love— both of which assert and affirm the militant masculinity of its singers.

Given the many sensitive themes touched on in Vandré's composition, the military's censorious response to it extended well beyond any possible influence imposed on the song festival's jury. One group of security agents even took to regularly casing the storefronts of music shops that played the tune, where passersby would sometimes stop to listen. "If anyone appeared to really enjoy the song, or if they didn't have identification with them," they were subject to harassment and arrest, wrote a journalist who reported their behavior.[7] Eventually officials banned outright any further sales of the record, and Vandré, fearing for his personal safety, fled into exile. Meanwhile at the end of 1968 regime officials took drastic steps to shut down all sources of opposition, ushering in the so-called years of lead (*os anos de chumbo*) characterized by institutionalized state repression and political exclusion.[8] Assembling an enormous security apparatus that relied on gross violations of human rights, the military regime struck at its opponents, especially the traditional aboveground student movement and the emerging clandestine lefts.

In this new context "Caminhando" became a powerful symbolic means of recalling 1968 and students' earlier political prominence, both for the state security forces and for students themselves. From 1969 on, the military regime's security agents kept a close eye on any references to 1968, including allusions to this song, as memories of 1968 permeated their records and inspired their actions against students. For their part, students initially made few overt references to 1968 or to "Caminhando," as they struggled to respond to an unprecedented wave of repression. But for some the music and its role in that earlier period continued to be a private source of inspiration. Aldo Rebelo, who would go on to become an important federal congressman in the 1990s and 2000s, remembers that as a student in 1975 he and others would retreat behind closed doors at their student center to listen to Vandré's music. And he recalls the sense of reduced risk they felt when they finally considered it safe to listen publicly to the song in the late 1970s and early 1980s.[9] In this latter moment, when students re-created former student movement institutions like the outlawed student union UNE[10], it was inevitable that Vandré's music would accompany their other commemorative acts, and "Caminhando" and other references to 1968 figured prominently.

The meanings of "Caminhando," like the meanings of 1968 itself, changed over time. If students in 1968 intended many interpretations when they sang the song, so too did those a decade later. This book is titled *Speaking of Flowers* in an attempt to capture these diverse, shifting meanings. The title highlights one of my central concerns: to examine the ways in which different generations of students spoke about these flowers, that is, how they recalled, imagined, shaped, and affiliated themselves with the meanings of the 1968 protests against the military regime.

At its broadest level, *Speaking of Flowers* is a book about university student activism in Brazil. Eschewing preordained views of the student activist as either naturally idealistic and self-sacrificing or a force of uncritical youthful rebellion—easy tropes that are largely constructions of the post-1968 period—the book questions the very idea of *student* activism. What makes students engage in national political affairs *as students* rather than through political parties or other means? And how have students constructed and defended their authority to do so? Scholars of student movements elsewhere have offered a rich range of explanations for the rise of student activism in the 1960s, from expanding economies that gave middle-class youth important purchasing and cultural powers, to the increased reach and speed of the media that broadcast galvanizing news to young people quickly and powerfully.[11] Notwithstanding the important attention given to the politicizing aspects of the university experience, most notably in those areas where a population boom in the 1950s led to overcrowding in the 1960s, there has been little treatment of why young people chose to organize as students, or how the idea of a "student activist" was constructed, challenged, and redefined over time. For the case of Brazil, Andrew Kirkendall's *Class Mates: Male Student Culture and the Making of a Political Class in 19th Century Brazil* documents the important early construction of student political authority in the nineteenth century, while João Roberto Martins Filho's *Movimento estudantil e ditadura militar, 1964–1968* demonstrates the need to understand the social category of students in this period as class based. I build on this work to not only bridge the temporal lacuna between these studies, tracing the historical construction of university student activism in Brazil throughout most of the twentieth century, but also to examine the multiple ways in which students themselves built, defended and modified their claims to political authority. I additionally explore the varying degrees of political recognition accorded to student activists, that is, the extent to which established political forces sought to utilize or exclude student organizations. In doing so, I trace how the class, race, and gender privileges through which student activists initially asserted their right to political participation gradually, if unevenly and incompletely, gave way to other institutional and symbolic forms of political authority. And I show how the political divides that led to the military coup d'état of April 1, 1964, and the ensuing twenty-one-year military dictatorship exacerbated contests over the appropriateness of student political participation at all.

Speaking of Flowers is also about the making of 1968 in Brazil. That is to say, it is in part a history of the year of 1968 in Brazil: the precedents that led up to it; the political struggles that took place during it; and the more general processes that help explain it. Scholars of Brazil agree that 1968 was a critical year, marking a sharp divide between the first four years of the military regime, when the initial military president promised moderation and a quick return to democracy, and the period after 1969, when, as students would later say, the dictatorship revealed its true face, or as others would joke darkly, the *ditabranda* [soft dictatorship] became a *ditadura* [hard dictatorship].[12] Indeed, 1968 signified both the high-water mark of student activism and provided an important catalyst for the dictatorship's oppressive turn. At the same time, Brazilian students' clarion calls to end a violent dictatorship turned out to be their Cassandra moment, as the regime's post-68 repression confirmed their earlier warnings. Thus the student protests of 1968 have inspired a wealth of commemorative and memorialistic attention and a number of important academic studies. This body of work has been very useful in documenting personal lived experiences of 1968, showcasing the variety of local manifestations that made up the larger story of 1968 in Brazil, and explaining distinguishing facets of that year, such as the critical role played by the press during violent standoffs between students and the military.[13] But several important features of 1968 remain unexamined, and *Speaking of Flowers* seeks to complement this literature with an exploration of them.

First, while generally all histories of 1968 in Brazil rightfully mark the March 28, 1968 death of a secondary student as the catalyst for massive student protest, few explain just why or how such an act of violence presumably undertaken to discourage student demonstrations had instead the opposite effect. As noted earlier, one cannot assume that young people automatically mobilize in response to acts of seeming injustice, hence it is valuable to ask why this particular incident generated the response it did. In so doing, I reveal the ways in which violence acted as a dialectical force that both propelled individual students to action and helped student organizations authenticate the very idea of student activism through appeals to students' collective militancy, martyrdom, and masculinity.

Secondly, *Speaking of Flowers* adds a much-needed analysis of gender to studies of 1968 and to the history of student activism more broadly by exploring the ways in which gender operated to define and authorize student activism. From the founding of UNE in 1937 to the reconstruction of the student movement in the 1980s, male and female students faced different behavioral expectations, and gendered ideas about appropriate forms of political activism marked the student organizations. In fact, the high degree of political engagement by women students in 1968 fomented deep social and political anxieties in Brazil and contributed to officials' fears that the national and international student movements posed a severe threat to the national order. The concern about participation in political and, on occasion, violent actions by female students was often expressed through specifically sexualized references, demonstrating the ways in which gendered tropes were used to denounce and constrain oppositional political activism. While this is not a book exclusively about gender or predominantly about women students, it rightfully explores the relationship between gender and the practices and symbols of power and reveals how gender is integral to the meanings and memories of student activism in 1968.

The third and final contribution to studies of 1968 in Brazil that I hope to make is an interrogation of the meanings of the international context of 1968. Certainly no author or commentator on Brazil in 1968 neglects to mention the concurrent explosion of student activism in other parts of the world that was a critical context to Brazilian events. Yet possibly due to the fact that popular views at the time suggested that Brazilian students copied their European or U.S. American counterparts, without explaining how such momentous and unidirectional influences occurred, most contemporary writers have shied away from exploring the impact of this concurrence.[14] Instead they have tended toward noting the international context without integrating it into the local narrative of 1968.[15] By contrast, *Speaking of Flowers* brings together national student movement activities in Brazil and the broader international experience of 1968 in other parts of the world, demonstrating that the worldwide arena of student activity impacted the reception and direction of Brazilian students.

In this sense, *Speaking of Flowers* also offers a critical intervention in the rise of studies of the global 1960s. Scholars have increasingly emphasized the global connectedness of 1960s-era protests, but have thus far focused most of their efforts on questions of causality, thereby missing other resulting effects of this global trend. Their excellent work seeking to explain why this outpouring occurred in so many places at the same time has moved understandings of the 1960s a long way from the above-mentioned, contemporaneous interpretations that often viewed student protests as copies of one another, such as *Time* magazine's unabashed assertion in May of 1968 that "when television carries pictures of students demonstrating in London or Manhattan, students in Amsterdam and Prague start marching."[16] Some have addressed this issue by examining shared demographic patterns and interconnected cultural and discursive flows. The diplomatic historian Jeremi Suri, for example, has argued that an "infrastructure" and "language of dissent" coalesced in the late 1960s, when large numbers of young people mingled in increasingly crowded urban universities and expressed themselves in new and shared ways.[17] Others have emphasized the similar political perspectives that many young people held in common. In his now-classic argument Immanuel Wallerstein proclaimed 1968 a worldwide revolution brought on by increased recognition and criticism of U.S. hegemony in the world-system.[18] Recent comparative work has sought to trace the specific routes through which student and youth activists in various countries exchanged political ideas and tactical strategies.[19] Taken together, this wave of scholarly attention to the global 1960s has radically transformed earlier visions of the era as marked by youthful cultural copying, while similarly belying the fears of many government leaders at the time that the demonstrations resulted from an international Communist conspiracy. Yet even among those who seek to explain the local particularities of a specific group of students, the underlying urge to address the extent to which international factors prompted or influenced local events persists. In her study of 1968 in Mexico, for example, Elaine Carey argues that while the Mexican student movement "was part of the international student protests" and Mexican students "embraced international revolutionary rhetoric," their actions must first and foremost be understood "as part of a continuum of social protests in Mexico."[20] In a nebulous relationship of spark and fuel, many scholars present students both as being motivated or inspired by international developments and as selectively utilizing them to act on their preexisting political sensibilities and plans of action.

My book suggests that scholars of the 1960s should historicize the very question of causality and should seek to understand the period transnationally. In other words, rather than simply asking about the degree to which local student movements were connected to or influenced by those elsewhere, we must examine how contemporaneous beliefs, fears, and suspicions about such connections affected the course of local events. In Brazil, the concomitant rise of student activism at home and abroad led to a kind of contradictory perception: while it increased attention and sympathy for the struggles of Brazilian students, it also hardened accusations that the student protests in Brazil were inauthentic products of foreign influence. Meanwhile Brazilian actors, both students and state security forces, drew on the international scene to reinforce their own discursive and ideological positions. The upsurge of student political culture and activism globally in 1968 was thus always both an exogenous and an endogenous force in Brazil, influencing the reception, direction, and ultimate meaning of the student movements there. In other words, the global 1968 was always a part of the local 1968 in Brazil, and, I suspect, elsewhere.

If this book is a history of the student movement leading up to and during 1968 in Brazil, it is also a history of what 1968 came to mean in subsequent years, It demonstrates that while 1968 as a period of mass student mobilization ended on December 13, when the military regime decreed its most authoritarian piece of legislation and effectively shut down most public displays of opposition, "1968" in quotation marks, the "1968" that swelled beyond the bounds of a temporal marker to become a broadly powerful and contested memory of massive, anti-regime student protest, was only created in the years following. As this suggests, by looking at the meanings of 1968 for later generations *Speaking of Flowers* necessarily explores the role of collective memory and its uses in subsequent political struggles, examining the mechanisms by which succeeding generations of students harnessed the symbolic power of 1968 in their organizing efforts, and tracing the accompanying transformations of meaning that resulted.

In its focus on memory, *Speaking of Flowers* builds on an exciting outpouring of innovative work on this topic. It takes as its starting point the now well-established understanding that memory is both subjective and collectively constructed. Hence it is a useful lens for exploring collective beliefs in a given historical moment and their change over time. It also builds on important scholarship about struggles over memory, and the many rich studies that show the ways in which memories emerge as areas of contestation or commemoration at specific historical, political, and cultural junctures.[21] Students of socially and politically divisive periods like the Latin American military dictatorships of the late twentieth century have produced rich studies of the protracted post-dictatorship struggles to define the repressive past, especially vis-à-vis efforts to challenge "official" memories with other alternatives, and they have offered insights into how societies have confronted collective trauma in the wake of atrocity.[22] Often this has meant examining the work of various groups to promote particular meanings of the past, social actors that sociologist Elizabeth Jelin has influentially termed *memory entrepreneurs*.[23] Most of this work looks at the post-dictatorship period and memory entrepreneurs' efforts to render sets of memories hegemonic on a national scale, so as to impact post-dictatorship policies and politics.

Speaking of Flowers departs from these important path breakers, even as it relies heavily on their insights. For I look at the uses of memory during the dictatorship itself, arguing that the construction of memories shaped the period of military rule as it was occurring, inspiring or allowing for certain kinds of actions at the time, and that memory's significance emerges well before the post-dictatorship era of public memory politics. By focusing on the internal uses of memory within groups—in this case those of post-68 generations of students and the security forces who kept tabs on them— my book also reminds us that memory struggles are not confined to national discussions about the politics of memory, truth, and justice, but also happen in much more quotidian ways and on much smaller scales, yet they nonetheless impact the actions of such groups and thus the history in which they participated. At the same time, by tracing the temporal lacunae of memory after 1968 in Brazil and then its re-appropriation by succeeding generations of students, it reveals the mechanisms by which successive generations of students transmitted and transformed collective memories of 1968, the changing political uses to which they harnessed these memories, and the ways in which student memories conflicted, literally and symbolically, with memories held by the state security forces. Finally, it explores the gendered dimensions of both social movement politics and collective memories, and the connections between political mobilization and commemorative practices. It reveals, for example, that students' ritualized tributes to fallen male colleagues both connected succeeding generations of students to a shared collective identity of political activism and forged a singularly masculine vision of 1968 martyrdom and militancy that limited their efforts. Ultimately it shows that struggles over memory can nourish and animate deliberate political strategies, and that invocations of the past can be both motivating and limiting.

Finally, this is a book about the military regime of 1964–85 in Brazil. The last several years have witnessed an important surge of historical interest in this period, as its legacy is a continuing source of both public and scholarly debate. On the one hand this has meant that numerous surviving actors, from military leaders to leftist revolutionaries, have granted extensive interviews and written memoirs. Indeed, personal memories continue to be an oft-used historical source.[24] At the same time, the long-standing efforts of activists and family members to uncover information about those who died during the dictatorship have led to the formation of important investigating committees that have published their results.[25] On the other hand, many archives within Brazil remain closed or tightly restricted, including many of those controlled by the armed forces and that contain further evidence of human rights violations.[26] Some historians in Brazil and the United States have turned to U.S. American sources to undertake research on the role of the United States both in supporting and in opposing the regime.[27] Others have found and probed important documentation on such topics as the role of the Catholic Church, the press, and the various groupings of the armed left.[28] Taken together, this wealth of scholarship has offered a relatively detailed picture of the factors and factions leading to the coup d'état of 1964 and of the major military personalities and perspectives that shaped executive-level governance.[29]

While no mention of the twenty-one-year-long military regime is complete without a corresponding reference to 1968, few have addressed the long-term history of the student movement before and after 1968.[30] My book emphasizes that students were important actors throughout the years of dictatorship. Young people were responsible for the most visible early manifestations of antidictatorship struggle—the student demonstrations of the late 1960s, especially those of 1968—and many students and nonstudents alike would later mention 1968 as a defining moment in their political trajectories. But they were also important actors in the years after 1968, attempting to reanimate the aboveground student movement and making up a large percentage of members of the clandestine lefts. Many of them developed a remarkable sense of political commitment at very early ages, foregoing class privilege for outlaw status. And they made important contributions to the period of political transition by re-forming many of their former organizations and participating in broader campaigns for such issues as amnesty for political prisoners and the eventual reestablishment of civilian rule. Examining the role of university students beyond 1968 thus helps explain students' sudden reemergence as vital political actors in the late 1970s and early 1980s. In short, the book uncovers a vibrant history of student movement activism long after the regime effectively shut down all avenues of public protest, the major student organizations dissolved, and universities experienced intense censorship and propaganda.

Students were also important *subjects* throughout these years. That is to say, the question of who exactly a student should be became the subject of much discussion, evaluation, and planning both before the 1964 coup and well after 1968. While the category of university student is, by its very nature, a shifting concept, as universities have not always meant the same thing in Brazilian (or any other) society or been attended by the same groups of people, my book reveals the extent to which this idea nevertheless became subject to unprecedented, heated political conflict in these years. Various actors, from businessmen to foreign experts to government officials and current students themselves, held conferences, published articles, created reports, produced films, suggested reforms, and, in short, attempted to analyze the role of students within Brazilian society and to advocate for changes in these roles.[31] As the assumed leaders of tomorrow, students were seen as a vital part of society, and political and ideological struggles to influence them were waged throughout the military period. Looking to the period before and during 1968 helps demonstrate the ways in which contests over students' rights to participate politically were an important indicator of disputes about the role of civil society as a whole. The book both reinserts the history of student movement activity into the history of the Brazilian military regime, and reveals the symbolic and material importance of student activism throughout the period of military rule.

Through its focus on students during the Brazilian military regime, my book seeks to contribute to understandings of authoritarian regimes more broadly, underscoring the strategic role of the cultural realm in challenging and legitimating such regimes. Without a base of popular, legal, or electoral legitimacy, authoritarian states run the risk of appearing to be regimes of naked domination and therefore need to foster public expressions of consent.[32] After the protests of 1968 marked students as the most visible source of opposition to the regime, the transforming and trumpeting of youth culture became a central focus of its concern, even as internal police reports show a constant preoccupation with preventing "another 1968." At the same time, post-'68 generations of students turned to cultural materials from 1968, such as popular protest songs and photographs, to mobilize a politics of memory as regime resisters when outright opposition was too difficult. Such efforts showcase the degree to which cultural expressions carried added weight in the absence of permitted political action.

In researching and writing this exploration of history and memory, I drew extensively on oral histories. I took advantage of the vast array of published and archived interviews with former student activists, such as the collection compiled by the Projeto Memória do Movimento Estudantil and the multiple edited volumes published in recent years. I also conducted various lengthy interviews of my own, for the most part consciously selecting students who were active in the period after 1968, as they often are the least represented voices in archives and published collections that tend to focus on 1968 itself. Yet if all oral histories (and indeed all primary sources) must be interpreted with care, the nature of my emphasis on memory demanded a particular kind of attention. In trying to historicize memories of 1968 or to understand what 1968 signified in the 1970s and 1980s, current memories and interpretations could have an obscuring effect. Thus I used these various interviews, alongside other sources, to document people's actions and strategies and then relied on contemporaneous documentary sources to interpret the role of memory in inspiring these actions.

Perhaps ironically, the final shape of this book was determined in one very unanticipated way by the interviews granted to me. In addition to providing me with gracious and careful explanations of their pasts, thereby offering me a dynamic perspective of my topic that I could not have otherwise enjoyed, those whom I interviewed unknowingly but markedly reformulated my central research question. For I did not set out to write about 1968 in Brazil. My original interest lay exclusively with the years of military rule after 1969 and the so-called mute generation, those young people who attended university during the mid- and late-1970s, when the presence of informants on campus and mandatory moral and civic education classes appeared almost normal. Historians have often portrayed this generation as essentially quiescent. Yet each time I sat down with my tape recorder and lists of questions about the activities in which they engaged in the 1970s, the interviewees always began their personal narrative in 1968. "In 1968 I was in the fourth grade," began one. "I went to my first marches in 1968; I was thirteen years old," began another. And so I learned to let my interviewees initiate their political life stories when they wished, and always they started in 1968. Through them I realized that the history of 1968 did not end with the close of the year and that the history of the 1970s, and indeed of modern Brazil, could not be written without it.

In addition to oral histories I have benefited from a wide assortment of textual sources. Students' voices can be found in the rich collection of student publications housed at the Edgard Leurenroth Archive at the Universidade Estadual de Campinas and in the personal collections of people like Daniel Aarão Reis Filho and Jean Marc von der Weid, students who were active in both the aboveground student movement and the clandestine lefts and who donated papers related to their political activities to the State Archive of Rio de Janeiro. They can also be heard, ironically enough, in the files of the Departamento de Ordem Política e Social (DOPS, Department of Political and Social Order), a branch of the Brazilian security forces tasked with investigating students. As security officers systematically confiscated samples of student newspapers, flyers, posters, and the like, these materials, still preserved in DOPS files, open a window onto contemporaneous student perspectives and self-presentations. In addition to confiscated materials, the DOPS-authored reports on student movement actions as well as their files on suspected subversives offer not only useful information on the vision of the state security forces but also a good sense of the general types of activities students managed to pursue. These collections lack the complete array of student-produced materials that escaped attention and preservation, either because they were securely guarded or because collectors deemed them unimportant. Nonetheless, the breadth of materials that have found their way into these archives is quite stunning and has enriched this book in multiple ways.

Another force that kept close tabs on the activities of the student movement was the U.S. diplomatic mission to Brazil through its embassies in Rio de Janeiro and, later, Brasilia and through its consulates in other Brazilian cities. The U.S. State Department paid special attention to university students in Latin America from the 1950s on, and Brazilian students were no exception. Embassy officials kept Washington informed of the state of student affairs, sometimes drawing on public discourse in local newspapers, but more often through insider conversations with military officials or students themselves. While these U.S. government reports tended to foresee student disturbances around every corner, read carefully they afford historians a unique contemporaneous insider perspective. At the same time, I carefully surveyed the collection of opposition newspapers at the Laboratório de Estudos do Tempo Presente at the UFRJ and turned to mainstream newspapers and magazines to understand public debates and understandings about student activities.

To trace this long history of 1968, I begin the book by exploring the history of student political organizing in Brazil in chapter 1, demonstrating the role university students played in Brazilian society from the formation of the first institutions of higher education in 1808 through 1955. I show that, as members of the economic and political elite, university students long enjoyed considerable social and even official, legislative support for their political activities. They nonetheless worked to guarantee their political authority in light of changing political trends, above all by forming and then strengthening the institutional authority of the officially sanctioned student union, UNE, a process that involved the consolidation of male students' predominance over the union and the establishment of a formal UNE headquarters building in Rio de Janeiro.

Chapter 2 examines the years 1955–67, when the very idea of student political activism in Brazil became contested in the context of the Cold War. It demonstrates that by the late 1950s changes in the national and international political context and in the composition of the student body itself led to more radical political postures on the part of the student movement as well as to a broader debate about students' proper place in Brazilian society. Following the military coup of 1964, the new government intervened repeatedly in student affairs, banning traditional student organizations and ejecting students from the UNE building, among other measures. This reaction in turn contributed to growing, if latent, student dissatisfaction with the regime.

The year 1968 is the subject of chapter 3, a period when university students burst forth en masse on the political scene, holding enormous public demonstrations to protest issues ranging from university conditions to police violence. Assembling record-breaking numbers of participants and garnering extensive and often sympathetic media coverage, the student movement became a primary source of opposition to the regime, criticizing not just flaws in government policies but also its legitimacy as a whole. Fundamental to this transformation was the role of violence, both as a central grievance against which students organized and as a collective and mobilizing experience in which they participated. The chapter shows how students came to see themselves as a hybrid of martyrs and militants, compelled to respond to the regime's repressive acts and uniquely poised to do so. It also demonstrates the threat this group appeared to pose to the military government and the steps the regime took to quell student dissent.

Chapter 4 moves to 1969 and the early 1970s, after the imposition of an extremely authoritarian piece of legislation, Ato Institucional Número 5 (AI-5, Institutional Act Number Five), made public student demonstrations virtually impossible and led to the collapse of UNE. The chapter traces the response of student activists as they began to realize that Brazil had entered a radically new and much more violent phase and that any student organizing on their part required new strategies. From this point forward, my book augments a social history of student political activism in the years after 1968 with a history of memory. As students and security forces negotiated their way in the period after AI-5, people from both groups came to invoke and construct memories of 1968, and those memories would become a fundamental part of how they responded to the new conditions. I point to a chain of commemorative practices throughout the 1970s in which students paid annual homage to those who had been killed by the regime, and argue that these events linked different generations of students to one another mnemonically and forged compelling experiential and symbolic connections with 1968.

I turn to the reconstruction of UNE in the late 1970s and early 1980s in chapter 5, when appeals to memory and claims to a legacy of 1968 fueled students' re-creative actions. In the context of a government-decreed political opening in which antidictatorship civic organizations proliferated, a new generation of university students called upon and reconstructed memories of the past in order to mobilize others and to legitimize their new involvement. By examining students' efforts to reclaim the UNE headquarters building, the chapter shows how certain memories of Brazil's military past were ignored or transformed. The chapter demonstrates how the continuing construction, transformation, and use of memories of 1968, even decades later, helped succeeding generations of students and other civil actors in the political regeneration of Brazil. Finally, the epilogue reflects on recent invocations of 1968 in Brazil and suggests how memories of this period continue to transform and to inform present-day concerns.

1

CONSTRUCTING THE "HOUSE OF DEMOCRATIC RESISTANCE"

Authority and Authenticity in University Student Politics, 1808–1955

As university student activists gathered in Rio de Janeiro for a National Congress of Students in August 1951 they received a booklet to help guide their stay: "O Rio para o Universitário: Roteiro Turístico, Cultural e Informativo" (Rio for university students: a touristic, cultural, and informative itinerary) (figure 1.1).[1] Containing helpful advice about navigating the city during the multiday event and suggestions for excursions to museums and other locales, the publication reflected the fact that, for many of the several hundred students expected to attend, it would be their first trip to the seaside capital and a significant event in their young lives. Further suggesting the momentousness of the occasion, the cover design centered around a photograph of a stately three-story building bedecked on either side with elegant palm trees and distinguished by the columns and caryatids on its second- and third-floor balconies. Below the picture was the caption, "A Casa da Resistência Democrática" (The house of democratic resistance), an unofficial moniker that would have done visiting students little good in locating the building at 132 Praia de Flamengo Street. But the attendees who carried this guidebook around doubtless needed no such clarification to recognize the site as the well-known headquarters of the União Nacional dos Estudantes (UNE, National Union of Students) and the reason for their meeting. For this was the fourteenth year in which students convened to elect UNE officers and debate their forthcoming agenda, and by now the prominence of the national union finally seemed secure. Meanwhile

FIGURE I.I. The UNE building at 132 Praia de Flamengo Street graced the cover of this UNE booklet from 1951. United States National Student Association Collection, Hoover Institution Archives

UNE's permanence and prestige found no better symbol than the solidity of its elegant headquarters.

As both the showcase for and a symbol of students' political authority the stately UNE building played an important role in the history of student activism in Brazil. Indeed, the building was quite extraordinary. A symmetrical, Palladian structure that faced Guanabara Bay in the historically aristocratic neighborhood of Flamengo, it boasted an elegant dining room for over sixty guests, a polished marble and wood bar, and a stately library with glass-doored bookcases. The house also possessed a game room replete with poker and snooker tables, a ninepin bowling alley, and, perhaps most breathtaking, an enormous rooftop veranda with unobstructed views of Flamengo Beach and the famous Sugarloaf Mountain jutting into Guanabara Bay. Built in 1929 for the Sociedade Germânia (German society), a typical immigrant association of the early twentieth century that sought to cultivate private social spaces for its members, the building was in fact the club's second, more luxurious domicile, constructed to replace an earlier building (1900–1929) located a few doors down. With Brazil's declaration of war against Germany in August 1942, however, all property belonging to the supposed enemy became part of the national patrimony, including the Sociedade Germânia structure. Almost immediately President Getúlio Vargas granted the building to UNE and to two other student associations, and students enthusiastically took over the well-outfitted space to make it their headquarters.

In the nine years since then UNE members had hosted innumerable meetings, congresses, and debates at 132 Praia de Flamengo Street as well as formal dinners, dances, receptions, and cocktail parties. They also came to run a subsidized student restaurant out of the dining room and a student theater from the ground floor. And to the immense organizational advantage of the union, the building literally came to house the UNE leadership, as the elected student officers not only managed UNE from the office space, but also lived in the modest top-floor apartment for the one-year term of their leadership. In this way the students who made up UNE directorates could hail from all over the country yet still reside in the nation's capital, close to one another and to the center of national politics. Although, as noted, two other student organizations shared the space—a local student association and a collegiate sports group—the structure on Praia de Flamengo Street soon became known as the UNE building (a sede da UNE) and was a source of reference for all who participated in the union as well as a physical validation of the student union's status.

For many people today whose image of student activism is colored by the innumerable photographs, films, and media accounts that came out of the 1960s, this earlier picture of formal gatherings in elegant buildings may appear incongruous with visions of student movements as centering around tumultuous street protests of rebellious young men and women. Indeed, after the coup d'état of 1964 that led to twenty-one years of military rule, Brazilian students in general and those organized around UNE in particular would become central protagonists in just the kind of violent student–police skirmishes and regular front-page news items that helped to paint this enduring portrait of student militancy. To understand how the student activism of this later period emerged, however, one must first ask how students came to see themselves as a group with special claims to participate in national political affairs, claims that would be fiercely challenged by the military regime. One must further interrogate what it meant to be a university student in Brazil, where students historically came from the elite male sectors of a highly stratified society, but where not only the social makeup of the student body would change but the very category of student would become increasingly contested. And one must explore the means by which students established and asserted their political authority through UNE, whose lavish building would so strongly come to symbolize student political activism that one of the military regime's first acts would be to deny UNE the right to occupy it, while one of its last acts would be to demolish the structure.

At the UNE Congress of 1951, however, the loftiness and location of the building both advanced and affirmed university students' political ascendancy. This authority was founded on their status as the sons of the elite, young men whose forays into political debates and associations in the nineteenth century seemed appropriate activities for those who would soon take their rightful place as leaders of the nation's affairs. The social and gendered exclusivity of higher education and its concomitant relationship to the political prerogative of university students extended throughout the Brazilian Empire (1822–89), when Brazil broke from Portuguese colonial rule to become an independent nation ruled by an emperor, and through the Old Republic (1889–1930), the period when the empire was replaced with a democratic republic. In the era of consolidation of central government ushered in by the Revolution of 1930, and continuing through the period of the Estado Novo (New state, 1937–45), the rapidly changing political context both required and offered university students new forms of political organization, nationally and internationally. A small group responded to the prevailing corporatist system by creating UNE and then worked to extend its influence and secure its authority. Among other measures, for several years they sought the political benediction of being granted official status, while also trying to participate in the intra-elite male networks of political decision making. If their efforts met with mixed results at first, in the climate of heightened political debate around the question of Brazil's role in World War II and the possibility of new presidential elections after the war, students were able to parlay their position as young leaders-to-be into greater official status, including the granting of their headquarters building. After 1945 students held on to this newfound prominence, notwithstanding various transformations in internal UNE leadership and in the ideological persuasion of those leaders as well as changes in the student body as a whole, including the increasing participation of women students. Throughout this period student political activism was neither reliably left nor right but constantly shifted according to the ideological views of the students and the political exigencies of the moment. Yet no matter who directed the union, its university student members came to believe they had both an inherited and a hard-earned claim to engage in political affairs, one built on both institutional and moral authority—a status nowhere better symbolized than in the prominence and seeming permanence of the UNE building.

The Men of Letters: Social Hierarchies and Higher Education

If decisions about who is granted or denied access to education are always political, the transparency of this fact in Brazil was never more clear than under Portuguese colonial rule. By prohibiting the establishment of universities in Brazil the Crown ensured that elite families would have to send their sons to Europe for this requisite leadership credential—usually to Coimbra University in Portugal—thereby fostering close intellectual and personal ties between future colonial leaders and the imperial center.[2] And it was sons who were sent to European universities, not daughters, as elite girls' education generally consisted of home tutoring in subjects like music, poetry, and French. Formal institutions of higher education within Brazil would not be permitted until the early nineteenth century. When the Napoleonic Wars forced the Crown to flee to Brazil in 1808, colonial Rio de Janeiro temporarily became the center of the Portuguese Empire, and the royal court, libraries, and other institutions took up residence in the Marvelous City. Rather than building full-fledged universities in Brazil, however, Portuguese intellectuals, inspired by ideas of the French Enlightenment that regarded such institutions as ideological apparatuses of the ancien régime, favored instead the creation of individual, highly autonomous, professional programs. Called *cátedras* (cathedrae) after the lifetime chair to which the professor in charge was named, these schools offered training in one main area of study. The first such programs arose almost immediately: 1808 witnessed the establishment of two cátedras in surgery —one in the capital of Rio de Janeiro and one in the former capital of Salvador da Bahia—as well as one cátedra in anatomy, also in Rio.[3] Two years later Rio gained a third cátedra, in engineering.

Following the return to Portugal of King Dom João VI in 1821 and the declaration of an independent Brazilian empire by his son Dom Pedro I in 1822, the process of opening new Brazilian cátedras continued, now augmented by the need for experts in law who would help govern the newly independent nation. To that end, in 1827 the emperor established the first two law schools in Brazil, geographically balancing them by founding one in the traditional northeastern stronghold of Olinda (later relocated to Recife in 1854) and another in the up-and-coming southern city of São Paulo. Over time additional cátedras emerged, and as they did they became grouped into academies or faculties, such as those of mining and metallurgy or philosophy, humanities, and social sciences.[4] Through the prominence of the families who sent their sons to study in these schools and the corresponding personal and social relationships students established, the programs conferred upon their graduates not simply specialized training but also the marks of social and political legitimacy. Lilia Moritz Schwarcz, an expert on nineteenth-century social and racial identity and citizenship, explains this phenomenon as owing in large part to the immense symbolic weight of the law degree in particular: "When the law schools opened their doors in 1828, the prestige of both the legal profession and the bacharel [those who held the bacharel degree][5] in Brazil began to mount. The source of the prestige lay not in the course of study, nor in the law profession as such, but in the symbolic mandate of legal professionals and in the political possibilities that beckoned. . . . The obtaining of the degree became synonymous with achieving social prestige and political power."[6]

Throughout the nineteenth century, as Andrew Kirkendall has shown in his study of the São Paulo and Recife Law Schools, the young men who enrolled there were well aware of their future leadership roles, and they actively struggled to define and legitimize their authority accordingly. He cites the student Estevão Leão Borrul, for example, who wrote in 1890, "Brazil will always be governed by men of letters, by the pen and the word—by the bacharéis, in short—because they were, are, and will always be the elite of the nation."[7] At some moments, defining their authority meant displays of literary dexterity as "men of letters," and at others it took the form of explicit political partisanship. Kirkendall notes that by the 1870s and 1880s, as the nation became embroiled in campaigns for the abolition of slavery (achieved in 1888) and the replacement of the empire with a republic (accorded in 1889), "Student republicans were in the forefront of calls to organize 'conferences in the public squares.'"[8] Notwithstanding these public appeals, nineteenth-century politics centered firmly around the maintenance of a highly stratified social order. Both abolition and the end of the empire, for example, occurred in tightly controlled ways that prevented any significant upheaval from below. Hence students' participation in calls for these kinds of progressive reforms were not incompatible with their elite status, but dovetailed with other elites' efforts to usher in what many had come to see as more modern political and labor structures. Parents and others might at times complain about excessive political activism distracting students from their studies, or lament that they did not yet know enough about the array of ideas at stake to commit to firm positions, yet a degree of political engagement was nonetheless generally accepted as appropriate conduct for those who would soon take on real leadership positions.

The exclusivity that characterized these early schools and undergirded the presumed authority of student activism remained the hallmark of higher education throughout the ensuing Old Republic of 1889–1930, when democratic elections replaced the former monarchy but suffrage remained extremely limited. This situation is unsurprising given the country's predominantly rural composition at the time and a political scenario in which large landholders dominated the governmental system via patron–client relationships. While the number of academic programs grew slightly in this period, admission remained tightly circumscribed, depending both on graduation from one of the scarce secondary schools geared toward university preparation and on passage of a rigorous entrance examination called the *vestibular*.[9] Despite the fact that technically women earned the right to enroll in courses of higher education in 1881, they nonetheless faced exceptionally high barriers in that few preparatory schools admitted female students. Women's secondary schooling was generally limited to teacher training at normal schools, which did not qualify their graduates to take the vestibular.[10] Although a handful of women nonetheless began enrolling in faculties in the late 1880s, the student body in the Old Republic remained overwhelmingly male.[11] The proportion of male to female students from 1907 to 1912 in the Federal District of Rio de Janeiro is revealing (tables 1.1 and 1.2). As access to education was higher there than in many Brazilian cities, this case may be considered an extraordinarily inclusive example, yet nonetheless the discrepancies are obvious, with women and girls making up just 25 percent of secondary school students and slightly over 1 percent of undergraduates. In 1910 only a small proportion of the overall population in the Federal District was made up of students of higher education (table 1.3). While the educational figures are not broken down by race, and Brazil never experienced the formal racial segregation that barred African Americans in the United States from attending many schools, the

TABLE I.I Secondary School Educational Enrollments in the Federal District, 1907–1912

	Male Students	Female Students
1907	3,721	1,221
1908	4,329	973
1909	4,596	1,460
1910	6,044	1,515
1911	6,579	2,469
1912	7,165	2,145

Source: Instituto Brasileiro de Geografía e Estatística, Estatísticas do Século XX, Rio de Janeiro, 2006.

existence of slavery in Brazil throughout most of the nineteenth century and the corresponding inequalities between white and nonwhite populations that marked the country resulted in a similar dearth of students of color.

Those lucky few who became students during the Old Republic continued to find ways to involve themselves in political pursuits, even if some complained that doing so seemed less exhilarating than during the excitement of the abolition and republican struggles. Such was the case of a group of São Paulo Law School students in 1903 who lamented the disappearance of "the old splendor of academic life . . . . [when] the voice of the academic tribune, in the public square, incited the people to revolt against social institutions that enshrined injustice."[12] Notwithstanding these nostalgic expressions, students not only participated in the major political events of the period, but usually found general acceptance for these pursuits. In his study of the São Paulo Law School, John W. F. Dulles has noted the many overlapping political alliances and arrangements made between former and current students in the first decades of the twentieth century as they engaged in the political debates of those years.[13] Elsewhere in the country students participated as well. During the military campaign of the mid-1890s at Canudos, Bahia, in which federal forces ultimately destroyed a religious community of peasants that they found threatening, the Faculty of Medicine of Bahia was transformed into a military hospital where professors and students volunteered to treat the wounded soldiers.[14] After the campaign, state and military officials erected a marble stone at the faculty

TABLE I.2 Higher Education Enrollments in the Federal District, 1907–1912

	Male Students	Female Students
1907	2,455	32
1908	3,045	27
1909	3,323	39
1910	3,243	62
1911	3,972	56
1912	3,630	53

Source: Instituto Brasileiro de Geografía e Estatística, *Estatísticas do Século XX*, Rio de Janeiro, 2006.

that read, "Through this marble Bahia eternalizes its thanks to the doctors, pharmacists and students who exercised their apostolic duty during the painful Canudos period in 1897."[15] Meanwhile students at the newly created Bahian Law School nearby critiqued the campaign, protesting the excessive military violence used against the residents of Canudos.[16] And when the São Paulo law students cited above sought to resurrect that "old splendor of academic life" by creating a new student association, the school's director had electric lighting installed in the main hall in time for their first meeting.[17] The newly formed Centro Acadêmico Onze de Agosto (August 11th academic center)—so named in honor of the founding of the school on August 11, 1827—was the first permanent student organization (one that continues to this day). It gave rise to later Centros Acadêmicos (CAs) across the country, centers that served as platforms for students' participation in national political debates, as well as for organizing social activities, producing student newspapers, and generally representing student demands to university authorities.

Brazilian students were not alone in their desire to form student associations and to use them to advocate their interests and to express their political positions. Both in the Americas and in Europe the early twentieth century witnessed an effervescence of national and international student organizing as students promoted and took part in a wave of international meetings and organizations.[18] Several Brazilian students served as representatives at the first International Congress of American Students, for example, held in Montevideo, Uruguay, in 1908. Among other resolutions, the 113 attendees voted unanimously that students should be able to elect

TABLE 1.3 Estimated Proportion of Population Enrolled in Higher Education in the Federal District, 1910

	Total Enrolled	Estimated Population	Estimated Proportion Enrolled
Men	3,323	435,237	0.8%
Women	39	435,237	0.009%
Total	3,362	870,475	0.4%

Source: Instituto Brasileiro de Geografía e Estatística, *Estatísticas do Século XX*, Rio de Janeiro, 2006, taking total population count for 1910 and estimating male:female division of 50/50.

delegates to represent them on university governing councils, supported proposals in favor of government-funded travel scholarships and residence halls for out-of-town students (*casas para estudiantes*), and decided to create a League of American Students. According to the historian Mark J. van Aken, while "an anti-Yankee spirit did not pervade the deliberations, . . . a Brazilian delegate gave a long report on the Monroe Doctrine which castigated the imperialism of William McKinley and Theodore Roosevelt and denounced the United States' intervention in Panama."[19] The new League of American Students sponsored two more international congresses, one in Buenos Aires in 1910 and the other in Lima in 1912.[20] In short, Brazilian students joined other Americans in efforts at political organizing, debating both student-specific issues like the need for residence halls and broader questions about Pan-American solidarity and the role of the United States in the region.

Later, however, when a wave of student protest erupted in neighboring Argentina in 1918, Brazilian students did not follow suit. Beginning first in Córdoba, Argentine students demanded deep reforms in a university system they accused of being "authoritarian, inefficient, clerically oriented and obscurantist," and they engaged in radical tactics such as attacking churches, vandalizing a Catholic newspaper, and, most notably, seizing and occupying the National University of Córdoba.[21] Coordinated by the recently formed Argentine University Federation, a national-level organization, the University Reform Movement, as it soon became known, quickly spread across Argentina. Similar movements followed in Peru (1919), Chile (1920), and Mexico (1921), seemingly inspired by Argentine students' actions and their distribution of the Córdoba Manifesto, a document directed "to the free men of South America" that called on them to "collaborate in the work of freedom that we have begun."[22]

The absence of this kind of cry for reform in Brazil helps elucidate the different situation that characterized Brazil in 1918. For one thing, Spanish American universities were much older institutions (the University of Córdoba, for example, had been founded in 1613) as well as being predominantly religious, and they were consequently seen as exerting an archaic influence in a way the secular Brazilian faculties were not. The Córdoba Manifesto colorfully refers to the universities as "the last chain of the old monarchical and monastic domination" that bound Latin America, a depiction that would not have found much resonance in Brazil, where, as we have seen, institutions of higher education were created in the early nineteenth century as colonialism itself was disintegrating.[23] Similarly, the fact that the Brazilian system of higher education was still organized exclusively around isolated faculties and contained no actual universities meant there were few shared problems that could connect students across the country in common grievance directed at a common source. Even if students had shared a set of concerns, no national-level student organizations akin to the Argentine University Federation that might have coordinated their efforts on a national scale existed in Brazil. Yet perhaps the most important reason Brazilian students did not pursue radical reforms at this moment is the fact that in Argentina many students came from the ascending middle classes and saw the universities as aristocratic impediments to their social inclusion, while the vast majority of Brazilian students hailed from the elite and benefited from the current political and university system. Since the 1880s the Argentine state had universalized primary education and extended and popularized secondary education, spurred by its early efforts at industrialization and the corresponding need for educated labor, and by 1918 higher education had become a primary means of social mobility for the growing middle classes.[24] Yet the universities remained tied to an older, hierarchical system characterized by professors with lifetime appointments, an antiscientific curriculum, and no student participation in university decision making. This latter aspect seemed out of step with current political trends, as just six years earlier Congress had passed the Sáenz Peña law, instituting universal, secret, obligatory male suffrage. In this context, Argentine students saw the universities not simply as ill-equipped to help them gain the training necessary to succeed in the nation's changing economy, but also as actively impeding them, a bastion of aristocratic ideals being defended at their expense. According to the analysis of the historian Natalia Milanesio, through their actions the student demonstrators demanded a gendered kind of recognition as men, embodying a new model of masculinity that privileged both violent rebelliousness and moral intellectualism.[25] Facing an uncertain future, Argentine students were willing to engage in radical tactics to ensure that their political voices were heard.

By contrast, in Brazil higher education served as a recognition of social status rather than as a vehicle for attaining it. In many ways Republican Brazil still reflected the social structure envisioned by the planter classes who had long dominated political life. Heavily agricultural (until 1920 about 90 percent of the population lived in rural areas) and stratified by race and class, the country was also divided along geographical lines as individual states strongly defended autonomous economies and political rights, while the federal government lacked institutional strength.[26] The political system was dominated by local and regional patronage networks, while formal means of political participation were extremely scarce for most of the population. Brazil had no equivalent to the Sáenz Peña law, and suffrage was severely limited. The historian Joseph Love has calculated that the highest rate of voter participation during the entire Old Republic, at the 1930 presidential election, was just 5.7 percent.[27] The fact that literacy was still a voting requirement when Brazil was over 70 percent illiterate in 1920 sets into further contrast the political power of those with access to a higher education.[28] Unlike Argentine students, Brazilian students generally benefited from the current political and university system. They also enjoyed a degree of political authority as students and assumed their influence would increase in the years to come.

Hence while in several Spanish American countries authorities in the 1920s struggled with the question of reforming the universities, in the same period federal and state governments in Brazil began to create universities for the first time. The first federal Brazilian university, the University of Rio de Janeiro (now the UFRJ),[29] combined the faculties of medicine, engineering, and law into one organization in 1920, becoming the conglomerating model other universities would follow, beginning seven years later with the state-funded University of Minas Gerais.[30] Because they arose more from administrative decree than from any expansion of facilities or opportunities, the rise of universities did little to alter the social composition of the students. Meanwhile, for the rest of the population even basic literacy was hard to acquire. In short, the possibility of obtaining some level of higher education remained in the hands of a very select few, usually those from wealthy families who had access to the private preparatory schools and who could afford the high cost of the vestibular entrance exam.

Indeed, Borrul's words about the elite nature of the student body rang true for a long time. Historically restricted to a select few, access to a university education implied a student's impending political and economic prominence. The bacharéis were the economic, gendered, and racial elite of the nation, and, appropriately, they learned how to wield their governing pens and words in student politics.

Making Politics Official:
Student Political Organizations from the CAs to UNE

After a military-backed political coup in 1930 put an end to the Old Republic and brought Getúlio Vargas to the presidency—whence he would govern as head of a provisional government until 1934, as a democratically elected president until 1937, and then, until 1945, as a dictator of the authoritarian Estado Novo regime—the student body and the nature of student politics began to change. Immediately upon assuming office Vargas and his supporters struggled to wrest power from the previously dominant states and to vest more control in the federal government. They also worked to shift the economy away from a reliance on export-led agriculture and to promote industrialization. As they did so, they sought to widen a base of support for such changes, including that of new groups from the urban and popular sectors. Among other early measures, in November of 1930 they created the first Ministry of Education and Health, whose task it would be to centralize and widen the educational system, including that pertaining to higher education. As efforts to accelerate national industrialization in the wake of the worldwide depression of 1929 meant an increased need for trained scientists, technicians, and bureaucrats, such measures were opportunely important.

One way in which the new ministry attempted to meet this need was to increase the number of students eligible for university study by gradually eliminating the two-tracked secondary school system that had previously directed students into either university-preparatory or technical lines of study. Students still had to receive passing grades on the vestibular exam, but university enrollment was no longer limited to those who had attended only certain secondary schools. Another way the ministry tried to increase access was by radically reducing the enrollment fees at federal universities, thereby virtually, if not officially, eliminating them and making entrance for those who qualified basically free of charge.[31] Undergraduate enrollment slowly began to increase in the ensuing years, though experiencing a slight dip at the end of the decade (table 1.4). Overall, however, in the twelve years from 1932 to 1944 faculty and university enrollment figures increased 21 percent and in succeeding years grew even more rapidly.

The Vargas administration not only set the wheels in motion for the expansion of the university system, but also impacted student political organizations in ways that would have lasting effects on the future of student politics in Brazil. One of the hallmarks of the Vargas period is the fact that he and his advisers espoused and enacted a corporatist philosophy by which they saw society as naturally organized around specific functions—a system perhaps most visible in their policies toward labor.[32] According to this perspective, the state's task was to minimize conflict between groups (such as that between labor and capital) and to pursue policies that would benefit the greater social body (hence the name corporatism, from the Latin corpus). It did this by encouraging the formation of officially sanctioned, noncompetitive, compulsory interest groups that would represent their members to the government and by offering them incentives, such as special perks and subsidies. At the same time, it imposed constraints on these groups in terms of the kinds of demands they could make and on their internal governance and leadership.[33] As Vargas's presidency coincided with the growing mobilization and organization of urban workers who could potentially either threaten or buttress his position, corporatist incentives and constraints offered his government ways of simultaneously currying support and stifling opposition.

University students constituted an important part of the social body, and they too experienced the incentives and deterrents of corporatism. Less than a year after Vargas became president, as part of a sweeping reorganization of the system of higher education, he legally mandated the creation, recognition, and funding of official student organizations, essentially guaranteeing students the right to organize collectively and facilitating their efforts to do so, while also precluding the rise of strong, unofficial student groups. Under the law the student body in each faculty was to "create class associations to defend their general interests and to

TABLE 1.4 National Enrollments in Higher Education, 1932–1952

Year	Enrollment	Year	Enrollment
1932	21,526	1943	23,786
1933	24,166	1944	26,004
1934	26,263	1945	26,757
1935	27,501	1956	28,464
1936	26,732	1947	30,715
1937	25,481	1948	34,544
1938	23,300	1949	37,584
1939	21,235	1950	44,097
1940	20,017	1951	45,803
1941	19,872	1952	48,266
1942	21,425		

Source: Instituto Brasileiro de Geografía e Estatística, *Estatísticas do Século XX*, Rio de Janeiro, 2006.

make the life of the collective agreeable and educational" and to "create and develop a class spirit." The term *class* in this sense did not refer to school spirit like that on display at collegiate sporting events in the U.S., nor did it suggest Marxist understandings of social class as defined by a group's relationship to the means of production. Rather, class became a common term used in corporatist systems across Latin America to delineate the various collective groupings that were seen to make up society, and this law of 1931 defined class spirit as "the submission of their individual interests to those of the collective."[34] With passage of the law, students within each faculty gained the legal right to form a student-run organization and elect a directorate that would both receive an annual budget and be recognized "as the legitimate representative organ, for all intents and purposes, of the student body of that institution."[35] In practice this meant that in some places preexisting CAs or similar student organizations rose to official status, while in others new organizations were created.[36] Many of the smaller, issue-specific student groups and clubs that had earlier characterized student organizing were essentially folded into or superseded by the new centers, as they enjoyed, first and foremost, legal recognition as the official representative student organizations and, additionally, the benefits of guaranteed funding and other perks.[37] Yet the law went even further, as it also decreed that within each university students could form a Diretório Central dos Estudantes (DCE, Central Student Directorate) made up of two representatives from each CA to represent their interests on the university level. And it established that the president of the DCE would sit on the university governing board (Conselho Universitário), an important gesture of student inclusion in decision making, even though in practice one student seat in a large council meant little real power.[38] Through this legislation students gained important rights to organize and benefits for doing so. This new system, echoing the general structure of the regime as a whole, attempted to streamline student political organizations into one hierarchical chain of command ultimately subordinate to university officials, posing limits on their political action and exposing student organizations to possible co-optation by authorities. While the Vargas government legislated faculty- and university-wide student organizations, it initially stopped there and did not of its own initiative promote state- or national-level student coalitions. Instead, students themselves launched such groupings a few years later, creating the first União Estadual de Estudantes (UEE, State Union of Students) in Minas Gerais in 1937 and, most importantly, founding UNE in 1937–38.[39] Given a context in which unofficial representational organizations were discouraged, it may at first seem surprising that students were able to form a new national union and that they would go on to create other UEEs in the years to come. Yet in the case of UNE, few officials (and perhaps few students too) foresaw the kind of political role the organization would eventually take on, and it was only after students presented officials with the fait accompli of a national union that Vargas and others had to decide how to respond.

For UNE grew out of the Casa do Estudante do Brasil (House of the Brazilian Student), a private charitable and cultural institution in Rio de Janeiro that offered inexpensive lodging and meals to students in need as well as hosting theater performances, art shows, and academic discussions.[40] Its founder and director was the feminist poet Ana Amélia Queirós Carneiro de Mendonça, the daughter of wealthy parents and the wife of a famous soccer player, who put her considerable social prominence to work establishing the Casa do Estudante in 1929 and securing government subsidies to pay for its activities. At least some activist students appreciated her efforts, for in 1930 they elected her Queen of the Students as part of their protest against the city's hosting of the Miss Universe pageant during difficult economic times.[41] By 1933 the Casa do Estudante headed an important publishing house, producing a monthly magazine called *rumo*, edited by the law student and future politician Carlos Lacerda.[42] It eventually produced books by and for students, including, among other titles, *Sensacionalismo*, prepared by the Centro Acadêmico Cândido de Oliveira (CACO) of the Rio de Janeiro Law School.[43]

If the Casa do Estudante do Brasil fulfilled one of the needs highlighted at the earlier International Congress of American Students (at which the argument was made for casas de estudiantes), by the 1920s new international student associations were actively promoting joint cultural activities as necessary aspects of student welfare. This was particularly true in the wake of the First World War in Europe, where students sought to restore cooperation after the war's divisions. In 1919 seven European student groups founded the Confédération International des Étudiants (CIE), headquartered in Brussels and "concerned primarily with non-political matters such as cultural exchange and better conditions for students in universities."[44] Throughout the 1920s the CIE gradually expanded, and its near-annual university games included ever-larger numbers of athletes. By the mid-1930s, as the group was actively encouraging other national student organizations to join, the Casa do Estudante too was seeking to increase Brazilian students' opportunities for international exchange. The Casa hosted two Polish student representatives of the CIE on their visit to Brazil in 1935 and then sent a Casa member, Clothilde Cavalcanti, to Bulgaria in 1936 to attend the CIE's annual meeting and request Brazilian membership. As member organizations were expected to have national, not simply local, representation, the CIE approved Cavalcanti's bid contingent on the Casa's convocation of a nationally representative body. (Presumably the CIE took this unusual step in order to bolster its own efforts, ultimately successful, to be named by the League of Nations as the official international student organization, as it was thereby able to increase its number of national members to forty-two.) Thus in August 1937 the Casa hosted just such a meeting, drawing representatives of thirty-nine student organizations from various areas of the country to create a Conselho Nacional de Estudantes (National Council of Students). In the seven-page statutes they drew up, they made clear that the council's goals were "cultural, educational, and sportive exchange" (Article 3); that it shared with the Casa titular membership in the CIE (Article 27); and that it would "not adopt or involve itself in political or religious issues, nor [would] it affiliate with student organizations that do so" (Article 31). As president of the new council's executive commission, students elected Cavalcanti.

Taking seriously the idea of fostering a national student dialogue, President Cavalcanti wrote to additional student organizations the next year, inviting them to a national congress in Rio. Noting that the Casa regularly attended international student gatherings at which young people put aside their associational differences in order to treat their common problems, the letter invited Brazilian students to come and "discuss, within the strictest camaraderie, our problems and our needs." Yet, true to the council's statutes, the invitation foreswore any political action, advocating instead "clarifying and demonstrating [problems] to the leaders of the Nation, who benevolently receive dignified and worthy suggestions."[45]

In this avowedly apolitical stance, the council shared the orientation of the CIE, which advocated addressing matters "concerning students as students, and not as members of the broader society."[46] In the context of Brazil, however, this orientation would soon be contested by other students. They would be fueled both by the fact that many had long seen themselves as important and legitimate political actors and by the declaration of the Estado Novo in November 1937 that abolished all political parties, thereby rendering political participation via electoral means meaningless, and corporatist and other forms of political pressure ever more critical. Thus at this second gathering in December 1938, held in Rio's grand Municipal Theater and distinguished by the attendance of Minister of Education Gustavo Capanema, the participating students (now from some eighty organizations), voted to replace the idea of the council, subordinate to the Casa do Estudante do Brasil, with an independent association, UNE, that was free to engage in political activities.[47] They elected an eight-seat directorate and drew up new statutes, Article One declaring the new organization to be "the maximum representative organization of all Brazilian students," superseding all others, and affirming in legalistic prose both the authority of student politics and UNE's monopoly on such authority at the national level. In a conciliatory gesture the authors added the notation that UNE had been founded through "the initiative of the Casa do Estudante do Brasil," but the new union's autonomy and its representative role were firmly asserted.[48] By the next year efforts were under way to form additional UEEs, following the strong hierarchical order established by Vargas yet directing all student organizational efforts toward

UNE: each faculty's CA was under the umbrella of each university's DCE, each DCE was to report to the state's UEE, and, finally, each UEE was to be represented by UNE.

This relatively autonomous structure may in part explain Vargas's ambiguous response to the new union. Although he declared his support for UNE soon after its foundation and quickly adopted the custom of inviting each newly elected UNE directorate to the presidential palace for a special luncheon, he delayed granting UNE the legal status enjoyed by CAs and DCEs for several years. Despite formal entreaties by the UNE directorate, made in person and by letter, requesting recognition, Vargas failed to vest UNE with official standing. The union had no formal guarantee of its status and no such comforts such as a physical center from which to operate. Instead, it funded its activities by imposing annual dues on affiliated DCEs and kept its offices at the Casa do Estudante do Brasil.

Another factor that helps explain Vargas's delay in recognizing UNE is the fact that very early on the UNE leadership included members with close ties to the Partido Comunista Brasileiro (PCB, Brazilian Communist Party), a party strongly at odds with the president. Founded in 1922 and officially outlawed in 1927, the PCB was very small when Vargas came to power in 1930, having hardly more than a thousand members.[49] But in the ensuing years the PCB (like communist parties elsewhere at this time) began to grow in stature as it pursued a popular front approach, actively seeking to forge alliances with other groups in order to widen the party's appeal and counter the growing threat of fascism. This strategy appeared to be highly important in light of a growing fascist movement within Brazil, the Ação Integralista Brasileira (AIB, Brazilian Integralist Action), or Green Shirts, so named for the green shirts they wore in their military-style public marches. Since its founding in 1932 the AIB enjoyed close ties with the Vargas government while its membership ballooned to over three hundred thousand, with particular support among the middle class and the military.[50] Communists and left-leaning noncommunists who opposed this right-wing turn formed a united front organization, the Aliança Nacional Libertadora (ANL, National Liberating Alliance). Though not technically run by the PCB, the ANL was headed by the PCB's most famous member, Luis Carlos Prestes.[51] As the leader of the 1920s Tenentes Revolt, a series of uprisings by junior army officers, Prestes symbolized the frustrations of midlevel sectors of society over their continued political exclusion. When the government shut down the ANL in July 1935 it enjoyed a membership of several hundred thousand as well, many of whom also came from the middle class.[52]

University students in the mid-1930s were thus confronted with a highly polarized political situation. Their options for political participation became even more limited after 1935, when the PCB launched a failed uprising against Vargas and accordingly suffered an immediate crackdown, and again after 1937, when Vargas decried a supposed new communist plot, one actually concocted by his own regime, and used this fallacious threat to cancel elections and inaugurate the authoritarian Estado Novo. Soon thereafter he prohibited all political parties, consequently (and deliberately) rendering the AIB illegal too. With formal means of political participation thereby made impossible, mobilizing via organizations like the illegal PCB had added appeal, and an important group of university students affiliated with Brazil's communist party.

This context also helps explain the eagerness of left-leaning students to become actively involved in UNE. For the closing down of the ANL had not dissuaded PCB members from pursuing a popular front approach. Rather, the need for such alliances only grew as European fascism began to take on stronger military overtones. Thus PCB members and other left-leaning students saw a national students' union as a much-needed opportunity to join together, and they quickly became involved. Almost immediately after UNE's creation it began to assume a position in national and international affairs. In 1938, for example, as conflicts in Europe and Asia threatened to turn to war and American representatives planned to meet in Lima at a Conference of American States, UNE sent written denunciations of Nazi-fascism to the Brazilian representative, Afrânio de Melo Franco.[53] By 1940, after Germany and the USSR signed a nonaggression pact, both the PCB and UNE were advocating neutrality. The union released a message "to the youth of Brazil and the Americas" warning that those who characterized the budding war as being fought to defend civilization were demagogues who "want to spread the conflict, hurling the whole world into the flames."[54] After Germany broke the agreement in June 1941, UNE would again take up the antifascist cry, advocating intervention on the side of the Allies.

Beyond the lukewarm reception from President Vargas, the union also soon found itself at odds with the Casa do Estudante do Brasil, despite the fact that the two organizations initially worked closely together. Not only did the Casa grant UNE office space in its building in Rio, but the two also continued to participate jointly in international student events, as when they hosted the Pan-American Student Conference in Rio in 1939. At least one long-standing Casa representative, the former council president Cavalcanti, was elected to the first UNE directorate, in her case as first secretary in charge of international affairs. Nonetheless, the relationship between UNE and the Casa soon broke down. By May 1940 ties between the organizations had deteriorated so badly that the Casa asked UNE to find its own office space, and the union was forced to leave. That same month the CIE dissolved when German troops occupied its Brussels headquarters and destroyed its offices and files.[55]

In the break between UNE and the Casa do Estudante do Brasil, political differences between the two organizations undoubtedly played a central role. We have seen that the Casa viewed student organizations as best being directed toward essentially cultural ends, while UNE almost immediately sought to enter into national political discussions. The Casa's report of 1939 complained that its efforts to create UNE had been "entirely disparaged by the student political orientation which some had imprinted on [UNE]."[56] Dulles has suggested that squabbles over who had the right to choose the Brazilian representatives to international student gatherings —UNE as the official member organization or the Casa as the organization that secured the necessary financing—contributed to the breakdown.[57] Yet in addition to any differences of political perspective and any specific power struggles, the gendered tensions that permeated this moment of student movement activism contributed to the break between the two groups. For UNE came to diverge from the Casa as it abandoned women's issues, turned toward an almost exclusively male leadership, and fostered a gendered political culture of male camaraderie and homosocial political networks.

Whatever its political reservations, the Casa had nonetheless offered a space for women students to discuss their needs, and it counted on female leadership both in the directorial figure of Queirós and in student leaders like Cavalcanti. By the late 1930s and early 1940s women were beginning to enroll in faculties and universities more regularly, especially in those areas considered to offer gender-appropriate training, such as programs in teaching and nursing.[58] As they did so, they realized they faced challenges that needed addressing. Thus at the council's national meeting in 1938, at which UNE was formed, one of the five major topics slated for discussion was devoted to women students, in particular the unique difficulties they

faced in entering the job market and professional associations, their domestic situations, and the potential role of women's groups in providing
assistance.[59] Yet within a year women-specific concerns disappeared from
the UNE agenda, and after Cavalcanti's term as first secretary expired no
women would be elected to the national directorate for over a decade.[60]

More revealing, when asked about the rupture between UNE and the
Casa many years later, several male participants placed responsibility
for it on Queirós, whom they described as overly dominating.[61] "[The
break occurred] because she wanted to enlarge [her position] within the
student movement," recalled the former student and UNE founder Irum
Sant'Anna. "She was just the director of a foundation. The Casa do Estudante do Brasil wasn't anything more than a foundation, and she wanted
to go farther forward, she wanted to be a student leader, without having
any credentials for that." Drawing an invisible boundary around the definition of a student, one that incorporated age, gender, and family circumstances, he added, "She wasn't a student anymore, she was a married
woman, she had a child, but she wanted to enlarge [her position]."[62] Even
José Gomes de Talarico, another student who took part in the founding of
UNE and who credits Queirós with giving a huge push to student politics,
later blamed the split on "her obsession with wanting to control the student movement."[63] That this perspective had some contemporary resonance appears likely, given an UNE publication from 1940 that turned her
earlier position as Queen of the Students into a form of sarcastic derision,
referring to her as the Queen, as if she had given herself the title.[64] To those
who fit the traditional mold of a student as an independent young man, the
attempts of a former female student to involve herself in student affairs
was seen as both overbearing and illegitimate.

Once UNE was deprived of its space at the Casa, the behavior of its
leaders sheds further light on what kind of cultural and gendered environment marked the union's early years. As recounted by the Brazilian journalist Artur Poerner in one of the most celebrated histories of the student
movement, the all-male leadership began to hold its meetings in various
bars in Rio de Janeiro, where they soon skirmished with male residents of
the area over the students' behavior with local women. Poerner wrote,
"These conflicts between students and marginals solidified, over time, into
typical features of the neighborhood, almost always arising out of the
advantages that the former had with women, in the gay late-nights that
ended the prostitutes' evening labor. The 'scoundrels' and the 'unlucky'

rebelled against the privileges students enjoyed at the brothels—50% discount, especially with the *francesas*."[65] According to the historian Sueann Caulfield, *francesa* was a term for higher-class European prostitutes who might or might not be French. She has demonstrated that in the early twentieth century a social hierarchy of prostitution developed in the red light district of Rio de Janeiro, the francesas occupying the highest rung.[66] Beyond Poerner's many allusions to the UNE leaders' status, such as his division of the men into "students" and "marginals," the reference to francesas suggests a further example of gender, class, and racial privilege. Embellished though his account may be, it speaks to the sense of early UNE leaders as being privileged young white men behaving like others of their status, with little room for their female colleagues. When UNE leaders did not meet in bars or brothels, they gathered at the home of Luís Pinheiro Paes Leme, who remained president of UNE for two years after the union was expelled from the Casa (from 1940 to 1942).[67] In that environment, it is not hard to imagine how, despite the important role of women like Queirós and Cavalcanti in laying the foundation for UNE, both the Casa in particular and women students in general might soon find themselves at odds with the new UNE leadership. And the split reveals a sense of the challenges facing those women students who sought to become involved in student politics, especially at a moment when literate women had only recently won the right to vote (in 1932) but could not act on that right between 1937 and 1945 owing to the cancellation of elections under the Estado Novo.[68]

Despite UNE's origins in the woman-led Casa and its initially unofficial status, the union soon reflected and engaged in the kind of intra-elite political diplomacy marked by close male relationships that characterized this period. Throughout the union's early years its leaders maintained extremely close ties with top-ranking political figures. The minister of education and other politicians continued, as they did in 1938, to attend the formal opening of UNE's annual congress, the event at which new directorates were chosen, and President Vargas regularly complemented these events with a formal reception of the incoming directorate at the presidential palace.[69] Moreover, direct personal ties often linked students and the government. As Talarico recalled, "Getúlio was very cordial, very kind. He was a likable man. Of course, whenever students were able to approach him, he received them very well, cordially. So much so that, for example, he tolerated or went along with the student movement from 1938 to 1942–43, when it had a huge influence from the left and the PCB. I cite as a fact that even Paes Leme, Wagner Cavalcanti, and Antonio Franca [known leftists and UNE leaders], all of them were received by Doctor Getúlio." Besides this general level of cordiality, Talarico noted, more specific personal relationships played crucial roles. For example, his friendship with Euclides Aranha, the son of Foreign Minister Oswaldo Aranha, often came in handy when UNE leaders wanted to speak with the president immediately. As Talarico said, "He [Euclides Aranha] had access to President Vargas and so every time a fellow student or colleague was arrested we'd go to the [presidential] palace to talk to Getúlio, and he'd always attend to us right away."[70] Social and familiar ties bound the president and university students, especially the UNE leadership, even when they held strong political differences.

Consistent with these kinds of interpersonal relationships and with the fact that under a corporatist system "conflicts [were generally] resolved through adjudication rather than through confrontations," UNE's political strategy in this early period tended toward advocacy and persuasion rather than active mobilization.[71] For example, at the UNE Congress in 1938 students prepared wide-ranging recommendations for restructuring the Brazilian university system, suggestions drawn heavily from the Argentine reform movement of 1918. But they did not engage in anything like the political tactics of their Argentine neighbors, such as militant strikes and university occupations. Instead, Brazilian students called their university reform positions suggestions and offered them to the minister of education for his perusal. When many of the suggestions went unheeded, they addressed the issue again at their third annual congress, resolving "to offer all possible cooperation to the Ministry of Education and Health in the elaboration of an educational reform."[72] In part these strategies were a result of the strict limits imposed by Vargas on all oppositional organizing and on the strategy of the PCB in seeking alliances rather than conflicts. Yet they also reflected students' privileged positions as members of the elite, for whom lobbying could be much more effective than confrontation.

In short, throughout much of the Estado Novo, social groups formed official organizations to advocate their interests, a process made all the more necessary in the absence of legal political parties and the increasing ideological polarization between communism and fascism. In this context, university students, whose political activism had previously enjoyed informal acceptance, worked to secure these earlier assumptions. They did so by calling on the intra-elite male networks of their friends and families, eschewing the leadership and programs of their female colleagues, and, most important, seeking to build an official students' union that would represent them nationwide.

Building Institutional and Moral Authority in the
Theaters of War and Peace

First in the face of deepening debates about Brazil's role in World War II, and then in the increasing calls to end the Estado Novo and resume presidential elections, UNE's status began to change. The heightened political debate and resulting need for visible public allies meant that several political factions, from President Vargas to those who sought his removal, turned to university students for signs of support and collaboration. In the theater of war, students who had long sought to solidify the authority of a national students' union found just such a stage to do so. And in the ensuing postwar period they worked to maintain their institutional authority and to advance a sense of moral authority as well.

Their first major success in this regard came when President Vargas finally decreed official recognition of UNE in February 1942, affirming the union's status as "the coordinating and representative entity of all student bodies in institutions of higher education in the entire country."[73] The timing of the gesture suggests that the decision had become symbolically useful in the context of war. In what Stanley Hilton has labeled "Machiavellian opportunism," for several years Vargas delayed taking sides in the looming international conflict in order to make shrewd use of the rivalry between the United States and Germany.[74] Meanwhile, tensions within Brazil escalated as several prominent figures in the government and the military seemed to support the Axis, while pro-Allied and antifascist factions began to take part in public demonstrations, events that included many UNE leaders. Just one month before Vargas recognized UNE, Brazil broke off relations with the Axis and allowed U.S. troops to set up military bases in the Northeast. Yet Vargas resisted declaring outright war, and tensions within Brazil continued. The decision to recognize the union may therefore have represented one way of currying favor with Allied supporters without fully committing to war. Indeed, Vargas began including a specific line in the annual budget of the Ministry of Education for UNE, a practice all successive governments would follow until the military regime of 1964–85.[75] The two gestures, especially the granting of formal status, gave an enormous boost to the union's claims to authenticity, as it could now proclaim to legally represent all university students, regardless of how many of them were active in it.

In addition to this source of institutional authority, the union soon achieved other victories. Support for Brazilian intervention on the side of the Allies grew in the months to come, especially after German forces sank several Brazilian merchant ships, and demonstrations broke out across the country. In this context, on July 4, 1942 (the date being chosen specifically to emphasize solidarity with the United States), members of UNE and several local student groups organized their own pro-Allied rally in the capital. When authorities fired the infamously repressive and pro-Axis police chief Filinto Müller two days before the event, students considered it a major accomplishment and turned out in record numbers, marching through downtown Rio with carnival floats portraying an imprisoned Hitler and carrying green-painted hens (*galinhas verdes*) intended to mock the green-shirted AIB members.[76] Although this watershed event numbered only slightly over one thousand students, a figure that would pale in comparison with later demonstrations, it was the largest (and perhaps most colorful) gathering they had yet assembled, and it garnered them extensive and positive press coverage.[77] According to one marcher, it won the attention even of U.S. President Franklin Roosevelt, who so appreciated the students' pro-Allied demonstrations in front of the U.S. embassy that he sent UNE a Victrola phonograph, delivered via U.S. Ambassador James Caffrey.[78] Coming on the heels of Vargas's official recognition of the union and shortly before the fifth anniversary of its founding, these demonstrations in July 1942 helped the union establish and project a position of national prominence. When, in August 1942, Vargas finally declared war on the Axis, the move confirmed that the union's pro-Allied position was shared with dominant political forces within the government.

The theatrical use of painted hens to label the Integralists as chickens highlights one of the multiple ways in which UNE leaders expressed their understanding of authority, especially in wartime, as revolving around rigid gender categories. It also offers an early example of how the idea of a student began to take on militant connotations. Despite the fact that the AIB had been banned since 1937 and essentially shut down since 1938, the group nonetheless served as a useful foil for critiquing the kind of militant masculinity it had earlier showcased as well as standing in for international fascism more generally. In calling them galinhas verdes, students drew on an old, well-known epithet for them, a moniker that used the figure of female hens to connote cowardice and effeminacy, as chickens are said to scatter at any disturbance, while their male counterpart, the cock, supposedly fights off competitors in fierce battles (and further displays his potent virility as the lone male in a plentiful henhouse).[79] As an insult always implies not just the faults of the insultee but also the presumed attributes of the insulter, UNE was not simply denigrating the weakness of the Integralists but simultaneously asserting its own masculine courage.[80] Much of the UNE leadership (still all male) followed up on these displays of masculine militancy by immediately volunteering to serve when the government announced it would be sending an expeditionary force to Europe.[81] Meanwhile the union initiated numerous wartime campaigns, such as sponsoring blood drives, selling war bonds, organizing metal recycling, and encouraging women students to volunteer as army nurses.[82] In the climate of enhanced militarism and nationalism that gripped Brazil in wartime, UNE became a vocal advocate of patriotic actions that drew heavily on gendered ideals about how society could contribute to the effort. The young men of UNE showed their commitment to the nation by evocations of courage and offers of military soldiering and by directing their female colleagues into their own gender-inscribed roles as medical caretakers.

The union's ascendant position during the war was further compounded and confirmed in August 1942, when President Vargas bestowed upon it the building at 132 Praia de Flamengo Street, a prime piece of Rio de Janeiro real estate recently expropriated from its German owners. While several groups vied for the former Sociedade Germânia headquarters, Vargas granted it to UNE, the DCE of the University of Brazil, and a collegiate sports group, the Conselho Brasileiro de Deporte Universitário (Brazilian Council on University Sports).[83] Offering the site to the country's young leaders-to-be was a shining example of wartime pageantry, celebrating Brazilian youth while symbolically taking aim at Germany and perhaps at the fascist models of youth emerging from the German society. It was also a relatively easy way to address UNE's long-standing requests for an office, made more exigent now that the union had been granted official status. The act reflected and reinforced UNE's growing national prominence and institutional ascendancy, as the building would become fundamental to many of the union's future activities, beginning with the occasion of its fifth annual congress the very next month. Vargas even accorded the union extra funds to help it hold the conference in grand style.⁸⁴ With a stately building to call home, UNE could now receive important visitors such as Minister Capanema at formal dinners and other occasions, rather than simply be received (figure 1.2).

Yet the authority of UNE did not stem solely from members' relationships with President Vargas. The union maintained close ties, even personal ones, with Vargas during much of the Estado Novo, notwithstanding the close alliance of UNE directorates with the PCB and the government's concomitant efforts to repress the party. But during the war years opposition to Vargas began to mount among much of the Brazilian political elite, who chafed at their exclusion from real political power and saw the current attention to fighting for democracy abroad as propitious for political and economic liberalization at home. UNE too made this shift. Once national political parties were again allowed to form and presidential elections were scheduled for December 1945, much of the UNE leadership threw their support behind the main opposition party, the center-right União Democrática Nacional (UDN, Democratic National Union), and its candidate Eduardo Gomes, in opposition to Eurico Gaspar Dutra, the official candidate of the progovernment Partido Social Democrático (PSD, Social Democratic Party), and Vargas's presumed successor. Meanwhile a group called the *queremistas* (for their slogan, "Queremos Getúlio," [We want Getúlio]) staged vociferous demonstrations urging Vargas to run under the Partido Trabalhista Brasileiro (PTB, Brazilian Labor Party), a party he founded as he increasingly courted working-class support. Indeed, Vargas's final months in office witnessed an ironic shift in which the president and the PCB's Prestes, who had long opposed each other, briefly became allies. The Electoral Code of 1945 allowed the PCB to function as a legal political party, and Prestes and other party leaders began advocating positions very similar to those of the queremistas. Within UNE, however, PCB-aligned students had lost ground. A powerful opposition group that supported a return to liberal democracy defeated the PCB-aligned directorate in July 1943, and in 1944 and 1945 the union joined the growing anti-Vargas chorus.

As a sign of how involved UNE became in these debates when a group of prominent lawyers, writers, and former congressmen formed an "antidictatorship society" called Resistência Democrática, they met to approve their "program of political action" at the new UNE headquarters building.⁸⁵ Indeed, one wonders if the Resistência Democrática had university students in mind when they wrote in their published manifesto that "men

FIGURE I.2. Minister of Education Gustavo Capanema at an UNE event in the union's dining room in 1942. Gustavo Capanema Collection, Fundação Getúlio Vargas

of our age" needed to save the next generation because it "[did] not have the preparation" necessary to guide Brazil democratically.[86] In any case, their decision to meet at 132 Praia de Flamengo demonstrates how connected UNE was to important factions of political leaders and how useful their meeting space could be in cultivating these ties.

While UNE leaders harnessed their potential as visible political allies during the war and the postwar electoral campaign, thereby helping to secure the institutional authority of the union, events in early 1945 spurred a subtle but meaningful shift in the way they came to articulate this position. On March 3 of that year a student activist named Demócrito de Souza Filho was shot and killed in Recife during an anti-Vargas protest. Both his death and the military's decision a few months later to remove Vargas from office would eventually augment UNE's claims to institutional authenticity with a sense of moral authority founded on unjust persecution and resistance. De Souza, a student at the Recife Law School and a member of the directorate of the UEE in Pernambuco, was one of many people who demonstrated in the anti-Vargas rally that day. After marching through the city, the group was assembled at a plaza to listen to a series of speakers when bullets suddenly began whizzing by, injuring several and instantly killing de Souza. The origins of the gunfire were unclear, but demonstrators blamed the police, who in turn claimed the shots had come from within the crowd itself. In any case, many observers criticized the federally appointed state leaders who had failed to maintain security. For many days after this event students in Recife and UNE leaders in Rio held additional demonstrations to protest the young man's death and they pressed the authorities to investigate. As they did so, they began increasingly to refer to themselves as democratic students, counterposing themselves to Vargas. Moreover, de Souza's death came to be heralded as a sign of students' political centrality, a kind of persecution that proved the strength of their threat to the authorities. The president of UNE, Paulo Silveira, wrote to Capanema two days after de Souza's death, asserting that "the liberty, security, and even the lives of democratic university students are seriously threatened, as at this moment there are no guarantees on the part of those in power that these events will not be repeated." Nonetheless, he went on, students were resolved to confront any such provocations by those seeking to disrupt the scheduled elections, as "the immense pain that is in our hearts will not dampen our just and righteous combat."[87] The death of de Souza worked to signal, to themselves and to others, students' seeming centrality in national political events and the sacrifices they were willing to make for a righteous cause. When, in October 1945, the military, fearing Vargas would block the upcoming elections, forced him to step down as president, UNE considered it another important victory, one that confirmed students' importance as political actors who had come to publicly oppose Vargas and to stress their commitment to democracy. Although students could not have realized so at the time, twenty years later the image of a student victim killed by state forces would become a central part of what it meant to be a student.

Although UNE's preferred candidate in 1945 was defeated by Dutra, the union continued to enjoy political prominence and authority that carried beyond the vicissitudes of presidential officeholders yet still made good use of intra-elite political networks. Elections for DCEs and UEEs became fiercely contested, while positions of leadership within UNE often served as stepping-stones to professional political careers. The affiliations of UNE leaders with the national political parties also intensified, as some student electoral slates, or chapas, hewed closely to the positions of the national parties. Between 1944 and 1946, as noted earlier, the union leadership shifted to a group who generally supported the UDN. From 1947 to 1950, by contrast, UNE leaders had close ties to a small, leftist offshoot of the UDN called the Partido Socialista Brasileiro (PSB, Brazilian Socialist Party). Indeed, some of the earliest figures from UNE's founding became important UDN politicians. Paes Leme, at whose home UNE leaders met in the early 1940s, served two terms as an elected state representative for the UDN during this period. From 1950 through 1955 the more conservative udenistas (UDN supporters) again gained control. Throughout this period other parties and affiliations found space within student politics. José Frejat, a student in the late 1940s who was elected president of UNE in 1950 and later became a journalist, a PSB politician, and a government minister, explained in 2004 that back then "you could have socialists [PSB], PTB, UDN, communists without a party." In other words, students with ties to many different political parties and groups participated actively in UNE. But, Frejat went on to affirm, "no one used us."[88] While his tone in this interview might be read as simple pride in the distinction between his generation and those that came later (who, as we will see, have been considered problematically tied to partisan agendas of the left), it also suggests a degree of defensiveness about the earlier generation's struggles with this relationship. For although student chapas in the late 1940s and early 1950s were not extensions of the national political parties, they did reflect students' participation in the national and ideological debates of the time as well as their continued close ties to official leadership. And they were at times critiqued for being too closely aligned to certain political parties.

Students strongly resisted accusations that they were partisan, as the charge could undermine their organizations' legitimacy as representative of students as a whole. Such was the case in October 1947, when UDN Senator Hamilton Nogueira complained to reporters that the PCB was essentially controlling UNE, as evidenced by union posters in favor of the nationalization of oil. Nationalization was a position the PCB had long supported. Yet it had been one of the agenda items at UNE's founding meeting in 1938, as that event had taken place shortly after Mexico famously nationalized its own oil production. By the late 1940s Brazilian oil production had increased to such a level that similar measures were proposed and the possibilities were widely discussed, now as part of a larger conversation over the degree of state intervention and protection necessary to promote development and secure national sovereignty. Both before and after the PCB, charged with being an antidemocratic party, was once again declared illegal in May 1947 it was one of the strongest promoters of nationalization. Having a left-leaning leadership, UNE too favored nationalist and protectionist policies. The union launched a National Pro-Petroleum Campaign and began plastering major cities with posters advocating nationalization. It was these posters that drew Nogueira's ire, leading him to assert that UNE was "full of communists." But it was his suggestion of UNE partisanship that outraged the president of UNE, Roberto Gusmão, who penned a note of rebuttal the next day.

What is most remarkable about Gusmão's response is the sense that Nogueira's comments required public redress. Like a gentleman defending his honor, Gusmão had his remarks read aloud in the National Congress and challenged Nogueira "to document any partisan attitude taken by the current directorate." He also used the occasion to emphasize UNE's democratic structure, which presumably made it incapable of exerting such influence. Calling Nogueira's comments "grave accusations," Gusmão wrote, "Your Excellency's statement reveals a total ignorance of the objectives of the university student entities. . . . The National Union of Students assembles students from all the schools of higher education in the country, without regard to political distinctions. The current directorate was elected by a wide margin of votes in a congress where all Brazilian students were legitimately represented." In case these references to structural democracy did not suffice, he invoked UNE's claims to moral authority as well, reminding listeners that UNE was in "the vanguard of the struggles for democracy in our country."[89] For UNE leaders like Gusmão, suggestions of UNE partisanship challenged the union's authority and required public response.

Denunciations of partisanship as an intimation of leftist influence were not confined to officials' views of students but pervaded discussions within the international student movement. After the dissolution of the CIE, student organizations from sixty-two countries, including UNE, formed the International Union of Students (IUS) in 1945. Headquartered in Prague, the IUS represented the collective hopes of an otherwise heterogeneous group that mutual cooperation could prevent a fascist resurgence. After February 1948, however, when communists gained control of Czechoslovakia and the burgeoning Cold War sowed mutual distrust between former allies, student groups from noncommunist countries accused the IUS leadership of partisanship and cooperation broke down. The United States National Student Association (USNSA), for example, wrote to UNE repeatedly in July and August 1948 suggesting they break with the IUS because of its "partisan political stand" and the fact that it "was more concerned with political considerations than with constructive student activities, such as travel and exchange, education, etc."[90] UNE never considered student interests to be limited to travel and exchange and decided not to leave the organization. More important, in their response to the USNSA they argued that influencing the IUS from within was more effective than abandoning it. Generously writing in imperfect but intelligible English rather than Portuguese, UNE General Secretary Sylvio Wanick Ribeiro wrote, "Whether the majority of members of the IUS does not think like its secretariat, there is a councill [sic] and a congress to which [w]e can appeal."[91] More provocatively, he continued, "If occasional majority determine a conduct line that may not be arranged to what we wish, or different than our conduct line, it might be very easy [to] not accomplish their resolutions and so to expect [to wait] until that majority disappear or then [until] our ideas predominate."[92] Both in its national and international affairs UNE responded to critiques of partisanship with appeals to democratic processes, thereby defending students' rights to participate politically.

Whether dominated by right- or left-leaning leadership, UNE members helped to maintain political authority in the 1940s and 1950s with a decidedly formal political culture. This was perhaps nowhere more visibly expressed than in the clothes they wore. Male students customarily attended class in suits and ties, while women students wore dresses. Such attire was a significant marker of class position and of the interrelated social prestige of university enrollment, and university students took care to uphold their collective status. At public demonstrations maintaining this sign of social respectability was especially important, as it spoke directly to students' presumed political authority. Photographs of protesting students show the men duly outfitted in elegant suits, while the increasing numbers of women who began to appear in such photos wore modest dresses and dress suits. And at national congresses, when students gathered in one place for several days and inevitably attracted a lot of attention, they took even more care with their appearance. As Genival Barbosa Guimarães, a student of engineering from Pernambuco in the mid-1940s, explained, "[We took] a lot of care and devotion [to how we dressed;] our clothing at the congress [of 1948] was suits and ties, and the women with dresses below the knee. Tight pants there? No, never."[93] Outfitted in the garb of the political establishment, university students could visibly assert their inclusion in this group.

As the increasing number of women in UNE photographs attests, this period witnessed women's heightened participation in UNE activities as they joined in events, served as minor officers, and attended the annual UNE congresses, albeit in lesser numbers than their male counterparts.[94] As they did so, the formal authority exhibited by UNE came to rely on strong notions of appropriate behavior for men and women, particularly those concerning female sexuality. If, a decade earlier, the absence of women meant that UNE directorates could carouse in bars and brothels and have this be seen as acceptable male behavior, by 1948 the presence of their elite female counterparts at UNE events transformed their expected behavior. Indeed, Barbosa's memories of women in formal attire at the UNE Congress in Rio in 1948 contrast with his fears of what people would say (*a língua do povo*) about the daring clothes and "high-cut shorts" some women participants wore to visit Copacabana beach. He further recalled that the women students stayed in a separate hotel from the men, seeking to avoid not just the potential for romantic liaisons but even the appearance of them. These precautions speak to concerns that mixed student gatherings would be seen as, at best, inappropriate and, at worst, injurious to female attendees. In either case, the appearance of scandal would besmirch all students' claims to responsible leadership, especially the men's, whose authority was in part predicated on paternalistic ideas about their ability to protect their female colleagues. Barbosa claimed that the mother of two young women delivered them specifically to his care ("Vou entregar as minhas filhas aos seus cuidados") and implied that he and other leaders felt responsible for the conduct of all students at the congress. In a final example of the mixture of the formality and paternalistic chivalry that permeated these gatherings, he noted that students followed a strict decorum at the meetings themselves, allowing women "the privilege of voting first" in the elections.[95] Whatever individual students thought about the potential freedoms to be enjoyed by traveling with their peers to distant UNE congresses, a powerful ethos of gendered decorum worked to patrol their behavior, thereby maintaining an air of serious respectability and further asserting the leadership of the male student majority.

In addition to these signs of formality, students continued to hold meetings and events at the UNE headquarters and other locales, where they met with high-ranking officials such as the president and the minister of education, events often duly photographed in formal splendor. So important a site of real and symbolic UNE authority did the building become that at times it emerged as the centerpiece of heated conflict. Such was the case in January 1949, when students in Rio de Janeiro protested a sudden increase in tram fares by climbing aboard trolley cars across the city to deliver fiery political speeches. At one tram stop, located immediately in front of the UNE building, a skirmish between the demonstrating student and a police officer erupted. Undoubtedly intensified by its location, the dispute escalated until a large contingent of police encircled the entire building while inside several hundred students jeered and waited. They had gone to eat dinner at the union's subsidized restaurant when the conflict broke out and stayed to see how the standoff would end. What is remarkable about the conflict is, first, how UNE President Barbosa responded when he arrived on the scene. According to him, he ordered that all the lights be turned on and almost all students be asked to leave, presumably both to showcase to the police that no disturbances were occurring and thereby prevent a police invasion and to illuminate the interior to journalists and others in case this did not work. He recalls saying, "Look, what is at play here is UNE and our headquarters; we have to preserve all of this."[96] That is to say, the immediate concern of the UNE leadership was the preservation of the building as a direct means of preserving the union. Yet the police resolved to seal off the building and, disregarding the remaining leaders' ingenious and truthful entreaties that they lived there, demanded that they leave the premises. The second remarkable aspect of these events is the fact that in the ensuing days, as students negotiated to have their building returned, several prominent politicians and officials publicly complained that the police had gone too far in encroaching on the students' physical territory. Carlos Lacerda, the former law school student who edited *rumo* in the 1930s but who was, by this time, a rising politician and newspaper owner with a strong anticommunist position, had a firm antipathy toward the current UNE leadership. Yet even he wrote critically about the police in his newspaper, the *Tribuna da Imprensa*, saying that even though he believed the union was controlled by communists, the police had gone too far in invading it.[97] Now over a decade old and located at Praia de Flamengo Street for nearly six years, UNE was unquestionably recognized as the authentic organization of university students, even by its political opponents, and its building a material proof of its sovereignty. It was perhaps fitting that once the building was returned, the students held a cocktail party to celebrate, inviting, among others, Lacerda.[98]

Emphasizing its stated commitment to democratic process was necessary to the union's continued legitimacy, as both the union's leadership and the nation's shifted from one political perspective to another. In January 1951 Vargas returned to the presidency, this time via direct popular elections and a campaign focused on renewed attention to the urban working classes. Throughout his term, however, the UNE directorate was headed by right-leaning udenistas, the party that most steadfastly opposed Vargas and that sought even to block his inauguration. Nonetheless the new UNE directorate still met with the president on occasion and posed formally for official photographers to document the event. Moreover, debates within the union remained vibrant. The historian Maria Paula Araujo asserts that pressure from the UEEs led UNE to continue to support the nationalization of oil, even though most udenistas, students included, had initially disagreed with the proposal.[99] After several years of debate in which support for nationalization increased on nearly all sides, Congress created the national oil company, Petrobrás, in 1953.[100] One can glimpse the degree of organized discussion that took place at the UNE Congress in Rio in 1951 in the notes made by Herbert Eisenberg, a USNSA representative who attended. Still concerned with Brazil's inclusion in the IUS and now possibly funded by the United States Central Intelligence Agency (CIA), the USNSA sent Eisenberg and another representative, Helen Jean Rogers, to try to persuade UNE members to leave the IUS once and for all.[101] In his notes Eisenberg expressed repeated astonishment at how loud the discussions became and how late into the night they extended—observations that would come as no surprise to even a casual observer of the contemporary student movement in Brazil, and that evince the high degree of debate that took place even during a period of seeming party dominance. Despite Eisenberg's view of the group as being divided between "unhappy Commies" and "Democrats," he could not help but express some admiration for the communists, noting, "Seems to be a strong Commie section and very hard working." Notwithstanding the strength of the "Commie section" and the amusing mixture of Portuguese and Spanish, or Portuñol, in which Eisenberg delivered his speech ("Apesar de estar aqui ha poco tiempo, estamos verdaderamente maravilhados con su pais"), both his and Rogers's comments were well received, he noted thankfully, while his mentions of Franklin Roosevelt earned a "very large hand." If the UDN leadership facilitated Eisenberg's and Rogers's participation, they nonetheless could not and did not unilaterally direct policy. Only after a congressional vote on the proposal did UNE decide to leave the IUS.[102]

The opposition of UNE to Vargas in this period did, however, lead it to take positions that would later become hard to reconcile with its narrative as a defender of democratic principles. For in the tumultuous final years of Vargas's presidency a small but vocal contingent of opponents began to argue that Brazilian democracy had failed and needed intervention in order to be restored.[103] Vargas had faced criticism since his election, some complaining that he manipulated both machine politics and ill-informed sectors of the public to win office. Opposition mounted still further after mid-1953 as he battled an economic crisis in part by renewing his commitment to *trabalhismo*, his laborite political philosophy that blended economic nationalism, a commitment to social welfare, and the political organization of the working classes.[104] When in June 1953 he appointed as new labor minister the thirty-five-year-old PTB figure and close family friend João Goulart, who many claimed was too close to militant labor leaders, tensions further increased. Nor did they subside after Vargas replaced Goulart eight months later, and instead only escalated in the face of a series of high-profile corruption charges against his administration. In this context, large protests broke out in several major cities. At one demonstration, students in Fortaleza critiqued "the electoral lie . . . and the misery of the purchased vote," as they protested a wave of seeming scandals.[105] The complaints escalated still further in August 1954 with charges that a close associate of the president attempted to assassinate Lacerda, who had become one of Vargas's fiercest critics and had turned his *Tribuna de Imprensa* into an important weapon against him. The attempt failed and resulted instead in the death of Lacerda's bodyguard, the air force major Rubens Florentino Vaz. At this point many groups began to call for Vargas's resignation. José Gregori, a student activist from São Paulo, later recalled leading other students in these protests in 1954 and even demonstrating in front of army headquarters, where they called on the armed forces to rise up against the president.[106] When the military eventually insisted that Vargas step down, he chose instead to end his own life, leaving behind a dramatic suicide letter and inspiring enormous and unanticipated outpourings of grief in which several hundred thousand people turned out for the various funeral processions, memorial services, and street demonstrations that marked his death.[107] For students who had opposed his presidency, the sudden turn of events—especially the show of popular support for the martyred president—eventually threw their position into question. In an interview in 2005 Gregori described his efforts at persuading the military to intervene as "the sins people commit in their youth." Another contemporary from São Paulo, Almino Afonso, looked back on that moment as a difficult one for students, saying, "We were in an extremely conflicted situation with that Vargas who was a symbol of repression, that Getúlio who seemed to be even a symbol of corruption, and the Getúlio who 'entered History' [through his suicide letter and death. . . . The student response] was all very conflictive and varied from person to person. It was a very difficult period, I'd say for the rest of our lives. Even today that history isn't easy to synthesize."[108] In 1954 leaders of UNE saw opposition to Vargas as consistent with their belief in democracy, even if they later would come to reconsider this perspective.

UNE's asserted commitment to democratic principles was thus one of the many meanings conveyed by the pamphlet from 1951 with which this chapter opened: the booklet that carried a picture of the UNE building and the phrase "The House of Democratic Resistance" emblazoned across the cover. The phrase and the accompanying photo were also an appeal to the union's burgeoning claim to institutional and moral authority—an image and slogan meant to call forth in one powerful set of signs UNE's acquisition of the building from supposed German enemies during World War II, the anti-Vargas and prodemocracy discussions that took place there in 1947, and the more general ways in which UNE cast itself as a force of democratic resistance to authoritarian threats. And while UNE leadership changed hands every year—shifts in personnel that often meant swings in political perspective as well, including the more problematic opposition to Vargas in 1954—the symbolic and material strength of this "house" as proof of the union's claim to political authority remained constant.

Just five years after this pamphlet was published, after the right-leaning leadership had been replaced by one that advocated much more leftist views, another UNE publication once again showcased an enormous photo of the building and captioned it once again the "House of Democratic Resistance" (figure 1.3). In fact, the UNE authors of 1956 went one step farther than their opponents in 1951, producing a second large picture on another page with the caption "The Republic of UNE: Free, Occupied, but Never Defeated" (figure 1.4).[109] For no matter who controlled the current directorate, students saw the presence and seeming permanence of

FIGURE I.3. Cover of the UNE magazine *Movimento* from 1956 proudly proclaiming 132 Praia de Flamengo Street the "House of Democratic Resistance." United States National Student Association Collection, Hoover Institution Archives

FIGURE I.4. A celebratory picture of the UNE building that appeared in *Movimento*. United States National Student Association Collection, Hoover Institution Archives

UNE and its building as the result of a long, collective effort, a house constructed and defended by several generations over time.

....

From the early nineteenth century university students in Brazil enjoyed considerable acceptance of their political activities, a status founded on their privileged social positions as the presumed political elite of the future. In the early twentieth century the system of higher education gradually changed, and enrollments increased for both men and women, although access to higher education remained an exclusive privilege for the very few. Even as the 1930s gave rise to federally recognized student academic centers, university directorates, and a national student union, students' claims to political authority still extended this earlier status in many ways. From the importance of students' personal relationships with high-ranking officials to their gendered perspectives on appropriate forms of leadership, student politics reflected the elite nature of national politics. Yet students also laid the foundation for an accepted and acknowledged political role for themselves, whatever their political persuasion.

Events surrounding World War II and the subsequent debates about the need to elect leaders democratically provided important platforms for students within UNE to assert themselves on the national stage as important members of the political elite. They did so via their shifting political affiliations, voting out PCB-linked members just as the party's new closeness with President Vargas suggested a prolonged period of elite political exclusion and allying instead with rising political factions like the Resistência Democrática. They also did so through their gendered appeals to war mobilizing, projecting a reassuring image of strong male leadership in a moment of national concern. Meanwhile UNE consolidated ever more fully its visibility in Rio de Janeiro with events held at its stately building and with its public participation in national debates. Throughout this period students exemplified both the consistency of class authority and the growing authority of the institution of UNE. If originally based on students' inclusion in intra-elite networks, this authority was increasingly built on the institutional strength of a well-established and housed union and on students' moral claims as democratic actors and supporters, even when those claims could appear to be in conflict with one another. Increasingly, too, their appeals to moral authority were buttressed by a sense of persecution and sacrifice, one seemingly at odds with their class status. In short, in the postwar period UNE held on to its prominence despite changing union and national leadership, bolstering its institutional authority with claims of moral authority as well.

If by the mid-1950s the House of Democratic Resistance symbolized for many UNE's institutional prominence and the authority of student political participation, in the decade that followed both the structure and the union it housed would take on new meanings as the UNE leadership veered decidedly to the political left and outside critics disputed students' authority to participate politically at all.

2

PROFESSIONAL STUDENTS AND POLITICAL POLARIZATION

Contested Revolutions in Brazil, 1956–1967

When Celia Guevara came to Brazil in late May 1961 to speak at the Federal University of Pernambuco in Recife, she preceded her famous son Ernesto "Che" Guevara by several months. In August Che, the Argentine-born revolutionary and Cuban minister of industry, passed through the country en route from a meeting of the Organization of American States (OAS) in neighboring Uruguay. He stayed for only a few hours, just long enough for President Jânio Quadros to decorate him with the Order of the Southern Cross, the highest honor Brazil grants to foreigners. Approved by a commission of government ministers who considered the decoration a reaffirmation of Brazil's position on Latin American self-determination, the award nonetheless prompted a storm of protest and helped lead to Quadros's abrupt resignation just six days later.

At first glance Celia Guevara's earlier sojourn to the northeastern city of Recife seemed a much simpler affair than her son's trip to Brasilia. Her invitation had been extended by students rather than by the president, and her arrival lacked the honor guard parade, military band performance, and official welcome at the new presidential palace that Che's stopover had entailed.[1] Her visit was no less contentious, however, ultimately leading to a seventeen-day strike by students and, most shockingly, the massive mobilization of troops of the Brazilian army, navy, and air force to break it up—a show of force so tremendous it made national and even international news for several days. One journalist at the time explained its importance by stating, "It would be incorrect to assert that only the University of

Pernambuco, the Army and the Government are involved in these events, for in fact the whole Nation feels the consequences of these incidents."[2] In this dramatic yet little-noted moment one can glimpse the rapidly changing terrain on which those students who welcomed Celia Guevara and those who involved themselves in similar political activities came to tread.

In this case the controversy began not when a student organization at the famous law school extended a speaking invitation to Celia Guevara, who was already in Brazil attending the Second Conference of Latin American Women.[3] Rather it started when Soriano Neto, the director of the school and vice rector of the university, infringed on the students' tacit right to do so by essentially prohibiting her visit. First he refused them the use of the main auditorium to host the talk, and then, when they planned to hold the event at the headquarters of their CA, he denied that too. Students at the school had long complained of Neto's authoritarian style and possible financial corruption, and they bristled at these latest imperious and arbitrary acts. Undaunted by his proscriptions, they secretly went ahead with the event on May 31, holding it in an unused classroom under the cover of night. The story perhaps would have ended there had Neto not found out about the furtive event and ordered the electricity to be cut, plunging the group into darkness midway through Guevara's speech. Attending students quickly ran to a nearby store for candles, and Guevara dramatically finished her lecture under the flickering light of dozens of small tapers.

Two days later, after Guevara had returned to Argentina, law students were still inflamed by the situation and declared a strike. They refused to attend class, occupied the law school building—surrounding it with large barriers and indignant signs—and demanded the rector's dismissal. Almost immediately students from other schools within the Federal University of Pernambuco and at the nearby Federal Rural University of Pernambuco began similar occupations, and Minister of Education Brígido Tinoco soon hurried to Recife to assess the situation.[4]

Student strikes were nothing new, of course. Neither were the occupations of university buildings, the symbolic burials of figures like Vice Rector Neto that the Recife students performed, or the rush of negotiating that quickly took place among local and national student and government figures. Although the forms of political protest had changed over time, Brazilian university students had long involved themselves in a variety of political activities, and the spectacle of demonstrating students was unexceptional. What happened next, however, marks the fallout from Guevara's visit as much more than a student demonstration typical of its time, even one compounded by the prominent involvement of the mother of an already mythical figure. For in response to the student strike, the national government exploded with a hitherto unforeseen display of force. President Quadros first authorized Minister of Education Tinoco to use whatever means necessary to end the occupation and then ordered army troops supplied with tanks, machine guns, and bazookas to station themselves around the campus and eventually around Recife itself. Within days he directed the air force to send planes to serve as reinforcements, and by June 10 he had dispatched a navy cruiser and two anti-torpedo ships to the city. For several days thereafter students and military troops faced one another in a tense standoff until finally, recognizing the impassability of the situation, students vacated the occupied buildings, vociferously singing the national anthem as they dispersed.[5]

What explains such an overwhelming military response to an apparently simple student strike against an overbearing administrator? The writers at the U.S. American magazine *Time* characteristically blamed Guevara, or "Che's red mother," as they called her, "a kind of Marxist Typhoid Mary, spreading violence wherever she goes," implying that her mere presence had set off the "student riot."[6] The Brazilian media paid less attention to her than to the fact that the topic of the forum at which she spoke was the recent agrarian reforms in revolutionary Cuba and that the meeting was also supposed to include Francisco Julião, the well-known Marxist founder of the first "peasant league" just outside of Recife. Led in part by Julião, since the mid-1950s peasants across the Northeast had begun to organize to demand agrarian reforms "by law or by force," as their popular slogan declared, and their efforts and land occupations attracted considerable attention and concern.[7] Indeed, on the very same day Guevara addressed the students in Recife, Federal Senator Fernandes Távora denounced Julião as an extremely dangerous demagogue who sought to "serve the interests of Moscow" by inciting the Brazilian people to insurrection.[8] If these responses diverge in the influential characters on which they focus, they nonetheless point to the Cold War fears that undergirded this moment in both American countries, Brazil and the United States, and that saw the combination of peasants, university students, and communists as potentially catastrophic.

For by the time these events occurred in Recife, many Brazilian, U.S., and other Latin American leaders had come to see the primary threat to national security as arising not from invading foreign troops but from internal revolutionary groups of the left. In this view, the very real destitution and dissatisfaction of the region's poorest classes could lead them to be swayed by calls for radical change and even for armed revolution. This anxiety had recently escalated with the success of the Cuban Revolution in 1959, in which the rural and urban poor of Cuba had sustained the guerrilla fighters and in which the official turn to socialism on May 1, 1961, confirmed the contrasting fears or hopes of those who observed the island. Outside of Cuba, few places garnered more Cold War anxiety than the Brazilian Northeast, the most impoverished area of the most unequal nation in Latin America. Just a few weeks before Celia Guevara's visit, a U.S. State Department official declared, "The eyes of the world are on Recife."[9] By June several U.S. congressional delegates as well as Edward Kennedy, the brother of President John F. Kennedy, conducted fact-finding visits to the state of Pernambuco. And the OAS meeting of August 1961 that Che Guevara attended before visiting Brazil witnessed the launching of the response of the United States to this situation: the Alliance for Progress, a program to offer targeted development and military assistance to Latin American countries in the hopes of preventing future revolutions. (Perhaps unsurprisingly, Cuba was the only OAS member not to sign the resulting charter and not included in the program.) In this context the scenario of Guevara and Julião together in Recife discussing agrarian reform provoked substantial alarm in many cold warriors.

As observers across the hemisphere looked warily at impoverished peasants, some in Brazil and elsewhere began to argue that university students, the sons and daughters of the Brazilian elite, were also vulnerable to and targeted by communist revolutionaries. In an editorial of June 10, 1961, titled "The Exploitation of Academic Youth," the newspaper *O Estado de São Paulo* warned readers that "red agents" were speedily directing their efforts at this group. The very same traits that made studious young people the vanguard of Brazil's political and social life—their freedom from "the prejudices and excesses of realism and objectivity that imprisoned adults"— made them "easy prey for adventurers specialized in enlarging and gilding their fraudulent plans, mobilizing the noblest and most generous sector of humanity for their unworthy campaigns." Moreover, they cautioned, if one carefully read the manifesto the striking students in Recife released when they ended their occupation, "one could clearly see the Communist hand" involved. The editorialists concluded that more astute attention to the fact that Latin America was now a Soviet target in the Cold War would prevent students from taking part in events like those of the previous week, actions that had "in no way strengthened the sympathy with which society customarily observes university students' civic activities."[10] For observers like these, the students' combative response to the vice-rector's heavy-handedness suggested there was much more at work (and at risk) than the usual student protest and that a miniature Cold War battle was brewing. In such a climate a student demonstration against an unpopular university figure could take on the appearance of a near national emergency, necessitating troops and tanks.

These concerns reflected attempts to understand a very real trend among university students and others in Brazil: the surging influence of leftist thought that marked the political culture of the late 1950s and early 1960s. Pernambucan students' interest in the agrarian reforms of Cuba, their invitation to the mother of Che Guevara to speak to them, the presence of Julião at their event, and criticisms of an autocratic university administrator were all part and parcel of wider discussions then under way about the nature and causes of inequality, both in Brazil and elsewhere. In events such as these, students and others fiercely debated the historic roots of Brazil's problems, the social and political structures that helped maintain the country in its current state, and the merits of various methods for charting a different future. Marcelo Ridenti, in his preeminent study of politically engaged artists and intellectuals of this period, has described the prevailing political and cultural atmosphere as one that was "pregnant with ideas about the people [o povo], liberation, and national identity—ideas that stretched a long way back in Brazilian culture but that since the 1950s brought with them the novelty of being mixed with leftist, communist, or laborite influences."[11] As students engaged in these debates, their student organizations became important forums for discussion and activism as well as an increasing cause for alarm among officials.

What the O Estado de São Paulo editorial reflects, besides the authors' anticommunist fears, is the sense that "the sympathy with which society customarily observes students' civic activities," that is, the considerable social acceptance of students' political activism, for which they had so long struggled, was now increasingly at risk. As we have seen, the privileged sons (and, later, the daughters) of the elite had, with the general approval of most observers, participated in diverse political activities since the early nineteenth century. This acceptance was deepened in the second quarter of the twentieth century as students strengthened their claims to both institutional and moral authority via legal guarantees and symbolic victories. By the time of Guevara's visit to Recife, however, the student body itself and the national and international political context within which students mobilized were undergoing major transformations. Just as the Republic of UNE was becoming most active, it became most threatened.

This chapter traces the growing influence of leftist ideas and organizations among university student activists between 1956 and 1967 exploring how the left came to hold such sway within the official student organizations, especially UNE. Officials, the media, and other observers of this process responded to the shift in ways that threw into doubt the appropriateness of any student political activism. For the Cold War context made students' political activities appear increasingly threatening, and they soon faced severe challenges to their right to organize. These impediments intensified still further after the implementation of military rule in 1964, when the new regime made concerted attempts to purge the student organizations of leaders it considered inauthentic, in the process disparaging the authority of organizations they led and the right of students to mobilize politically at all.

Revision, Reform, and Revolution

The formation of peasant leagues in the mid-1950s by Julião—that controversial attendee at Celia Guevara's Recife speech—served as a harbinger of an immense swell of revolutionary cultural and political activity that surged across Brazil in the late fifties and early sixties. Large numbers of peasants, urban and rural workers, low-ranking members of the military, intellectuals, artists, and members of the Catholic Church began to reconsider Brazil's long-standing economic, social, and political inequalities in the face of local and global transformations and to propose radical new solutions. In academic discussions and through cultural productions people debated theories of dependency, cultural imperialism, colonialism, and neocolonialism. University students actively participated in this dynamic wave, joining forces with other groups and forming alliances via their student organizations.

Some of the domestic impetus for this turn lay in a deep disappointment with the failure of Brazil's recent economic development to lead to meaningful social change. Nothwithstanding the multiple signs of prosperity and economic growth under the presidency of Juscelino Kubitschek (1956–61), including the construction and inauguration of the new, modernist capital of Brasilia in 1960 and the successful development of an automobile industry in São Paulo that began churning out Ford, Volkswagen, and General Motors vehicles, these efforts had not eradicated the extreme inequalities that marked the country. Moreover, this expansion was financed through deficit spending, and, when growth stalled, the country was soon wracked by high inflation and rising, untenable government debt, leading to increases in the cost of living and decreases in public spending that might have cushioned the blow.[12] Bitter disputes broke out over the degree to which foreign investment could lead to domestic economic sovereignty or whether it kept Brazil locked in a position of dependency on international interests. In this context, when fares on the Canadian-owned tramway lines in Rio de Janeiro doubled in May 1956, UNE organized massive protests, blocking the tracks at various points across the city (in some places by placing tables over them on which students played chess or ping pong), holding symbolic burials of the mayor who had approved the increase, and, at one point, hosting a mass meeting at the UNE building where leaders spoke from the balcony while those assembled out front sang multiple choruses of the national anthem.[13] Members of Congress complained publicly about police interference at that event and, in a further show of support for students, when the fare increase was cut by half, much of the press called it "the first popular gain against inflation."[14] Another set of student demonstrations two years later further showcased this climate. When U.S. Secretary of State John Foster Dulles visited Rio in 1958 to discuss the two countries' economic relationship, UNE students protested. Taking advantage of the fact that Praia de Flamengo Street was the main route for his motorcade, they draped their building with black mourning crepe and hung signs reading (in English), "Go Home Dulles!" and (in Portuguese) "Petrobrás is Untouchable."[15] Complaints of economic imperialism, especially by the United States, held special appeal in this context.

Politically, many on the left were coming to doubt that Brazil's democratic institutions were capable of reconciling opposing factions and maintaining the stability necessary to effect meaningful change. After the long Vargas era that began with a coup d'état, extended through an authoritarian dictatorship, and ended with the dramatic suicide of a sitting president, Brazil was facing an extended period of crisis. The election of 1955 that brought victories to Kubitschek and his vice presidential candidate,

João Goulart, on a joint PSD/PTB ticket was highly contested, as important figures from the UDN saw the candidates' earlier connections with Vargas as evidence of authoritarian tendencies and their popular sector votes as the result of manipulation. The two took office only after a so-called preventative coup, in which Army Marshall Henrique Lott deposed the acting president amid concerns that he and sectors of the military were planning to prevent Kubitschek's inauguration. At the next election, in late 1960, popular frustration with the status quo and a broad search for solutions resulted in an unusual split-ticket result wherein Quadros, the candidate of a three-party coalition anchored by the UDN, was elected president, while Goulart, hailing from the opposing PSD/PTB, again assumed the office of vice president. Quadros had presented himself as a true political outsider, notwithstanding the UDN support he enjoyed, and his populist appeal stemmed from what the historian Thomas Skidmore has called "the hope of radical change through the redemptive force of a single leader's personality."[16] Meanwhile the electors' vice presidential choice reflected their unwillingness to eschew the *trabalhista* promises of the Vargas legacy. When Quadros abruptly resigned the presidency only seven months into his term, the protracted dispute over Goulart's ascendency to the office that followed demonstrated still further the weakness of the country's political institutions and the tenor of distrust and division that subjected them to frequent interference. Goulart, in China on an economic mission at the time, returned to Brazil only after ten days of intense negotiations between political and military officials and the approval of a constitutional amendment that limited the president's powers by temporarily creating a parliamentary system of government. To many observers who sought deep changes, political institutions could not be relied on to respect the popular electoral will, let alone to represent their interests against powerful sectors of society. In short, many believed that the government could not effect meaningful change on its own and that real transformation would have to happen from the bottom up.

At the same time, the international context offered multiple examples of what Marcelo Ridenti has called "liberating Third World alternatives for humanity."[17] From the Cuban Revolution in 1959 to the independence of Algeria in 1962, many Brazilians took inspiration from the multiple "living examples of underdeveloped peoples rebelling against global powers" and actively sought new solutions to enduring problems of injustice and in-

FIGURE 2.1. Students from UNE and UBES (the union of secondary school students) decorated 132 Praia de Flamengo Street for the visit of U.S. President Dwight Eisenhower in 1960. *Correio da Manhã* collection, Arquivo Nacional

equality.[18] The Cuban Revolution in particular generated widespread enthusiasm among university students. When U.S. President Dwight Eisenhower visited Rio de Janeiro in 1960 and city officials plastered "We Like Ike" signs (in English) in conspicuous locations throughout the city, UNE students turned again to the prominence of their building, draping a huge banner over the front proclaiming, also in English, "We Like Fidel Castro" (figure 2.1).[19] Meanwhile glowing references to the revolution blossomed in the student press, such as in *A Época*, a magazine produced by CACO. A May 1962 edition contained not only a poem by the Cuban writer Nicolás Guillén commemorating José Martí and Fidel Castro but also an article written by a Brazilian student who calls Cuba a model for Latin American students: "Happily the Cuban Revolution brought new mentalities to the people of Latin America. . . . After three years of the Cuban Revolution, the proletarian masses, students, and intellectuals of all of Latin America have the undeniable example that the anti-imperialist and anti-feudal struggle is the initial stage that will bring diverse nations of the Continent to a just and democratic social state."[20] Seeing the Cuban Revolution as a peculiarly

Latin American model endowed socialist ideas with added legitimacy and offered students an important symbolic alternative to the former models of Europe and the United States.

During this period the growing prominence of leftist thought in the Latin American Catholic Church, especially the rise of what would eventually be called liberation theology, played a fundamental role in influencing many young people and in transforming the leadership of UNE.[21] In simplest terms, liberation theology interpreted the Bible from the perspective of the poor, seeing the Christian mission as a fight against poverty and social injustice. In its call to action to combat systemic sins, it both drew from and paralleled revolutionary Marxism. Many of the students who became involved in Catholic youth groups in the late fifties and early sixties similarly came to view a theology that did not seek to address the nation's extreme social and economic inequalities as hypocritical and even immoral, and they began to translate these ideas into student politics.

Two national organizations played decisive roles in student politics: the Juventude Universitária Católica (JUC, Catholic University Youth) and, later, Ação Popular (AP, Popular Action).[22] Though not originally a political organization, JUC nevertheless came to have a dramatic impact on leftist student politics. Individual JUC members in the growing student movement gradually began to band together, drawn to one another by a shared set of values and beliefs. As the influence of liberation theology grew, extending the circle of those with similar beliefs, they increasingly did so in conjunction with secular leftist groups. This growing alliance proved fundamental for the 1955 election of a leftist slate of candidates to the directorate of the União Metropolitana de Estudantes (UME, the Rio de Janeiro metropolitan union that was akin to the UEE state unions owing to Rio's status as the capital when UME was founded). In addition, JUC's extension nationwide proved important a year later when it helped elect leftist candidates to UNE too.

This foray into student politics soon led to a self-titled political sector of JUC that organized directly within the student movement, establishing areas of strength in the states of Minas Gerais and Bahia and in the city of Rio de Janeiro.[23] By 1961 a JUC candidate, Aldo Arantes, now leading a broad coalition of leftist groups, including important communist organizations, won the UNE presidency. In so doing he received extreme criticism from the Catholic Church hierarchy, who not only disagreed with liberation theology but also saw Arantes's communist alliances as especially threatening. When he went on to reaffiliate UNE with the IUS (the so-called partisan organization seen in chapter 1), the cardinal of Rio de Janeiro expelled him from JUC and prohibited all future members from running for student political office. In 1962 disaffected JUCistas consequently formed AP, an organization independent from the Church and one that would have a major role in UNE elections for the remainder of the decade.

Besides Catholics who critiqued a theology that preached toleration of social inequalities, other thinkers began to emphasize the power of education to either encourage conformity with the status quo or to offer the means by which to understand and transform the world. Quite possibly the most important person in this regard was Paulo Freire, an educator in Recife who came to national prominence for his work in popular education and literacy training, including his success at teaching sugar cane workers to read and write. As literacy was then still a voting requirement, his efforts were straightforwardly political. Moreover, he believed that education could have more pointed political significance too by encouraging democracy and self-determination. Freire argued that the hierarchical relationship between active teachers who deposited information and passive students who stored it, wherein both saw the world as already known and unchanging, ought to be rejected. In its place he advocated a reciprocal relationship in which teachers and students taught and learned from each other and in which education itself would be "a practice of freedom."[24] As he later explained, "We wanted a literacy program which would be an introduction to the democratization of culture, a program with men as its subjects rather than as patient recipients, a program which itself would be an act of creation, capable of releasing other creative acts, one in which students would develop the impatience and vivacity which characterize search and invention."[25] In the course of these interactions participants analyzed their own reality, thereby learning to perceive the social, political, and economic constraints posed on them, a process he called conscientização (roughly, "consciousness creation"). Freire's pedagogy paralleled aspects of liberation theology and anticolonial ideas of collective self-determination, and it influenced generations of students. Large numbers of them joined Freire-modeled literacy campaigns as volunteers, spending their vacations promoting literacy and political consciousness among rural workers in remote areas of the country. Moreover, Freire's general attention to dialogical consciousness raising became widely influential. The historian

TABLE 2.1 Educational Enrollments, 1960–1968

	1960	1965	1968
Elementary	7,458,000	9,923,183	12,353,000
Secondary	1,177,427	2,154,430	3,205,851
Undergraduate	93,202	155,781	278,295

Source: Graham, "The Growth, Change and Reform of Higher Education in Brazil," 281.

Heloisa Maria Murgel Starling calls conscientização "the magical word of the era" and artfully describes the period of the early sixties as a moment when the entire country se conscientizava ("created its consciousness").[26]

Students in Brazil also began to mobilize around the troubled system of higher education. Herein lies part of the pragmatic explanation for the Catholic students' political success in these years, as they were some of the staunchest critics of the system and made education reform a central political platform. Moreover, their rise to prominence coincided with a boom in university admissions (table 2.1), as larger numbers of young people began to enter the universities than ever before, very often as the first members of their families to do so. The increased supply of secondary school graduates, owing to the educational reforms implemented earlier, meant that more students qualified to enter university. At the same time, Brazil's developing industrial economy led to increased opportunities for those with university training, a demand further fed by the rising expectations of middle-class students (and their families), who sought both future employment and the social status that came with a university degree.[27] Notwithstanding the considerable expansion in the number of positions available at the universities, those who sought access to universities vastly exceeded this total, as officials simply could not keep pace with the rapid increase in demand. In fact, a growing number of students who received passing marks on the vestibular entrance exam and hence technically earned admission to university found themselves barred from registering owing to overmatriculation, above all in the most sought after areas of medicine, engineering, and chemistry. Nicknamed excedentes, or "surplus students," their numbers increased with each passing year until, by the early 1960s, they began banding together in public protests against a system that deemed them qualified to enroll but denied them the chance to do so (figure 2.2).

FIGURE 2.2. *Excedentes*, or "surplus students," camped out at the Ministry of Education to demand that university enrollments be increased. *Correio da Manhã* collection, Arquivo Nacional

Meanwhile the young people who were able to matriculate found a system of higher education far removed from their expectations and needs. Enrollments had been augmented quickly and without a corresponding growth in university infrastructure. Consequently classes were overcrowded, libraries lacked sufficient books, and laboratories proved inadequate and outdated. Many additionally complained that the education provided was archaic and authoritarian, marked by paternalistic and nepotistic professorial relationships, with little room for student involvement in governance. Built around a limited number of powerful professors with lifetime appointments, the universities seemed to promote outdated curricula that were largely irrelevant to the country's current challenges and impervious to new approaches. In the face of this situation Catholic students joined others around the country to mobilize a campaign for university reform, sponsoring conferences, drafting proposals, and spearheading a large rush of student political involvement around these educational issues, including an extensive strike in 1962 to gain student representation in university governing bodies. Because most of the best and most coveted universities fell under federal administration or, in the case of the University of São Paulo, under the governor's control, students' criticisms did not remain confined to their specific faculties but became translated into state and national policy objectives.

These reform-based activities not only reveal how JUC and, later, the AP rose to prominence among students, but also underscore the new role many university students came to articulate and defend as one they themselves could play in Brazilian society. As more students versed themselves in ideas like those of Freire and liberation theology, and as they no longer came exclusively from the uppermost classes but now stretched into the middle class, they brought a critical eye to an elitist university system they believed was mired in antiquated, foreign paradigms. These students criticized not just the obsolete facilities and professorial structure but also the pedagogical content, one that failed to address what they termed Brazil's social realities. Correspondingly, they often associated university-centered issues with broader political ones, recognizing that efforts at university reform divorced from other changes would do little to resolve the social roles universities played. For example, in a pamphlet first circulated widely around faculties and universities in mimeographed form before being published in a book edited by UNE, the author and professor Álvaro Vieira Pinto criticized Brazilian *cátedras* for imitating the Sorbonne and viewing themselves as guardians of universal knowledge rather than educators. He continued with a radical reconsideration of the potential of university reform itself: "The university is one piece of a general device of domination through which the dominant class exerts its social control over the rest of the country. And if that is the essence of the university, then right away we can see that the problem of reforming it is political and not pedagogical."[28] According to this perspective, changes in university-specific issues required political action and would have wide-ranging consequences for society as a whole.

This viewpoint undergirded the extensive campaign for university reform that students developed in this period. In 1961, 1962, and 1963 UNE (now with many AP supporters in its leadership and numerous JUCistas in attendance), sponsored three National Seminars on University Reform at which attendees drafted position papers offering analyses of Brazilian history and suggestions for reform.[29] What emerges from these statements is students' vision of a Brazil in crisis, plagued by centuries of international exploitation and the resulting social injustices at home and saddled with a university system designed to keep the Brazilian people in a perpetual state of alienation from the country's social and political realities. In place of this paradigm, students proposed a model of the university as a transformative social actor. Their position papers at times refer to a "democratizing university," a "socializing university" and even a "revolutionizing university." They explain that "University Reform has as its goal the transformation of the university structure in such a way that the University becomes a bulwark in the struggle for the Brazilian revolution and not an organization that, in addition to being anachronistic, is impeding development in Brazil."[30] Freire's influence is clearly discernible in these references to education's obstructionist power. A pennant some students created in 1962 for that year's seminar graphically conveyed these ideas. Drawn in a modernist style that evokes Socialist Realism, four muscular students grip an enormous lance to pierce and shatter the word *university*, as if in doing so they were collectively doing away with outdated impediments to modernity (figure 2.3). In students' position papers, appeals to conscientização as a liberating and revolutionary pedagogy are also clear, such as when they wrote, "The University should widen its action in community problems; it should act insistently alongside the working masses, the laborers and peasants." Yet in these anthropomorphic verbal images of universities striding beside workers, images complemented by the pennant figures of students in undershirts rather than suits and ties, one can see not just the transformative role students envisioned for these institutions but also the vanguard role they began to assert for themselves. For they went on to say that the university should "seek . . . to awaken in them [the working masses] the consciousness of their rights, the consciousness of the breadth and width of their collective and individual possibilities, developing them and stimulating them." Indeed, elsewhere in the paper the authors outlined exactly who would provide the impetus for such radical changes, arguing, "Students must be the principal agents in this transformation."[31] Notwithstanding the problematically inchoate image of workers and peasants demonstrated here, these visions of the transformative potential of education inspired increased political engagement among students as a collective body and reflect the radicalization of their goals in this period.

Students also began to emphasize the potentially revolutionary role of popular culture as a force that could and should reflect the country's needs and aspirations. The Brazilian essayist and cultural critic Heloísa Buarque de Hollanda says "the incredible 1960s" were deeply shaped by "debates about the recruitment and revolutionary effectiveness of the poetic word, of

FIGURE 2.3. Pennant for the 2nd National Seminar on University Reform, 1962. This banner may have been made for University of Pernambuco (UPE) students, or it may refer to recent strikes at UPE. Pennant in the PMME collection; photograph by the author

the word that, at that time, appeared very powerful, a tool even, in plans for taking power."³² This period saw the rise of Cinema Novo, in which young filmmakers sought to counteract the passive consumption of Hollywood fantasy with films that encouraged critical awareness by combining avant-garde aesthetics and revolutionary content to create a stark portrait of Brazil. These years also witnessed the prominence of the Teatro de Arena in São Paulo, a theater company run by the dramaturge Augusto Boal that produced a series of successful nationalist plays written by Brazilian playwrights. Artists and students both began to argue that the relationship between political organizing and cultural production and promotion was crucial, while the search for an authentic national popular culture was intimately connected to national development. Their alliance in these efforts took concrete shape in late 1961 in the form of the Centro Popular de Cultura (CPC, Popular Culture Center), a combined effort by a group of politically minded writers, actors, and musicians and the leaders of UNE to produce and disseminate what they called popular revolutionary art, or art that would both reflect and speak to the mass of the population. They staged street theater at the entrances to factories, published pocket-sized books of poetry and short stories at affordable prices, produced a record of bossa nova tunes called *O Povo Canta* (The people sing), and sponsored young filmmakers in their productions. They also sought to learn about popular culture through their experiences. As the intellectual publication *Revista Brasiliense* explained in an essay of 1962, the CPC intended to "open the way which will lead to an authentic popular culture by learning from popular aesthetics, and by identifying with the aspirations, the emotions, the problems, the anguish, and the thought of the popular masses."[33] In addition to promoting cultural events throughout the Rio de Janeiro region via the CPC and beginning the construction of a large CPC theater inside the UNE building, students and artists created a program called Flying UNE. For several months in early 1962 and again in 1963 they took their politically engaged cultural productions on tour to remote areas of the country, where they could take part in interactive revolutionary theater with rural workers and peasants while simultaneously laying the groundwork for the founding of a dozen regional CPCs, many housed in universities.

As these examples of UNE activities imply, participation in the union increased in the late 1950s and early 1960s. While technically all university students were represented by UNE, specific figures of just how many actively engaged in UNE decision making or activities are hard to determine. One estimate is the number of delegates who attended the annual congress. Each faculty was allowed to send two delegates and one alternate, chosen by local elections and accredited by their state's UEE (although not every faculty had the resources or interest to do so). Genival Barbosa, elected UNE president in 1948, claims to remember the exact number of votes cast for and against him, asserting that, in all, 398 people voted in that election, of whom 60 were women.[34] Assuming his recollection is accurate, one might estimate that roughly 400–600 people attended and that around 15 percent were women. One can then compare that with the number of attendees in 1961, a year when the USNSA again sent representatives to the UNE Congress and left detailed notes. In this instance they sought to convince UNE to join the International Student Conference, a relatively new organization designed to counteract the IUS (and, like the USNSA a recipient of covert CIA funds). As Joe Love, one of the three representatives explained, "It was sold on the basis of neutralism. Since UNEb [UNE-Brazil] was already a member of the IUS, it could only maintain its neutrality between the two camps by entering the ISC."[35] In his notes, Love not only expresses relief that UNE agreed to become a full member but also observes that 868 delegates and alternates attended the event. Another USNSA representative, Bob Aragon, added that "almost one-third of the delegates" were women.[36] While Aragon's figure may be an approximation, Love's specific number probably derived from announcements made at the congress itself. On the basis of these observations, it appears that between 1948 and 1961 the number of students who participated in UNE congresses grew by as much 100 percent, as did the percentage of those who were women.

Reading further into Aragon's report on the trip, one gets a sense of the ways in which the nearly 33 percent of delegates who were women provoked certain kinds of alarm. On the one hand, Aragon's claims that they were conspicuous bespoke more about his own gaze than about any behavior on their part. "One could not help noting the contrast between the fashionably dressed delegates at the UNEb and the drab attire of most women at the [US] NSA Congresses," he reported, as if the clothing of women activists everywhere were impossible to ignore.[37] Although he did not interpret the scene in this way, his observation nonetheless points to the degree to which formal attire, even in this period of heightened political radicalism, continued to be an important indicator of political authority for congress participants. (His comments also suggest a great deal about his assumptions about his USNSA female colleagues, but that topic is beyond the scope of this book.) On the other hand, his interpretations of what he saw revealed gendered concerns about students' vulnerabilities. From his perspective, the elegant clothes worn by female Brazilian students implied a lack of political seriousness, and he claimed that "for most of them the emphasis was on social events and fashionable dress rather than on issues central to the Congress."[38] These comments were made in the context of his and Love's broader report on UNE, a document that nearly quivers with Cold War fears. They noted that the union had become an incredibly powerful force in Brazil, had a luxurious headquarters, a generous annual budget from the federal government, and additional support from Petrobrás, which, for example, had paid for colored pamphlets distributed at the congress. They also suggested that a few strong, communist-run state delegations could easily convince the other delegates to follow them. As evidence of this, Aragon invoked the large number of women delegates, claiming that "most delegates were inexperienced and motivated by non-political factors."[39] In this view, the very presence of women—illegitimate political actors whose true ambitions were directed elsewhere—rendered UNE vulnerable to undue ideological influence.

Students of both sexes fiercely debated Brazil's revolutionary future in these years. In addition to participating in UNE activities, a small number of them began to join the clandestine lefts, the multiple and competing covert leftist political organizations noted in the introduction. The most self-evident choice for left-leaning students was the historic PCB, still officially banned but seeking to restore its legality. After a period of vehement opposition to President Kubitschek, one that included proposals for armed opposition, the party switched course in the early 1960s. It viewed the political ferment then taking place as evidence of useful divisions emerging within the dominant classes and saw Goulart's government as having "revolutionary potential." If the burgeoning social movements, especially the rural and urban workers, could only push them hard enough, Goulart and other nationalistic leaders would break with those groups most compromised with feudal or imperialistic powers, create a Popular Front alliance with the left, and implement deep reforms. These reforms, in turn, would create the necessary developmental conditions for the future Brazilian revolution and, eventually, the institutionalization of socialism.

Rivals of the PCB soon emerged to critique this perspective and form their own clandestine organizations. Following the Sino–Soviet split, in 1961 an assemblage of socialists, Trotskyists, and others founded the Organização Revolucionária Marxista-Política Operária (POLOP, Revolutionary Organization of the Marxist-Workers Line), while the following year a group of dissident leaders broke off from the PCB to create the Maoist Partido Comunista do Brasil (PCdoB).[40] Both groups thought the PCB's focus on peacefully pressuring the government to implement reforms was a tragic waste of opportunity, as the political agitation of recent years demonstrated the potential for immediate revolution, not reform. Instead they called for armed struggle—a theoretical position that neither group put into practice at the time but that nonetheless marked POLOP and the PCdoB as distinct from the PCB. As explained by Daniel Aarão Reis Filho, a historian of the revolutionary lefts in Brazil who had personal experience as an activist in several leftist organizations and in the student movement in the 1960s, they critiqued the PCB's belief that the current government could effect the necessary reforms that would lead to revolution: "This being the case, what was there to hope [for] from the legal game of their institutions?"[41] In POLOP's view there was no such thing as true opposition within the bourgeoisie, who would never jeopardize the capitalist system by agreeing to meaningful changes like agrarian reform. Instead, the responsibility for ushering in social reforms lay with the working classes, who had to reject the false promise of class collaboration. Reis described POLOP's perspective on the situation: "The country was facing a crossroads: either it chose an alliance with the dominant classes, or [with] a Unified Front of workers. Either the consolidation of capital or socialism. Either reaction or revolution. The struggle for socialism stopped being a far-off objective and became an immediate concern."[42] The PCdoB shared many of POLOP's concerns (and indeed their many similarities made them almost indistinguishable to outsiders) but differed in that it saw Brazil as bound for an intermediate phase before socialism, with a small role for the dominant classes under a popular revolutionary government. Yet both saw revolution as imminent and requiring only a vanguard party to make it happen. "The overthrow of Jango [a nickname for Goulart] and a revolutionary regime change were called for," wrote Reis. "The people already spoke 'openly' of revolution, although without a clear sense of 'how to make it happen.' "[43] Indeed, all three groups—the PCB, the PCdoB, and POLOP—agreed that Brazil was on an irreversible path toward socialism. Through their efforts they could speed it up or through their errors slow it down, but they firmly believed in utopian visions of a fair, just, and equal society as Brazil's inevitable future. Theirs was a vision highly attractive to many university students, and, indeed, a large portion of POLOP members hailed from the universities.

Even for the vast majority who did not join one of the organizations, the ideas and discussions generated by the rise of the clandestine lefts infused university life. As Antônio Amaral Serra, a UFRJ law student in 1963 and a future member of the AP, later reflected, "What was interesting is that the [political] positions were really clear. For example, one Saturday you'd come to the faculty and there'd be a poster like this: 'Meeting of the Communist Party base.' In another room: 'Meeting of the PCdoB.' It was all really obvious, and everyone had their positions."[44] That these discussions were being carried on was physically apparent to anyone, even if not everyone followed the subtle philosophic differences that emerged between the groups. Serra went on to explain, "My first year in school I participated in a really modest way because I wasn't yet clear in my own position. That many ideas was a little overwhelming."[45] He was not the only student who felt overwhelmed by the effervescence of political discussion and study. The future student leader Franklin Martins also recalls the vagueness with which he first turned to socialist ideas in the early 1960s: "I was a person of the left, socialist, but with a confused aspect. . . . I didn't become a Marxist; I hadn't studied enough Marxism for that, but it was attractive to me. Communist ideas were attractive to me. . . . It wasn't from some theoretical agreement [that I felt this attraction], because I didn't really know it deeply. . . . [But b]ecause in that period the Communists were the ones who most decidedly fought against injustice."[46] Martins's comments offer a sense of the appeal of communist ideals in this context, while his and Serra's recollections both speak to their widespread circulation among student sectors.

The late 1950s and early 1960s were a period of intense political and cultural discussion and action that involved many university students. They conducted literacy drives, promoted popular culture, and campaigned for reforms in the university system. Many debated leftist ideas and strategies for addressing what they called Brazilian realities, and a few of them joined revolutionary groups like the PCdoB and POLOP. They also voted into UNE office students who reflected this trend, even as some began to complain of a gap between leaders and followers. As they did so, and as Brazilian society itself became more polarized politically, new debates about the authenticity of student political activism emerged. Some sectors of society saw these transformations as threatening distortions of students' appropriate roles and took steps to delegitimize any political participation.

Let Students Study: Responses to Radicalization

As students engaged in these debates and promoted deep educational and cultural changes, fierce and powerful critics began to question their authority to do so. If before this moment one could always find those who disagreed with the political positions students adopted, during this period some began to publicly challenge the rights of students to participate politically at all. As in the Celia Guevara case, they proposed that young people were especially vulnerable to communist influence and should avoid political activity entirely.

The Instituto de Pesquisas e Estudos Sociais (IPÊS, Institute of Social Research and Study), a private foundation formed by staunchly anticommunist business executives in 1962, was one influential group that believed this and made the depoliticization of students a top priority. To this end, IPÊS funded the publication of books, produced short films to be presented at movie houses before feature films, and hosted conferences and symposia on educational questions.[47] Whereas leftist students critiqued foreign educational models that ignored Brazil's problems, IPÊS offered a different vision of the dangers of foreign influence and the importance of national duty, one in keeping with the organization's own brand of nationalism. In this view university students were obligated to preserve and advance Brazil's many accomplishments, improving rather than transforming the country. They should take full advantage of their educational opportunities, devoting themselves exclusively to study and steering clear of disruptive distractions such as allegedly imported political ideologies like communism. IPÊS stressed the national duty of university students to dedicate their efforts to mastering technical skills that would help Brazil develop and argued that political activities not only detracted from this duty by squandering time but also exposed students to the dangers of what they called strange, foreign influences. In the film that uses this expression, the student-narrator asserts, "A student is a student, and he only has responsibilities to books, to himself and to the future of Brazilian society. . . . Students always inherit the typical aspects of our culture, they are the citizens who are most conscious of the Brazilian way of life, those who have the obligation to know our problems deeply and to understand them through national ideas, without any strange, foreign influences. To flee from that is to fall into ideological chaos. . . . A student's mission is cultural, patriotic, democratic. That's why I, as a Brazilian university student, say, 'Let students study.' "[48] In this perspective, not only were students who organized politically not real students, they were exogenous forces disturbing the natural, studious peace of the university. As such films were directed beyond the campus arena to the general moviegoing public, so too were its messages. Rather than critiquing students' specific political positions, IPÊS films sought to undermine the legitimacy of student political activity itself.

The phrase most often used to depict such allegedly illegitimate students was *professional students*, an expression that hints at both the conspiratorial/performative nature of supposed communist agents trained to pose as students and the financial rewards, as opposed to moral and humanistic ones, they presumably gained for this work. Certainly not limited to Brazil, elements of this idea appeared throughout the late-1950s and early 1960s, for example, accusations that Mexican student activists were really *fósiles* (fossils), spending an excessive number of years in the university and reenrolling each term not for educational reasons but for the chance to organize politically.[49] This idea could be seen as well at the leadership seminars sponsored by the U.S. State Department in 1959 and designed to bring Latin American student leaders to the United States in order to change "unfavorable and suspicious attitudes" among them. In their postseminar evaluations the U.S. officials reported that most of the Brazilian participants were "student politicians, who were in the universities primarily for political purposes."[50] Raymundo Eirado, president of UNE in 1959, recalled criticisms of the union's leaders for being so-called professional students—"students who never moved on from school, who never passed their exams, who repeated years, who just stuck around"—as so strong that his directorate changed UNE rules to prohibit reelection and thereby avoid such accusations.[51] And in an IPÊS-sponsored publication of a few years later that railed against UNE for being an "instrument of subversion," the author asserted that UNE leaders were working in the interests of Bolshevik agents "from whom they probably receive money" and repeatedly argued that the union spent much more than it received in government funds, paying its leaders large salaries and lavishing expensive vacations on them.[52]

The activities of IPÊS were not confined to students. The organization sponsored extensive political propaganda designed to undermine popular support for President Goulart, portraying his government as multifariously corrupt, incompetent, and dangerously leftist. Nor was the institute's voice the only one raised in criticism of Goulart in this period. On the contrary, it reflected a swelling chorus of civilian and military leaders who considered the Goulart government and the growing popular mobilization it engendered a threat to Brazilian national security. For example, IPÊS was joined by the Instituto Brasileiro de Ação Democrática (IBAD, Brazilian Institute of Democratic Action), a similar assemblage of business executives that also sought to influence political debate. In the IPÊS/IBAD defense of a nationalist, "traditional" culture against a perceived international communist threat, they echoed the teachings of the Escola Superior de Guerra (ESG, Higher War College), a kind of pedagogical think tank in which civilian and military elite together examined the interconnections between capitalist development and national security.[53] IPÊS and the ESG also shared considerable overlap in terms of their members, such as Gen. Golbery do Couto e Silva, an ESG professor who simultaneously headed an important intelligence-gathering section in the Rio de Janeiro branch of IPÊS.[54] Finally, since at least 1962 U.S. agencies such as the United States Information Service took part in efforts to delegitimize and destabilize Goulart, for example, by financing the electoral campaigns of his opponents in the parliamentary elections of 1962.[55]

In its defense of a so-called traditional culture, the IPÊS helped support the formation of a women's group, the Campanha da Mulher pela Democracia (CAMDE, Women's Campaign for Democracy). In the words of the political scientist Sonia Alvarez, CAMDE and other right-wing women's organizations employed "traditional symbols of feminine piety and spiritual superiority, morality and motherhood" to implore the military "to perform its 'manly duty' and restore order and stability to the nation."[56] If women student activists were not directly named, one might nonetheless see their growing participation in an increasingly left-wing student movement as one part of the disorder that required remedy.

Within this increasingly polarized context U.S. representatives and others expressed concern about the potential for an ideologically entrenched UNE leadership, one empowered by the wealth and status of the union to, at best, misrepresent students as a whole and, at worst, manipulate them. Such a sentiment could be discerned in the observations of the USNSA at the aforementioned UNE Congress in 1961, when the U.S. observers worried aloud about the inordinate influence of the highly organized communist sectors, the special vulnerabilities of women students, and the large government subsidies they believed the union received. Similar allusions surfaced regularly within Brazil as well, such as the calls for a congressional investigation into how UNE used federal funds, a proposal voiced amid criticism of supposed communist control of the union following the UNE Congress of 1962 and the election of Vinicius Caldeira Brant, a JUCista.[57] Moreover, other groups arose to provoke UNE, such as the Movimento Anti-Comunista (MAC), a group supposedly made up of students but whose membership was rumored to include police officers, and, after 1963, the Comando de Caça aos Comunistas (CCC, Communist Hunting Command), a similar group in São Paulo.[58] MAC specifically targeted the wealth and symbolism of the UNE building in January 1962 when it sprayed the outside of the headquarters with machine gun fire and painted the walls of the building with the initials M.A.C.[59] The contention behind all of these criticisms and acts of violence was that, for some, a communist leaning by UNE was by definition illegitimate and could not possibly represent the real opinions of Brazilian students were it not for external influence.

Within the student sector criticisms also arose about a gulf between the leaders and the student masses (a massa estudantil). Reis, then a student activist who later in the decade would join a group that opposed both the PCB and the AP, critiqued the UNE directorates of the early sixties. In an interview in 2005 he said, "The leaders [of the student movement] agitated things a lot; they had a very fast pace. [But] they cared very little about organizing students within their year of study, within their classes, what we would later call organizing the base."[60] While his comments are colored by his opposition status and the later organizing strategy he advocated, Reis's general sense that the leadership was not fully supported is backed up by isolated incidents of real conflict between students. In June 1961, for example, police troops again surrounded the UNE building, this time to protect it from a student attack. A group from the Escola Nacional de Engenharia (National School of Engineering) believed that UNE supporters had thrown rocks at their school the day before, and they assembled at Praia de Flamengo to retaliate.[61] The political scientist João Roberto Martins Filho has shown that in various regional elections at the end of 1963 and beginning of 1964 students opted for candidates who had run on moderate or even right-leaning platforms, in opposition to the left-leaning UNE, particularly in the state unions of Pernambuco, Minas Gerais, and Bahia and in the UME of Rio de Janeiro.[62] The same holds true for the state union of Paraná.

These divisions became more manifest as the tenor of political debate in Brazil strained even further during Goulart's efforts to define and promote a series of deep reforms. Referred to as reformas de base (base reforms), these included agrarian reform, changes in the tax system, education reforms, and others. In addition, he advocated the abolition of literacy requirements for suffrage and endorsed nationalistic economic policies such as state control over certain enterprises and limits on foreign remittances. Yet Goulart vacillated widely in trying to implement these ideas, balancing appeals to his popular base, who supported deep changes, with efforts to gain support from his opponents, who favored a more moderate approach. In one sense this strategy paid off, as the president mustered enough support to hold a national plebiscite in January 1963, in which voters chose to restore the presidential system. Equally true, however, is that his inconsistencies frustrated many otherwise supportive observers, who pointed out that his radical rhetoric did not often match his more moderate decisions. As Reis poignantly noted, "The president's zigzagging tormented allies and enemies. . . . Everyone doubted the president's intentions." Goulart's changing position added further incentive to those groups, including the leadership of UNE, who thought the president needed to be pushed in order to fulfill his potential.

Meanwhile the political divisions that marked other sectors of Brazilian society intensified. In 1963 the destabilization efforts of civilian groups like IPES and IBAD escalated until they grew into a budding conspiracy to overthrow the Goulart government, one that included both civilians and high-ranking members of the military.[63] By the end of that year the U.S. government had drawn up a secret contingency plan purporting to lay out the appropriate response should there be any attempt, from the left or right, to change the governing regime in Brazil. In effect, as the historian Carlos Fico has shown, the plan actually contained the predictions and proposed policy of its authors, one that entailed close, covert contact with the anti-Goulart conspirators, assumed that sizable democratic forces with considerable military support would soon mount a resistance, and proposed an initial noninterventionist posture after the event coupled with covert or overt support to the interventionist forces.[64] All of this would be borne out a few months later. In the meantime, however, signs of a civilian–military interventionist movement proliferated, and some of the clandestine lefts began discussing armed resistance to any such attempts.

In these tense final months of Goulart's presidency criticisms of UNE and divisions within the student movement emerged most forcefully. Leaders of UNE became part of a vocal leftist coalition with labor unions that urged even deeper reforms, regularly sharing the podium with labor leaders and left-leaning politicians at protest rallies and demonstrations. At the same time, large numbers of other students, like many of the middle and upper classes generally, expressed growing suspicions about Goulart, fearing the reformas de base belied a radical nationalist takeover of the country that would abolish Brazil's constitutional democracy.[65] So while on March 13, 1964, Goulart shared the stage in Rio de Janeiro with UNE leaders, among others, in a massive rally to support his reforms, six days later hundreds of other students assembled at a huge counterrally in São Paulo organized by CAMDE and called the March of the Family with God for Liberty. When rumors of the impending military coup inspired UNE leaders to decorate their headquarters with a large banner reading, "Students mobilized against the coup" and to broadcast radio announcements asking students to be on a state of alert, scores of other students promised to support the military if it intervened.[66]

The first few years of the 1960s thus corresponded with a period of intense political activism on the part of UNE on the one hand and of growing vociferous criticism of its activism on the other. What bound these two developments was their focus on the authority of students and their unions to engage in these political actions. Nor did such divergences remain at the level of discourse but spilled forth in a flood of escalating tensions during the early months of 1964. Thus on April 1, 1964, the military deposing of President Goulart could not fail to leave an impact on the student movement. Nor would the ensuing transformations in the student movement itself fail to leave an impact on Brazil.

The Smoldering Aftermath of the Day of Lies

After weeks of increasing tensions and rumors of military intervention, students and CPC artists gathered at the UNE building on the night of March 31, 1964, to debate what to do. The night before they had canceled the long-awaited inauguration of the new four-hundred-seat theater on the third floor, a project several years in the making, postponing the scheduled play and instead using the theater to discuss the impending national crisis. They were in the midst of this discussion around midnight when a passing car sprayed machine gun fire into the building, wounding the actor Haroldo de Oliveira in the leg. One group quickly took him to the hospital, while others barricaded the doors and prepared for the possibility of more attacks. They would come, but not until nearly two days later well after word of the successful military coup had become official.

In the late hours of March 31 and early morning of April 1 soldiers from Minas Gerais marched on Rio de Janeiro in an attempt to overthrow Goulart.[67] The Rio-based First Army that was sent to stop them instead joined the revolt. When São Paulo's Second Army did so as well, Goulart's fate was sealed. Following a few days of desperate negotiating but no actual fighting, his supporters admitted defeat, and Goulart flew to Uruguay in exile. Unbeknownst to the many who had urged the military to undertake this coup d'état, these acts ushered in what would become the longest, most repressive military regime in Brazilian history. Newspapers supportive of the intervention originally celebrated the fact that the overthrow took place on April 1, otherwise known as the Day of Lies (a facetious holiday much like April Fool's Day in the United States), but military officials later redefined both the event and its temporal genesis, thereafter referring to it exclusively as the Revolution of March 31.[68]

To UNE members and CPC artists, however, April 2 became the more obvious marker of radical change, for on that day crowds of coup supporters assembled outside the UNE headquarters to celebrate, first by attempting to break down the doors and reach those still barricaded inside and then, when that failed, by setting the building on fire.[69] Luis Werneck Vianna, one of the small group inside the headquarters that day who hoped to protect it from potential attacks, later described the historic building as being encircled by people jeering and throwing things while residents in the high rises next door watched from their windows or chimed in to heckle and boo: "There was a festive air about it, as if the city had been liberated from some oppression."[70] Vera Gertzel, one of several women who formed part of the defense group, had a similar impression. When the situation out front became too menacing, the men made their female colleagues leave.[71] Ironically, Gertzel and the other women hitched a ride out of the area in a van driven by two marines. As they drove down Praia de Flamengo, the women saw UNE go up in flames. Gertzel described their experience: "They [the marines] stopped the car to watch the show. Isolda [Cresta] began weeping when she saw the scene. And me, pinching her, telling her to shut up and be quiet. And those guys just watching the fire. When we went through [the tunnel to Copacabana], all those horns celebrating the coup. The climate was that of a party."[72] Another participant, Carlos Vereza, similarly recalled how "little by little, more and more cars arriv[ed] in front of UNE with guys from the middle class of that period, tanned, eating hot-dogs with Coca-Cola and saying 'that the communists had been defeated, that Jango [President Goulart] had fled. . . . ' Those people hooted, threw things into the barricade that could start a fire."[73] In the climate of celebration and abandon that gripped the coup's supporters, UNE's building was not only destroyed but its very destruction was banal-

FIGURE 2.4. Barricades burning in front of the UNE building on April 2, 1964.
Agência JB

ized, turned into a show for the happy marines and others. In fact, the spectacle was not limited to those in the immediate area but extended to television viewers as well. One local TV news program sent an announcer to broadcast live from the scene, where he not only excitedly described the events unfolding around him but also invited the public to join in.[74] The building at 132 Praia de Flamengo Street, once seen as a formal confirmation of students' political authority, had become a symbol of dangerous radicalism that needed to be destroyed, and the military coup against Goulart became the catalyst for this purging fire (figure 2.4). Roberto Amaral, UNE vice president in 1961, evocatively recalled the burning of the building as the defining moment of that day. Seeing it, he said, "it was as if I [myself] were being burned. . . . Because UNE had huge symbolism for me, that building where I had lived, catching fire, those documents we had catalogued. The coup, for me, was the burning of UNE."[75]

As one might expect given the divergence of opinions leading up to April 1964, students' responses to the coup varied. In Rio de Janeiro, where Carlos Lacerda, now the governor of Guanabara, played an active role in advocating intervention,[76] hundreds of students gathered at the Governor's Palace, ready to take up arms to support the overthrow.[77] Hundreds more paraded in the Rio version of the March of the Family with God for Liberty, planned weeks earlier in order to encourage intervention but ending up as a celebration of the completed act. Meanwhile in another part of the city students congregated at the National Law School, which they hoped to defend in case of attack, but they soon found themselves surrounded by military troops. In the ensuing standoff seven students were injured and one killed[78] before a supportive army captain stationed his tank between the police and the university and urged the students to go home.[79] In Recife similar skirmishes led to the deaths of two more students, while young people in Brasilia and Belo Horizonte suffered injuries as well.[80] In general, however, the planned resistance among the lefts never materialized, as the much-promised arms with which groups like POLOP and the PCdoB had intended to defend the government failed to appear. Despite the appearance of a strong militant left, the coup d'état was accomplished quickly and unilaterally.

The military in Brazil had intervened politically in the past, as when it forced the removal of Getúlio Vargas from office in 1945 and staged a preventative coup in 1955 to assure the inauguration of the newly elected President Kubitschek. Yet in these prior incidents a democratically elected civilian presidency soon followed. In 1964, however, as Skidmore explains, important sectors within the military, soon deemed the hard-liners, "wanted to stop the merry-go-round in which recurrent military interventions since 1945 had been followed by the rapid return to civilian rule. As the hard-liners believed this strategy solved nothing, they wanted no more direct presidential elections until they had changed the rules. They especially wanted the more dangerous actors removed."[81] Manipulating rather than strictly following constitutional procedure for replacing the president, the head of the Chamber of Deputies, Ranieri Mazzilli, became acting president in accord with the Constitution, giving Congress thirty days to elect a new president who would serve out Goulart's term. At the same time, Gen. Artur de Costa e Silva of the army, Adm. Augusto Rademaker Grunewald of the navy, and Brig. Francisco Asis Correio de Melo of the air force, created an extraconstitutional junta called the Supreme Revolutionary Command. After considerable private debate among military officials and their civilian allies, on April 9 the command issued what would be the first of several Atos Institucionales (AIs, Institutional Acts)—unconstitutional executive decrees that created extensive new powers. Asserting that "the civil and military movement that just opened up new perspectives on Brazil's future

... is an authentic revolution" and, as such, is the "most expressive form of popular will," the preface of the act maintained that "the victorious revolution, as an expression of popular will legitimizes itself."[82] The text of the decree made military officers eligible for public office, gave the executive vast new authority, including the power to unseat elected politicians and to suspend the political rights of anyone for ten years, and diminished the powers of Congress and the Judiciary. It also set the date for the election of a new president a mere two days later. This haste ensured that Congress would support the military's chosen candidate, Gen. Humberto de Alencar Castelo Branco, as indeed it did.[83] President Castelo Branco took office on April 15, with the PSD politician José Maria Alkmin as vice president and a cabinet made up almost exclusively of civilians, mostly from the UDN. Like the joint civil–military movement that brought it to power, the new regime ostensibly combined civilian and military forces as well as constitutional and extraconstitutional acts, even as these founding events presaged increasingly authoritarian military control.

For many of the various social and political movements active during the Goulart period, the immediate consequences of this transfer of power included severe repression and the quick dissolution of their organizations. Beginning almost immediately the new regime launched Operação Limpeza (Operation cleanup). Ostensibly designed to purge the country of alleged subversives, the roundup focused on the PCB and other left-wing groups, supporters of the ousted president, and those in his government accused of corruption.[84] According to the historian Maria Helena Moreira Alves, in the first months after the coup as many as 50,000 people were arrested: "Roadblocks were set up and house-to-house searches were conducted for all persons included in previously prepared lists. . . . The large football stadium of Rio de Janeiro . . . and a number of Navy ships . . . were turned into gigantic, temporary prison camps."[85] Main targets included union leaders, teachers, organizers in the Catholic movements, intellectuals, agrarian workers, and members of the military itself. Indeed, 421 military officers were forced into the reserves, while 24 of 91 generals were purged.[86] Some 2,000 public employees lost their jobs, almost 400 people had their political rights suspended, and another 2,000 found themselves subject to Inquéritos Policial Militar (IPMs, military police inquiries), extrajudicial investigations into suspected subversive activities.[87] In the Northeast the peasant leagues suffered especially brutal repression. Military personnel there rounded up both organizers and sympathizers, beating, jailing, and at times torturing and killing them.[88] Though initially considered most prevalent in the Northeast, reports of torture soon surfaced in other areas as well, eventually leading to a series of heavily critical exposés in the *Correio da Manhã* newspaper and, consequently, a military investigation into the practice. The military report admitted that a few cases had occurred, though only in the first few weeks after the coup, but the *Correio da Manhã* offered evidence that the practice continued.[89] (In the next two years official denunciations of torture did subside.)[90] Finally, to survey threats to the new regime more efficiently, the government created the Serviço Nacional de Informações (SNI), an exceptionally powerful intelligence agency that reported directly to the president. Headed by General Golbery do Couto e Silva, as noted a former member of IPÊS, the service compiled its first information files on the basis of IPÊS archives, which it took over. Meanwhile the army, navy, air force, and part of the federal police all maintained their own intelligence bureaus, as did the state-run political police forces first established by Vargas and known to all as the DOPS, the militarized state police forces (*polícias militares*), and even the intelligence divisions of various federal ministries.[91] These various state security forces became numerous, overlapping, and extremely active.

The student movement, as an especially public and vocal ally of Goulart, felt the effects of this radical change in government. Besides the attacks on the UNE building, police and others soon invaded the offices of local and state-level student organizations around the country, inflicting physical damage and removing mimeograph machines, typewriters, and archives while university rectors took advantage of the situation to expel or suspend so-called inconvenient students.[92] Over seven hundred members of UNE underwent IPMs, as did the union itself, eventually leading to a nearly four-thousand-page report arguing that the union had been trying "to Change the Political and Social Order established in the Brazilian Constitution through subversion, including violent means."[93] The situation was sufficiently threatening to the current UNE president, José Serra, that he sought refuge in the Bolivian embassy. Serra (no relation to Antônio Serra), remained there for three months before going into exile until 1978. (The advanced degrees in economics he earned abroad, at the Universidad de Chile and Cornell University, would later help him in his return to political life in the 1980s and beyond, including two unsuccessful campaigns for president in 2002 and 2010.[94]) Numerous other student activists also went into exile in 1964, so many that Reis later noted, "The disappearance of the entire leftist vanguard of the student movement that had been developing since the late 1950s was really shocking."[95] In both material and symbolic terms the effects on the student movement were sudden and deep.

Beyond the purging of individuals and the disruption of organizations, the legitimacy of the student organizations themselves, especially UNE, came under fire. The investigations noted above received much attention in the local press, as did other accusations against UNE, casting a dark shadow over the organization. José Serra later recalled, "After the coup they decorated my office with a photograph of Stalin, displayed in all the papers as if it were mine. They said that President Goulart had paid us in dollars, kept a luxury apartment for us in Rio, and gave us a car with a chauffeur."[96] Though personally troubling for Serra, the broader impact of these stories was the ways in which they cast doubt on the legitimacy of the organization as a whole. The long-standing preoccupation with UNE's institutional benefits—such as the small apartment for its directorate in the UNE building and the annual subsidy for its activity—appeared here in exaggerated form, intimating that the union was directed from afar and that its leaders were corrupt. By this token, even well-meaning student members, it was implied, had inadvertently labored against the nation's interests, manipulated by inauthentic UNE leaders.

Hence, just a few months after the coup Minister of Education Flávio Suplicy de Lacerda sent a letter to President Castelo Branco proposing the eradication of UNE and the UEEs and their substitution with new entities. Congress passed the new legislation in November, a complete reorganization of the entire structure of student organizations that had existed since the 1930s and 1940s. Nicknamed the Suplicy Law after its author, Minister Suplicy de Lacerda, this regulation did not technically outlaw UNE and the UEEs, but it did mandate new state and federal student organizations, rename CAs as Diretórios Acadêmicos (DAs, Academic Directorates), and order deep transformations to the faculty-level and university-level DCEs. Unsurprisingly, the Suplicy Law strictly prohibited student organizations at any level from engaging in political "action, demonstration, or propaganda" and from "inciting, promoting, or supporting collective absences from scholastic work."[97] It also placed them firmly under the control of their respective universities and the Ministry of Education, and gave existing organizations sixty days to transform themselves to fit these criteria.[98]

The text of the law reveals the extent to which officials sought to prevent presumed professional students from controlling the new organizations, as it made voting obligatory for all full-time students (and only full-time students), required that all candidates for student office similarly be enrolled full time (reverting to part-time status after election would immediately end the student's term in office), and prohibited reelection to the same post.[99] The law exposes the minister's concerns about students' potential financial powers as well—especially the fear of foreign financing—by requiring an annual detailed accounting of each organization's income and expenses and threatening directorate members with "civil, penal, and disciplinary responsibility" for any "international or inappropriate use of funds."[100] Officials had especially high hopes for the new national-level organization, the Diretório Nacional de Estudantes (DNE), and expected it to quickly render UNE obsolete. In the weeks leading up to the law's passage, Suplicy de Lacerda described its aims as nothing less than "saving the university, constituting an authentic elite, and leaving UNE aside."[101] The Forum of University Rectors concurred, declaring their support for the law, which, they argued, "would restore lost dignity to the student representative organizations."[102] In legislative terms, officials mostly ignored UNE at first; after stripping it of its official status and accompanying budget, many believed it would soon disappear or be reorganized into the DNE.

If the government's goal had been merely to replace the leftist student movement leadership with more moderate actors, then this law would have made little sense. From the first public announcement of Suplicy de Lacerda's proposal until at least several months after the law was passed, students who had won metropolitan or statewide leadership positions by opposing the leftist direction of UNE and who might therefore have been prime candidates for constituting a so-called authentic elite in the student movement, campaigned vigorously against it, to no effect. Just two days after news of the proposal appeared in the *Jornal do Brasil*, leaders of UME, wrote a telegram to Castelo Branco (a copy of which was published in the newspaper) stressing their belief that the "great majority of national students" had "patriotic principles and democratic ideals" and requesting that the "unheard of" step of "marginalizing Brazilian youth" be reconsidered.[103] Apparently UME requested support from the USNSA on this matter, for U.S. students also sent a telegram to Castelo Branco shortly thereafter (with copies to several Brazilian newspapers) urging that "no action be taken to destroy the status of UNE."[104] Several days later they received a response from the UME officials Antonio Figueira and Humberto Rodrigues thanking them for their statement, asserting that "with that act you are certainly helping us to preserve our struggle for democracy and freedom" and signing off with a note of solidarity in English: "We shall overcome."[105] In addition to these lobbying efforts, Figueira and others tried to reclaim UNE. Leaders from UME and three other state unions that had opposed the leftist UNE directorate—those of Pernambuco, Minas Gerais, and Paraná—met in July to form a temporary, four-person directorate.[106] Tellingly, the two immediate items on the new group's agenda were, according to Artur Poerner, reclaiming the burned UNE building and defeating the Suplicy Law.[107] Both goals reflect how important the legacy of UNE was, even to those who opposed its recent leadership. Lest their differences with the exiled UNE leadership appear slight, the creation of this temporary directorate sparked a furious flyer signed by "the UNE directorate" that accused them of allying with the dictatorship's stooges (interventores) and attempting to impose "a false and cowardly leadership onto the student movement."[108] It is significant that this early flyer labeled the new government a dictatorship, a term that few then dared to employ publicly.

Notwithstanding the angry flyer and the Suplicy Law's passage in November, the temporary directorate held another meeting a few months later, at which they chose as UNE president a law student named Alberto Abissâmara.[109] He intensified their efforts, meeting personally with Minister Suplicy de Lacerda and, when this proved fruitless, arranging a secretive rendezvous at an art museum to speak with two U.S. embassy officials.[110] According to the embassy report, Abissâmara had personally explained to the education minister that the newly configured UNE supported the military government, but the minister was "still out to crush the organization." Abissâmara further complained that ever since that meeting he found himself under federal surveillance.[111] Given multiple opportunities to return UNE to supportive student leaders, the government refused.

Instead, eminent voices within the military government sought to proscribe any kind of political involvement for students. Much as they refused to return executive power to civilians in an effort to "stop the merry-go-round" of temporary measures, so too they sought to end the political influence of university students. In addition to the specific limits imposed by the Suplicy Law, the thinking behind this policy is revealed in the results of the police inquiry into UNE, which was completed in October 1965. The military and police investigators pinpointed one particular UNE document from 1959 as a "masterpiece of political and subversive display" that marked the turning point for the union on its one-way path of subversion. The UNE passage they cite reads as follows: "Besides being an organization that seeks increased privileges for students, the União Nacional dos Estudantes ought to be a movement, a demonstrating body for the political thoughts of Brazilian students in the face of the important problems that confront our country and the people of our land." This, the authors argued, was a calamity, for "the important problems were always accentuated in the sense of changing the social structure, a goal emphasized by all the directorates from that day forward."[112] In this view, the major "subversive" turning point for UNE was when it began to deliberately take on issues beyond students' needs as scholars and sought instead to represent them as citizens.

At the same time, military figures publicly asserted that students were simply too young and inexperienced to involve themselves in political matters. For example, at a graduation speech at the University of Bahia in 1965, Minister of Planning Roberto Campos told students "not to seek premature political leadership with the pretension of setting directions without previous experience."[113] This paternalistic message echoed that of the earlier IPÊS film on students, which suggested their responsibilities were only to books and the future. From this perspective students should never advocate political causes because they were, by definition, unprepared.

Perhaps not surprisingly some of the measures the regime adopted soon alienated many otherwise supportive students and incensed those who already opposed it. In addition to repressing specific organizations like UNE, the excessive intervention of the new government in university affairs bred resentment and anger among students and professors alike as entire campuses came under the regime's heavy hand. Just a week after the coup the University of Brasilia endured a military occupation by four hundred soldiers. Troops aggressively inspected departments and libraries, closing down vast areas and confiscating materials they deemed subversive and arresting professors and students. The architect who had helped design Brasilia, Oscar Niemeyer, graced the top of the list of those sought, while others included students active in their CAs.[114] Soldiers invaded the University of São Paulo also, and for several months military personnel ran the Federal University of Minas Gerais.[115] Professors too were purged en masse, as special investigative commissions were installed at all federal and state universities and schools (as well as at all government agencies and corporations) to conduct IPMs. Headed by military-appointed panels from within the university and informed by confidential army reports, these commissions investigated allegedly subversive professors and compiled lists of those to be dismissed, creating a climate of distrust and acrimony among colleagues.[116] Even casual forms of student dissent proved dangerous. When a small crowd of students at the University of Brazil booed Castelo Branco during his appearance there in March 1965, army officers identified and imprisoned five of the culprits. For many students, including those who previously did not participate in the student movement, the sudden appearance of military officials on campuses, observing classes and directing administrators, proved deeply unwelcome.

Hence after a brief period of disarray, the Suplicy Law ironically contributed to students' efforts to sustain UNE. According to Jean Marc Von der Weid, then a first-year student of chemical engineering at UFRJ who would eventually become an AP member and the president of UNE, the mandatory elections facilitated their endeavors in that they essentially forced all students to discuss the situation in order to decide how to vote.[117] Thus when UNE organized a national referendum to see if students "accepted the . . . restrictions or if they wished to support an illegal UNE," he recounts, "approximately 98% of students voted to support the illegal organization."[118] By July 1965 even U.S. embassy officials were reporting that the law was becoming a "key factor in student opposition to the government," resulting in "growing student alienation and disaffection and the gradually growing strength and influence of the radical leftist AP and, to a lesser degree, the communists."[119] Building on this momentum, UNE held a small congress that month in which another left-leaning directorate was chosen, one that again had close ties to the AP as well as to other clandestine leftist groups. By the end of the year, when student dissatisfaction had become so obvious that Minister of Justice Gen. Juracy Magalhães sought to open a dialogue with students, UNE refused, making appeals to a collective memory of accumulated grievances that would soon become commonplace for the beleaguered organization.[120] "They are talking of approach and understanding, but what they really want is to make us forget the cries of our colleagues," they wrote. "They want us to forget the three thousand University students who have been arrested, expelled, and expatriated since April 1964. They will ask us to forget the episode . . . [when a student] had one of his hands crushed."[121] In January 1966 Castelo Branco signed a decree suspending UNE for six months, the time necessary for federal prosecutors (the Ministério Público Federal) to legally disband the organization.[122] Officials instructed journalists to henceforth refer to the illegal group exclusively as "the ex-UNE."[123] Also in 1966 the government reassigned UNE's still-damaged building at Praia de Flamengo to national programs in theater and orchestral music (the Conservatório Nacional de Teatro and the Conservatório Nacional de Canto Orfeônico). The theater was so badly burned that students could not lean against the walls without getting covered in soot.[124] Yet such measures did little to dampen the enthusiasm of UNE leaders, who still ran the union from various locations and remained publicly known as UNE officials. They continued to organize public UNE activities and mocked the ex-UNE label by calling it the clandestine UNE instead, a clear reference to the clandestine lefts. For despite the legal restrictions against it and the joke of its having gone underground, UNE maintained its presence as an active, aboveground student organization, one whose existence was not only well known but needed to be in order to maintain its legitimacy.

The eventual establishment of the DNE did not transform this situation, but only highlighted the growing disillusionment of even those students most inclined to support the new government. Six months after the first DNE directorate assumed office in January 1966, after an unopposed election of only one slate of candidates, one of the DNE vice presidents, Paulo Nunes Alves, spoke informally with U.S. embassy officials about the unending difficulties they faced.[125] These ranged from the repeated refusals of the new minister of education, Pedro Aleixo, to meet with them to the fact that their promised funding never arrived, leaving the officers to personally pay the DNE's expenses. The report concludes, "Nunes said that unless the GOB [Government of Brazil] radically alters its policy, the moderate leaders associated with the DNE will be swept out of office. . . . Nunes and his colleagues were not optimistic over prospects that the Ministry will change its attitude. Unfortunately, their description of the total lack of dynamism in the Ministry of Education coincides with the Embassy's own assessment."[126] Undoubtedly stemming from these failures, in early 1967 a new Ministry of Education decree replaced the Suplicy Law with Decree-Law 228, abolishing all state- and national-level student organizations, including the DNE. Henceforth only faculty-level DAs and university-level DCEs were allowed to operate, as long as they followed the strict regulations set out in the decree, including the continued prohibition against political involvement of any kind.[127]

Despite the loss of much of the earlier leadership and the repressive atmosphere that made many students apprehensive about getting involved, a small committed group became eager to reorganize the student movement. For some younger members, the eradication of the old guard even offered new opportunities to make their mark. Antônio Serra remembers the climate as one in which a few students at his university said, "Okay, let's put this back together, let's start it all over again. We have to start it all over. It didn't work that other way, so we're going to start with a new plan."[128] Indeed, the fact that new students who took up the slack were mostly unknown to the government's security agents meant that they often worked in relative liberty, at least at first.

As this new generation of student activists worked to rebuild the shattered student movement, they debated the extent to which earlier leaders' failure to ground themselves in specifically student concerns had contributed to a widening gap between leaders and the rest of the student body. And as those who advocated increased attention to university-centered grievances began to gain traction in several important student organizations, students in various parts of the country began to stage demonstrations. Although they faced numerous constraints, throughout 1964 and 1965 students went on strike at least sixteen times in eight states to protest university issues, from the mandatory retirement of certain professors to the poor quality of teaching.[129] When news emerged of a joint arrangement between the Ministry of Education (MEC) and the United States Agency for International Development (USAID) to reform the Brazilian university system, extended protests against what students saw as the privatization of education followed. Indeed, when the federal universities first began charging small matriculation fees, student activists complained bitterly that this was the first step in such privatization plans. By 1966, as matriculation fees began to rise and the excedentes problem increased, they undertook more public forms of protest, from camp-outs by surplus students to a few street marches led by UNE.

Students' denouncements of the so-called MEC–USAID plan became at once a defense of the public university system and a criticism of U.S. interference in national affairs and of the tight relationship between the United States and the military regime. As this critique suggests, the emerging new leadership did not by any means advocate foregoing attention to national and international political issues. No student leaders of any public profile sought to adopt the 1920s' perspective of the CIE, in which student organizations should address only matters involving "students as students" (see chapter 1). Part and parcel of defending institutions such as UNE was protecting students' hard-fought claim to political participation. This only became more important in the context of a military government that curtailed other forms of political engagement. But student activists disagreed on tactics. Some argued they could best mobilize other students to take part in political actions during this difficult time by focusing on issues that most directly impacted them. Others worried that too much attention to educational policy would dilute critically necessary efforts to contest the regime. They also disagreed, often quite fiercely, on political perspective, despite the fact that those students most active in restoring the student movement concurred in their strong opposition to the military regime and in their firmly left-leaning views.

In their disagreement students mirrored the divisions and debates of the clandestine lefts themselves, which suffered a major crisis in the wake of the coup. Their organizations became the target of government intervention, and bitter disputes broke out within their ranks over their responsibility for the coup and the lack of resistance to it. One line of thought within the PCB held that the lefts had been too impatient and that their radical posture had helped to bring about Goulart's overthrow. Others criticized the PCB's attempted alliances with bourgeois groups that had presumably left it weak when military intervention came.

These splits widened as people disagreed about what role the lefts should take in the context of what they all now agreed was a military dictatorship. Several prominent figures of the PCB, such as the executive committee member Carlos Marighella, advocated immediate military training to overthrow the regime and pursue the revolution, while others in the party leadership firmly opposed this tactic. Marighella ultimately left the party and formed a new clandestine organization at the end of 1967, a group that would soon be called the Ação Libertadora Nacional (ALN, National Liberating Action), one of the first organizations to put into practice the idea of armed struggle. That year the ALN staged holdups of banks and armored cars that appeared to be the work of regular thieves but were instead intended to fund the future revolution.[130] Meanwhile further divisions occurred across the lefts. In 1966 and 1967 alone, three of the four major groups that predominated in 1964—the PCB, PCdoB, and POLOP—suffered splits that resulted in fourteen new clandestine organizations. (The fourth group, the AP, would also split in 1968.) Of these fourteen, two were mostly student-run organizations based in what is now the state of Rio de Janeiro, the Dissidências (DI-GB and DI-RJ), so named because they were dissident offshoots of the PCB. Other student Dissidências emerged elsewhere in the country but were soon folded into some of the larger clandestine groups.[131] If many of these new groups concurred on the need for armed revolution, very few took practical steps in that direction at this point.

As observers, discussants, and members, students across the country both followed and participated in these heated debates and reorganizations. To explain just how they became involved with the clandestine lefts, it helps to recognize how important the organizations were in offering intellectual explanations of the country's current situation and its prospects. Those who joined such groups describe the process as one that interconnected thoughtful political engagement, personal growth, and social relationships. José Gradel, a secondary student in 1966 when he joined POLOP, recalls the fluidity with which politically motivated students entered into discussions organized by various clandestine groups: "There were classes. We would go to someone's house, the house of someone older than ourselves, someone in university, who would give classes on historical materialism, excellent classes."[132] Even after joining POLOP, he regularly went to classes held by the Dissidência and felt an affinity with this group too despite disagreeing with certain of their interpretations. "We would be connected to these groups, even if we weren't an 'organic' part of them," he noted.[133] José Genoíno, who eventually joined the PCdoB, took up arms against the regime and endured a five-year prison term marked by torture and abuse, likewise recalled the importance of fluid intellectual debate in these early years, noting, "All the organizations of the left . . . sold books and publications within the universities. This wasn't legal, but it was public and it really facilitated our relationship with these organizations."[134] For many, personal friendships played a central role as well. Gradel had friends in several groups and said that those relationships as well as romantic crushes he harbored for various female members greatly influenced his decisions to take part. In his memoirs Herbert Daniel similarly wrote about the importance of friendship in bringing him into POLOP in 1967, saying it was his friend Ângelo who "broadened me [my consciousness]" ("Foi Ângelo quem me 'ampliou' ").[135] His use of the verb *ampliar*, common in that context, suggests the intellectual exhilaration many young people claimed to feel as they collectively searched to make sense of Brazil in the post-coup years.

If the new student activists at first operated in relative obscurity, as they became better known they too suffered government persecution. The presidency of UNE switched hands twice after July 1965, as the president stepped down, the first vice president who replaced him was arrested, and the second vice president, José Fidelis Sarno, had to assume the office. If the majority of students did not get directly involved, they recognized the organizing taking place as well as the repression their colleagues faced. Antônio Serra explained that "at some moments we felt really isolated, as if we had no more social base, no more support. It was as if we had become very dangerous figures, very disquieting ones, and people tried to avoid us."[136] Sometimes this response was expressed via dark humor. With so many former student leaders in exile in Uruguay, when a new generation of student activists at the National Law School began holding heated political discussions in a nearby bar (botequim), everyone at the school quickly nicknamed the place Uruguay.[137] If on the one hand the joke reveals how visible the purportedly clandestine actions of student activists were, on the other it suggests the sense of rebellious identity being forged by a new generation of students.

Meanwhile sources of dissent appeared in other sectors. Economically, the new government's efforts to combat inflation and spur international investment led to much criticism. Its corrective price hikes for services such as public transportation and commodities like bread, for example, were immensely unpopular.[138] Politically, despite early assurances that Castelo Branco would merely serve out Goulart's term and then hold new direct elections for president in late 1965, Congress and the president soon passed a constitutional amendment postponing them until November 1966. This action won swift condemnation from many but especially from one prominent figure who sought the presidency for himself, the governor of Guanabara, Carlos Lacerda. An early supporter of the coup, Lacerda soon became an outspoken critic of many of the regime's policies. When he won the UDN's presidential nominating convention in late 1964, his candidacy disrupted the otherwise close relationship between Castelo Branco and the UDN.

Some voters expressed their dissatisfaction via the gubernatorial elections in October 1965, granting absolute majorities to antigovernment candidates in four politically and economically important areas: Guanabara, Minas Gerais, Santa Catarina, and Matto Grosso.[139] The internal government crisis this generated gave rise to AI-2, which mandated the future indirect election of the president, the vice president, and all governors, arguing that "the Country needs tranquility in order to do its work . . . and one cannot have peace without authority."[140] Among other measures, the act abolished all existing political parties. They were replaced with two official parties, the opposition party, Movimento Democrático Brasileiro (MDB, Brazilian Democratic Movement) and the progovernment Aliança de Renovação Nacional (ARENA, Alliance for National Renovation), or, as some students quickly took to calling them, the Yes! party and the Yes, Sir! party. As another round of elections approached, the regime released yet another AI, its third, in February 1966, decreeing the appointment rather than election of mayors in state capitals and other cities deemed to be important to national security.[141] By the end of 1966 Lacerda had not only renounced his presidential bid, but also launched an opposition movement he called the Frente Ampla (Broad front), advocating a return to popular democracy. As his efforts at first gained little traction, the military government mostly ignored him. Yet they recognized that political opposition was growing. At the presidential election in November the MDB was so outraged with the regime's political interventions that it boycotted the campaign. The electoral college within Congress thus dutifully elected ARENA's and the military's candidate, General Costa e Silva, to a four-year term. Costelo Branco closed his term with AI-4, revoking the current constitution.

In this context of growing dissent, student activists in UNE managed to hold onto the union and prevent its collapse. Despite strict prohibitions against it, in July 1966 they organized for UNE's annual congress to be held in Minas Gerais, and at least some students saw the climate as sufficiently receptive to sell fund-raising bonds in downtown Belo Horizonte.[142] Not even the arrest of several of them deterred the group, as, much to the chagrin of the police reporting on their activities, "on the same day [of the arrests], various university students returned to the city streets to keep on selling bonds."[143] Meanwhile the outgoing president of UNE, José Fidelis Sarno, had the institutional capacity to call on the union's alliances with other student organizations around the world. Writing on official UNE letterhead, he sent them news "about our struggle during this third year of Military Dictatorship and National Betrayal installed in Brazil" and informed them of the planned UNE Congress. He even invited them to send "fraternal delegates" to the event as witnesses to what he was sure would be government repression.[144] As his letter demonstrates, UNE had by now definitively labeled the military-led government a dictatorship. Most important, the union won an important symbolic victory when, despite fierce government opposition, it managed to hold its congress and elect a new directorate. Troops visibly occupied central areas of Belo Horizonte, inadvertently drawing attention to this latest incursion against what had long been a student prerogative. Students instead assembled secretly in the basement of a Franciscan church, initiating what would become a series of clandestine UNE congresses and the resulting cat-and-mouse games of intrigue they inspired. With the help of priests the attendees staggered their arrivals over the course of a few days, and by entering and exiting the church during Mass and mixing in with other worshipers the students escaped detection. The police estimates of 200–250 participating students paled in comparison to the 800–900 who had attended the legal, public UNE Congress in 1961.[145] But both by holding the prohibited event at all and by successfully electing a new directorate at the customary time students were able to assert that the institution and tradition of UNE continued, no matter the legal prohibitions against it.

Students also successfully mobilized to their advantage sectors of the media, which still operated with little or no censorship. A number of student leaders and actors in the clandestine lefts also worked as journalists, and they took pains to make sure that student demonstrations received ample coverage in the papers. Newspapers in Rio de Janeiro like the *Correio de Manhã* and the *Jornal do Brasil* as well São Paulo's *O Estado de São Paulo* became increasingly critical of the government. According to Reis, as they did so they came to support student protests to such an extent that they exaggerated their significance: "Sometimes we would hold lightning demonstrations [very fast speeches delivered quickly before a crowd which then dispersed] on Rio Branco Avenue. I'd climb up on a lamp post and make a speech to ten or fifteen people, our friends who were there. They were radical speeches, fast ones, and then we'd take off running, a little excited but also sad that it had been so small. The next day the story would appear in the first section of the JB [*Jornal do Brasil*] 'Students protest . . . ' and we'd be encouraged. I mean, the newspaper reverberated our actions and presented us with a force we didn't have, in truth; but that fed us." Sometimes journalists offered more direct support, as Márcio Moreira Alves did, for example. A well-known reporter for the *Correio da Manhã* and a regime opponent, he had investigated and denounced the multiple cases of state torture that took place in the wake of the coup, ultimately publishing the results of his findings in a controversial book that was initially banned.[146] By late 1966 he decided to run for Congress as a federal legislator from Rio for the MDB. According to reports of the DOPS political police, in September of that year he helped a group of students prepare for a demonstration not only by hosting the planning meeting in his home, but also by walking with them through the plaza outside, where he deliberately stopped to say hello to the several undercover police agents working there.[147] Presumably Alves knew them from his years as a journalist and from his status as someone currently under surveillance. By greeting them he was able to reveal their presence to the students.

When students suffered police repression, media coverage could elicit sympathy and solidarity for their plight. After the police invaded a meeting of São Paulo's UEE in September 1966, arresting over 150 students, the dissemination of the story via the newspapers as well as the organizing reach of UNE and other student organizations led to ten days of violent protests around the country. Students soon nicknamed these events the *Setembrada* after the month in which they took place. If events such as these earned them a degree of public sympathy, they also frightened some potential student participants, and large demonstrations diminished significantly in 1967.

Nonetheless, by the inauguration of President Costa e Silva in March 1967, the student problem, as officials called it, had become so salient that the new president made promises to initiate a dialogue with them a prominent part of his inauguration speech. Even Carnival that year, the month before his swearing in, had been marked by the student crisis, as surplus students danced in the parade carrying protest signs. And although Costa e Silva tried to remedy some of the excedentes' complaints by offering extra financial support to universities that allowed them to enroll, the measures were small and only further fueled discontent among other students who suffered increased overcrowding with no improvement in facilities.[148] Several months later UNE supporters held yet another clandestine national congress, this one in Vinhedo, São Paulo, where they elected as UNE president yet another AP candidate, Luís Travassos. Their new platform radically asserted, "The student movement, . . . workers and peasants [have] a common enemy: imperialism and the dictatorship that expresses its interests."[149]

Finally, at the end of 1967 Costa e Silva created a commission to study the problems plaguing Brazil's higher education system. The commission was headed by Col. Carlos de Meira Mattos, a close adviser to the president and the former commander of military forces in Brasilia who had briefly, on then-President Castelo Branco's orders, closed Congress in 1966. The Meira Mattos Commission was inaugurated in January 1968, presumably when summer vacation would prevent further student protests over this controversial choice.[150]

....

By the time of Celia Guevara's visit to Recife in 1961, university students and university student politics in Brazil were undergoing tremendous transformations. By the late 1950s and early 1960s the ideological polarization of the Cold War combined with a much greater expansion of the student population than ever before to create a vigorous national debate about the proper role of university students. On the one hand, a highly active and visible student leadership joined with artists, workers, and others in an effervescence of leftist political activity, adopting radical reconsiderations of the role of the university and of students themselves in transforming Brazilian society. On the other hand, powerful forces, concerned with internal threats to the nation, began to proclaim that students should avoid political activity altogether.

The coup d'état of April 1, 1964, put a quick end to this activity and drove out many of those who were behind it. In their place a new generation of student activists eagerly stepped into the vacuum of the student movement's departed leadership and struggled to rebuild. The new students shared the leftist ideals of their predecessors but disagreed with aspects of their governance that had ignored the majority of student concerns. At the same time, the military government tried to transform the student movement by eradicating the former student organizations and intervening in university life. Both strands—the re-creative and, ironically, the destructive —slowly worked together to foment student opposition to the military regime and its incursions into student life. If nonetheless a large contingent of students, by deliberate decision or by default, still shied away from participation, by the end of 1967 student dissent simmered beneath the surface. In the summer months of January and February, between the academic years 1967–68, few observers would have imagined that the student movement would soon burst forth on the political stage.

3

FROM MARTYRDOM AND MILITANCY TO MEMORY

1968 in Brazil

On March 28, 1968, the Guanabara state police shot and killed Edson Luis de Lima Souto, a young secondary school student purportedly about to engage in a street demonstration in downtown Rio de Janeiro. Newspaper reports gave conflicting accounts as to whether the group of some three hundred to six hundred mostly secondary school students assembled outside of the Calabouço, a student restaurant, had just initiated a protest march against the poor conditions there or whether some of them were merely attempting to organize one. Nor were they clear about what exactly led the police to enter the building that day. What was transparent, however, was the fact that soon after the officers arrived some of them began shooting. Before people could flee the scene several students were injured, and one passerby suffered a bullet wound to the face. The shot that killed Edson Luis went through the heart.[1]

The killing of Edson Luis, a poor student from the northern state of Pará who worked and sometimes lived at the Calabouço, set off an enormous surge in student mobilizing as almost immediately young people across the country protested his death in massive demonstrations. Their actions shocked officials who had considered the problem of the student movement to be dissipating. Just one day before the shooting Gen. João Dutra de Castilho, a regional army commander, had espoused confidence that student demonstrations would not disrupt the upcoming commemorations of the coup d'état of 1964 that brought the military regime into power—what the military, as noted earlier, called the Revolution of March 31—casually asserting that it was "useless for a small minority to try to perturb the country as they'll find no climate for that."[2] While it was true that the outlawed UNE and other suspect student organizations had not entirely disappeared and that the short-lived DNE had failed miserably as a government-sponsored alternative, student protests in the last year had become relatively small affairs, drawing reduced numbers of participants. While groups like the *excedentes* had recently staged several creative demonstrations to draw attention to their plight—for example, they held an ironic party protest (*festa-protesto*) to celebrate the one-year anniversary of their having been denied enrollment—none had galvanized mass numbers of students. Nor did the clandestine lefts—those extralegal revolutionary organizations that counted many student movement leaders as members—produce much cause for concern, as they had undertaken few public actions so far. And although tumultuous student strikes in Poland had recently become front-page news in Brazil, stories of Polish students' criticism of the Communist Party in power there appeared unquestionably foreign to the Brazilian situation. Notwithstanding the political radicalization of some Brazilian students, many presumed that the great majority of them, like others from their social class, generally if quietly supported the military government. Thus when General Dutra delivered his assured comments on March 27 few would have guessed that 1968 would soon become forever marked by an upsurge in massive university student demonstrations in Brazil and around the world.

The death of Edson Luis not only spurred an immediate, nationwide response it also mushroomed into nine tumultuous months of violent confrontations between students and police that would resound throughout the ensuing seventeen years of military rule as students became the most visible and emblematic symbol of opposition to the regime. During the period basically encompassing the March-to-November academic term, the concerns and grievances of a wide variety of student sectors—notwithstanding their frequent disagreements with one another—coalesced around a shared opposition to the dictatorship, as they fittingly referred to the military government. As student activists built on the momentum generated by Edson Luis's death, they implicitly and explicitly staked new claims to students' political authority, recasting themselves as a hybrid mix of martyrs and militants, both compelled to respond to the regime's repressive acts and eagerly poised to do so. Meanwhile military officials and others cast students' behavior as decidedly unnatural, provoked by nonstudent influences. These charges became further animated as student protests in other parts of the world became front-page news in Brazil. When, at the end of the year, the military took even more drastic steps to end student movement activity, enacting the most authoritarian piece of legislation of its twenty-one-year rule and plunging Brazil into its most repressive period, it marked a turning point in the history of the Brazilian military regime. It also augmented appeals to (and charges of) student militancy and martyrdom and ensured that the demonstrations of 1968 would assume a key place in collective memory.

In many ways the explosion of student protests in 1968 and their role in transforming both the history and memory of the student movement began with Edson Luis's death. Beyond the very real emotional responses generated by his murder, student leaders' skillful harnessing of the event's richly symbolic contours granted them a uniquely powerful opportunity to mobilize others. At the same time, they tapped into and helped reveal a swelling middle-class opposition to the regime that chafed at its continued political exclusion and was particularly open to public demonstration. The escalating police violence that followed the shooting of Edson Luis served to galvanize this opposition, as, far from subduing student activism, it helped propel it forward. In a process similar to that described by Edward Escobar in regard to the Chicano movement in the United States, a paradoxical "dialectics of repression" emerged in which increasing police violence aimed at silencing students became instead the central issue around which they organized and through which they earned public sympathy.[3] For weeks after Edson Luis's death student demonstrations assembled record-breaking numbers of participants, transforming the student movement into a source of regular debate, discussion, and speculation. The media catapulted students' violent clashes into front-page news; the military sought ever firmer ways of quelling the protests; and the clandestine lefts exalted the possibilities offered by such mass displays of aggressive resistance. The repression students encountered would become one of the hallmarks of the year and one of the defining ways in which 1968 would later be remembered.

The ways in which students' engagement with this dialectics of repression during the remainder of the March-to-July semester helped to harden the divisions explored in chapter 2, whereby some believed university students to be uniquely authentic political actors while others considered them dangerously vulnerable to outside manipulation. From students' increasing recourse to violent tactics to their disruption of gendered norms for women students, their actions in 1968 reanimated debates about the role students should play in society. At the same time, as student demonstrations in other parts of the world began to escalate and turn violent, the international scenario became an inextricable part of the local experience of 1968 in Brazil. Some figures took the concurrence of student unrest in various places at once as evidence that university students, owing to their combination of social privilege and youthful vigor, were naturally inclined to rebel against injustice and specially positioned to take on a vanguard role. For others, student protests elsewhere in the world offered confirmation of, at best, aberrant and un-Brazilian influences on the nation's youth or, at worst, an international communist conspiracy perpetrated by subversive agitators infiltrating student ranks. As police repression and student protests continued and even intensified throughout the first semester just as massive student demonstrations around the world also headlined the news, fierce disputes about the authenticity of student political activism reemerged as central political contests.

As the ongoing dispute about what constitutes authentic student behavior intensified, violent incidents between students and the police marked a final turn in the dialectics of repression and the boundary between the aboveground student organizations and the underground lefts became increasingly murky. For in the second half of the year fewer and fewer students chose to defy new bans against public demonstrations and to confront the steadily increasing police violence levied against them. Those who did were the students most connected to the clandestine lefts, fueled by their commitment to a long-term struggle for radical change and their sense that the state's recourse to violence pointed to its present weakness and imminent future collapse. At the same time, more of the lefts formed armed wings and began to undertake armed actions. As they did so, the security forces came to conflate the underground armed groups with the aboveground student organizations, that is, with known, legal, or formally legal organizations such as UNE that attempted to operate openly and that most students wanted to preserve. Once they had what they considered definitive proof of this connection, their response to all aboveground student movement activity—regardless of its connection to the lefts—changed radically, and 1968 as a year of student protest was brought to an early close.

The shooting of Edson Luis occurred around 6 P.M. in front of a student restaurant in downtown Rio de Janeiro called the Calabouço, or Dungeon. Located just east of downtown, near the former site of a seventeenth-century slave prison (whence its name derived), the Calabouço served state-subsidized meals daily to several thousand economically disadvantaged secondary and university students and offered other services such as tutoring. For over a year news of the restaurant had sparked controversy, as the city planned to host the twenty-second annual meeting of the International Monetary Fund (IMF) at the Museum of Modern Art, which was very near the rowdy student locale. In preparation the governor of Guanabara, Francisco Negrão de Lima, ordered the Calabouço to be relocated and the surrounding area renovated. As one of the opposition governors elected against the regime's wishes in 1965, Negrão de Lima faced loud denunciations by students for this seeming act of betrayal in prioritizing the IMF meeting over them. Partially to quell this criticism, the new restaurant opened quickly, even before construction had been completed. But such haste only made the situation worse. For months the continuing construction work resulted in leaking sewage and infestations of cockroaches, worsening the already poor food served there.[4] "I went [there] a lot, so I can say this," affirmed Bernardo Joffily, now a member of the PCdoB and in 1968 a secondary student who dined at the Calabouço. "That food was really foul . . . , 'un-swallowable.'"[5] Long before the shooting of Edson Luis there, the Calabouço symbolized student dissatisfaction.

Unsurprisingly, the Calabouço was also a renowned center of student political activism, in part due to the irresistible audience of potential political recruits in the form of the many students who dined there. The restaurant even had its own student organization, the Frente Unida de Estudantes do Calabouço (FUEC, United Front of Calabouço Students), with a particularly militant leadership. Headed by Elinor Brito, a secondary student with a somewhat unusual name for a man, the FUEC regularly held boisterous demonstrations in protest of the restaurant's squalid conditions. "Everyone would be eating . . . in that huge room," Joffily recalled, "and suddenly a student would stand up on his chair and say, 'Companheiros, I just discovered a cockroach in my soup, in my beans, on my tray.' And we would bang our forks. It was all prearranged, everyone knew it; no one had to explain what was going on. Everyone would bang their forks against their trays and make that immense noise of protest against the discovered cockroach."[6] These noisy cafeteria protests would soon find their way outside, where Calabouço students became notorious for causing sizeable disruptions in the surrounding area. While accounts differ, most sources assert that on March 28 students were merely planning a march when the police invaded. Yet they all agree that in the gunfire that erupted a bullet struck and killed Edson Luis.

In explaining the wave of student protest that followed Edson Luis's death and extended throughout much of the year, observers both at the time and in hindsight have rightfully seen his murder as a catalyst. Yet they have also tended to view the seemingly spontaneous student outburst that followed his death as the foreseeable and even inevitable consequence of such a blatant act of injustice. Such a perspective does little to explain the surge and more aptly reflects constructions of young people as easily and even naturally mobilized by certain triggers. In fact, throughout the year the police would kill three other students and seven additional bystanders, yet no massive student demonstrations ensued after these deaths, notwithstanding the concerted efforts of student activists to encourage them. After one such death, U.S. embassy officials mistakenly believed the event was likely to touch off a new round of protests, warning Washington that students had "another martyr" around whom to rally.[7] Yet no such rallies took place. Understanding the immediate response to Edson Luis's killing —and thereby making sense of the rush of student activity that marked 1968 in Brazil and the long-term meanings accorded to these events—requires that one consider carefully the specific circumstances of his death, the responses to it, and the aftereffects of those responses.

When one does so, it becomes apparent that, through a mixture of emotional spontaneity, clever strategy, and circumstantial fortuity Edson Luis's fellow students responded to his death in ways that helped transform a singular atrocious act into a rich set of symbolic meanings. Immediately after the shooting a group of shocked and alarmed fellow students rushed the boy to a nearby medical center, where doctors pronounced him dead.[8] The group then carried his body on their shoulders to the Guanabara State Assembly, bearing him past awestruck state legislators to the front of the room, where they stretched out the bloodied corpse on a regal wooden table.[9] Students had as allies several supportive legislators, and the State Assembly offered both a nearby refuge and the promise of official witnesses to the students' corporeal evidence. Their choice of location was also a strategic one, as, according to Brito, they knew the press would be in attendance at a formal event being held that day, and media coverage would help them denounce this act.[10] The incidental fact that Edson Luis had been killed nearby made all of this possible. Carried along by both outrage and political acumen, students brought the incontrovertible truth of the boy's dead body to a highly public space in order to denounce the police actions and the state they held responsible.

Once inside, student leaders continued their skillful use of symbolism by transforming the State Assembly and the young man's body itself into tangible platforms from which to declaim the murder. In one controversial move, Brito and other FUEC members insisted, over the objections of some student factions, that the corpse not be removed for an autopsy, as authorities might not return it. Instead they demanded that the procedure take place inside the legislature, symbolically and spatially transforming a medical exam into a political act.[11] They then converted the legislative arena into an unofficial wake, keeping vigil over the body throughout the night and displaying it to the hundreds of photographers, journalists, additional students, and other mourners who arrived to witness the events and spread the news of the boy's death. Media-savvy students surrounded the corpse with candles, placed flowers in the boy's hands, and covered his waist and legs with a Brazilian flag while leaving his bare chest exposed—a compelling image of youthful male vitality denied. They also plastered the table and the body itself with the unavoidable cynosure of dozens of handmade signs, messages that found their way into the many photographs that captured the event (figure 3.1). Mostly written on sheets of paper torn from school notebooks and three-ring binders, these signs proffered such statements as "Here lies the body of a student killed by the dictatorship" and "This is putrid democracy." Meanwhile outside the assembly building thousands of people began to gather. The president of UME, Vladimir Palmeira, rushed to the scene, where photographers snapped pictures of him speaking before the raised banner of Edson Luis's bloodied shirt.[12] Other students formed small groups to traverse the city denouncing the death. As word of the killing circulated, theaters halted their performances in acts of solidarity while horrified audiences offered accordant applause. As a sign of how quickly the news spread, funereal flowers began to arrive at the State Assembly from all corners of Brazil. One newspaper reported that by two A.M. eighteen anonymous wreaths had been delivered, and by the following afternoon the number had grown into the hundreds.[13] The next day

FIGURE 3.1. The body of Edson Luis de Lima Souto in the state legislature, where students bedecked his corpse with signs and held them up for photographers.

photographs of the poignant scene filled the morning newspapers, and students across the country initiated protest marches of mourning and solidarity.[14]

Students' adroit attention to the symbolic aspects of Edson Luis's death extended into the next day when, still at the State Assembly, they held an official wake for thousands of visitors that drew on the language of religious martyrdom and schoolboy purity in its presentation of the young man. Inside an open casket the boy lay ensconced in flower petals and long-stemmed carnations, his body entirely covered except for his head (figure 3.2). This display brought to mind the coffins of very young Catholic children, who are similarly buried amidst flowers, as the blossoms' fleeting beauty and delicate impermanence emphasize the youthful purity that is supposed to guarantee them, as people too young to have yet committed human sin, a place in heaven.[15] A Brazilian flag once again lay across Edson Luis's waist, suggesting the national dimensions of his personal tragedy, while over his legs someone carefully placed the geometry notebook he had with him when he died, a potent symbol of his status as a student.[16] Invariably students labeled him with the general term *student*,

FIGURE 3.2. Edson Luis's body was covered with flowers at his wake. Note the open geometry notebook placed at his feet to emphasize his status as a student and the national flag folded near his waist.

referring to him as "the student Edson Luis," rather than specifying what school he had attended or clarifying that he was a secondary rather than a university student. The more universal category emphasized the general sense of youthful promise cut short, while also implying a need for broad-based solidarity. At his funeral later that day both ideas intertwined in the multiple banners proclaiming "Poder Jovem" (Youth power), a phrase that at once emphasized the crime of cutting down a young man in his youth and the contested depictions of students as being too young to be authentic political actors.

This casting of Edson Luis as an abstracted student and symbol of innocent youth rather than as a particular individual was facilitated by the fact that few people knew him before he died. After his death newspapers struggled to provide a simple biography for him, writing one day that he had lived in Rio for several years and claiming the next that he had only recently arrived. Some confusion reigned even over his name, whether it was Edson or Nelson.[17] Many students claimed to know who he was, but no one publicly declared themselves a close friend. This may have resulted from the extremely tense circumstances of the moment, in which talking openly could have put the speaker at personal risk (real or perceived). But even DOPS agents struggled to find out more information about him. They had no files on him before he died and hence no way to contest the portrayal of him as an innocent victim. As the social scientist Maria Ribeiro do Valle asserts, Edson Luis "didn't carry those adjectives that were so dear to police searches, like 'subversive leader,' 'communist,' or 'agitator.'"[18] While one official sought to publicly taint all Calabouço students by denouncing the FUEC leader Brito as a "well-known agitator," such accusations did little to tarnish Edson Luis himself.[19] Perhaps in pursuit of incriminating material, DOPS officials interrogated arrested Calabouço students about the deceased young man, but in their report they could find nothing illuminating to say about him and instead merely intimated that FUEC leaders had cared little for him before he died.[20] In death Edson Luis became a household name, but the person Edson Luis remained an enigma, and his name and photographed corpse became symbols of dictatorial repression against innocent students.

Ironically, it was the boy's status as an indigent student far from home that allowed his fellow students to fiercely safeguard their control over the proceedings, thereby emphasizing his death as a distinctively student bereavement, that is, as a loss sustained by students rather than by his family. Besides keeping strict vigilance over the boy's body on the night of March 28, students refused to accept the funds offered by state legislators to pay for his funeral the next day. While opposition politicians in the State Assembly had kept vigil alongside the students that night, using the occasion to deliver fiery speeches critical of the police and the regime, student leaders turned down their offer of financing, claiming it would be a sad irony to let the state pay to honor a death it had caused. Instead, groups of young people traversed the city throughout the night to collect donations from drivers and pedestrians, stopping cars at intersections, boarding city buses from which they hung black, funereal flags, and combining fund-raising with broadcasting the news. Nor would they accept any planning help from the Department of Transit and even rejected the offer of a fire truck to bear the heavy coffin during the funeral, an event that included a three-hour march through city streets and drew upward of fifty thousand participants.[21] Instead, they themselves organized and or chestrated the event,

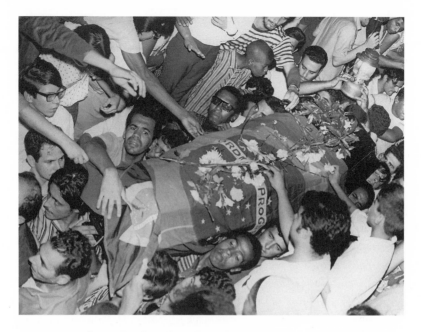

FIGURE 3.3. Edson Luis's funeral was directed and controlled by students. Here, volunteer pallbearers carry his flag-draped, flower-strewn coffin to the São João Batista Cemetery. *Correio da Manhã* collection, Arquivo Nacional

a long procession through Rio de Janeiro to the São João Batista Cemetery, the casket carried by various male pallbearers whose photographs appeared prominently in the national papers the following day (figure 3.3). As most of Edson Luis's family members lived far from Rio they were unable to contest the decisions being made.[22] The resulting effect was that the death of Edson Luis became a quintessentially student affair, thereby gaining an additional symbolic meaning as a demonstration of students' organizing powers and collective autonomy.

To the extent that Edson Luis's personal biography entered into discussions of his death, what mattered as much as his innocence was his status as a poor student from Pará who had come to Rio de Janeiro to study. The symbolic significance of his presence in Rio was crucial for a student movement that had long sought to criticize flaws in the national educational system and their relationship to Brazil's perpetual inequalities. With no good secondary school in Pará (and hence an infinitesimally small chance of gaining admission to a university), Edson Luis had needed to move to the home of his relatives in a Rio suburb in order to pursue his studies.[23] His presence thus transcended the geographic boundaries of the city and became emblematic of a national problem. At the same time, his poverty highlighted the continued inequalities that plagued Brazil, as the circumstances of his death magnified his family's economically humble background. The Calabouço was supposed to offer support to students like him, and instead his presence there led to his death. Edson Luis not only ate daily at the subsidized restaurant and took part in the subsidized tutoring sessions, but also, it seems, worked unofficially at the restaurant to pay for these services. He even came to avoid the long trek to his relatives' house by sleeping in a small area between the restaurant and the tutoring classrooms.[24] The figure of Edson Luis thereby became a symbol of the problems the new regime had failed to address and of an idealized interregional and cross-class solidarity among students.

Students elsewhere reflected and reinforced this sense of national solidarity by mobilizing in cities across the country and by referring to the death as an affront to the nation. The DCE at the Federal University of Paraná, for example, hoisted a huge black banner proclaiming, "Our grief is not just for the assassinated student but for the whole Brazilian Nation."[25] At the funeral in Rio they sang numerous choruses of the national anthem. And in slogans and banners students portrayed the boy's fatal misfortune as a personal and even collective sacrifice. For example, multiple signs at the funeral read, "Brazil, your children are dying for you," a phrase that transformed Edson Luis into the general and collective children of Brazil while implying a deliberate act of martyrdom in stating that they "are dying for you" (figure 3.4).[26] Another saying displayed on numerous banners, "He could have been your son," was a gendered invocation of the idea of a national sacrifice, one akin to the wartime image of a nation's sons at risk. Meanwhile the ubiquity of the slogan "In mourning the struggle begins," (neste luto começa a luta) a clever play on the words luto (mourning) and luta (struggle) presaged a deliberate upsurge in student mobilizing (figure 3.5). As student demonstrations of outrage and solidarity quickly took place in almost every major city in Brazil, they further created the sensation and the effect of a national problem and a national response.[27]

Most intriguingly, in various places students engaged in nearly instantaneous efforts to memorialize him. On the very day of his funeral young people collected funds to commission a sculpture of him to be placed in front of the Calabouço.[28] In Brasilia students tried to rename a section of

FIGURE 3.4. Protesting Edson Luis's death, students hold a national flag and a sign that reads, "Brasil: Seus Filhos Morem por Você" (Brazil: your children are dying for you). *Correio da Manhã* collection, Arquivo Nacional

FIGURE 3.5. Students in downtown Rio de Janeiro protesting Edson Luis's death, many with signs referring to luto and luta. *Correio da Manhã* collection, Arquivo Nacional

the University of Brasilia campus after him.[29] Representatives of various student organizations soon petitioned state and federal congressmen to make March 28 Student Day, an official holiday that would, they said, "always be a reminder of the assassination of Edson Luis by the Guanabara State Military Police."[30] Only days after the young man's death, students mobilized not simply to protest his murder but also to preserve and sustain his memory.

Yet Edson Luis's death resonated well beyond students, feeding into broader currents of frustration with the military regime and generating a wider response. The increasing limitations on political expression, from the cancellation of direct presidential elections to the abolishment of all preexisting political parties, meant that many political figures and others had long-standing grievances they were eager to address, and the blatant murder of a young student offered just such an opportunity. On the day of the wake the U.S. embassy in Rio telegrammed the U.S. Secretary of State's office to report that opposition politicians were using the incident to criticize the regime. "Mood of crowd in front of Guanabara Assembly where body being displayed is ugly—crowd being harangued by flow of opposition speakers attacking state and federal authorities. . . . Posters attacking 'Dictatorship' prominently displayed," they reported ominously.[31] The national press presented similar stories of political figures who made use of the moment, including those from opposing political camps. The former governor of Guanabara Carlos Lacerda, for example, proclaimed, "It's not right that in this country a young person is killed because he demands his right to study, to feed himself, to have an opinion," thereby criticizing both the economic and educational difficulties left unresolved by the regime and the limited political expression it allowed. Governor Negrão de Lima expressed some support by promising students they could hold the funeral without police interference. (The U.S. embassy secretly hid eighteen police in its basement, presumably in case of student vandalism.)[32] During the funeral cortege the student-led crowds received multiple signs of support, such as flower petals and confetti tossed from high-rise apartment buildings in the upper-middle-class neighborhoods of Flamengo and Botafogo or candles lit in the windows as it began to get dark.[33] As Antônio Serra recalled, "Everyone turned out their lights and put candles in their windows. It was fantastic. You could see all those windows, all with candles, and the funeral procession going by."[34] Even if not everyone lit candles, the large number who did hints at the ways in which this death afforded an outlet for those who wanted to speak out against the excesses of the regime.

Students' insistence on viewing the killing as a national incident paradoxically coincided with the federal government's efforts to disclaim direct responsibility for it. The day after the shooting Minister of Justice Luís Antônio da Gama e Silva released a statement asserting that "responsibility for public order within the States of the Federation belongs to the governors who direct their police," thereby implicating the opposition governor Negrão de Lima rather than the regime.[35] An official investigation of the event led to multiple allegations against the students themselves or unknown agitators within their midst, from the assertion that rock-throwing students forced the police to defend themselves to the charge that students fired the first gunshot.[36] The fact that the death nonetheless became a national topic of conversation and theme of protest suggests that most observers paid little heed to these official justifications, seeing the killing as symptomatic of national problems for which the regime was ultimately responsible.

While the outlawed UNE had no means of fomenting such a national response, the event nonetheless served to strengthen and legitimize the national union and the hierarchy of student organizations beneath it. At the funeral an UNE representative exuberantly told a journalist that "in killing a student, the police succeeded in reorganizing the student movement and creating authentic leaders overnight."[37] If that statement was a touch optimistic, the event certainly led to nearly instant celebrity for regional student leaders like Brito and Palmeira, who helped direct the well-publicized events of those days. As a sign of how relatively unknown the two men were outside of student and security circles before this date, the newspaper O Dia initially referred to them as Luis Brito and Flademir Palmeira and called them both FUEC officers.[38] This kind of error would soon be inconceivable as the two became household names. For their part, they conscientiously struggled to reassert the centrality of UNE, such as when they broke into the UNE building during Edson Luis's funeral processional to deliver speeches from the balcony. As Palmeira later explained, "It was on the way. So since we were passing the UNE building, we went there. We climbed up in the window, made a speech. We said that UNE was resisting; [that] it was directing our movement. It wasn't always exactly the truth. . . . But we were part of the group that was trying to build up UNE, so we wanted to strengthen it. We stopped there to make a presence for

FIGURE 3.6. The UNE building draped in a black flag of mourning the day after Edson Luis's funeral. *Correio da Manhã* collection, Arquivo Nacional

UNE."[39] Others, presumably students affiliated with UNE, followed up on this act by climbing into the building the next day to hoist a black flag of mourning from the balcony, pictures of which appeared in newspapers (figure 3.6). In fact, the general lack of UNE direction meant that, at least initially, it was difficult for officials to categorize the student response as being driven by inauthentic professional students. Despite the fact that UNE played little organizational role in students' response, its appeal and prominence were strengthened.

Other student organizations too made use of the event to affirm their vitality and significance. One group after another declared itself to be on "mourning strike" and held solidarity marches. In just one article in *O Estado de São Paulo* for March 31, the author notes separate protests launched by four CAs, one DA, one cultural association, and the São Paulo UEE.[40] Often these demonstrations linked the death of Edson Luis with other long-standing grievances, such as the legal prohibitions on UNE and the UEEs, proposed hikes in student fees, and problems within the education system as a whole, using both sets of issues to criticize the military regime they held responsible. For example, in Minas Gerais students protested his death by assembling before several Federal University of Minas Gerais faculties recently closed by university officials, physically connecting his murder in Rio to their local problem.[41] And in Brasilia student activists burned down the stage where the upcoming celebrations of the regime's fourth anniversary were to be held, leading to conflicts with the police. The overall result was a flourishing of activity by student organizations that helped to validate both their local and national importance.

The sudden mobilization of thousands of students animated the hopes and plans of the clandestine lefts, which had close ties to many of the student organizations. Indeed, by 1968 nearly all of the major student leaders held deep and important connections to the clandestine lefts. None of these organizations could claim responsibility for the outpouring of student responses to the Edson Luis killing, but they read the mass mobilizations as a positive sign of political frustration with the regime, and they saw the strengthening of the student organizations as potentially beneficial to their own efforts.

An indication of how successfully students had coalesced as a body was that officials took to labeling some protests "nonstudent" events in an attempt to discredit them. A few days after the above-noted students in Brasilia burned down the stage, the mayor released a note defending police repression of future protests, asserting, "It's obvious that since Friday [March 29] the real students have shied away from these events, and those who remain are interested in taking advantage of this situation so as to subvert the public order."[42] Security forces similarly announced that, because of "infiltrated elements" within the student movement the "authorities can no longer consider these demonstrations student demonstrations."[43] By labeling the events inauthentic, officials inadvertently acknowledged the legitimacy of "real" student protest. Even if both students and nonstudents participated, the general sense of students' collective right to protest was strengthened.

Rather than end the demonstrations or render them inauthentic to student participants, the police repression intended to stop them often served to further animate students, even when that violence led to additional deaths. Much like Escobar observed of the Chicano movement in the United States at around the same time, the escalation of police violence in Brazil served not to subdue student activism but to help propel it forward.[44] Just in the period

FIGURE 3.7. Large numbers of students and other community members attended the Seventh Day Mass for Edson Luis in Candelária Cathedral in Rio de Janeiro. *Correio da Manhã* collection, Arquivo Nacional

between Edson Luis's death and the Seventh Day Mass held for him in Rio a week later three more people were killed, two in Rio and one in the state of Goiás, and many more were injured.[45] At one point conflicts between students and the Guanabara state police in Rio became so intense the army intervened, sending twelve hundred troops with tanks to "assume control of the city."[46] At the Seventh Day Mass at the famous Candelária Cathedral, another enormous event and one that counted on the public support of much of the clergy, police occupied large swaths of the downtown in anticipation (figure 3.7). Then, over the pleas of the attending priests, mounted officers with sabers drawn charged the mourners as they attempted to exit, once again filling the newspapers with shocking photographs—this time of police attacking the fleeing congregation. Even the U.S. embassy in Brasilia, which generally credited the authorities for implementing control judiciously, called the photographs damaging, reporting that the mounted police "looked like Cossacks riding roughshod over the populace" and noting that "nightsticks would have been more potent physically and less damaging psychologically."[47] These events and the numerous images of them published in newspapers the next day prompted further indignation and criticism from students and others around the country.

For many students these examples of police repression were not simply complicated side effects of their protests but a transformative, motivating force in itself. In other words, the experience of facing threats of police violence became part of the mobilizing dynamic that moved large numbers of students to participate, as the physical risks and challenges they confronted, and in which they participated, helped them demonstrate to others—and to themselves—their commitment to the idea of a student movement as a necessary force of political opposition to the military regime.[48] It would therefore be misguided to reduce the rhetoric surrounding a student martyr to that of a merely discursive political strategy used by a few student leaders. Rather, the trope of collective self-sacrifice became a series of real and symbolic collective acts of self-sacrifice. For many students, the slogan "He could have been your son" also meant "He could have been me," as the killing of the previously anonymous Edson Luis—in fact, the very haphazardness of his death—implied that none of them were immune from such a fate. Hence their decisions to turn out in great numbers for the multiple marches of solidarity across the country signified their conscientious decision to potentially risk their lives in order to repudiate his death. While they may have considered the risk a relatively low one, the explicit contradiction inherent in protesting the assassination of another protester meant that joining in student marches could be truly dangerous.

If the degree of physical risk was at all in dispute, it was quickly affirmed as police repression increased. Newspapers reported on students' protracted discussions about whether or not to defy bans on student rallies and noted how, in at least one case, news of injuries and deaths in the city of Goiânia persuaded students in Brasilia to confine their acts to campus.[49] The papers also relayed police officials' threats of their willingness to use violence against students. For example, O Estado de São Paulo quoted one police officer in Brasilia in April as saying that if students there protested, the consequences could be very grave, as, in his words, "the men are under a lot of emotional pressure and in a conflict it will be almost impossible to restrain them."[50] Through stories like these the police sought to frighten and deter students from demonstrating. The fact that so many students ignored these warnings speaks to the mobilizing urgency of the moment and suggests that demonstrating despite the risk of police repression was a way for students to assert their commitment to the issues at stake.

In sum, the killing of Edson Luis on March 28 led to an enormous outpouring of student political mobilizing and national attention. The symbolic resonance of his death and the astute responses of local student leaders who managed the event dovetailed with growing middle-class frustration with the military regime. Hence the violent repression that befell Edson Luis brought the student movement notoriety, engendered a strong moral grievance with the state, and created a central rallying point for several intense days in March and April of 1968 and long thereafter. It also galvanized students across the country to feel themselves at risk, and to put themselves at risk, of violence and possibly even death. Although some observers criticized their behavior, students demonstrated, both symbolically and literally, a spirit of student commitment that hinged on their ability to confront and withstand physical repression. In the weeks and months to come, as reports of other young people involved in violent confrontations around the world increased, this news would both help to establish the centrality of the student demonstrator as a contemporary, critical political actor and threaten to divest Brazilian students' struggles of their own authenticity as it added fuel to the idea that real Brazilian students did not engage in such actions.

The Universal Rebellion of Youth

During the remaining weeks of April and throughout most of May and June student demonstrations continued at a rapid pace as formerly weakened institutions like UNE resurged as important organizational and symbolic centers. No longer simply protesting the death of Edson Luis, students assembled in groups large and small for a variety of reasons, from criticizing the closing of the Calabouço to demonstrating support for a brief labor union strike in Contagem, São Paulo. Across Brazil they carried banners asserting "Youth Power," while "Down with the Dictatorship" graffiti and signs of support for UNE became ubiquitous on walls and buses. The police continued to use force in their efforts to contain student demonstrations, yet, students' public actions, consistent with the dialectics of repression, often became reactions to prior repression. They also began engaging in violent tactics of their own, such as countering the police with sticks and stones, an assertion of student militancy that carried decidedly gendered connotations. Concurrent with these developments, violent student upris-ings broke out in other parts of the world, provoking new questions about the nature of student activism. In fact, the student protests of 1968 were always a transnational experience as the contemporary comparisons they generated impacted the ways in which Brazilian students were understood. In short, both of these developments—the deepening of student mobiliz-ing in Brazil and that of students abroad—combined to harden the divi-sions between those who saw Brazilian student political activism as the natural manifestation of their youth and social position and those who considered it a non-Brazilian aberration stemming from outside influence.

In the weeks immediately preceding Edson Luis's death, students in Spain, Italy, Belgium, Poland, and Japan had faced off with police in univer-sity occupations and street demonstrations. At the time, the Brazilian me-dia generally presented this news as interesting international develop-ments quite extraneous to the everyday lives of its readers. In the days after Edson Luis's death, however, stories about student protests abroad became more commonplace, and journalists began implicitly and explicitly linking this surge to the one taking place in Brazil. They made note of anything that might resemble common themes or influences, such as references to the Vietnam War, the Chinese Cultural Revolution, or politically radical au-thors like Herbert Marcuse and Regis Débray, then being discussed by young people elsewhere. In early April reporters diligently reported that protesting students in Minas Gerais shouted, "Our example is Vietnam,"[51] while those in João Pessoa burned a U.S. flag and yelled, "Down with American imperialism."[52] Later that month the photo-magazine *Manchete* published a photo-essay of student–police conflicts in Sweden, Belgium, the United States, France, Italy, and Japan. Entitled "The Universal Rebel-lion of Youth," the piece implicitly alluded to interconnections between the six countries, while its editorial placement next to a story about Edson Luis's funeral enfolded the Brazilian case into the tableau of "universal re-bellion."[53] After massive demonstrations broke out in Italy and West Ger-many in mid- and late April and strikes by students and workers gripped France in May, reporters explicitly decried the presumed intrastudent con-nections. An article in *O Estado de São Paulo* explained that "without doubt" demonstrating French students had received "a certain contagion" from their German counterparts and noted that the rector of the University of Paris had the police remove all the "pro-Chinese, pro-Castro and anti-Soviet students," thereby implying that these global connections were well-known.[54] It mattered little that direct material ties between students rarely appeared: the simultaneity of their mobilizations and similarity of their social position as students led many media sources to pronounce them connected. Among other consequences, this had the effect of magnifying local developments, making them appear part of a global phenomenon.

In contradictory ways the media coverage also had the effect of diluting local issues, subsuming them in sweeping statements about youth unrest everywhere. The author of "Universal Rebellion of Youth," for example, wrote, "A common thread ties all the movements: they want to overthrow the *establishment*" ("establishment" in English in original).[55] Such statements demonstrate the limits of generalizing across student demands. In one sense, young people *were* all struggling against the established power systems in their respective communities, whether authoritarian university administrations, racist institutions and practices, an unaccountable military, or a repressive dictatorship. Yet such lumping together of vastly different agendas into the rubric of overthrowing the establishment suggests a knee-jerk response to authority, while code switching to English for one word implies that students everywhere were imitating or highly influenced by English-language actors or authors. In other examples, descriptions of an international context of dangerous student mimicry hinted at pernicious implications for Brazilian youth. "The eyes of the Latin American 'student' look to the European outcomes, especially those of France, for the guidelines for their next steps," wrote one correspondent. "From the Latin Quarter to Latin America, the threads are already being tightened. Only the good sense of the young generations and the prudence of the older generations can cut them."[56] Media coverage such as this left the impression that Brazilian students' actions were trendy copies of the latest vogue behavior rather than the authentic political expressions of specific local actors.

To some observers the international rise of student activity was evidence of young people's natural disposition toward political activism, especially when confronted with news of injustice or an uncertain future. The federal legislator Ernani do Amaral Peixoto, a politician generally supportive of the students, asserted in an interview in 1968 that the only real problem with youth lay in the media's ability to depict travesties around the world, making rebellion practically inevitable.[57] Archbishop dom Serfim Fernandes de Araújo, the rector of the Catholic University of Minas Gerais, expressed similar ideas about young people's proclivity to fight for social justice when he released a statement declaring that today "in the world we are witnessing a constant pressure on students, especially university students, in their efforts to construct a more humane society."[58] Such explanations often rested on a sense that young people were especially sensitive or passionate. A visiting Jesuit priest who met with university students in Recife and Rio said they had impressed him with "the authentic enthusiasm of their young souls" and their "concerns for the future."[59] And a foreign correspondent writing about events in Paris and Nanterre, France, wrote that they reflected "the real anguish of a generation that is increasingly concerned about its future."[60] For observers such as these, the mix of national and international student unrest confirmed essentialist ideas about youth everywhere as compassionate and concerned.

Yet for others, especially Brazilian government and military officials, the international context fueled long-standing suspicions that students were being inappropriately influenced or even inauthentically directed by others. Security agents repeatedly indicated that so-called student demonstrations were often orchestrated by people who merely posed as students. Speaking to reporters about student protests of Edson Luis's death, DOPS director Lucidio Arruda said, "Students are being directed by outsiders, who prepare these agitations and then disappear." Linking these fears to the international situation, he went on, "They are Communists, and they're doing the same thing in various countries, like Uruguay, Chile, and Italy."[61] A few weeks later Arruda again cast doubt on the student nature of a political action, telling reporters he was not convinced that those arrested at the UFRJ for submitting a petition to the rector were really students and hence would not release their names.[62] Former minister of education, sponsor of the Suplicy Law, and then-rector of the Federal University of Paraná Suplicy de Lacerda echoed this charge after demonstrators tore down a sculpture of him, dragged it around with a rope, and used it to decorate one of their barricades. "I don't know if they're students or not," he told reporters," but they are positively bandits and savages."[63] And when *Veja* magazine asked Gen. Luís França de Oliveira, secretary of public security in Guanabara, what had happened to the "romantic protest" of the Brazilian student movement's past, when students yelled nationalistic slogans and the press called their marches parades, he replied that students today are "directed by outside forces," adding "The worldwide subversive movement we see now is eloquent testimony to this assertion."[64] Nor were these ideas designed only for external consumption. Internal security reports often expressed the belief that other groups were actively exploiting Brazilian students. A report in June adamantly affirmed, "The continuing agitation that has been disrupting the student sectors throughout the country, causing serious damage to the culture and education of young people, is the consequence of a subversive plan previously elaborated by the Communist Party."[65] Even generally sympathetic figures sometimes formed similar conjectures. Father Deolindo Valiati, the education director of the Brazilian Religious Conference, argued that while the real cause of student rebellion in Brazil lay in problems with the university system that deserved redress, he suspected that an international organization of the right or the left was behind the most recent demonstrations.[66] For these figures the confluence of student activity in Brazil and elsewhere in 1968 confirmed fears that nonstudent organizations with international ties, above all the Communist Party, lay behind the upsurge.

For Brazilian students themselves the rise of student movements elsewhere presented an ambiguous dilemma. They enthusiastically followed the news from abroad, sometimes collecting clippings about other student movements and displaying them on university bulletin boards. At the same time, however, they struggled to distinguish themselves to the reporters and others who inevitably asked about links between themselves and the other movements. One sociology student told *Veja* magazine that the specific commonalities among students from different countries were few, stating, "We in sociology have been accompanying these student crises all over the world and we've discovered that the only constant in all of them is the lack of attention to young people's small demands by adults who are fixated on defending outdated concepts."[67] In a separate interview UNE President Luís Travassos and Vice President Luiz Raul Machado were asked about connections between their struggles and those in Europe. Denying any such relationship, they added, "We do think [the] European students' struggle is fair. . . . But in the international sphere UNE's position should be to enter the anti-imperialist fight of the student movements in Asia [and] Africa."[68] Their comments point to the anti-imperialist position of many of the clandestine lefts, especially that of the AP, to which they both belonged. But they also reflect the ways in which Brazilian students worked to keep the focus on their own political aims and not be subsumed into generalizations about youth uprisings in Europe or elsewhere. Students could occasionally tap into fears about youth unrest abroad in order to advocate certain concessions. For example, in early June a spokesperson for the DCE of the UFRJ pressed for leniency from military authorities by pointing out that students in Rio were "not taking the French line." That is, they were not overturning cars or using similar methods and thus should not be harassed.[69] The following month Machado used the specter of France to taunt the regime and mobilize other students. Speaking to an enthusiastic crowd at a large rally, he said, "Our generals can relax. What happened in France won't happen here—It's going to be much worse."[70] In short, the international rise of student uprisings could at times inspire students in Brazil and at others could muddy understandings of them. But throughout the year they were an integral part of the context in which Brazilian students operated.

If the international situation reanimated debates and reinforced ideas about students' suitability as political actors, the steadily augmenting violence that came to mark Brazilian student protests only further animated these discussions. Student–police conflicts became notoriously violent as the police employed tear gas and nausea gas, small bombs, water cannons, horses, regular and electrified nightsticks, and even gunfire to limit the demonstrations. Some arrested students reported being tortured by their captors, and many young people came to refer to the police simply as the repression.[71] As students continued to demonstrate in the face of such coercion, some observers began to describe them as self-sacrificing and righteous, willing to withstand abuse to stand up for their ideals. Carlos Lacerda, for example, wrote of their "combativeness, heroism, and faithfulness to liberty and honor," going on to say that "if some of them commit excesses, we need to remember that they are fighting unarmed and they represent, within the submissive flock, a sign of protest, a stone of scandal."[72] This perspective was augmented by newspapers that carefully reported on the many injuries students suffered in these encounters, paying particular attention to the multiple cases of gunshot wounds. And while a portion of this coverage was critical of students for participating at all, much of it comprised a dose of admiration for their persistence in the face of such odds. The David and Goliath aspect of students' confrontations with the heavily militarized police could make them appear selfless, risking physical harm for some larger purpose.

Many students gradually decided to confront rather than avoid the mounting force, in a dialectics of repression that intensified the struggles. In her analysis of students' comments to journalists in 1968, Ribeiro do Valle has detected their growing "option for confrontation and a climate of combat" in the weeks after Edson Luis's death.[73] Olga D'Arc Pimentel, a student activist from Goiânia, later described the decision to use force as one students felt obliged to undertake: "We decided to change tactics. You're going to oblige us? Then let's go, now everyone is going to go prepared. And we all did. The girls with bags underneath the skirts of their uniforms, full of rocks. Then when the army would start to line up, there came that rain of rocks."[74] Her recollection of this moment alludes to both a deliberate decision to "change tactics" and the sense that students only followed the military's lead, raining rocks on an army that was readying itself for battle (figures 3.8 and 3.9). Whether or not the decision to begin doing so was quite so clear as she maintains, as the year wore on many students did begin arming themselves for street protests with makeshift weapons like sticks and stones, rocks and corks hurled in slingshots, Molotov cocktails, and firecrackers for startling police horses. Others stationed themselves in the windows of high-rise buildings, where they could throw heavy objects, from ashtrays to a water cooler. Indeed, more than one police report complained of this tactic, and at least one officer was killed when hit in the head by a typewriter.[75] The sociologist Martha Huggins found that student demonstrators also threw marbles on sidewalks to trip up police and at times even outfitted themselves with iron spears and tear gas.[76] One newspaper noted that students took to shattering acetate music records, as the pieces could be "thrown great distances with precision."[77]

Students also began to verbalize their commitment to using force. By May 11 students in São Paulo openly told journalists they would physically defend the university building they were occupying, asserting that while they had no plans "to fight with anyone, . . . if the police come here we will take them on."[78] A student flyer released a few weeks later encouraged its readers as follows: "If there is repression, get into the fights. Throw paperweights, bottles, sticks and stones. But act in groups, because when we're organized we do things better and with more security."[79] Of course, violent acts by students were not new. As early as July 1966 security forces claimed to have confiscated "crude bombs and Molotov cocktails" from a raid on a student center.[80] Nonetheless the broader tactical debates in 1968 about the utility of collectively adopting violent strategies marked a watershed for the student movement as more and more students deemed such an approach necessary or desirable.

For some students a new and defining hallmark of authenticity became their militancy, even in the face of unequal confrontations. When the long-

FIGURE 3.8. Male and female students collect paving stones from a construction site to throw at police. *Correio da Manhã* collection, Arquivo Nacional

FIGURE 3.9. A woman protestor throws a stone at a police van as it turns a corner. *Correio da Manhã* collection, Arquivo Nacional

awaited Meira Mattos Commission report on the state of higher education in Brazil was delivered to the minister of education in May 1968, UME published a flyer fervently deriding its idea of government-promoted "leadership training" for young people. The union argued instead that "leaders [should] arise out of the struggles waged by their groups" and that students needed "an authentic and combative" leadership, one conscious of students' responsibilities to the nation.[81] In this perspective, legitimate student leaders proved themselves in battle by fighting in defense of the country as a whole. Both in word and in deeds acted out in street conflicts, many students argued that an authentic student movement ought to be combative.

Yet as student–police conflicts intensified they took on decidedly gendered aspects that cast student demonstrations as mostly male affairs. Newspaper descriptions of the clashes, peppered with accounts of daring hand-to-hand combat and streets transformed into war zones, presented an image of male struggle that mentioned women only occasionally, and then generally as unexpected additions to the central protagonists. For example, when students in Curitiba took over the rector's office at the Federal University of Paraná, O Estado de São Paulo described the office as having "fallen [to] a group of 100 young men and a few women" (um grupo formado por 100 rapazes e algumas moças).[82] When the petition-wielding UFRJ students noted earlier were arrested by DOPS agents, a relatively mild situation, the Jornal do Brasil reported, "Yesterday afternoon DOPS arrested 14 students at the UFRJ Rector's office, including two young women" (duas moças).[83] Such stories appropriately made clear that the demonstrating students included both men and women even as they tacitly indicated the novelty or newsworthiness of the women's participation.

Women made up an increasing proportion of students in the universities, and they were active and important participants in the student movement of 1968. Yet they also occupied an ambiguous position both vis-à-vis their male colleagues and in terms of how they were viewed externally. Although the Brazilian government did not keep statistical information on university enrollments by sex until 1970, the fact that 41 percent of graduating university students that year were women denotes that in 1968 they probably made up a similar percentage of the student body.[84] Within the various faculties there was a much greater gender imbalance, as women constituted a large majority of the humanities and arts and letters students, while men predominated in the mathematical, biological, and social sci-

TABLE 3.1 Total Enrollments by Gender and Area of Study, Beginning of
Academic Year 1971

	Male Students	Female Students
Exact Sciences	37,711	5,408
Biomedical Sciences	16,556	8,729
Human Sciences, Arts, and Letters*	11,730	30,868
Social Sciences	44,676	14,552
Total**	115,024	61,844

*In 1971 Human Sciences and Arts and Letters were two different areas of study, but for
purposes of clarity they are combined here.
**Total figures also include students enrolled in two or more areas, not included here.
Source: Serviço de Estatística da Educação e Cultura, Anuário estatístico do Brasil 1972. Rio
de Janeiro: IBGE, vol. 33, 1972.

ences (tables 3.1 and 3.2). Nonetheless, the larger overall proportion of
female students would lead one to expect greater opportunities for women
to take part in the student movement and an even greater probability that
they held leadership positions in those faculties that had large female
enrollments. Beyond these numerical possibilities, photographic, anec-
dotal, and documentary evidence all attest to women's role in the aboveground student movement activities as well as within the clandestine lefts.
A quantitatively reasonable estimate hails from attendance at the UNE
congress later in the year, when about 22 percent of the attendees were
women.[85] Women were active in the student movement but received little
recognition for it.

Beyond the gender of the individual protagonists, authentic student
activism itself was sometimes presented as a masculine endeavor, especially as student protests became increasingly violent. Alongside the rocks
and gas canisters, police and students often lobbed verbal barbs at one
another, taunts that challenged one another's masculinity. For example, as
students at one demonstration scattered into small groups only to reas-
semble again a few minutes later (called lightning demonstrations), a
colonel told journalists that this was a "protest march of cowards" because
they would not confront the police head-on.[86] Most colorful is a description of a street protest that appears in at least three accounts of 1968.[87]
In the version of the anecdote drawn from the bestselling memoir *O que*

TABLE 3.2 Percentage of Students Who Were Women, by Area of Study,
Beginning of Academic Year 1971

Exact Sciences	12
Biomedical Sciences	34
Human Sciences, Arts, and Letters*	72
Social Sciences	25
Total**	35

*In 1971 Human Sciences and Arts and Letters were two different areas of study, but for
purposes of clarity they are combined here.
**Total figures also include students enrolled in two or more areas, not included here.
Source: Serviço de Estatística da Educação e Cultura, Anuário estatístico do Brasil 1972. Rio
de Janeiro: IBGE, vol. 33, 1972.

é isso companheiro? (What's up, comrade?) by Fernando Gabeira, then a
member of a clandestine leftist organization with heavy student membership, he writes of a police device students mocked with the nickname the
Brucutu (figure 3.10). A special vehicle designed to spray powerful jets of
water to disperse crowds, the Brucutu had been much discussed in the
newspapers as it was being built. Yet Gabeira recalls that the first time the
police brought out this famous new weapon, directed it at students, and
turned it on, only a small amount of water trickled out of the hoses—to the
unrestrained laughter of its intended targets. Gabeira wrote, "I remember
the psychoanalyst Hélio Pellegrino, that marvelous character, screaming in
his big voice, in the middle of [a downtown street], 'People, the Brucutu
lost its erection!' [*Gente, o Brucutu brochou!*]"[88] In this bawdy taunt, not only
did the protesters label the military's failure as, literally, male sexual impo-
tence, but even the students' name for the presumably powerful water
cannon evoked a problematic kind of masculinity. For Brucutu was the
Brazilian name for the cartoon figure Alley Oop, a thick-headed caveman
who rode a dinosaur. The name had recently returned in the lexicon of
popular culture owing to a popular song by Roberto Carlos, the chorus of
which said, "Look at the Brucutu . . . He is always well armed and he fights
with pleasure. . . . He carries a hammer and he loves to hit." Through their
use of the nickname Brucutu students insinuated that the military adopted
a distorted form of unthinkingly violent masculinity, while Gabeira's overall narrative firmly characterized the students as formidable opponents

FIGURE 3.10. A *Brucutu*, in action. Designed to spray powerful jets of water to disperse crowds, this special vehicle was also the focus of student jokes. *Correio da Manhã* collection, Arquivo Nacional

who had managed to throw the police off course, necessitating the Brucutu. Even the telling of Pellegrino's joke suggests a male social space, for this scene of him publicly screaming—in his "big voice"—the vulgarity *brochar* (to lose one's erection), apparently to great laughter, evokes an image of shared masculine humor. In short, the rising importance of physical combativeness as an indicator of student authenticity contributed to defining student militancy as masculine.

Given this situation, when women visibly participated in violent conflicts they provoked special consternation among officials and other observers. Security agents carefully preserved the flyer that urged students to "get into the fights," appending it to an eighteen-page internal report on the threat of future student disturbances. Especially noteworthy is the report's lamentation that at one demonstration, "regrettably, we saw girls carrying cans of rocks that were used by their male companions for throwing," as if it were inconceivable to the agents (and possibly to the students themselves) that women could throw the rocks too.[89] U.S. embassy reports made special note of women's roles, noting in a telegram of June 1968 that they witnessed young people going to a protest holding sticks rolled up in newspapers, while girls carried stones in their handbags.[90] The reports indicate that, even if most descriptions of street conflict centered on men, women did take part. When they did, they attracted special attention and concern.

Even when physical violence was not at issue, definitions of appropriate student movement activity and leadership could take on gendered tones. The fact that Palmeira was married was often remarked upon in the press, usually with the implication that this reflected a degree of responsible maturity. After his arrest in early August, his wife, Ana Maria, was interviewed by at least one national publication. While she herself was active in the student movement and had met Palmeira through their shared political organizing, the interviewer described her as "the wife of a student leader." Ironically, in the same interview she made it a point to declare that she would continue to work in the student movement even after he was arrested, "not as a woman who is upset because her husband is imprisoned, but as a colleague who also fights against the dictatorship."[91] In this case, marriage accorded his leadership added gravitas and respectability while stripping her of political agency. In fact, nationally known women student leaders were few, while their male colleagues often became household names. Women certainly gained leadership positions at the faculty level, especially in the areas with sizeable female enrollment. And in a few exceptional cases, such as those of Catarina Meloni, a vice president and then (disputed) president of the São Paulo UEE, and Helenira Resende, an UNE vice president during the presidency of Travassos, they filled important regional or national leadership positions.[92] But in terms of nationally known leadership, the great majority of students in such positions in 1968 were male. UNE president Travassos, UME president Palmeira, and the leaders of almost every other state union (UEE) and the preponderance of the most active university-level organizations (DCEs) were all men, and newspaper coverage of student movement leadership predominantly focused on these figures.

Where women students' behavior attracted most attention was in the area of sexuality. In 1968 students and other young people in Brazil, like their counterparts internationally, came to question long-standing values about sexual and emotional intimacy while the technological advance of the birth control pill allowed young couples to act on their beliefs with much less risk of pregnancy. "The order of the day," as the historians Maria

Hermínia Tavares and Luiz Weis have said, "was 'questionings' . . . of the disdainfully labeled 'bourgeois marriage,' understood as the apex of hypocrisy and of the inequality of erotic opportunities between the sexes."[93] Some women found the possibility of more open romantic relationships liberating. Maria Augusta Ribeiro recalled, "I dated half the student movement. . . . I was very flirtatious [namoradeira] and loved the huge freedom."[94] As her comments indicate, romantic relationships often blossomed between young people who shared political goals and spent time together furthering them. José Gradel, another student activist, attested to the importance of "personal and emotional affinity," including romantic attraction, in students' decisions to join one or another political faction. Noting that when faced with a choice between "this group where the people treat me well and where that pretty girl is, and that other group where the son of a bitch who always scores against me in soccer is," he would choose the former.[95] (In fact, Gradel and Ribeiro both joined the same organization of the clandestine left and eventually married one another, one of the many intimate relationships to come out of this period.) This does not mean that all or even most university students necessarily engaged in more open sexual activities. The journalist Zuenir Ventura notes that in hindsight the sexual revolution of 1968 was probably more discussed and written about than acted upon.[96] The actress Marília Carneiro told Ventura of sage advice given her at the time by her friend Heloísa Buarque de Hollanda, then a well-known figure in Rio's social and intellectual scene: "We have to act like we put out for guys, but we don't really have to put out for guys."[97] In part her statement alludes to the sense among some young people that their ideas about sexuality were forward thinking and thus acting like they "put out" meant asserting a kind of progressive attitude. Indeed, when excedentes from the Pontifical Catholic University in São Paulo (PUC-SP) demonstrated by camping out in the campus gardens, they intimated as much by provocatively claiming that "the chaplain and spiritual counsel are going to consider the co-ed nature of our gathering immoral."[98] Carneiro's statement, however, also reveals the pressure young women felt from their male colleagues to engage in sex. Palmeira jokingly recalled that women students who held onto their virginity were derisively nicknamed "museums," an example of social pressure masked as humor.[99] The student activist Vinícius Caldevilla has said that he wasn't the only man at the time to have both an official, chaste romance with a woman from the country club society of his upbringing and, at the same time, embark on "passionate affairs with colleagues from the university, political militants."[100] His comments speak to the ways in which such sexual explorations held different connotations for male students, who could easily lead both lives, and their female colleagues, who could not. For while both young men and women contributed to the transforming of sexual norms, female students bore inordinate social scrutiny for doing so.

One notorious case of intrastudent romance both exemplifies this double standard and demonstrates how paternalism undergirded the performance of student leadership. In this case José Dirceu, the São Paulo student who disputed Melloni's claim to the presidency of the UEE-SP and who was repeatedly portrayed as a rake, had a tryst with an attractive young woman named Heloísa Helena Magalhães. When other students accused Magalhães of being a DOPS agent and orchestrated a press conference to denounce her, the story briefly became a media scandal.[101] The romance between Dirceu and Magalhães took place during a student occupation of a São Paulo university. When students discovered evidence that she might have been working for DOPS, including a police ID card that certified her abilities with pistols and revolvers, they decided to use the occasion to denounce the agency. Inviting the press into the occupied university, they accused DOPS of taking advantage of the young woman's rural upbringing and naïveté in convincing her to undertake this task while simultaneously "returning" her to her parents' custody. They also readily divulged the nickname they had given her—the Golden Apple—a moniker that evoked the tempting entrapment she supposedly used to snare the beguiled and unsullied Dirceu. Most remarkable about this tale are the sense of paternalistic chivalry that marked students' actions in returning Magalhães to her parents and the way they played on fears of unrestrained female sexuality to denounce the DOPS's supposed tactics of infiltration. In both cases they tried to reaffirm their own suitability for leadership, presenting themselves as having put a halt to another's sexual manipulation (whether by DOPS or by Magalhães) and having reestablished paternal/parental order.

For some observers, students' experimentation with sexuality became an important sign of their very inauthenticity as political actors, for it demonstrated how far removed they were from Brazilian norms. Mirroring other debates about the rise of student movement activity elsewhere in the world, students' sexual ideas and behaviors stoked fears of foreign influence. A flurry of articles on such topics as sex education, abortion, birth control, and the use of bikinis filled the pages of newspapers and magazines. In "Nudism and Sex: Is the World Implanting a New Morality?," carried in *Manchete* magazine, the authors lamented the new "revolution of sex, . . . a type of atomic bomb, of highly explosive material, destined to destroy society and subvert customs." Like the numerous analyses of heightened student political activity at the time that pointed to deleterious foreign influences as a causal factor, the source of this revolution, the article argued, was the advertising and media images emanating from industrialized countries. Their effects were felt the world over, especially by the young, as "many [young people] dispense with devoted feelings and dedicate themselves to brief relations, in the style already called *snacks* [in English in original], an analogy to quick meals taken at luncheonette counters."[102] Exaggerated or not, such articles were not uncommon. Moreover, within the ESG a chorus of voices began to express alarm at the level of violence in which students engaged and to suggest that this turn stemmed from external communist influence and via a subversive sexual agenda. As the historian Benjamin Cowan has shown, metaphors of seduction "became standards of ESG discourse, constantly used to describe the ways that communist 'activists' exploited the weakness of Brazilian students, who inevitably lacked the will to resist leftist blandishments." The heart of this problem "lay [with] young people's innate passivity, irrationality, and susceptibility to subversive 'penetration' through 'seduction' [*sedução*] and 'enticement' [*aliciamento*]."[103] Similarly allusive language pervaded President Costa e Silva's speech to students at the National Institute of Telecommunications, in which he said, "Those young individuals who throw themselves at sterile agitation and at diffuse movements of revolt and protest [do not] perceive that what throbs in their spirit is not new but rather old and invalid."[104] Public media reports, private ESG ruminations, and presidential speeches such as this reflected the profound sense of unease prompted by young people's sexual and political explorations in a climate of international student activism and violence.

The rise of student–police violence around the world impacted the clandestine lefts as well, contributing to or reinforcing the decision many made to form armed wings that would engage in military training and undertake armed actions. Carlos Marighella's aforementioned ALN, for example, had begun to carry out armed actions the previous year, robbing banks to fund the future revolution. It was soon joined by other groups, including the newly formed Vanguarda Popular Revolucionaria (VPR), an offshoot of

POLOP that counted among its membership a sizeable number of students. While the ALN and VPR actions were controversial and spurred deep discussions among the lefts about the timing, strategies, and models for this turn to militancy, many organizations (with the strong exception of the PCB) came to agree that armed actions were necessary. To them the violence used against students around the world appeared a last-ditch effort of weakened powers that be. In one report of the situation, for example, from the PCdoB, the authors wrote, "The intensification of struggle across the world and the revolutionary content it is taking on constitute one of the characteristics of our current situation. . . . In its agony, capitalism has become more ferocious and commits heinous crimes. Whether this be in the villages and jungles of Vietnam, Laos, Indonesia, Colombia, and Venezuela or whether it be in the avenues and plazas of Paris, Madrid, Rome, Berlin, New York, Tokyo, and Rio de Janeiro, indiscriminate and criminal violence reigns. The civilization of the moribund imperialism is the civilization of the nightstick and tear gas."[105] Equating military struggles in places like Vietnam and Colombia with the violence of street protests in cities like Paris and Rio, the authors painted a global picture of a changing tide in which imperialism and capitalism were both on the cusp of defeat. In this context students' repeated clashes with state security forces were welcomed not just as a sign of capitalism's "agony" but also as useful, practical experience and vital psychological preparation for the inevitable revolutionary confrontation with the state. In this sense the concurrence of violent student protests around the world in 1968 contributed to the ways in which the lefts saw university students as expedient political actors. At the same time, students' valorization of physical resistance to the police reflected and resonated with the lefts' growing advocacy of armed conflict.

By mid-June evidence of both egregious police repression and seemingly intractable student "disorder" had so fully preoccupied observers that one editorial could find just one "poor, sad consolation . . . the fact that we're not alone in this land of student agitation, which is a constant in the world today."[106] Despite months of urging for dialogue between students and government officials, such meetings had still not taken place. Sectors within the military made known their belief that President Costa e Silva should refuse any such discussions as long as students continued to demonstrate in the streets, as it could only be an affront to his authority to speak with them in these circumstances. For their part, students remained heavily divided about the possibilities of such an encounter, some arguing

that such legitimizing conversations were incompatible with an antidictatorship struggle and others hoping the occasion could lead to the securing
of real goals such as improved funding for the universities. In the meantime, grievances on both sides continued to accumulate. Hundreds of
students were in prison, several student leaders now traveled with body-
guards and slept in undisclosed locations in order to avoid arrest, and
student demonstrations met with almost immediate police repression.
Military officers continued to interpret the rising student violence as being
linked to external influences and accused them of plotting "vast schemes
in the French mold,"[107] while the minister of justice threatened that government authorities were not going to let Brazil become a new France,
"even if that means we have to use force."[108]

The deteriorating situation became most evident in the final weeks of
June as several days of police repression in one city once again prompted
outpourings of solidarity elsewhere. In this case previously latent public
support turned into actual public participation in a series of street skirmishes in Rio de Janeiro. Police there had worried that people caught in the
middle of street protests would blame the security forces for the disruptions rather than students, who, they claimed, instigated confrontations
and then quickly disappeared.[109] They became even more uneasy after June
19, when employees in the highrise buildings downtown leaned out of
windows to boo the police and applaud the students, while others deliberately came out into the streets to watch the commotion.[110] The next day a
student assembly led to dramatic altercations with the police when nearly
five hundred exiting students were beaten and arrested, notwithstanding
the mediation of university officials and police promises to the contrary.[111]
And at demonstrations to protest this action on June 21, groups of bystanders joined in the ensuing police confrontations, leading to the deaths
of three people, the injuries of dozens more, and the arrests of one thousand (figure 3.11).[112] Students quickly dubbed the day Bloody Friday, while
DOPS reports lamented the sight of "students and popular sectors con-
fronting the police together with sticks and stones" and "popular sectors
applauding the students and jeering the police."[113] These events in Rio
provoked yet another national outcry and additional solidarity demonstrations.[114] Three months after the death of Edson Luis, the dialectical cycle of
repression between students and the state still operated to mobilize not
just other students but even otherwise casual observers.

In fact, public outrage over this series of incidents became so pro-

FIGURE 3.11. Mass student arrests in Rio de Janeiro in June 1968, like this one on June 20, sparked a new round of protests. *Correio da Manhã* collection, Arquivo Nacional

nounced that it led to what would be the largest single demonstration in Brazil in 1968. After multiple groups expressed their support for such an event, from mothers of imprisoned students to university professors, Governor Negrão de Lima and President Costa e Silva granted the demonstration official authorization and the promise of no police interference, paving the way for mass attendance. On June 26 over one hundred thousand people, including musical and theatrical celebrities, coalitions of nuns and priests, and tens of thousands of others joined students in the largest and most important show of public support for students and of public criticism of the military regime since the coup (figure 3.12). Amply photographed and commented upon in the national press, the March of the 100,000 as it soon became known, represented the extent to which violence against students had propelled and channeled others' displeasure with the military regime as a whole. It also displayed the vanguard role of students in giving expression to this dissent and their ability to direct a peaceful, orderly event of such magnitude. Those who took the most prominent roles in the march became virtual celebrities (to such an extent that some later worried that the "deification" of Palmeira would impede the larger student movement, while police reports complained that he was "deliriously applauded every time he opened his mouth").[115] Glowing news stories and numerous photographs filled the newspapers the next day, from the wide-angle views that showed off the magnitude of the crowds to the images of famous musicians uncomplainingly following student requests to sit on dirty city streets in order to hear their speeches. These visual

FIGURE 3.12. The largest demonstration of 1968 brought together one hundred thousand people in downtown Rio de Janeiro to protest recent violence against students.

snapshots became part of the national experience of the March of the 100,000.[116]

The peaceful nature of the March of the 100,000 did nothing to relieve the security forces' anxiety about the threat student demonstrations posed. In a report of the Rio de Janeiro DOPS dated July 2 the authors admitted to the "indisputable ability" of those who had directed the famous march "with perfect order and discipline." But rather than seeing this as a hopeful sign, to these police officials it only proved the manipulative powers of the student leadership, who just a few days earlier, they said, had promoted bedlam (que atuo na baderna). "The orderly . . . way in which they carried out [the March of the 100,000] revealed the political meaning that the violence [of earlier demonstrations] obscured," they warned. "Once again we call attention to the fact that 'UNE' and 'UME' were the names most frequently shouted and applauded by the crowd. The students' attempts to rally the popular masses around these student organizations are taking shape. This, in our view, is one of the most serious aspects of the issue, for which

FIGURE 3.13. Students participate in the March of 50,000. *Correio da Manhã* collection, Arquivo Nacional

the authorities should be attentive, as it is well known that within [UNE and UME] can be found the most recognizably subversive elements. . . . [E]ither the Authorities shut these [student organizations] down definitively, or the farce will work once again, requiring constant vigilance."[117] From their perspective, the longer the state tolerated student demonstrations, the greater were the risks that other sectors of the population would be deceived into supporting subversion.

Officials of DOPS must have been dismayed when, the day after their report, some three thousand students in São Paulo gathered in protest and the next day students in Rio assembled fifty thousand (figure 3.13). (They soon called this event the March of the 50,000.) National leaders were certainly displeased, for after several days of discussion about the possibility of declaring a state of siege President Costa e Silva and the National Security Council officially prohibited all further public protest demonstrations. In an official note released to the press they asserted that "the revolutionary principles of the 31st of March of 1964 have been systematically disrupted by the actions of subversive and counterrevolutionary elements whose motive is to promote social unrest and disturb the public in order to overthrow the regime." And they warned that any attempt to "return to the climate of agitation" would lead the government to adopt "exceptional measures" without delay.[118] Unbeknownst to all, however, the March of the 50,000 would be the last massive demonstration of the year. Many students soon dispersed for the July winter vacation period, and when classes resumed in August for the second semester of 1968 student protests diminished in size.

When Edson Luis died in March few would have predicted that 1968 would become defined by student protests around the world. By July 1, however, student demonstrators at home and abroad had become so familiar that the *Jornal do Brasil* published comments on its front page that five months earlier would have been inconceivable. A French philosopher proclaimed that students in Brazil had "Frenchified themselves" (*se afrancesaram*) by adopting tactics like street barricades, while those in France had been "Latinamericanized" for taking on strong political roles.[119] In between these two moments, Brazilian students had mobilized in enormous protests, provoking serious discussions about their political, sexual, and militant behaviors, while reports of demonstrating young people elsewhere around the world informed and, at times, inflamed these national debates. Divisions hardened between those who saw student political activism as natural and authentic and those who believed it to be an aberration of foreign origin. Meanwhile violent confrontations between students and the police escalated in a seemingly ever-spiraling relationship, contributing to and giving expression to growing dissatisfaction with the regime.

Sílvia and Her Companions:
Conjoining the Aboveground and Underground

After the July winter break, the second semester gave rise to a final, divergent turn in the dialectics of repression. On the one hand, the period witnessed a noticeable diminishment in the size and frequency of student protests. With a few notable exceptions in support of a labor union strike in Osasco, São Paulo, in July and in protest against the arrest of Palmeira in early August, student public demonstrations became much smaller than they had been just a few weeks earlier. Much of this owed to the powerful ways in which the security forces implemented the ban against them. After Palmeira's arrest, for example, over thirteen thousand military troops occupied the streets of Rio to limit students' response.[120] Soon thereafter, when students in Salvador demonstrated against a rise in bus fares, six of them, plus one passerby, suffered bullet wounds and another was bitten by a German shepherd police dog.[121] Similar confrontations occurred in Fortaleza, Goiânia, and Belo Horizonte.[122] Meanwhile rumors of severe mistreatment of imprisoned students circulated. Speaking of the fear of being imprisoned by the DOPS, one student who had recently been arrested and released explained to reporters in July 1968, "You know, we always imagine torture, violence and mistreatment, as well as harsh interrogations."[123] While he offered such comments in order to affirm that this had not occurred to him, his fears reflected common beliefs at the time. Such beliefs were only augmented by the large numbers of currently imprisoned students and by the seemingly greater proclivity of the state to arrest those who defied the protest bans.

On the other hand, this situation served to intensify the commitment of those students and others with sympathies for or ties to the clandestine lefts. As we have seen, the clandestine lefts were small organizations built around a few committed members. Marcelo Ridenti has calculated that the sum total of those accused of participating in one of these organizations in the 1960s and 1970s was only 3,698, 1,897 of whom were also accused of joining one of their armed wings. Current students or young people who had recently left school made up a good portion of these numbers—some 30–50 percent of the accused.[124] Clearly, the vast majority of students did not join the clandestine lefts. But the organizations were nonetheless influential in stimulating political debates, including questioning the appropriateness, feasibility, and necessity of violence. As we have seen, since at least March some students had argued that police repression called for a degree of militant response. By the March of the 100,000 in late June the political aspects of this debate had become prominent enough that, in one much-remarked moment, sectors of the crowd competed with one another in chanting "Only an organized people [o povo organizado] can defeat the dictatorship" and "Only an armed people [o povo armado] can defeat the dictatorship." The contours of the debate extended to musical preferences, such as the aforementioned outcry at the September song festival when Geraldo Vandré's song and call to arms, "Don't Say I Never Spoke of Flowers," won second prize.[125] But the state's increased use of violence in the second semester also led to diminished numbers of willing protestors. As Gradel later explained, "One is willing to face bullets for socialism, but not for increased education funding."[126] Yet the situation encouraged others, especially those who believed in the transformative potential of violence. When army troops occupied the streets of Rio in August, for example, UME released flyers proposing that "the people" create their own army, arguing, "for the violence of the people and against the violence of the dictatorship."[127] The rhetoric of UME and the outrage of Vandré fans speak to the rising appeal of armed struggle for some young people and the degree to which those who continued to protest in the streets held strong sympathies with the clandestine lefts.

For their part, the armed wings of the clandestine lefts undertook additional expropriatory actions, as they called them—bank robberies and burglaries of weapons caches—in the second half of the year, although few people recognized them as the work of the lefts. Police repeatedly expressed confusion about whom to hold responsible for the thefts, as some considered them the work of sophisticated bandits, while others thought they originated from either the clandestine left or right.[128] The forty-seven armed actions undertaken over the course of the year represented the armed lefts' growing conviction that revolution was imminent, while contributing to the sense among some that the situation in Brazil was becoming increasingly unstable.[129]

Adding to this tense climate, underground groups from the right emerged and mobilized to discourage student activists and other left-leaning groups by attacking institutions with which they disagreed. The CCC, for example, staged two violent attacks on actors and audiences at performances of a controversial play called *Roda Viva*, first in São Paulo in mid-July and then in Porto Alegre in early October.[130] Other clandestine right-wing groups exploded bombs at media centers, such as publishing houses and the headquarters of the Associação Brasileira de Imprensa (Brazilian Press Association) as well as at other theaters.[131] As this kind of violence became more unpredictable, public demonstrations appeared to become highly dangerous.

Perhaps the incident that most reflected a changing mood regarding the increasing violence was an altercation in October between two adjacent universities in São Paulo, Mackenzie University and the Faculty of Philosophy of the University of São Paulo, an event that led to yet another student fatality. In this case the São Paulo student José Guimarães was shot, presumably by Mackenzie students. But rumors circulated that the CCC had provided the Mackenzie students with their weapons and that the police had actively supported the Mackenzie side or at least refused to intervene. Yet what is most remarkable about this death is the extent to which students attempted to replicate some of the practices that had followed the death of Edson Luis but how different was the response to their efforts. As soon as Guimarães's body was carried off in an ambulance, students in São Paulo took to the streets with his bloody shirt and, as in the case of Edson Luis, held it aloft as a flag of protest. Shouting, "They killed a student," the students marched through the streets of the city, stopping to offer fiery speeches and tweaking the Edson Luis slogan "In mourning the struggle begins" (*Neste luto começa a luta*) to "Our mourning is our struggle" (*O nosso luto é nossa luta*).[132] But in this case family members of the deceased student lived nearby, and they quickly intervened, preferring to mourn their loss in private rather than allow for a large, public funeral. Guimarães's brother retrieved the corpse from where it had been autopsied, and his family held a private funeral at their home (figure 3.14). Security forces, eager to prevent a repeat of the events of March and April, encircled the house and allowed only invited guests of the family to enter.[133] When São Paulo students realized what had happened, they parked a mortuary car in front of the house in protest, using an empty coffin and candlesticks for added effect. According to Dirceu, some even proposed stealing the young man's body from the cemetery in order to rebury it in their own funeral. (They were dissuaded).[134] Guimarães's death led to large protests in São Paulo the next day but never resulted in the kind of national out-pouring of solidarity or mourning that had followed Edson Luis's murder (figure 3.15). In part this reflects the fact that some considered the event an example of student extremism rather than one of state repression.[135] It also reflects the general decline of the student movement in the second half of the year.

Despite the fraught climate and the growing divisions between students, the annual UNE Congress was such a symbolically important demonstration of students' historically constructed political authority that student leaders decided to defy prohibitions against it and hold the meeting in secret in October.[136] For weeks beforehand students across the country secretly elected delegates to represent them at the congress, and then around one thousand people made the difficult trip to a remote clandestine location in Ibiúna, in the interior of São Paulo state, for the multiday affair. The number of attendees is remarkable given the recently displayed commitment of the police to preventing such gatherings as well as their violent efforts to seize much of the current student movement leadership, who would be in attendance. It was also just the sort of symbolically provocative

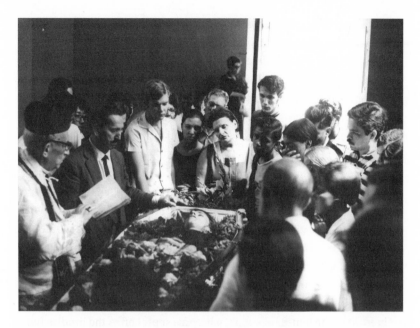

FIGURE 3.14. Although the wake for José Guimarães was private, pictures of the boy's flower-strewn body appeared in the newspapers. October 5, 1968. *Correio da Manhã* collection, Arquivo Nacional

FIGURE 3.15. Students in São Paulo disrupted traffic as they marched in protest against José Guimarães's death and in support of the upcoming UNE Congress. *Correio da Manhã* collection, Arquivo Nacional

event that security agents would seek to prevent. Indeed, as one journalist explained, "Various military sectors and federal intelligence agencies reached two important conclusions [about this year's congress]: 1. participants would discuss subversive means and formulas; 2. for it to take place would be an affront to authorities."[137] Even if many of those who attended had close connections with or sympathy for the clandestine lefts, the congress offered UNE a chance to reassert and reanimate its appeal to the aboveground majority.

Rivalries between the lefts and the student leaders affiliated with them, however, threatened to derail the entire event. In such a tense atmosphere, everything would have had to run perfectly for the conference to go undetected. Instead, the opposite occurred. First, it began late. Although most participants had arrived at the rural location by October 6, much of the current leadership, embroiled in a bitter debate back in the city of São Paulo concerning an excess of delegates from Minas Gerais and the resulting charges of fraud, did not reach the site until four days later. Their delayed arrival meant food supplies became stretched to the limit as hundreds of people needed to be fed for several extra days. If students were already testing their luck by hoping that hundreds of young people gathered in a small farming community would go undetected, their sudden need to buy extra bread and other supplies from local merchants only added to their precarious situation. In this very direct way, the congress showcased the extent of the divisions among leaders and the gulf between the leadership and others, as the leaders became so mired in internal disputes that they left everyone else vulnerable to detection for several days.

To make matters worse, it began to rain and would not stop. The open-air meetings the organizers had envisioned became impossible in the persistent rainfall, as the earth-cut benches carefully carved the week before quickly turned to mud. Owing to the lack of shelter, students were forced to sleep in shifts, packed tightly together and even sitting up to conserve space, crammed into barns and stables and under a makeshift tent. Released from jail in time to attend, Palmeira later described the scene: "[It] was really a mess. It rained into the canopy they had improvised, the mud entered our shoes, everyone was wet the whole time, no one could stand it."[138] Perhaps the soggy climate contributed to people's contentious mood, as arguments both political and logistical raged, especially regarding the continued debate about the legitimacy of some delegates. After the first full day of discussions on October 11, and despite an increasing uneasiness that the group would be discovered, elections still had not taken place. Even students' own security reports announcing that heightened police activity in the area almost certainly meant an impending raid went unheeded in the air of mistrust that the various factions felt toward one another, some believing the reports to have been fabricated in order to hurry on the election at an advantageous moment for their opponents.

In the early morning hours of October 12 when federal soldiers and DOPS agents descended on the muddy farm, they found a strained and sodden group, trapped by geography and mud, unable to escape. The next day the whole ordeal hit the front pages of the newspapers with a splash, as did the images of the wet and weary students, wrapped in blankets as they were marched fifteen kilometers over muddy back roads to the buses and trucks waiting to ferry them to jail. While newspapers initially reported over twelve hundred detentions, the final figure proved to be slightly over seven hundred, as some of those captured were journalists and others were undercover police agents.[139] São Paulo's secretary of public security, Heli Lopes Meireles, gleefully admitted to reporters, "We didn't expect to arrest so many people all at once."[140] Perhaps even more significant was the fact that, despite their efforts to escape and to blend in with other students, nearly the entire UNE leadership found itself in police custody. So too did those students who had already joined, or soon would join, one of the organizations of the clandestine lefts. Security forces photographed and documented each apprehended student, creating a veritable police gallery of student activists. As Maria Augusta Ribeiro recalled, "Not everyone in the student movement was supportive of the armed struggle, but we were and we shouldn't have gone. We were all documented."[141] Most intriguingly, DOPS officers made a separate photo album of women students detained at Ibiúna, as if they merited special examination (figure 3.16).[142] Meanwhile a host of detectives remained at or returned to the muddy meeting site to comb for evidence of students' subversion, eventually displaying their triumphant finds, from revolutionary pamphlets to birth control pills, to waiting reporters.[143]

If the police raid on the UNE Congress reflects some of the many internal divisions within the student movement, the response by some of those who did not attend highlights how important defending UNE remained. In the period immediately following the mass arrests, press coverage of students and public student activity resurged. In part the media interest stemmed from the dramatic nature of the events themselves, both in terms

FIGURE 3.16. Officers of the DOPS placed the photos of women students arrested at Ibiúna in a special album. DEOPS Collection, Arquivo Público do Estado de São Paulo

of the torrential rains and the miscalculations that turned a highly organized clandestine meeting into, in the words of one participant, a virtual
"booby trap, where the police came in and spooned us up like rabbits,"[144]
and because of the sensational escapades of several students leaders who
attempted to escape.[145] (The fact that several prominent newspapers sent
what one would now call embedded journalists to participate in the rainy
student congress, and that they also fell victims to the police dragnet,
undoubtedly helped color their stories and spark readers' interest.)[146] More
significantly, though, the renewed press coverage corresponded to students' resumption of some degree of public protest after a period of relative quiet and tumultuous internal debate (figures 3.17 and 3.18). From
Recife, where two thousand demonstrators camped out on the patio of one
university, threatening to remain there until their colleagues were released
from jail,[147] to Rio de Janeiro, where one thousand students broke into the
former UNE headquarters building to physically demonstrate that UNE
had not disbanded, it quickly became clear that although students no
longer commanded huge crowds, there still existed a determined core independent of those under arrest (figure 3.19).[148] Even in Alagoas, where
students prided themselves on adopting less confrontational styles than
their counterparts in other areas, they held a fund-raising campaign among
motorists to help the detainees.[149] Notwithstanding internal divisions and
a mostly incarcerated leadership, in late 1968 students organized a coordinated series of protest demonstrations, albeit in reduced numbers. Defending UNE and the student movement remained a vital enterprise.

After the soggy UNE Congress, officials' suspicions that the student
movement as a whole served, knowingly or unknowingly, as a proxy for the
clandestine and armed lefts were only strengthened by the coincidence of a
second major event that took place on October 12. As students in Ibiúna
were facing arrest, in the city of São Paulo a U.S. Army captain and Vietnam
veteran named Charles Chandler died instantly when an unidentified man
sprayed his car with machine gun fire. Before fleeing the scene, the at-
tacker scattered leaflets explaining the political motivation behind the killing. Proclaiming to have served "revolutionary justice" against a "war
criminal" currently training counterrevolutionaries in Brazil, the flyers
marked Chandler's assassination as the work of one of the clandestine
armed lefts. Almost immediately Public Security Secretary Meireles declared a connection between his death and the student movement. Claim-

FIGURE 3.17. A student spray paints a sign protesting the arrests made at the UNE Congress. Morales, photographer. *Correio da Manhã* collection, Arquivo Nacional

FIGURE 3.18. Students at a Rio de Janeiro medical school protest the arrests at Ibiúna with a Brazilian Statue of Liberty. October 23, 1968. Osmar Gallo, photographer. *Correio da Manhã* collection, Arquivo Nacional

FIGURE 3.19. Students hold a protest from the balcony of the former UNE building in October 1968. The façade is still charred from the fire in April 1964. *Correio da Manhã* collection, Arquivo Nacional

ing that the pamphlets found near his body proved similar to writings confiscated at the UNE Congress, he told the press that congress participants might be implicated in the killing.[150]

Notwithstanding the fervent inquiries of both Brazilian and U.S. investigators, by early November officials had produced no evidence of student involvement in Chandler's death, and no arrests had been made. Nonetheless another coincidence further fueled their growing suspicions about the interconnections between students and the armed lefts. On November 8 the police arrested nineteen-year-old Paulo César Monteiro Bezerra, who confessed to having participated in the robbery of an armored car in Rio de Janeiro a few hours earlier. Throughout the year a series of bank robberies and holdups in several southern cities had provoked considerable alarm, not to mention prurient curiosity about a mysterious blonde woman who had taken part in several of them, even though most believed the holdups to be the work of career thieves. In fact, just a few days earlier, after the robbery of the Banco Ultramarino in Rio, police officers categorically denied that the expertly handled four-minute operation could have been carried out by "terrorists," hinting instead at professional international criminals or fellow bankers working an "inside job."[151] Yet when, by chance, they captured Monteiro, he acknowledged he was a student and, after eight hours of detention (eight hours of severe torture, according to his lawyer), he not only confessed to having participated in the robbery but also revealed both its political nature and the involvement of the ALN founder Marighella and a blonde woman named Sílvia.[152] Within days the São Paulo police force began to reevaluate their investigations of thirty-four recent bank robberies, now believing them to be linked to Marighella's group.[153]

Following Monteiro's confession, the media began to focus on exotic descriptions of Sílvia and published rumors of her supposed romantic entanglements with Marighella and others. Meanwhile the police began to call repeated attention to Monteiro's status as a student, as if he could provide the long-sought link between the above- and belowground movements. The first newspaper reports referred to him almost exclusively as "the student Paulo Monteiro," and only after later journalistic research did it become apparent that Monteiro was not actually a university student but had only been taking preparatory courses for the *vestibular* entrance exam. Sílvia, for her part, appeared sometimes as a medical student in Ceará and sometimes as a philosophy student in São Paulo, despite also being reported to be thirty-five years old, quite a bit older than most university students.[154] In this, newspapers followed the lead of investigators, who quickly came to focus their efforts on the student movement and on the student status of some of the robberies' perpetrators.

To complicate the story still further, within days the Rio de Janeiro DOPS came to reassess a fatal car crash on the same night as the Marighella-led armored car robbery. The crash had resulted in the deaths of two other São Paulo students: João Antonio dos Santos Abib Essab and Catarina Helena Ferreira. Originally judged an accident by police, the wreck was relabeled as "an important detail in the national plan of subversion."[155] Officers reassessed the case and now not only proclaimed they had identified the students' vehicle as the one used in the robbery of both the armored car and the Banco Ultramarino, but also purported to have found in its trunk a machine gun matching the type used in Chandler's assassination. That the two deceased students had attended the philosophy program at the University of São Paulo, a department with a reputation for student political activism, seemed to further mark them as guilty of subversion. Secretary França immediately informed the press that Abib played an active role in the São

Paulo student movement, particularly within the UEE of São Paulo; and Ferreira, although not officially involved in the UEE, was implicated by the fact of being his girlfriend. In one fell swoop security forces publicly linked Marighella, the ALN, and the recent spate of politically motivated bank robberies with both the aboveground student movement and politically active students generally, allying them all in one, grand "national plan of subversion."[156] That these connections proved mostly incorrect does not detract from their powerful symbolism at the time.[157] Security forces had long expressed their suspicion that behind the façade of the student movement lay a direct link to the clandestine armed lefts, and they took these recent confessions as added confirmation of this belief.

Other opposition figures also faced attempts by the regime to stifle them, as the High Military Command began proceedings within the legislative Chamber of Deputies to revoke the parliamentary immunity of Marcio Moreira Alves for a series of speeches he had delivered. In the past, motions to revoke immunity had occasionally reached the Chamber when legislators were suspected of crimes like electoral fraud and tax evasion. But in this case they meant to prosecute Alves for his words. In criticizing the regime for a violent invasion of the University of Brasilia in August, Alves had proposed a "boycott of militarism" by those girls "who dance with the cadets and date the young officers." As he explained, "The women of 1968 must deny entrance into their houses to those who revile the Nation, they must refuse to accept those that keep silent, and, thereby, serve as accomplices."[158] The complaint against him said his speeches were "highly offensive to the Armed Forces and [were delivered] with the obvious intent of demoralizing them, aiming to struggle against democratic order and national institutions."[159] In the context of the intense political and gendered tensions of 1968, his emasculating suggestion that women respond to the military in the manner of Lysistrata was intolerable.

By early December, as the Chamber of Deputies entered extra sessions to deliberate on Moreira Alves's case, rumors of a possible new Institutional Act permeated discussions of national politics. In fact, as Maria Helena Moreira Alves has argued, President Costa e Silva and his advisers probably wrote the text of what became AI-5 months earlier (as far back as July), waiting for the appropriate moment to introduce it.[160] Less than two weeks before its release, Costa e Silva had threatened to put forward such a measure. During an improvised speech at a presidential reception for ARENA congressmen he warned, "Provoked, I will react, as I do not accept the defiance of those irresponsible ones who want to bring Brazil to disorder and chaos. . . . It must be understood that every action generates a reaction. Don't think that you can agitate all you like against our institutions and that we will stand there with our arms folded. Don't confuse tolerance with toleration. We are strong and our reaction will also be strong. . . . If [you] really understand the seriousness of this, you will certainly cooperate to resolve it with order and legality."[161] In the days that followed, government officials sent mixed signals about how they would respond should the Moreira Alves vote not go their way. In one issue of the *Jornal do Brasil*, two contradictory stories appeared on the same page. In one, Costa e Silva denied the possibility of a new Institutional Act, citing the swirling rumors as coming from "elements who are interested in disrupting the government, disturbing the order of the country."[162] Alongside this was an article on the birthday party of his fellow coup planner and current intelligence director, Emílio Garrastazu Médici, in which Médici was quoted as proudly proclaiming, "We will make as many revolutions as are necessary" to ensure Brazil's future.[163] Though unofficial, signs of a new turn in military Brazil were everywhere.

Yet even then, with numerous signs of a regime hardening, observers predicted much future student organizing. Universities around the country began holding the vestibular for the new academic year, which always led to surplus students, and both the Brazilian press and the U.S. embassy again began to speculate on the seemingly inevitable resurgence of the student movement. A *Jornal do Brasil* editorial sarcastically quipped that "the student leaders are in prison, perhaps to guarantee, with their absence from classes, some room for the mass of excedentes which is coming."[164] The U.S. embassy predicted, "When this year's surplus applicants, who the *Jornal do Brasil* estimates at 35,000, run up against the hard, insoluble fact of overcrowded schools, the student leadership can expect to gain some new converts to it cause." They went on to report that their student informants foresaw 1969 as an even more promising year than the previous one. The consular official William Belton cautiously noted, "Student activists in general feel that 1968 was a most successful year for them and that, even though the Ibiúna [UNE] Congress was smashed, its mere occurrence represents a major victory. There is a belief that 1969 will be an even better year for the student movement, if UNE can regain the momentum lost in the attempt to decapitate it and thus provide the mass of marginal participants with a sense of triumph over the 'dictatorship.'" Nor did U.S. officials chalk up this sense of confidence to youthful optimism, for in the same report they warned of "a program of activism and perhaps agitation in the forthcoming vacation period" (January-February).[165] One must be cautious in reading too literally these consular and embassy reports, as U.S. officials' apprehensions about student disturbances often caused them to overstate the risk. Nevertheless, their observations reflect general impressions culled from the media and their conversations with others, all of which suggested that, despite the setback at Ibiúna, the student movement had an active future ahead.

Finally, in the midst of the intense showdown between the Chamber of Deputies and the military leaders over Alves's immunity and amid the swirling rumors of a new Institutional Act, student activists organized their last major action of the year: a campaign to free the remaining two hundred incarcerated students before Christmas.[166] With the support of various prominent figures and organizations, including the vice rector of the UFRJ, several priests, the Order of Lawyers of Brazil, the Medical Association of Guanabara, and a number of labor unions, students flooded the courts with requests for habeas corpus and other legal petitions. At the same time, they began a campaign to visit their imprisoned colleagues en masse and encouraged supporters to send thousands of Christmas cards to the jails, all in an effort to gain publicity for their cause and to appeal to the judges' holiday sentiments.[167]

After weeks of debate, an attempted filibuster, and an ensuing extension of the congressional session, on December 11 the president of the Chamber of Deputies moved to end discussion on the question of Alves's immunity and call the vote the next day. Newspapers that morning fully expected the measure to revoke his immunity to pass, with most estimates guessing the vote would be around 190 to 170. Whether from conviction or intense government pressure, a majority of legislators pledged to back the measure. Instead, in an intensely ritualized procedure, the legislators denied the request. Since discussion had been closed the day before, only three people were allowed to speak: the majority leader, the minority leader, and Alves himself. Following their brief words, each legislator, one by one, entered a booth and cast a secret ballot. With 369 legislators voting, the process took two hours and forty minutes, the slowest in the chamber's history. Despite the periodic cheers when well-known opposition figures cast their ballots, once the votes began to be counted, the floor—and the gallery of over one hundred visitors—fell deadly silent. Within ten minutes of counting, the regime's loss already started to become clear. One hundred seventy-eight votes were needed to defeat the measure, and as the total reached 150 everyone in the room rose to their feet. When the figure hit 178, a cry went up as people began cheering, laughing, and hugging each other. A young woman in the gallery started to sing the national anthem, and others immediately joined in. Soon the song swept over the house, drowning out the clanging bell of the majority leader, who, in vain, demanded silence. The final vote tally was 216 against, 141 in favor, and 12 blank votes—a resounding victory for Congress and the right to dissent, and a symbolic defeat for the military.[168]

While the legislators congratulated one another, Alves moved quickly. Handing out to journalists a prepared statement calling for the restoration of democracy, he later explained that "through a forest of outstretched hands and smiling faces, [I] moved toward the rear exit of the House, where I had arranged for trusty friends to whisk me away."[169] The night of December 12 passed tensely, as people braced themselves for the government's response, while behind closed doors President Costa e Silva "silently presided over a military revolt," as hard-line officials demanded a strong response.[170] Meanwhile radio and television stations received specific orders prohibiting them from reporting on the case or the ensuing crisis. Military and police forces were ordered into a state of alert, and armored tanks moved briefly onto Brasil Avenue in Brasilia, then were quickly retracted. One army commander told journalists they were simply troops returning from military exercises, but an inside source admitted "a small problem with military discipline."[171] The uneasy climate lasted well into December 13, as the president and the twenty-three members of the National Security Council met at Laranjeiras Palace and studied the text of AI-5, the passage of which, Vice President Pedro Aleixo asserted, would mean "instituting a process equivalent to a real dictatorship."[172] Among its twelve articles, AI-5 gave the president the right to suspend Congress for an indeterminate amount of time; to intervene freely in the governance of states and municipalities; and to declare a state of siege for any period of time; and it restored his authority to unseat elected officials and suspend anyone's political rights for ten years. It also ended habeas corpus rights for a cavernously wide variety of crimes, from "political crimes," to "crimes against the social and economic order."[173]

Vice President Aleixo's concerns were ignored as the group approved AI-5, and that evening Minister of Justice Gama e Silva read an official announcement over the radio that put an end to the speculation and rumors. "Clearly subversive acts," he proclaimed, "stemming from the most distinct cultural and political sectors, prove that the juridical instruments which the victorious Revolution granted to the Nation for its defense, development and well-being are serving as the means to combat it and destroy it."[174] With this, the military government promulgated AI-5, and with Supplementary Act No. 38 closed Congress, thereby definitively ending 1968 and sending the nation into a period of even deeper political, cultural, and military repression.

....

On December 12, 1968, as the student Arthur Carlos de Rocha Müller joyfully walked out of the DOPS prison in Rio de Janeiro where he had been held since his arrest at Ibiúna, a photographer caught him taking one last glance over his shoulder.[175] According to his wife, Ana Maria Müller, it was not nostalgia for the place where he had spent the last two months that inspired the backward look, but a shout from a DOPS officer, Mauro Borges. As Arthur Müller turned back in response Borges grinned and said portentously, "See you tomorrow." It was the eve of AI-5's release, but the group leaving the prison did not yet know this. "There we were thinking it was just a provocation," Ana Müller recalled. "But after that moment I only laid eyes on Arthur some time later, for reasons of security."[176] That she would remember this episode years later as a moment of personal and national foreshadowing reflects the way in which AI-5 has come to be seen as a severe rupture between 1968 and the difficult years that ensued. Yet the levity within her dark anecdote, coupled with the frozen snapshot of their smiling, youthful faces, helps one visualize the nascent, even expectant, spirit with which many students in late 1968 stepped away from the Ibiúna incarcerations and into what then seemed a future full of promise.

If defined as a period of fervent student protest, then 1968 neither began on January 1 nor ended on December 31. What it lacked in temporal neatness, however, it more than made up for in political and cultural significance. Student movement activity in 1968 proved to be unlike any that had come before, not simply assembling record-breaking numbers of participants and holding innumerable demonstrations, but also offering the most visible and recognizable opposition to the military regime to date. If all political movements have to assert a claim to their authenticity, at the dawn of 1968 students in Brazil had particular hurdles to overcome. Structurally they had to rebuild student organizations that had lost their leadership, physical headquarters and belongings, official status, and ultimately even their legal right to function. And they had to do so after an extended campaign against not just their leaders and ideas but also against students' basic rights and ability to act politically. Finally, they did so in a context in which political organizing by any civil group, not just by students, was essentially prohibited.

As the national and state student unions remained illegal and their activities banned, those who challenged such prohibitions necessarily contested the state's legal definitions of authentic student activity. Student activists argued this directly in slogans and speeches, both in response to the state's efforts to shut them down and as part of their internal struggles over leadership and direction. Many observers in the media and elsewhere supported this general view of students as authentic, even besieged, political actors, and references to young people everywhere as inspired to act by real or perceived injustices proliferated. At the same time, the clandestine lefts became fully convinced that harnessing a sense of militancy on the part of young people was critical to their revolutionary success, and they further contributed to these debates with their influence and interventions. Other voices, however, fiercely disputed this perspective and understood the contemporary rise of both Brazilian and global student movements as testament to unnatural, foreign influences. Such was the case with many of the government officials who sought to shut down student organizing, explicitly explaining their actions in these terms. So too did this perspective infuse other media reports, as journalists' conflation of local and global developments often rendered Brazilian students' actions mere copies of students' activism elsewhere. For those who saw the rise of student activism as an unnatural development, the violence that characterized these mobilizations and personal behaviors evinced a dangerous breakdown of social norms.

Fundamental to student mobilization was the dialectical role of violence that, among its other effects, highlighted the propensity of the military regime to resolve social issues through force. Meanwhile the confluence of violence in other student movements around the world that year reflected and impacted the Brazilian students' political potential, offering them added attention and distraction. And the struggles of Brazilian students to redefine gender expectations sometimes ran up against similar critiques by those who saw such changes as emanating beyond the nation. In the momentous months of 1968 Brazil's university students thoroughly destabilized the political and cultural context of military-ruled Brazil.

In the second semester of 1968 mass student protests tapered off. Yet this reduction did not represent any broad decrease either in students' belief that they had the right to political participation or in their support for their traditional organizations like UNE. Indeed, when the union appeared most under siege, students rallied to defend it. Yet escalating state efforts to violently repress student demonstrations, as well as the commitment of those students aligned with the clandestine lefts to respond in turn, resulted in fewer nonaligned students engaging in large public actions. Ironically, as the distance between the underground-aligned student leadership and the aboveground student "masses" grew more pronounced, state security officials became convinced that little distinction separated the two. They repeatedly held that student movement participation in practically any form constituted a direct path to armed subversion. When such officials found seeming proof of this connection in the form of an alliance between an alluring female bank robber named Sílvia, three students from São Paulo, and ALN leader Carlos Marighella, they moved to definitively end the student activism of 1968 as quickly and permanently as possible.

Nonetheless, on December 12, 1968, just one day before the release of AI-5, when Arthur Müller and others like him stepped out of their jail cells and onto the city streets, it was with a clear eye to the future. The year 1968 may have been a particularly dramatic one, but it was to be the launching point to their next struggles. Only in the ensuing months and years of persecution and disintegration would they take another backward glance.

4

DARK WEATHER

The Post-'68 Storm, 1969–1973

"Dark Weather. Suffocating Temperature. The air is unbreathable. The country is
being changed by strong winds. Max. 38°C in Brasilia, Min 5°C in Laranjeiras."
—Front-page weather report in the heavily censored *Jornal do Brasil* for
December 14, 1968

If the journalist Zuenir Ventura has called 1968 "the year that did not end,"
and the historian Carlos Fico has labeled it "the year that ended badly," one
might also consider it the year that ended a few weeks early.[1] For, looking
back, December 13, 1968, seemed to mark an immediate turning point
between the strident effervescence of 1968 and the stifling heaviness that
followed. Just one day earlier, as the congressmen and gallery at the Chamber of Deputies were bursting into song and applause over their moral
victory in the Márcio Moreira Alves affair, nearby at the Supreme Court the
justices were voting in their own momentous case. Writs of habeas corpus
for four important student leaders imprisoned since the raid at Ibiúna on
October 12—the university students Vladimir Palmeira, José Dirceu, and
Luis Travassos and the secondary student Antônio Guilherme Ribeiro Ribas—came before the court. Although the students' lawyers had filed many
such requests in the two months since their arrests only to have them
rejected, they had reason to be optimistic this time. Under the National
Security Law, prisoners could be held in preventative detention for no
longer than sixty days, and it had been just that long since the events at

Ibiúna. Indeed, in the previous two days seventy-nine other students had won their release and gone home.[2] Nevertheless, Palmeira, Dirceu, Travassos, and, to a lesser extent, Ribeiro had become such recognizable symbols of the student movement that their fates were by no means certain: would they be discharged or would their prominence as student leaders overshadow their legal rights?

Much to the delight of the students and their attorneys, the court unanimously approved their applications and gave the go-ahead for their release.[3] But just as Alves's and the deputies' victories of December 12 were short-lived—for Alves had to flee into hiding the same night while the December 13 declaration of AI-5 and of Supplementary Act No. 38 shut down Congress—so too were the students' celebrations curtailed. Although the court voted on December 12 to free the students, the official orders to release them were not processed until that same fateful Friday the thirteenth, and by then AI-5 made injunctions based on the habeas writs irrelevant. Travassos, Dirceu, and Palmeira would remain in jail until September 1969, when they and twelve other prisoners were exchanged for the kidnapped U.S. Ambassador Charles Elbrick. Ribas would stay in prison until June 1970.[4]

Yet back on that hopeful summer day in late 1968, of the four incarcerated students only Palmeira knew with certainty that, regardless of the legal outcome, he would not be allowed to walk free. Anticipating the judgment, military personnel transferred him on the night before the court decision, moving him from the army prison where he had been held with the others to a navy penitentiary. Even had the habeas petition succeeded, Palmeira would have been liberated by the army only to be reapprehended by the navy, who also had orders for his arrest. Years later, when Palmeira described his prison transfer on the eve of AI-5, he recalled an expression used by his mother at the time: "God writes straight through crooked lines," she had told him. "She was right," he later reflected, "because if they had let me out at that moment very soon after I would have been dead."[5]

Dramatic as this statement may sound, Palmeira did not exaggerate by much. Brazil after AI-5 became a drastically more dangerous place for anyone who actively opposed the military regime—and even for those who had done so in the past. Although four other Institutional Acts preceded it, AI-5 marked a radical departure from the previous five years of military rule and reflected the outward expression of a protracted power struggle within the military government—a significant though by no means decisive battle between soft- and hard-liners that many would later label the coup within the coup.[6] References to the historically unprecedented degree of state repression that marked the military dictatorship point primarily to the years after 1968. For it was in 1969 and the 1970s that the vast majority of cases of clandestine detention of political prisoners, state torture, and the forced disappearance of the regime's opponents took place. In addition, various underground groups from the right gained increased license in the post-AI-5 climate, at times using it to assassinate known opposition leaders, including students.[7] The heady days of 1968, when one hundred thousand people peacefully gathered in downtown Rio de Janeiro, officially ended on December 13, 1968, replaced by a period of increased danger and mistrust, the infamous "years of lead."[8]

Those exhilarating days of 1968 were not just a moment of relative political freedom when compared with what was to follow; they were also a turning point for the state security forces, who came to see the student demonstrations of that year as a causal factor in the rise of the clandestine armed lefts (see chapter 3). In the following years, state security officials frequently referred to 1968, keeping a close eye on former student activists and cautiously lumping together the most diverse types of student activities as "68-like." Indeed, they came to regard otherwise innocuous-seeming student activities as clear acts of subversion and employed this label widely for all kinds of student-related events. Military officials took advantage of the extensive powers granted by AI-5—oftentimes supplementing them with extralegal activities—in an effort to dismantle the student movement. In doing so, they demonstrated what Sonia Alvarez has argued, that militarism and institutionalized violence rest on patriarchal foundations.[9] For security officials often justified their efforts as necessary steps to protect "useful innocents" like students, in the process casting the regime as a paternal figure. Most provocatively, throughout this period they drew often on collective memories of 1968 as dangerous reminders of chaos narrowly averted and against which they remained vigilant. Such memories surfaced almost immediately among security agents and became important, if fluid, references throughout the post-1968 period. The memories of 1968 contributed to the unleashing of a previously inconceivable wave of repression against young dissenters.

If the state security forces came to invoke their memories of 1968 very quickly after AI-5, the same cannot be said of students. For a long period they generally did not make references to 1968 as a year to emulate or as a model for action. While 1968 had been a moment of tremendous growth and dynamism in the student movement, for many it was laudable precisely because it promised future activism in the hope of effecting political change. In other words, the mass mobilizations of that year had never been an end in themselves, and thus 1968 was not immediately seen as a success to be commemorated. Moreover, few immediately recognized just how drastic a rupture AI-5 would turn out to be and just what was to follow. Certainly as the act was promulgated many figures had a clear sense of foreboding about the future, one eloquently and cleverly displayed in the fictionalized weather report carried in the *Jornal do Brasil* and cited at this chapter's opening (see epigraph above). At 38°C (100°F) the federal capital of Brasília would have been scalding, while Laranjeiras Palace in Rio, where President Costa e Silva signed AI-5, would have been impossibly cold at 5°C (41°F) as well as implausibly consistent with the number of the act. The passage demonstrates the editors' use of dark humor in the face of somber events as well as the clever ways they occasionally managed to elude the censors. (The same front page was dotted with classified ads, signaling to readers that several news articles had not enjoyed the same fortune and were removed.) Yet even after the act came into effect, Palmeira and his colleagues desperately sought release from jail, not just for the obvious reason of wanting freedom from forced and difficult confinement but also because they fully expected and intended to continue working in the student movement. For students who were born a decade or more after the institutionalization of UNE and therefore saw themselves as time-honored political actors and who most recently had seen their organizations not simply persevere but actually grow to unprecedented prominence notwithstanding the efforts of a military regime to silence them, AI-5 initially appeared to be yet another hurdle to clear, albeit a formidable one. And 1969 beckoned as the future of their movement, not the year of its demise.

Only as the new reality became unavoidably clear did cultivating collective memories of 1968 gradually become important to students. As student activists responded to the onslaught of efforts to dismantle the student movement and as the student body itself changed over time, they were forced to recognize the extent to which AI-5 had altered their political possibilities. From trying to defend any kind of presence for UNE to turning to more cultural forms of dissent, some students continued to insist on their right to engage in political activity, while others begged off even the appearance of political involvement. Meanwhile the student body changed because of the normal progression of graduation and due to expansion, as university enrollment continued to grow steeply in the early 1970s, now admitting increasing numbers of women and working-class students. For this large, quickly changing group, 1968 did not immediately become a point of focus. Nonetheless, some among them did implicitly invoke that year each March 28 when they staged annual commemorations of Edson Luis's death. By marking the date he died they tacitly called forth 1968 itself and students' then-central role in protesting the military regime. At the same time, they challenged the regime's self-positioning as a paternal protector by calling forth its role in the killing of an innocent. They also repositioned themselves in an ongoing fight against the dictatorship, at once emphasizing their moral position as victims of state repression and the continuity of their movement in the face of severe restraints. In this way successive cohorts of students at once affirmed and continuously recreated their connection to the mass movements of 1968. When another, symbolically similar student death in March 1973 led to a new wave of protest and commemoration, the connection strengthened further.

Thus at that transitional moment between the two concentric coups d'état, security forces almost immediately invoked memories of 1968, while for students 1968 signified little more than the numerical designation of the quickly closing year. In other words, if 1968 as a period of mass student mobilization ended on December 13, then the "1968" in quotation marks, the "1968" that swelled beyond the bounds of a temporal marker to become a broadly powerful and contested memory of massive antiregime student protest, was only created in the following years. As Michael Pollak argues, understanding memories of the past requires that one move beyond treating social events as things and "analyze *how* social events *become* things, how and by whom they are solidified and given durability and stability."[10] More expansively, Elizabeth Jelin encourages scholars to "historicize memory," noting that the significance of past events is not constant. "Nor," she writes, "is there a clear and direct linear relationship between an event and the chronological passing of time, in the sense that as time passes the event falls into historical oblivion to be replaced by more recent events."[11] Indeed, in the case of university students in Brazil, 1968 did not immediately emerge as a cherished mnemonic reference and then gradually recede in importance over time. Rather, something closer to the reverse is true, as the year only came to take on special significance after the transition to the post-AI-5 world made undeniable the gulf between a 1970s present and the 1968 past, real or imagined. As the experiences of both the state security forces and students confirm, the meanings of the past are constantly subject to contestation and reinterpretation. Exploring how, when, and for whom memories of 1968 became solidified into "1968" helps one understand the role students would have in the remaining years of military rule—both as objects of debate and intervention and as active subjects in their own right. The fierce ideological and cultural struggles to define just who Brazilian university students should be and what roles they should play in society did not stop at AI-5 but intensified, now indelibly marked by the experiences, understandings, and misunderstandings of 1968.

The Specter of 1968: Settling the Subversive Storm

Even before 1968 had come to a close on the calendar, at least one Brazilian official went to work to prevent a repeat of that year by enlisting the guidance of the French police. In December 1968 Antonio Carlos Caillanova, the director of the Brazilian National Institute of Criminology, took advantage of a criminology conference in Paris to meet with French security officials about their experiences with student protesters earlier in the year. For two days they discussed the lessons the French police had learned, including both the reasons they had originally been unable to control students and their current, detailed plans to ensure that "another May 1968 would not be tolerated." In the report Caillanova soon filed in Brazil with the Ministry of the Army he explained that French security forces had at first underestimated the students, particularly their capacity for improvisation. They fell prey, for example, to such student antics as tossing paper bags full of cement or talcum powder from rooftops in order to obscure the vision of oncoming police; and they were tripped up by students' strategy of stringing fishing line through the hallways of occupied university buildings, a foot off the ground, so as to make entering troops stumble and fall. The French police had likewise failed to devise a plan of counterattack or to adequately coordinate their forces. Yet they learned from these mistakes, Caillanova wrote, and "currently there is planned, in the most minuscule details, a repressive, violent action [Action de Frappé] which will be unleashed at the first sign of new disturbances." This plan comprised a combination of concrete actions, such as immediate occupation of university buildings and the isolation of those that students managed to take over by cutting off all access routes and shutting off electricity, telephone, and water services. The plan also included more symbolic actions. For example, the French police advocated "employing large quantities of troops in the repression (one must show, right from the start, that we mean business, and [we must] intimidate by our initial [display of] troops)." They also recommended mounting counter-propaganda campaigns against known student leaders: refusing to treat students as equals and questioning the legitimacy of their leadership. After detailing these general lessons, Cailla-nova ended his report with a few specific suggestions. To combat the talcum powder sacks, police should use masks. Against the fishing line, a motorcycle preceding troops down the hallways would suffice. Helmets, slash-proof tires, and the ample use of nightsticks were also highly recommended. Finally, he wrote, fire extinguishers fired directly at students' legs "theoretically should offer excellent results, removing the individual from combat for six to eight days with multiple, irritating and slow-healing but nonserious injuries."[12] Whether the Brazilian Ministry of the Army followed through on all of these recommendations is unknown. But Cailla-nova's extended conversation and ensuing report demonstrate the early interest some Brazilian officials had in preventing another 1968 and point to the ways in which police efforts to prevent future student uprisings took on transnational dimensions.[13]

Learning from the experiences of other countries' police forces may have been useful, but efforts to dismantle the Brazilian student movement would require strong, local measures, and military officials moved quickly to implement these. Most significant, on February 27, 1969, right before the start of the academic year, Costa e Silva drew on the powers of AI-5 to issue Decree-Law Number 477, a form of executive legislation that did not require congressional approval and went into effect immediately on being signed. The law prohibited students, teachers, and even staff at all public and private schools and universities from participating in a long list of activities, including strikes, unauthorized marches and protests, or using any part of school property for vaguely defined subversive purposes.[14] Punishments for infractions were severe. Teachers and staff faced immediate dismissal and a five-year prohibition on acquiring another position in the field. Students risked expulsion and a three-year moratorium on re-enrollment plus a five-year ban on accepting any publicly funded scholarships. Responsibility for enforcement originally fell to school and university directors, who had forty-eight hours from receiving a complaint about an individual to investigate and possibly discipline the accused. But soon the Education Ministry amplified this section of the decree to include as responsible parties "any other authority or person," thereby paving the way for officials from the various state intelligence and security forces to intervene in student cases.[15] Meanwhile the regime continued to extend its authority more generally through the issuance of further Institutional Acts in February 1969, reducing the number of justices on the Supreme Court (via AI-6) and suspending upcoming elections (through AI-7 and AI-8).

Military officials also worked to limit the influence of students who had been politically active the year before, often bypassing the law in order to do so. At the start of the 1969 school year, for example, the U.S. embassy in Rio reported that universities around the country faced strong pressure to blacklist alleged subversive students: "A number of our contacts have told us of extra-legal orders to school directors that certain students deemed subversive are not to be enrolled." As part of this endeavor, claimed the U.S. consulate in Salvador, directors at both the Federal and Catholic universities there were given blacklists of such students.[16] At the University of Brasilia administrators denied readmission to over one hundred students, in most cases because of their prior involvement in political activity. At the Federal University of Bahia, nearly all of the students arrested at Ibiúna were barred from reenrolling.[17] In the northeast more generally, the Sixth Military Region Command assembled a collection of nearly two thousand faces from films of 1968 student protests and then circulated the pictures to school authorities for identification.[18] Officials of DOPS involved university rectors in their information gathering, requiring them to furnish the names of students involved in local student organizations.[19] Meanwhile any known activists who appeared at universities other than their own or who continued to visit their former faculty after graduation became subject to close scrutiny. Such was the case with several monitored students at the UFRJ who were assumed to be "promoting subversive activities."[20] In these and other ways officials worked behind the scenes to ensure that the most politically outspoken young people were barred from university campuses and that those who remained were carefully monitored. At the same time, they used the powers of AI-5 to unofficially punish those they saw as being responsible for the protests of 1968.

In a similar gesture, security forces began to retroactively prosecute students for subversive incidents that had occurred 1968. In March 1969 DOPS officers called in journalists and other witnesses to help them identify students who had briefly occupied the former UNE headquarters in October 1968.[21] In April they began proceedings to try a student under the Law of National Security for a speech he had delivered eight months earlier. Newspaper reports point to a Kafkaesque trial in which the contents of the speech in question were unknown. As one journalist wrote, "The prosecutor affirmed that the student climbed onto the bumper of a bus . . . , on which occasion he pronounced a discourse of a subversive character. The representative of the Public Prosecutor declared furthermore that, although his words were not understood clearly, owing to the shouts of demonstrators, isolated exclamations such as 'Viva,' 'Gorillas' [the pejorative nickname for soldiers], 'Down with the Dictatorship' and 'more funds' could be heard."[22] The precedent set by seeking to prosecute Márcio Moreira Alves for his speech now fell upon students' words as well. Around the country student activities from 1968 suddenly became the target of legal proceedings.[23] Moreover, several students faced convictions in absentia: for example, the military court sentenced the newly elected president of UNE, Jean Marc von der Weid, to two years' imprisonment for supposedly setting fire to a police vehicle in June 1968, an in absentia conviction that triggered repeated police attempts to arrest and imprison him.

As such examples of subversive blacklists and subversive speech imply, after AI-5 the definition of subversion became so wide that practically any kind of student political organizing fell into this category, while the government's labeling of individuals with the moniker had real consequences for those involved. Certainly student political protest and charges of subversion had been linked in earlier years, but if, prior to AI-5, the label *subversive* was generally applied to those with an assumed connection to the clandestine lefts, after AI-5 the charge expanded to include a wider variety of behaviors, paralleling the expanded list of activities prohibited to students. As Decree-Law 477 now specifically forbade students from engaging in anything that resembled political organizing, charges of student subversion also came to indicate participation in almost any kind of collective action. By May 1971 DOPS reports contained long lists of student organizations that were closed through Decree-Law 477 for having "a political-ideological character" and for "promoting antagonisms between students, faculty and administrators through subversive propaganda," demonstrating the enhanced license the regime now had to close down organizations it labeled subversive.[24] These reports also named each student elected to office within the organization, meaning that their names now figured in DOPS' vast files and could easily be drawn upon to substantiate any future allegations of subversion. That same year the military government narrowed still further the list of acceptable student activities by requiring intense government oversight of any student gathering. Another decree mandated that any kind of student assembly—"congresses, conferences, symposia, seminars, scientific, cultural or sporting competitions, special classes or any other type of meeting"—be approved by the Ministry of Education and Culture ninety days in advance and be the subject of a report filed within thirty days.[25] When Minister of Education and Culture Jarbas Passarinho later reminded university rectors of this requirement in a letter, he explained the need for it in terms of the threat of subversion. "I recognize the delicacy of this matter, given that we don't intend to impose silence on the students, but it must be noted that . . . the lefts are planning . . . , through strictly student issues, to develop new leadership directed toward subversion."[26] For figures like Passarinho, "strictly student issues" were a slippery slope toward subversion, and this threat justified the tight control of all student behavior.

Another provision of Decree-Law 477, its proscription against acts "contrary to public order or morality," showcases the ways in which political and sexual subversion continued to be linked in this period. As we have seen, in 1968 students' presumed sexual experimentation and flaunting of gender proscriptions against female militancy had appeared to some as real threats to the social order. The decree-law's prohibition against indecent conduct alongside its banning of political acts like strikes reveals the extent to which anxieties about the relationship between the political and the so-called moral order continued to be interconnected after AI-5. These ideas can also be witnessed in the realm of censorship, as another new decree of 1969 revised previously haphazard censorship rules and now included provisions for censoring materials based on either political or moral standards.[27] Among other consequences, this led to the banning of films and television shows with certain kinds of sexual content. The new censorship laws also forbade any criticism of the Institutional Acts, government authorities, and the armed forces and, most importantly for students, expressly prohibited reports on student or worker movements.[28] This not only limited student activists' chances of reaching out for popular support but also effectively ended the national waves of solidarity demonstrations that had so galvanized students in the preceding year.

Indeed, throughout this period some military officials not only continued to link sexual and political subversion but had increasing license to act on their concerns. Benjamin Cowan has argued that sectors of the Brazilian security establishment, especially those affiliated with the ESG, became "morally panicked" over the supposed connections between young people's political and sexual behaviors and managed to keep these preoccupations at the center of national discourse. As he explains, "A network of intellectually and institutionally intimate power-brokers and activists maintained a reactionary, morally panicked perspective that tended to conflate communism, subversion, and armed resistance with sexual radicalism, delinquency, and degeneracy, in an apocryphal construction of contemporary youth's perilous follies."[29] An intriguing figure in this regard was Antônio Carlos da Silva Muricy, army chief of staff between April 1969 and December 1970 and one of the coordinators of secret talks between high-level members of the military and the Church hierarchy.[30] Publicly he made numerous statements to the press about the connections between students' political and sexual behaviors. In 1970 he authoritatively declared to the *Jornal do Brasil* that young people entered subversive activities because of four factors, including parental disinterest and "social maladjustment." He added that young male subversives had a tactic of recruiting women by "winning young girls away from their families and incriminating them so that they could not return." He further added that "the young terrorists engaged in great promiscuity and [that] venereal diseases and illegitimate births [among them] were high."[31] By taking up the apprehension over students' sexuality that had been so prominent in 1968 and connecting sexual promiscuity to subversion and terrorism, Muricy tacitly argued that threats to both moral and political order had to be confronted. He also singled out women activists for solicitude. As the promiscuity of men was rarely seen as cause for alarm, his stated anxieties about indiscriminate sexual activity and pregnancy implicitly signaled fears of sexually vulnerable and uncontrolled young women. Most important, as Cowan details, Muricy and others like him did far more than impact national discourse through such comments, but also helped shape military policy toward young people.

In their newly empowered efforts to dismantle the student movement, military officials not only issued sweeping decrees like Decree-Law 477 but also ordered more vigilant on-the-ground observation of students' activities. This included monitoring of student voices by keeping close tabs on their classroom discussions. Undercover police and military agents disguised as students were not new to the post-AI-5 period. In earlier years students and professors had frequently complained of their presence on campus, particularly the many soldiers who monitored classroom behavior and discussions. But after AI-5, such vigilance as well as other forms of direct intervention in the universities increased. Files in DOPS literally overflow with agents' reports from this period, often on the most minor details, such as one which noted that a particular professor "refers to the Brazilian Government in an ironic manner"[32] and another warning that leftist professors leave the classroom "to drink water" when they know students want to make a prohibited political announcement.[33] Meanwhile DOPS' notes on student assemblies and meetings often include full attendance lists, suggesting their presence at these events too.

The military sought to purge faculty members deemed intellectually suspicious from the universities too. While in 1964 dozens of professors faced "involuntary retirement," a new and deeper wave of such dismissals rippled through the academic community in 1969. These forced retirements exemplify the military's hardened attitude toward dissent. For example, back in October 1965, when 15 University of Brasilia (UnB) professors faced sudden dismissal, 210 of their colleagues (totaling 90 percent of the UnB faculty) tendered their resignations in protest the next day. Almost immediately officials reinstated them all. But when, in April 1969, the minister of education and culture posted a list of 42 federal employees who faced mandatory retirement, including 3 University of São Paulo (USP) professors, the reaction was quite different. Vice Rector Hélio Lourenço de Oliveira of USP protested that, as USP was an institution run by the state of São Paulo, the professors were not federal employees and should not have been included in the purge. Two days later he received his response: officials published a new list just for USP in which they officially dismissed or retired those 3 plus 20 additional professors and Oliveira himself.[34] Similar processes took place throughout Brazilian higher education as the purges continued, some through additional Institutional Acts (No. 9 and No. 10).[35] By June several rectors voluntarily resigned, actions that many viewed as a response to the impossibility of administering universities in such a climate. Raymundo Augusto de Castro Moniz de Aragão, rector of the UFRJ, quietly accepted the resignations of two vice rectors before tendering his own, with no public explanation, in July. According to the historian James

Green, not all of those affected were suspected political threats as "the military placed [some] faculty members' names on the purge lists for reasons of internal university politics, rivalries and jealousies that had little to do with broader political issues."[36] Nonetheless the effects were the showcasing of military power within the formerly autonomous domain of the universities and the loss of large numbers of professors.

A report of the U.S. consulate in Recife demonstrates the effect of these various interventions on student life. In August 1969 it listed four types of punishments being meted out to students accused of subversion: citations, a notice that a student is suspected of subversive activity and needs to present a defense; suspensions, usually for a period of three years, as prescribed by Decree-Law No. 477; legal trials; and convictions. The last two were typically for violating the Law of National Security of 1967, a law that specified over thirty-eight crimes against national security, such as "publicly inciting subversion of the political-social order."[37] Of all the students in the state of Recife, consular officials claimed, one in ten suffered the direct effects of one of these four forms. The report also noted the existence of practices more difficult to calculate, such as the denial of scholarships, the barring of matriculation, and so forth. "The results of the attempts to neutralize student organizations, from the Government's point of view, have been gratifying," they concluded. "Pressures against the organizations, coupled with punitive actions against key student activists, have made it extremely unpopular to be a student leader."[38]

As they undertook these measures, military officials frequently justified their efforts in paternalistic terms, asserting their authority and good intentions in the language of a father addressing his children and portraying their actions as efforts to defend the Brazilian family. This was the case with the public declaration of General Muricy noted earlier in which he said that one of the causes for young people's entrance into subversive activities was parental disinterest. Indeed, the figures he gave about the number of prisoners held in custody for subversive or terrorist activities revealed a very young group: of the five hundred prisoners the army acknowledged it was holding, over half were current or recent university students and their average age was just twenty-three. Similarly, his protective tone in warning readers that young male subversives won girls away from their families through "incrimination" (that is, sex) conveyed the message that the military's actions against such men were efforts to safeguard the sexuality of the nation's young women, much like traditional notions of a father's role.[39] Most dramatically, on at least one instance the secretary of public security in São Paulo, Antônio Erasmo Dias, appealed to students' fathers and mothers when he assembled the parents of forty-seven detained students at a DOPS office in order to warn them that their children were being used as "useful innocents" by Communist forces and that their activities would have "negative consequences on the Family and the Fatherland." Explaining to the parents that his decision to address them was inspired by a sense of paternal duty to protect students and keep them from "the inglorious destiny of a shallow grave," Colonel Erasmo Dias said he needed to rest assured that "we are fulfilling our obligations as fathers, as heads of families." He invoked the disciplinary side of paternal authority, adding, "The law gives us arms to defend ourselves, and we will, for this is our obligation to Society, Family and Fatherland!"[40] Appeals to patriarchal order and authority such as these reveal how the military sought to justify, to themselves and others, what would otherwise seem to be an excessive assault on the nation's youth.

Paternalism also suggests an offering of guidance and education, and the regime's attempts to redirect students through official programs like Projeto Rondon and mandatory moral and civic education classes reveal other mechanisms by which officials sought to dismantle the student movement and transform the student body. The volunteer program Projeto Rondon was named after the early twentieth-century figure Cândido Rondon, a celebrated commissioner of telegraph lines and paternalist protector of Indians whose swashbuckling journeys into Brazil's Amazonian interior (once as host to U.S. President Theodore Roosevelt) represented the promise of both Brazilian modernity and masculine adventure. Developed with the material support of the military regime but often presented as a program that began independently, Projeto Rondon took university student volunteers to remote areas of the country during school vacations to live among the nation's most isolated and theoretically underdeveloped residents. Students were supposed to assist with medical, engineering, and other tasks while gaining hands-on experience in their areas of study, thereby furthering the regime's larger goals of national development through both the short-term services they provided (such as medical care) and the long-term benefits of the experiences and knowledge the students acquired. The program's coordinator in 1970, Lt. Col. Hermínio Affonso Friede, exemplified the paternal guidance Projeto Rondon offered when he noted in an essay that youth today were fighting for the right things—peace, an end to racism, and an end to underdevelopment—but needed guidance. Projeto Rondon intended to supply this: "With a new philosophy of support for youth, Projeto Rondon takes on its perfect form through the active, conscious participation of youth, responding to its pleas and anxieties, and giving youth today the responsibility for seeking solutions to national problems, so that in the near future young people can offer their professional contribution to the well-being and development of the Brazilian Nation."[41] In addition to redirecting youthful energies away from urban protest into the seemingly safer venues of rural volunteer work and realigning them to be in accord with the regime's developmentalist agenda, other officials stressed that the Rondon experience would forge true leaders out of this generation. Minister of the Interior Rangel Reis argued that Projeto Rondon succeeded in "forming a young leadership with a background in national reality."[42] Those who took part in the project, he explained, "become immunized against any kind of contestation since those who protest are a minority who have not yet opened their eyes to the responsibilities they will have in the future."[43] Official program literature stressed this idea by repeatedly pointing out that firsthand experience of the hardships and deprivations of the interior would irrevocably instill in students a sense of their responsibility for the nation's future. Through physical challenges, direct experience and knowledge, and a sense of military esprit d'corps, Projeto Rondon would form vigorous young people able and aware of their responsibility to lead the nation.

At the same time, Projeto Rondon represented a gendered model of appropriate leadership, forged through physical confrontation with the wilderness, cultivated via paternalistic relationships with its residents and symbolically represented in the Rondon name and in the literal and mythological location of the frontier. Its early participants were all men, and the oft-referenced stories of the first group's trips into the interior emphasized the bravery and dedication of these early pioneers, as they were called. Even though women students soon joined too, for the first several years official and media coverage reproduced decidedly masculine narratives of physical adventure and predominantly highlighted male participants. By the early to mid-1970s, however, as officials recognized that education, a field dominated by women, needed to be a crucial part of the developmentalist aims of Projeto Rondon, references to women participants began to grow. Reflecting and perhaps also creating reality, these women were typically portrayed in classrooms, with children and families, teaching hygiene, literacy, and domestic skills. In the nineteen years Projeto Rondon operated (between 1967 and 1985), some 350,000 students took part in one form or another, while official and media coverage of the program broadcast its messages of appropriate youthful leadership much more widely.

In a similar example of the regime's efforts to reeducate students, in September 1969 the government issued another Decree Law, this one establishing mandatory moral and civic education classes for students at all levels, from elementary school through postgraduate training.[44] The classes were designed to teach students both their "rights and duties as Brazilians" and to help them cultivate values such as "obedience to the Law."[45] As Benjamin Cowan has argued, beyond these aims the program's architects and champions viewed moral and civil education "as a direct response to the perceived sexual and moral subversion of the nation's youth" and an explicit "weapon to be deployed against the ever-vilified *guerra revolucionária*."[46] Indeed, the text of the law suggests the inextricable mix of gendered and political goals it held out for students' transformation. It aimed to encourage the "veneration of the Fatherland [*culto á Patria*], its symbols, traditions and institutions" as well as to help students improve their characters, in part by focusing on "dedication to family."[47] Succeeding president Gen. Emílio Garrastazu Médici, would later echo the importance of family to moral and civic education requirements when he explained, "We are always paying special attention to the family and to the moral and civic molding of the Brazilian man."[48] While the impact these classes had on students is impossible to calculate, the regime-mandated focus on family, fatherland, and obedience can be seen as evidence of the ways in which gendered and political goals for students' redirection went hand in hand.

When official programs seemed too heavy-handed, security officials tried to appeal to students by inventing fake student organizations and posting their pamphlets around campuses. Officers of DOPS sent multiple copies of one such flyer to numerous school directors in 1971, asking them to distribute them "with all due discretion" in highly frequented areas in the hope that "this information will help develop and activate a process of subversive counter-propaganda." In this case, the faux organization, Movimento Revoluciónario de Participação, adopted a youthful tone by employing slang like "Oh man!" (*Ora bolas!*) as it mocked an upcoming demonstration "by our classmates" against "possible repression that exists in our Country," thereby attempting to cast into doubt the existence of such repression.[49] Beyond this, the flyer offered an alternative political view to its presumed student readers, proposing that class-based critiques of the bourgeoisie were outdated and hypocritical, as students were themselves destined to become bourgeois. The planting of fake flyers like this one was not aimed simply at preventing specific demonstrations like the one referred to above, but also at influencing and redirecting students' thinking more broadly.

Undergirding the regime's attempts to persuade, redirect, or reeducate students lay a corollary to paternalism: the regime's power to punish wayward youth (and others), especially through its heightened use of physical repression. In addition to the violent ways in which, since the previous years, the police had already begun to break up student gatherings, after AI-5 the severe torture of detained activists became an increasingly common practice. In one early instance, reported by the U.S. embassy in Rio as coming from "a reliable contact," DOPS officers invaded the UFRJ Chemistry Department on June 4, 1969, seeking von der Weid, UNE's president. When they could not locate him, they instead apprehended the president of the school's Diretório Acadêmico, a student named Walmir Andrade de Oliveira.[50] Calling themselves a death squad, the agents tried to pressure Andrade de Oliveira into revealing the UNE president's whereabouts. They took him aboard a boat and interrogated him in the middle Guanabara Bay, the picturesque body of water that surrounds several of Rio's famous beaches. There, according to the U.S. report, "[The] captors proceeded to peel his thumb with [a] razor blade 'like a banana.' They then stuffed his mouth with sand, taped it over, and threw him into [the] bay during the night."[51] Andrade de Oliveira nonetheless swam to shore and sought medical treatment at a local hospital, whence his story quickly spread among students and professors. Indeed, that may have been the underlying purpose of the agents' treatment of him—a dramatic example for others of the danger in protecting figures like von der Weid and in heading the DA.[52] Von der Weid's visits to the campus often provoked near terror in his fellow students, in all likelihood because of stories like that of Andrade de Oliveira.

If this incident highlights security agents' attempts to send a dramatic message to Brazilian students, it also points to the military regime's concern for its international image and to its desire to present itself as having resolved the problem of student protest that had so dominated the national and international news in 1968. The fact that DOPS officers threatened and tortured Andrade de Oliveira shortly before Gov. Nelson Rockefeller of

New York visited Brazil is no coincidence. Appointed by U.S. President Richard Nixon to lead a "listening trip" to various countries of Latin America, Rockefeller planned to spend three days in Brazil in mid-June 1969. In 1968 the arrival of such a symbol of U.S.American influence would inevitably have provoked large student demonstrations around the country, and, in fact, throughout other areas of Latin America students vehemently protested his tour. Yet Brazilian officials, eager to showcase the social and political order established by AI-5, sought to prevent any public demonstrations while Rockefeller was in the country. In the weeks leading up to his arrival, the students who planned to protest the visit emphasized the governor's alleged financing of biological warfare agents used in Vietnam, distributed leaflets calling on students to assemble in particular areas, and labeled his tour "a symbol of capitalist exploitation."[53] But in anticipation of Rockefeller's arrival, the Costa e Silva government arrested hundreds of alleged subversives and issued strict press rules mandating that it only divulge positive news about the trip.[54] The fact that Rockefeller's visit to Brazil was the last stop on his tour and that observers had scrutinized the student protests elsewhere in Latin America and had wondered aloud if there would be similar disturbances in Brazil probably gave military officials an extra incentive to prevent such a scene.

Also hoping for a smooth visit, U.S. embassy officials in Rio nevertheless expressed shock at the new nadir in student–government relations that the visit revealed. In its report on the Andrade de Oliveira incident, the embassy downplayed the risk student protests posed to Rockefeller and criticized the military tactics, stating, "Security authorities appear to have held a seriously exaggerated concept of the possibility of student demonstrations posing [a] real security threat to Rockefeller. In recent weeks they have demonstrated inability or unwillingness to differentiate between terrorists and outspoken student opponents."[55] U.S. officials may also have been dismayed that the police response in the Andrade de Oliveira case impaired their efforts to arrange a meeting between Rockefeller and students in Rio. James Green has shown that the embassy did arrange a meeting between the governor and seven students, possibly, he explains, "as a diplomatic signal from the Nixon administration to register its dissatisfaction with some of the military government's policies" or "as an attempt [by the Rockefeller staff] to reframe the images emanating from the Latin American trips since they had been getting bad press at home." Yet these seven students, he notes, "emphasized to Rockefeller and to the press that they were not student leaders," as that group was in jail or in hiding.[56] Indeed, the report on the Andrade de Oliveira incident demonstrates that the embassy eagerly wanted student leaders to attend, for they bemoaned the fact that, owing to this case and students' sense that it was linked to the upcoming visit, "the chances of student leaders meeting for dialogue with Rockefeller or advisors have sharply decreased. Even close friends among student leaders who had previously agreed [are] now refusing to partici- pate under any circumstances."[57] A few days later embassy officials re- peated their belief that the chances of any serious threat to security during the Rockefeller visit were few, noting, "In Rio there is no—repeat—no evidence of [a] direct working relationship between terrorists and [the] leadership of [the] student movement." They asserted further that "police and military intelligence services have so penetrated [the] student sector that it [seems] difficult [to] imagine how even several hundred could as- semble without [the] authorities receiving advance notice." In their view, student plans to protest had little to do with any "intensity of feeling against [the] mission or personal hostility toward the governor" and everything to do with a "long-awaited chance to renew open defiance" of the government of Brazil and to resume their "ancient struggle against [the] 'dictator- ship.'"[58] In other words, embassy officials may have originally believed they could temper student protests via a meeting with Rockefeller, but they were essentially precluded from doing so by the overreactions of the state security forces. In any case, the U.S. diplomats recognized that the police had effectively eliminated students' ability to carry out large protests.

When Rockefeller arrived, the police heavily patrolled the areas sur- rounding the governor's meeting places, quickly and violently disrupting the few attempted student gatherings. The small pockets of lightning demonstrations that students managed to assemble served only to empha- size the extent to which the multipronged efforts of the regime had effec- tively destroyed the possibility of 1968-style mass protests.

While stories of abuse like that of Andrade de Oliveira rightfully rippled through student and U.S. diplomatic circles, this was just one example of what began taking place covertly on a much wider scale. Other pernicious cases of state repression, including the continuing and extensive use of torture, increased dramatically in 1969 and the 1970s. As we have seen, the regime employed torture against its opponents during its first two years in power, reducing such use after news of the practice came to light, only to resume and possibly intensify such efforts in 1968. After AI-5, however, pervasive, severe, and institutionalized torture, though officially and repeatedly denied and even condemned, became the central weapon in the regime's assault on it opponents, real and perceived. The number of cases in which defendants in military courts proclaimed to have been tortured gives a sense of this increase, even if the figures are by no means all-inclusive in that they leave out the many cases of victims who did not report being tortured to military courts or never even saw a military court. In the nearly four years from April 1964 through December 1968 there were 308 cases in which defendants attested to having been tortured. But in the two years 1969 and 1970 there were 1,027 and 1,206, respectively.[59] And the numbers remained high, with some fluctuation, throughout the rest of the decade of the seventies. Behind this growth lay the rise of new, additional security agencies and institutions that carried out this turn in strategy, most notably Operação Bandeirantes (OBAN, Operation Bandeirantes), a São Paulo–based organization and physical site headed by army officers and formed by presidential decree in July 1969. Funded by national and international businesses such as Ultragás and the Ford Motor Company (who supported OBAN's appeals to help in the "fight against subversion"), OBAN required all police agencies to share intelligence with it, and then "acted" on this information (in the euphemistic language employed at the time) through torture carried out in the OBAN center.[60] The army built additional repressive apparatuses in 1970 known by the acronym DOI-CODI for Destacamento de Operações de Informações–Centros de Operações de Defesa Interna (Information Operations Detachment–Internal Defense Operations Centers).[61] For the regime, this turn to state-sponsored terrorism appeared to be brutally effective in the short term, leading to the eventual decimation of various opposition groups. In the long term the effect on the reputation and authority of the military as a whole, to say nothing of the fissures it wrought on the nation more generally, was profoundly damaging.

Although the central targets of this new repressive infrastructure were purportedly the clandestine lefts, the consequences for students extended well beyond those with direct participation in these groups. It is the nature of state terrorism that, while the ultimate goal is to eradicate real or perceived threats to the regime in power, the mechanisms for doing so involve subjecting a great many more people to suspicion and abuse.[62] To the extent that Brazilian officials linked the aboveground student movement to the clandestine and armed lefts, both affiliated and unaffiliated students became especially threatened with and subject to barbarous treatment and potential death. The state security forces' turn to systematic torture must therefore be understood as one of the means by which they tried to dismantle the aboveground student movement.

One of the consequences of the increased state repression was that it led to some of the most well-known public acts by clandestine leftist groups to save their imprisoned colleagues from torture and possible death. And as the first and most publicized of these cases involved several well-known figures from the student protests of 1968, the event quite possibly confirmed security agents' fears of a link between the mass protests of 1968 and the armed actions to follow. The event occurred when members of the Ação Libertadora Nacional (ALN, National Liberating Action) and the former student-led Dissidência of Rio, now transformed into an armed movement called the Movimento Revolucionário 8 de Outubro, (MR-8, so named after the day of Che Guevara's assassination), kidnapped the U.S. ambassador to Brazil, Charles Elbrick, on September 4, 1969. The militants stopped the ambassador's car as he was being driven to work, pushed aside the driver, and spirited Elbrick away to an apartment rented for the occasion.[63] They then released a note to the military government giving it forty-eight hours to broadcast via radio, television, and major newspapers a prepared statement explaining their actions and to release fifteen prisoners of their choosing. Part of the statement read, "These are fifteen revolutionaries among the thousands who suffer torture in the prison-barracks throughout the country . . . leaders in the fight against the dictatorship. Each one of them is worth one hundred ambassadors, from the perspective of the people." The list included the three university student leaders held since the Ibiúna congress—Palmeira, Travassos, and Dirceu—as well as a former student activist who had recently joined the armed struggle, Maria Augusta Ribeiro, also held since Ibiúna and the only woman in the group.[64] While most of those chosen had deep ties to MR-8 or the ALN by this point, their age and recent student status confirmed for security agents the particular threat presented by students. More important, their prominence in the mass protests of 1968 helped cement the regime's link between these events and the armed actions of 1969 and beyond.

The coincidental arrest of von der Weid on the eve of Elbrick's kidnapping is an example of security agents' quick linkage of the UNE president to those involved in the ambassador's abduction. As noted above, several former student movement figures were included on the list of fifteen pris-

oners to be exchanged, but von der Weid was not. His captors assumed
that this omission might be emotionally difficult for him and taunted him
with the news, bringing in newspaper clippings to show him the list and
claiming that his friends had betrayed him. As von der Weid describes it,
the guards' insults did hit home, if inadvertently. For while the vast majority of people on the list had joined the armed struggle and had some
connection to the ALN or MR-8, one, the former UNE president and AP
member Travassos, did not. As von der Weid recalled, he thought to himself, "Man, if they hadn't released Travassos I would say it was just a
guerrilla thing, and we're not part of that, so fine, we're left out. But if they
released Travassos, then why not me?"[65] As he learned later when one of
the ALN members involved in the event was arrested and joined him in
prison, they simply hadn't known he was imprisoned. His arrest coincided
so closely with the ambassador's kidnapping that those who orchestrated
the prisoner exchange did not know about his detention.

The regime's hardened approach was strengthened when, shortly before the group of fifteen exchanged prisoners boarded a plane to Mexico
and the ambassador was safely released, the government issued two more
Institutional Acts, Nos. 13 and 14. The first granted the government the
power to permanently banish from the country anyone it chose, beginning
with the exchanged prisoners. The second legalized the death penalty in
Brazil. In a weighty symbolic precedent, the first person condemned to die
would be a student, nineteen-year-old Teodomiro Romeiro dos Santos,
convicted of killing an air force sergeant.[66]

While the enactment of AI-5 signified a shift in the power balance
within the military regime toward the hard-line faction, events like the
Elbrick kidnapping and prisoner exchange further legitimated their position within the military. Hard-liners gained an even stronger hand within
the regime when the former national intelligence director Gen. Médici, a
figure with deep ties to the state security forces, replaced a gravely ill
President Costa e Silva in October 1969. Though originally hidden from the
public, in August 1969 Costa e Silva had suffered a stroke that left him
unable to speak and partially paralyzed on his right side. The steps taken
to replace him demonstrate the extent to which hard-liners had become
powerful within the regime, as they were able to orchestrate this substitution notwithstanding a constitutional line of succession that precluded it.
Rather than allow Vice President Pedro Aleixo to assume office in his place,
the high command of the armed forces issued AI-12, temporarily replac-

ing the office of president with a military junta. Throughout September and much of October the junta maintained this position as officials monitored Costa e Silva's condition and engaged in heated internal discussions of possible substitutes. Once it became clear that Costa e Silva could not return, they settled on Médici and again turned to the power of an Institutional Act (No. 16) to authorize the succession for a new term until March 1974 (AI-15, issued by the junta a month earlier, had changed the date of certain municipal elections). On the same day the junta also issued what would become the military regime's last Institutional Act (No. 17), mandating that members of the armed forces who threatened internal cohesion would be moved to the reserves, thereby assuring an end to internal disagreements over the choice of Médici.

With a Médici administration in power and in the wake of the Elbrick kidnapping, the offensive against the regime's opponents intensified even more. Within weeks of Médici's assumption of office the torture of imprisoned activists had produced enough information that agents were able to set a trap for the ALN leader, Carlos Marighella. On November 4, 1969, security forces ambushed and killed him in São Paulo, documenting their success with gory photographs of his bloodied corpse in newspapers the next day, a visual warning to other potential opponents. Other clandestine organizations soon felt the effects of this turn as well, facing increasingly severe repression. In response to this general situation, several groups from the armed lefts borrowed from the Elbrick model, attempting to save their imprisoned comrades and their struggling organizations by eventually kidnapping the Japanese consul, the West German ambassador, and the Swiss ambassador in 1970 and exchanging them for ever-larger numbers of prisoners (including von der Weid in January 1971). By the end of that year all of the leftist organizations that had turned to armed struggle and that counted on one hundred or more members had been destroyed, with the exception of the PCdoB.[67] Smaller groups continued to mobilize throughout the first years of the decade while sectors of the PCdoB struggled to establish a rural guerrilla stronghold in the Amazonian region of Araguaia, but the regime's repressive wave had taken a decided toll on the clandestine lefts.

Yet even during these years when the gap between those who participated in the clandestine armed lefts and those in the student population at large widened cavernously, DOPS officers continued to worry about possible connections between student protests and armed struggle. Indeed, agents' memories of 1968 as a dangerous point of origin for the radicalization of the lefts became a steady frame of reference in their current efforts. Signs of this appear in the sworn statements of detained students and former students collected by DOPS officers. By the early 1970s these statements had adopted a decidedly formulaic narrative that repeatedly linked participation in the mass protests of 1968 to armed struggle. Such declarations represent officers' reports of information extracted (usually under torture and intimidation) from prisoners. While the reports are often signed by the student in question, they are most appropriately seen as a combination of the officials' overarching interpretative structure supplemented by personal details about the detainee furnished under pressure. Typed on official letterhead and written in the third person, they consistently describe very similar chains of events for each individual: beginning student movement activities at some point in the mid- to late-1960s; participation in the demonstrations of 1968 (often including a list of each major protest event attended); gradual familiarity with student leaders (again, including specific names); and, finally, the moment of conversion to armed struggle, including the name of the student leader who had facilitated it. One of the more succinct statements, from March 1970, reads, "In 1968 she participated in marches, however indecisively, as she clarifies that she did not have direct participation in said movements, that she only participated in the mass movements; that in April 1969 she decided to radicalize her position, having talked about this with Franklin Martins [a student leader in 1968]; that he offered the deponent various options within the Organization."[68] The names and dates vary from one report to the next, but the general arc of progressive radicalization—one that includes participation in the marches of 1968 or personal connection with a recognized figure from 1968 or both—remains virtually identical. This abundance of nearly indistinguishable narratives reflects DOPS officials' conviction that both the demonstrations and student leaders of 1968 had lured innocent young people into joining the clandestine armed lefts. In the case above, as in others like it, the officers did not ask the testifier why she decided to "radicalize her position" or to explain what constellation of intellectual, personal, or contextual factors led her to do so. Instead the implicit assumption in this and other interviews was that exposure to key events or figures from 1968 led seamlessly into political participation with the armed lefts. These numerous reports reveal that that DOPS agents believed student movement activities that in any way resembled those of

1968 needed to be prevented, as they constituted a slippery slope to armed struggle.

The long shadow of 1968 also touched the many students who were not suspected of joining the armed struggle but who were guilty merely of being part of one of the remaining aboveground student organizations. Officers of DOPS monitored anyone who was involved in such activities but paid particularly close attention to those who had taken part in the mass student demonstrations of 1968. The pervasive fear of a return to 1968 helps explain the following sensational police descriptions of a few graduate students who came under investigation by undercover officers in September 1970: "José Carvalho de Noronha—ex-president of the Carlos Chagas Diretório Acadêmico, intelligent, sure of himself, a declared leftist, he is commanding those who seek to reorganize the ex-student movement in their faculty . . . João Machado de Souza—an opportunist and adventurer, qualities which won him election to the directorate of his Centro Acadêmico . . . Nelson Remy Gillet—a fifth-year student, capable of uncommon argumentative powers. They say he's been prepared by the Communist Party to entice new converts, something he has been achieving with his customary ability."[69] As former participants in the student demonstrations of 1968, these young people provoked alarm by their renewed presence on university campus as doctoral candidates. Even taking into account the fact that this group of graduate students very well might have had connections to or sympathies with the clandestine lefts, the spy reports about them reveal a nearly irrational angst on the part of the investigators. They read more like pulp fiction than bureaucratic paperwork, offering no actual evidence of any clandestine affiliation yet still harboring a sense of intrigue and danger absent from most other DOPS reports. The same might be said of the army's analysis of a student newspaper in 1971. Entitled simply "Students' Newspaper" (*Jornal dos Estudantes*) rather than one of the more provocative titles other student groups used, the publication proffers some typical student complaints, specifically about the poor food and high prices in the university cafeteria. Army officers combed through this minor newspaper carefully, presenting in a five-page report their conclusion that the paper was actually designed to "fill students with a feeling of revolt." More alarming, they noted, "the editors are using [the newspaper] to create agitation within student sectors, complaining about restaurants and the price of food (a tactic similar to the sad episodes that took place in 1968) and supporting a boycott of the cafeteria food."[70] That those who complained about bad cafeteria food and a handful of graduate students who had once participated in the 1968 protests appeared so potentially threatening in this new era—notwithstanding the lack of evidence that they actually had any impact on others—is understandable only if one recognizes the way security agents remembered 1968 as a period of anti-regime chaos that quickly grew out of their control.

At times police concern with a repeat of 1968 bordered on the absurd. Such was the case in a mysterious episode of November 1973 when a group of around eighty students paraded through downtown Rio de Janeiro behind a banner proclaiming, "We Want a Love Song" (Queremos Canto do Amor) (figure 4.1). For about an hour and a half they marched through the major streets of the city "without any apparent motive" (according to the police) singing a "disfigured" version of a song called "The Marvelous City" (a reference to Rio): "Brasil vai para a puta que o pariu / Cidade Maravilhosa lata de lixo do meu Brasil / Arauta Arauta o Brasil é filho de puta"[71] (Brazil, go back to the whore who birthed you / Marvelous City, can of garbage of my Brazil / Glitch, glitch, Brazil is a son of a bitch). A DOPS officer dutifully photographed and reported on the students' brief promenade, noting that they appeared to be between sixteen and nineteen years old, but that their educational institutions were impossible to identify as the marchers "dressed in plain clothes" (trajavam-se à paisana). Presumably the mufti notation referred to the fact that, despite being in their late teens, the group did not wear the school uniforms that were de rigueur for all high school students at that time, public or private. Yet the reporting officer's choice of the expression à paisana, with its implicit covert military implication, rather than the much more common phrase ropa de dia a dia (everyday clothes), hints at the sinister quality he perceived in this situation. And despite the infantile lyrics of the students' song, the reporting agent claimed the event was orchestrated by older, "nonstudent elements" who supposedly directed things from a distance. Lest anyone miss the potential threat of this "love song protest," the police author concluded with the following warning: "In communicating such information this command alerts you that, in the beginning of '68, the student demonstrations also began this way, turning into a true urban guerrilla experience, planned and practiced by the leftist organizations that have done so much harm to the daily life of this city."[72] By invoking memories of 1968 the report offers a glimpse of the constant reference and looming specter that year continued to provide security officers as they surveyed student activities.

FIGURE 4.1. Students demonstrate in 1973, proclaiming, "We want a love song."
Arquivo Público do Estado de Rio de Janeiro

In short, by the time AI-5 was declared, military officials had come to see the mass protests of 1968 as a subversive tool designed to lead good students astray and hence the aboveground student movement as inextricably connected to the clandestine armed lefts. Throughout 1969 and the early 1970s security forces used the new and extensive powers granted by AI-5 to prevent a repeat of 1968, trying to shut down all student politicking via new restrictive measures and extensive, institutionalized violence, including torture. As they did so, they cast themselves as paternalistic guardians of social order, offering protection and administering punishment as necessary. In the process they paid special attention to anything that resembled 1968, and agents' notes on student activities reveal their powerful recollections of that year as a dangerous precipice to which Brazil had come threateningly close as well as their view that even relatively limited political organizing by students constituted a subversive act. The lingering symbolic power of '68 colored security agents' interpretations and reports and served to justify their assault on even the most benign student activities.

Sad Marches

A passage from Fernando Gabeira's memoir, although written years later, echoes contemporary understandings of the immediate post-AI-5 period: "Dear Mother: after you and the others from the Popular Commission abandoned us (or were you abandoned by us?) things started getting worse and worse. We didn't notice. We thought everything was so normal. The [military] men prospered because the war required it; people disappeared because there was a purification going on. Advocating violence became the magical word of the day. And it marked from then on our short, sad and sometimes bloody marches."[73] Despite the hindsight clarity with which AI-5 is today considered a stark turning point, the transition from the radio declaration of the act to the ensuing years of lead actually proved to be more gradual. Students had high expectations for 1969, and, notwithstanding some well-founded trepidation, many initially did not allow the threatening new political situation to prevent them from carrying on with their organizing activities. Despite early and deeply troubling political maneuvers such as the closing and purging of Congress, the reduction of the Supreme Court, and the suspension of upcoming elections, at first, as Gabeira notes, daily life for many appeared to be "so normal."

Two months after the announcement of AI-5 and shortly before the declaration of Decree-Law No. 477 a U.S. embassy official spoke with Milton Castro, a law student active in the student movement. The young man described his colleagues as more cautious about the risks of physical repression but just as determined—if not more so—to continue their efforts. "Almost all students are deeply upset by the Fifth Institutional Act and are now even more resentful of the military's intrusion into the nation's political life," the ensuing report declared. While Castro admitted that students were afraid of being beaten and were increasingly told by their parents to "stay out of trouble," he also revealed that the authoritarianism of AI-5 had made them angry. His comments formed the basis of the following embassy analysis: "[For students,] there is a necessity to keep the student movement alive and to demonstrate that repression will not silence all of the military's critics. Students in Brazil feel a deep responsibility to act as the political conscience of the nation. Not only are they better educated than other groups in society, but they are more free from the social and economic constraints which inhibit other groups from political expression."[74] Despite possible foreboding about the act, in early 1969 students continued to believe and to argue that as the privileged and educated children of the elite they not only had a responsibility to take political action, but also would enjoy some protection because of their status.

Consistent with this perspective, for the first several months of 1969 some student activists continued to organize and to employ many of the same tactics they had used earlier. In Rio de Janeiro, for example, where both the aboveground student movement and the clandestine lefts had been especially influential in 1968, student activists there were reluctant to revise their approach. The students in UME published magazines with provocative titles such as *Resistência* and *Combate* and debated promoting "mass actions" and "struggles for faculty autonomy," campaigns that closely resembled those of the year before.[75] Other groups, such as the DA of the UFRJ engineering school, vehemently protested when the rector shut down the student organization's office, distributing pamphlets and flyers around campus that said the military regime was behind the rector's action and that promised to initiate "a Week of Protest against the Dictatorship."[76] Not entirely unlike the year before, the police proved quick to intervene, though with a seemingly heavier complement of troops. When the engineering students began a demonstration in April 1969 in response to rising food prices, for example, five truckloads of state military police invaded the campus and arrested thirty-four participants.[77] Perhaps to avoid such a response, students at the Pontifical Catholic University of Rio de Janeiro (PUC-RIO) who wanted to protest the threatened expulsion of three of their colleagues held a silent one-day strike (students simply stayed away from the campus but did not picket or distribute flyers), and 90 percent of the study body participated.[78] Other groups also continued to challenge the boundaries of tolerable student protest, organizing several brief public assemblies in downtown areas one May afternoon. Of these events the U.S. embassy observed, "Except for [a] relatively small number of pamphleteering operations, this is [the] first time Rio students have taken to streets since [AI-5]."[79] On the surface, at least, student activities in 1969 initially appeared diminished from their heights of the year before but were not altogether different.

As the U.S. embassy comments suggest, however, the situation students faced was not entirely the same, despite their efforts. Although UNE members managed to reconvene their disrupted annual congress in order to carry out the unfinished elections, they did so in much reduced form. Rather than hosting one large gathering at which students could discuss issues and vote en masse, they instead held a series of regional meetings primarily to elect a new directorate. These meetings dragged on between November 1968 and March 1969.[80] By the time the election was finalized at an assembly of about one hundred people—with a victory for the AP-led slate of candidates that included von der Weid as president and nine others as vice presidents—the lack of open discussions had weakened the organization.[81] Moreover, the new leadership was unable to ameliorate this deficit later or to foster a real presence before other students. As Rosa Maria Feiteiro Cavalari has shown, for any member of the UNE directorate to even turn up at a student event was a security ordeal: "Unexpected appearances of the UNE leadership at certain schools were common then, as was their participation at specific events without informing the leaders of the host organization. It was an attempt to prove that UNE still existed and was still active, despite the increased repression. However, this did little to contribute to organizing students."[82] Von der Weid recalls these appearances as "almost provoking terror," as the visited students worried about the police repression that might follow such an appearance.[83] In the months after the election, the union lost several of its vice presidents: "The UNE directorate quickly lost two or three. . . . Imprisoned here or there, some simply stopped being part of it. The situation was becoming so overbearing that people dropped out."[84] Those AP members who saw their maintenance of the UNE leadership as a potentially important political asset worked hard to safeguard the victory embodied in the election of the president and tried to maintain the prestige and permanence of the student union in the new year. Nonetheless, UNE was weakening. Von der Weid described UNE as being "semi-clandestine" before AI-5 but "really clandestine" after it.[85] Yet UNE's legitimacy always centered around its position as an aboveground organization. Founded specifically to represent all university students, UNE's public visibility—whether through the symbolic weight of a grand headquarters building or through its centrality in leading public demonstrations—was critical to its authority. For the leadership to have to operate under such limited conditions, from its circumscribed election to its ability to coordinate with other student organizations, signified a major diminishment of the student union's potency. Well before von der Weid's arrest, a "really clandestine" UNE was almost no UNE at all.

If the implications of AI-5 were not immediately obvious to students who saw 1969 as the future of their movement, within a few months the transformations wrought on student politics became impossible to ignore. Through the strict prosecution of student activists via existing laws, the legislation of new forms of oppressive controls, increased state intervention in university affairs, and intense physical repression, within a few months military officials had managed to impair student political activities to such a degree that violence as "the word of the day," as Gabeira called it, became more and more of a reality.

These changes meant that the possibilities for student political organizing, closed off in the months after AI-5, became even more constrained in late 1969 and the early 1970s. The remaining aboveground student organizations endured interventions and severe limitations, and their connections to the increasingly beleaguered clandestine lefts became more limited. The sociologist Marcelo Ridenti says that many of the clandestine lefts themselves dedicated less attention to the universities, some because they abandoned the idea of a mass movement as a path to revolution and others because AI-5 simply "left no room for organizing within schools, neither for leaders nor for the 'advanced masses' [the leaders' most politicized supporters]."[86] Even when they tried to maintain a presence in certain universities, the effort proved to be more and more difficult. Ricardo Salles, a member of a clandestine organization when he took the vestibular in 1971, remembers that he was admitted to two Rio de Janeiro institutions, the Federal Fluminense University (UFF) and PUC-RJ, and chose the latter because of the greater possibility of political organizing there. Salles said, "In PUC [in the early 1970s] there was still an incipient student movement. There were DAs that were still open; these diretórios were occupied by the left. In truth, then you still had people who participated in the diretórios from the Brazilian Communist Party, from the Communist Party of Brazil, people from Ação Popular who hadn't yet been hit by the repression, and a few independent people, those who didn't belong to any group."[87] Nevertheless, even this lingering presence proved difficult to maintain. Salles's own clandestine organization came under DOPS scrutiny, and he and the other members were imprisoned in early 1972. Following his release a month later and a court trial in 1973, he shied away from further political activity on campus for several years, profoundly marked by his prison experiences. Nonetheless the diretórios at PUC continued to function. Geraldo Siqueira Filho had similar experiences at the Universidade de São Paulo (USP), where he also enrolled in 1971, hoping to organize new members for a Trotskyist organization. The university "was pretty much a devastated land," he recalled, "with many people who had gone underground, many who were in prison or in exile. . . . I had had no idea it was so bad."[88] In other universities the aboveground organizations met with even more severe restraints. At UFF, the school Salles chose not to attend, the diretórios also remained opened. But in 1973 over fifty UFF students, including the president of the DCE, were arrested. After much debate about what to do, their colleagues wrote a letter to the university rector asking for his support in gaining their release. Instead of helping them, he called the letter disrespectful and meted out strict punishments to its signatories. He also suspended the DCE and five other participating organizations for three months, closed their snack bar and movie house, took over their student housing office, and established a committee to determine whether or not they had misused funds.[89] At USP, according to Siqueira, the DCE itself held secret meetings in 1971, as if it were one of the clandestine organizations of the lefts. It too eventually folded when all of its leaders were imprisoned.[90]

Meanwhile this period gave rise to an economic and cultural climate that both directly and indirectly discouraged political dissidence. The early 1970s coincided with an economic boom that became known as the Brazilian economic miracle. Increased foreign lending led to spectacular levels of economic growth, much of it enhancing the consumptive power of the middle classes. Trumpeting this, the Médici administration embarked on a colorful public relations campaign that celebrated its successes and maligned its critics. Slogans such as "Brazil, Love It or Leave It" (Brasil: Ame-o ou Deixe-o) and "Go Forward, Brazil!" (Pra Frente Brasil!) soon appeared on posters and car bumpers across the country. When, in June 1970, the Brazilian national soccer team won the World Cup for the third time, the first country in the world to do so, the government carefully involved the team's stars, especially Pelé, in its campaign. At the same time, the government encouraged a large expansion of the university system, including huge growth in private universities. This opened up educational possibilities for women students and working-class students. Between 1969 and 1975 men's enrollment doubled and women's quintupled.[91] For many of these new students, who were often the first in their families to enter university, their and their families' prospects seemed to depend on academic success, and they were therefore less likely to risk involvement in wider political struggles.

In this context, von der Weid's arrest signified a devastating turning point for the aboveground student movement, as it led to the implicit and then explicit collapse of UNE. For if UNE was already, in his words, "really clandestine" before his arrest, after his arrest the union went totally underground. With von der Weid's absence, one of the remaining vice presidents and fellow AP member Honestino Guimarães assumed the UNE presidency. But by this point the student union had almost no public presence, could not convene national or even regional congresses to decide policy, and essentially existed in name only. Guimarães himself had personally gone underground shortly after the declaration of AI-5, living clandestinely to avoid arrest and of necessity discontinuing his studies at the University of Brasilia. He also joined the AP (renamed in 1971 the Ação Popular Marxista-Leninista [APML, Marxist-Leninist Popular Action]), further reducing his ability to lead an aboveground student organization. As we have seen, throughout UNE's history students asserted the union's authority by maintaining the visibility of the organization and leadership. Once the union and its leadership had to become deeply hidden UNE ceased to function as a national organization that represented students. So inoperative did UNE become that Guimarães remained its nominal president long beyond the expected end of von der Weid's term, as no more elections were held. Upon Guimarães's own abduction by security forces in 1973, no one took over the position of president. Instead, both he and UNE vanished; Guimarães never emerged from the torture centers, and his name now appears on the lists of the disappeared. The organization that students had promoted and defended since 1937 finally collapsed, as the group formerly assumed to be an incubator of the nation's political future became understood as a current threat to the nation's military leadership.

In such circumstances, some students found the slightest whiff of involvement with the aboveground student organizations frightening. When, in 1973, a law student in Vassouras, Rio de Janeiro found himself promoted as a candidate for publicity director of an aboveground student group, he went straight to the police. Explaining that he wanted "to express his incompatibility with this position in order to prevent any future misinterpretations," he declared that "he would not serve in such a position, even if he were elected."[92] For him and others like him, even the hint of affiliation with the student movement could appear risky.

Other students, however, found ways to maintain very active political lives, many of them turning to cultural forms to express their political perspectives. At times they used cultural events to advance a determined political message, such as the concert of previously censored music held in Rio in 1972. Hosted by students from PUC, they labeled the occasion a "symbolic act of protest."[93] Even when not articulated as specifically political, students often turned to the cultural arena to voice their right and need to act collectively and engage politically. Indeed the very means by which students organized cultural events implied a certain amount of political action, especially in the climate of the early 1970s, when students had to receive official permission for any kind of collective gathering outside of class. That this occurred and that the police paid strict attention to such matters are evidenced by the sheer quantity of student requests for permission to host events that fill the DOPS archives. For example, at the faculty of philosophy and social sciences of the UFRJ a full one-third of the student body (220 students) in 1970 signed a petition requesting "a time and place for the practice of artistic activities, such as film screenings and the staging of short theatrical plays." Alarmed, the DOPS officers who reported on this development wrote, "We can infer from this that a subversive-type leadership is beginning to act." They reasoned that, because the school would not be able to grant the request, the leaders obviously sought "to create a climate of dissatisfaction . . . as the first step to mounting political protest actions."[94] Although on the one hand the DOPS' panicky note reveals security agents' concern that this request for a cultural forum was really a political ruse, on the other its interpretation missed the larger issue at stake. That 220 students would sign their name to a petition symbolizes an act of political organizing in itself, one that required organization, direction, and discussion. Had they also been allowed to assemble and discuss film and theater, that too would have constituted an important space for the fostering of political awareness and group consciousness. Cultural events, although still scrutinized and at times censored by security agents, remained a potential arena for political protest, expression, and conversation, and students throughout the 1970s worked to carve out such spaces for themselves.

When actual mobilization was too dangerous, student newspapers and other publications similarly came to serve as venues for self-conscious expressions of political aspirations. Again, the very process of creating a newspaper could serve as an important form of dialogue among students. One editor expressed this idea in the first issue of a student paper, writing, "Vague or not, with possible limitations to its pretensions of communication and engagement at the student level, the most important thing was still obtained: its publication."[95] Other student newspapers voiced similar complaints, like an editorial from 1971 lamenting the fact that students were barred from discussing the topics that most affected them, such as university reforms and proposed tuition charges, and mocking the regime's gendered self-representation as exceedingly masculine. The editors wrote, "There are many people who would like you to not think, who would like you to just repeat 'everything's going well in our virile Fatherland.'"[96] Instead, they urged, students should speak out about these issues at their departmental organizations. Another university newspaper from that same year tried to persuade fellow students to reopen some of their aboveground organizations "because we know that [they] are the expression of our concerns." The police cover letter attached to this example in the DOPS files labeled the article "subliminal propaganda."[97] Presumably the desired student organizations were not allowed to reopen. Organizations that did remain operative typically found that the level of student participation dropped considerably. Such dissatisfaction with student political organizing would grow in the years following, influencing students' behavior toward the end of the 1970s. Imperfect and heavily censored, student newspapers nevertheless flourished during these dark years.[98]

The love song protest discussed earlier also offers a glimpse of aboveground student activity during the height of state repression. In this whimsical march, held despite strict prohibitions on public demonstrations, a large group of young people devised a provocative method of flouting the ban. As nothing in the newspapers or DOPS files points to any repeat performances, it is difficult to know exactly what the demonstrating students' intentions were; but it seems reasonable to suppose that beneath the seemingly playful exterior lay deliberate political implications. Although the reporting officer did not notice the reference, the phrase "We Want a Love Song" most probably alludes to Carlos Drummand de Andrade's poem "International Congress of Fear" (1940), copies of which had been distributed at a university play in nearby Niteroi a few months earlier.[99] If indeed the demonstrators were alluding to Drummand de Andrade, then their seemingly farcical protest would have disguised a profound critique of the current repression in Brazil. The poem reads as follows:

Provisionally we will not sing love,
Which has taken refuge below the subterranean.
We will sing fear, which sterilizes the embraces.

We will not sing hate because this does not exist.

Only fear exits, our father and our companion

The great fear of the backlands, the seas, the deserts,

The fear of soldiers, the fear of mothers, the fear of churches.

We will sing the fear of dictators, the fear of democrats.

We will sing the fear of death and the fear of after death.

And afterward we will die of fear

And on our tombs will grow yellow and fearful flowers.[100]

The theatrical production at which copies of this poem were passed out was called *Achtung*. That politically engaged students would have attended this play (or that an apolitical student audience might have been inspired by it) seems highly probable given the DOPS description of it. Granted, the portrayal comes from the DOPS officer sent to investigate the piece, who generically labels it very sympathetic to communists. Yet his report nevertheless reveals a daring presentation for Brazil in 1973, and one that reflects students' understanding of the practices of state terrorism then common. One of the acts, he writes, "Presents a communist being horribly tortured in order to make him 'speak.' They ask him where his leader is, what group he belongs to, what he does. The one being tortured, throughout all that they asked him, only responded with the following: 'I am a medical student!' Saying nothing more, he suffered until he died."[101] While the play's protagonist may not have actually been a communist, as security officials used that term loosely and frequently, the scene of a tortured student appears less open to exaggeration by the DOPS. Moreover, as we will see, the recent well-known death by torture of a São Paulo student closely paralleled and no doubt inspired this depiction. In short, the play is an example of how some students in the leaden years of the early 1970s used cultural forms to stage political critiques, while the love song protest suggests the possibility of a clever student follow-up to this message. The play and the love song protest also point to DOPS officials' alarm about anything that resembled 1968, notwithstanding their ignorance of the possible connections between this specific play and protest.

In addition to these indirect means of expression, some students directly protested against the expulsions, arrests and mistreatment of their colleagues, often doing so in ways designed to minimize incurring risk to themselves. For example, students commemorated their suspended or expelled classmates by placing flowers on their empty chairs in an anonymous effort to draw attention to their absence.[102] Others distributed published materials to help divulge news about imprisoned colleagues. This was especially important in the first few days of a person's abduction, as it soon became obvious that this period was the most brutal, when security forces tried to extract timely information that could be used to capture other suspects before anyone noticed the detainee's absence. Only after that period had ended might officials admit they had the person in custody. Indeed, in some cases it was never admitted. Thus as friends and colleagues realized that someone had been taken, they oftentimes tried to alert others. When six UFRJ medical school students were abducted from their homes in April 1971, for example, other students shifted into action, distributing an informative flyer throughout area hospitals listing their names and the date of their capture. According to this document, they also formed committees to go to the press, the National Council of Brazilian Bishops, the Brazilian Lawyers' Association, the Guanabara State Medical Association, the Medical Union, and the Medical and Surgery Society, all in an effort to disclose the news and seek support. In one pamphlet they wrote, "We protest . . . in order that concrete measures be taken to locate our colleagues, to break their state of incommunicability, and to determine what kind of treatment they have been receiving."[103] In another they argued that while students presently could not prevent such deplorable events from occurring, they could at least try to improve their classmates' prison conditions by spreading the word about their arrests.[104] At certain schools arrested students counted on the help of powerful allies, such as the vice rector of the PUC-RJ, a figure now remembered for having advocated fiercely on their behalf, regularly pressuring the government to admit students' detention (and thus halt or at least limit their torture).[105]

If the cases mentioned above allowed protesting students a degree of anonymity, a sampling of the more exposed methods students employed demonstrates why many chose to remain unidentified. When the demonstrators were known they put themselves at risk. For example, in late 1970 a student from the Federal University of Rio Grande do Sul died in police custody in a highly suspicious suicide. When other students requested that a Mass be held for him and wrote a letter in protest, they were charged with breaking Decree-Law No. 477 and were expelled from the university for three years.[106]

In sum, student political activity took on a very different shape in the early 1970s from what it looked like just a few years earlier. In the repressive climate wrought by a hard-line government led by President Médici, both the aboveground student organizations and the clandestine lefts suffered deep losses. Neither set of organizations was able to sustain a vigorous campaign of student political action. Yet some students still found concrete means of political expression, at times turning to cultural and other forms and at times promoting outright protest of the abuse of their colleagues.

In Mourning the Struggle Begins

In this period of unceasing investigation of and intervention in student groups, the hosting of cultural events, creation of university newspapers, and organizing around arrested and abused colleagues all offered a means of continuing political expression. Although these proceedings marked a departure from the intense student activity of 1968 that had filled headlines and mobilized thousands, a change one might expect student activists in the early 1970s to lament, students did not make frequent references to that prior epoch. Of the many student flyers and newspapers filed away by DOPS agents (or later donated to archives), very few from this period mentioned 1968 at all. When they did, it was typically by questioning how the student situation had changed and consequently what tactics a new generation of students should adopt. In other words, 1968 may have been analyzed, but it was rarely invoked with nostalgia or commemorative purpose. A pamphlet the police picked up in 1973 at the State University of Guanabara, for example, read in part as follows: "1968 will not return, that is, the objective situation today is different from that which allowed for the movements of 68. We must seek to understand this new reality, . . . to understand that our struggle is to rehabilitate the movement, not to reapply the forms of struggle of the recent past, to organically recompose the University Movement and not to make the student organizations act as in the recent past."[107] In this view, 1968 continued to be a reference for students, even if it was one of contrast. Unselfconsciously assuming students' familiarity with the subject, it labels 1968 the "recent past," one that clearly figures as part of its readers' own experiences as participants or observers. Despite the huge changes the student movement had undergone, 1968 was still a common memory and reference point for students in the early 1970s, as many current students had direct or secondary experiences with the events of that year. As they continued to organize politically through a variety of forms, the rupture with 1968 could best be understood, as this publication presents it, as one of form, not of purpose.

Students in the immediate post-AI-5 years may not have made frequent, direct references to 1968, but they did make regular, indirect ones by recalling and commemorating the death of Edson Luis. Student documents from this period make numerous references to him; pamphlets often ended with the expression "Viva Edson Luis and Down with the Dictatorship!"[108] Moreover, each year students commemorated the anniversary of his death with public demonstrations and speeches. Given the intense police scrutiny of student activities, these initial protests on March 28 were generally small affairs, often limited to anonymous postings of flyers and some brief assemblies of students. But the size and scope of the demonstrations grew over time, and, more important, the regularity and consistency of student actions to mark the date served to establish and reestablish ties across generations of students. Indeed, March 28 came to anchor a student-created vernacular calendar that they cyclically observed. On one level these commemorations represent an important example of continued political expression by students in the post-AI-5 years. On another level the regularity and continuity of these demonstrations ritualistically linked students throughout the demobilized 1970s to the earlier and far more robust responses to his death, simultaneously joining them to the mass student movements of 1968.

Within the context of increased state terrorism in the early 1970s, any marking of Edson Luis's death meant not simply defying state prohibitions against such gatherings but also a critique of the repressive state itself. Commemorations of the young man's death inherently called attention to the government's well-accepted role in his murder and, by extension, its continued, less openly acknowledged role in the current deaths of many more students. Students' commemorative efforts thereby constituted meaningful political activities. Moreover, because the date of Edson Luis's death corresponded so closely with the anniversary of the coup itself on March 31/April 1, commemorating it offered students an opportunity to connect this event to the continuation of military rule and to tie attacks on the student movement to a wider national problem. In March 1970, for example, students at UFRJ distributed flyers entitled "March 28: National Day of Struggle against Dictatorial Repression" in which they proclaimed that the country had lived through "six years of terror." Listing a series of "crimes against the Nation," they included the death of Edson Luis as one of many. The flyer also notes the specific instances of torture suffered by imprisoned student leaders such as von der Weid, as well as those of nonstudents like a mother superior from Ribeirão Preto. Nevertheless, the authors stressed that students had a distinctive responsibility to remember March 28, ending the flyer as follows: "Brazilian Students! March 28 has a special meaning for us. Second anniversary of the death of Edson Luis, assassinated by the military regime while defending the *Calabouço* restaurant, it's the National Struggle against Fascist Repression."[109] Initial commemorations of March 28 became a rich means of marking the accumulating crimes of the dictatorship as well as highlighting students' particular role as both martyrs and militants. In underscoring this date, students reinscribed themselves into an ongoing resistance struggle, at once emphasizing their moral position as victims of state terrorism and proclaiming the continuity of their movement in the face of severe restraints.

As the flyer hints, these commemorative acts served to enfold newer generations of students into a collective memory of struggle against the dictatorship. As groups of student activists continued to organize small protests and other acts of resistance, they called on the symbolism of Edson Luis to forge ties between classmates who may have recently entered the university with events that preceded them. In doing so, they stressed the naturalness of the connection, attempting to ease the seeming gap between the generation of 1968 and their own and to emphasize instead a continuity between the two periods. Three years after Edson Luis's death student activists at the philosophy faculty of the UFRJ circulated a detailed flyer that began by calling attention to a recent increase in undercover agents on campus. The authors then posed a rhetorical question, asking why there would be such vigilance during an apparently tranquil moment. "Why is the Dictatorship so scared?" they queried. Proceeding to give a detailed response, they simultaneously asserted that their readers already instinctively knew the answer: "Because this period is marked by three important dates. Dates that don't go unnoticed by us or by anyone." To explain these dates the authors repeated the tactic of assuming a shared understanding even as they were simultaneously educating their readers: "The first of these is March 28, Day of student protest and of struggle against the Bourgeois University. Why? Everyone remembers. That was when Edson Luis died, assassinated by the Dictatorship that tried to prohibit our struggles and our protest. . . . The second is April 1, which the gorillas continue trying to commemorate on the 31st of March. . . . The third is May 1 [International Day of the Worker]." They concluded the pamphlet by reminding their readers of the importance of commemorating these dates, especially that of the death of Edson Luis: "We learned much from our past losses. This is why we knew to commemorate March 28 on the same date. . . . [And the government] knows that students won't let these dates pass by [without doing something]."[110] The reference to the International Day of the Worker suggests that the pamphlet may have been issued by student members of the clandestine lefts, some of which, as we have seen, continued to try to organize at certain universities. Edson Luis made a particularly good subject for such an appeal, as he himself had not been a member of the clandestine lefts and thus any organization could legitimately invoke him without giving away its identity. Yet no matter who issued them, the collective effect of commemorative pamphlets such as this one was that they offered a symbolically rich platform from which student activists could call attention to their cause and could also help to forge or reinforce ties with newer students, thereby sustaining, if not regenerating, a shared identity of resistance in the aftermath of AI-5.

As the UFRJ philosophy students noted, security forces did pay especially close attention to university areas in the weeks leading up to March 28. At the first anniversary of Edson Luis's death they noted the "highly subversive" bulletins students posted calling for a general strike. Reporting on the flyers, they focused almost exclusively on the prohibited activities in which students planned to engage: "[The bulletins] refer to the anniversary of the death of the student Edson [Luis], and much student agitation is expected. If they hold [their proposed] strike, [there will be] much tumult in the streets in an attempt to demoralize the authorities. This movement will also serve to test Law 477."[111] Some reports predicted even more dangerous actions. Army intelligence claimed to have received information that "antirevolutionary and communist elements" were planning to commit various acts of terrorism and sabotage on the anniversary. Among other actions, these groups supposedly planned to derail trains, cut power lines, rob businesses, and assassinate government officials.[112] Afraid of a repeat of the disorder of 1968, security forces kept a close watch on protests and "tumult," increasing their vigilance on each March 28 that followed.

Indeed, by 1971 the police from the southern state of Paraná had added March 28 to their list of "Communist festive days" and to their "Calendar of Communist events," advising officers to be on extra alert around that day.[113] While their labeling of the date of Edson Luis's murder as "Communist" may have been wholly inaccurate, they correctly recognized the date's pervasive political meaning, one now regularly noted in the same manner as other key dates on the calendar.

Nearly five years to the day after Edson Luis was shot in one of the many street protests so typical of 1968, another young student was killed in the sadly characteristic way of this later period: he was tortured to death. On March 16, 1973, Alexandre Vannucchi Leme, a fourth-year geology student at USP, was abducted by security forces and taken to the DOI-CODI detention center in São Paulo, where he was repeatedly tortured. Like the student prisoner in the *Achtung* play performed a month later, Leme supposedly shouted, "My name is Alexandre Vannucchi Leme and I am a geology student!" as he was dragged past the cells of other prisoners on the way to his final and fatal torture session.[114] When news of Leme's imprisonment, torture, and death leaked out, it precipitated an outcry among students and clergy from his home state of São Paulo and soon led to a fresh wave of commemorative protests.[115]

The death of Leme was a brutal event in which a popular young student was barbarously murdered, and the official explanations for his death were so utterly implausible as to arouse doubt in even the most credulous observer. As the historian Kenneth Serbin explains, security agents created two differing descriptions of his death. The first was intended for public consumption and was released to the press around March 22. This version denied that Leme had ever been in police custody, claiming he was hit by a truck as he attempted to avoid arrest. The second admitted that he had been arrested but claimed he soon committed suicide; this was the explanation given to other DOI-CODI prisoners who had witnessed the commotion around his cell on March 17 and the removal of his bloody corpse. To further convince them of this story, guards slit Leme's throat and conducted a search of the other cells for sharp objects.[116] Neide Richopo, a fellow prisoner of the DOI-CODI when Leme died, later testified that even these suicide stories multiplied. She declared that "she witnessed the death of a boy in the DOI named Alexandre; that she heard his screams of torture all day, and that the following day he was found dead in his cell. And after that the interrogators presented at least three versions about his death being a suicide, when the official version was totally different from these three: it was that he was run over."[117] That officials created alternate explanations for the press and for those currently imprisoned would not have immediately come to light were it not for the fact that security agents unwittingly told both versions to the boy's family. Detective Edsel Magnotti insisted to Leme's father that his son had committed suicide, while a few minutes later Detective Fleury contended he had been hit by a truck.[118] In their report to the State Department, the U.S. consulate's version combined these two stories, offering the fantastical conclusion that, while fleeing from police, Leme committed suicide by throwing himself in front of a truck.[119] Adding to the dubiousness of these multiple and illogical explanations was the fact that Leme's family was not informed of the boy's death or allowed to see his body. Leme's father first learned of the arrest through a classmate of his son, who, recognizing the importance of the first days of imprisonment, called him at their home in Sorocaba to alert him to the abduction. The family only knew for certain that their son had died when they read the official notice in the newspapers on March 23, by which point Leme had long ago been hastily and anonymously buried in a pauper's cemetery. Their requests to have his body examined and reburied were refused.[120] This particular fact—the denial of the corpse to the family —appeared to many to be proof of both foul play and government callousness, and it would become a central theme of the subsequent protests. Finally, not only did officials' explanations fail to credibly identify the cause of his death, but also their repeated allegations that Leme had been a dangerous member of the ALN and guilty of several crimes were unconvincing.

Soon after news of Leme's death became public, clergy members and students alike initiated acts of public condemnation and mourning. The bishop of Sorocaba, dom José Melhado Campos, addressed the issue of the boy's corpse directly in a letter published in the church paper, in which he asked why the victim's body had not been returned to his family and requested that someone take responsibility for what had happened. A few days later, at a Mass held for Leme in the city of São Paulo on March 30, Cardinal dom Paulo Evaristo Arns echoed the idea in a clearly metaphorical sermon about the return of Jesus' body to his mother after his death.[121] Not unlike the 7th Day Mass for Edson Luis, Leme's Mass drew large crowds. Estimates put the number of attendees between three thousand and five thousand, making it the largest such gathering in years. This is all the more remarkable given the proliferation of photograph-taking security agents in attendance, and the inadequacy of attendees' efforts to protect their identities by covering their faces with prayer sheets.[122] (Indeed, in later months, security files on São Paulo students would indicate whether or not they had attended the Mass.)[123] Some of the attending students wore black arm bands in protest, as they had taken to doing in the agitated days leading up to the Mass. Other actions at USP included the distribution of flyers denouncing the murder by the police and the draping of large black banners on university buildings. U.S. American observers called the response to his death "the strongest student political action in recent years" and expressed concern that further confrontations could take place.[124]

In light of the precarious context for any kind of large protest demonstration, especially one that involved charges of state torture on one side and accusations of student participation in the armed struggle on the other, the obvious question is why so many students would expose themselves. Serbin argues that Leme's status as an extremely popular young man at USP helped fan the protests but says that the most important factor was the belief among students and the clergy that he had nothing to do with the ALN. Because Leme was one of the only (if not the only) USP students killed who had not first gone underground and lived a clandestine life, Serbin suggests that his supporters did not know of his ties to the ALN. He shows that Leme, in fact, served as a political coordinator for the organization, providing an important link between the underground movement and aboveground groups with whom it sought to forge ties, such as progressive Catholics and students. Yet clergy members' conviction that this was untrue (along with his family's important position within the Catholic Church) was precisely what allowed high-ranking priests to advocate on his behalf. This, Serbin shows, meant that bishops such as Campos, who firmly opposed communism, could publicly protest Leme's death.

The combination of egregious police behavior with Leme's apparent lack of culpability clearly incited some students to join in the protests. Geraldo Siqueira, by then a third-year USP student, later recalled how enraged he and others were by the discrepancies in the police claims. By 1973, he said, "denouncements of incarcerations and assassinations had already accumulated. But then, in the Vannucchi [Leme] case, the police version was really brazen. They implicated him in a robbery for a day on which he was having surgery. Another action they ascribed to him took place when he was on a trip with his classmates from geology. All of this provoked total indignation."[125] And if these police distortions, in Siqueira's view, angered other students, then the active participation of the clergy may have provided cover for the students. Twenty-five priests, including Cardinal Arns, officiated at the Mass for Leme on March 30. Moreover, the Mass was held in the Catedral da Sé in downtown São Paulo, a prominent location that the clergy and students believed would afford the attendees some degree of security. The combination of outrage and the support given by the Church filled the pews.

Whether or not many students knew of Leme's ties to the ALN, his seeming innocence and lack of well-known ties to any clandestine group proved decisive in the expression of public indignation around his death. In recent years students had learned of multiple cases in which student activists in the clandestine lefts had suffered inhumane treatment and even death at the hands of their state captors. The fact that students did not similarly protest these abuses did not imply that they believed the activists guilty of anything that merited such treatment. Rather, any possible involvement with the clandestine lefts by a victim made it much harder to protest on his or her behalf. Indeed, the very fact that security agents repeatedly pointed to Leme's presumed participation in the clandestine group as an implicit justification for his torture and murder speaks to the extremely hostile climate of Brazil in 1973. In such a context there was no possible way to protest his death without also affirming his noninvolvement with the clandestine lefts. On one level, to have acknowledged his ties to the ALN would have been tantamount to conceding that his death was, at least in the eyes of some, justified and unworthy of investigation. On a more practical level, had Leme been a known ALN collaborator, students and others who protested his death would have risked being seen as ALN supporters or collaborators themselves. Instead, the absurdity of the official explanations for his death, combined with the lack of any police evidence linking him to terrorist activities, gave São Paulo students a firm basis on which they could finally give voice to long-standing complaints of repression against students. His apparent innocence opened up the small space within which they could harness clergy support and publicly protest such abuses. Thus rather than dismissing the discursive battle over his guilt or innocence as being irrelevant to the question of police abuse of a suspect, they took part in the debate. To counteract police charges that he was a student activist, they emphasized Leme's academic excellence, especially the fact that he received the top grade in the country on the vestibular for geology, as the presumption was that only "real" students dedicated themselves to academic pursuits.

While the lack of clear ties linking Leme to the ALN fostered the practical conditions for protests by students and clergy alike in 1973, the importance of his innocence transcended these immediate circumstances and lent it great moral weight and symbolic meaning. In fact, the significance of the case extends well beyond the admittedly extraordinary act of several thousand attendees at his funeral and into the realm of memory. Steve Stern's instrumental concept of "memory knots" helps one understand this phenomenon. In his study of Chile after 1973, Stern explains that "specific human groups and leaders, specific events and dates, specific physical sites all seem to stir up, collect and concentrate memory, thereby 'projecting' memory and polemics about memory into public space or imagination." In other words, if memories of the past, especially the traumatic past, usually lie latent in the public consciousness, under certain circumstances they are brought explosively to the surface. Stern draws on the metaphor of the human body to imagine a knot in the stomach when one is nervous, "a nerve-and-muscle mass that spasms and cries out for relief . . . and break[s] the 'normal' flows of everyday life and habit." He then explains that memory knots on the social body "also interrupt the normal flow of 'unthinking' reflexes and habits." Expressed theoretically, he states, "Memory knots are sites of society, place and time so bothersome, insistent or conflictive that they move human beings, at least temporarily, beyond the *homo habitus* postulated by anthropologist Pierre Bourdieu. Expressed colloquially: Memory knots are sites where the social body screams."[126]

The death and funeral of Alexandre Vannucchi Leme throbbed within the Brazilian body politic with a resonance analogous to the murder and commemoration of Edson Luis de Lima Souto. On a purely objective level, few could miss the obvious parallels between the two cases, both understood as the flagrant murders of innocent young men by an out-of-control military state. More profoundly, however, students who knew of Edson Luis from the annual commemorations of his death suddenly found themselves experiencing a strikingly familiar, if previously only imagined, scenario. Whether they actually attended Leme's funeral in São Paulo or merely discussed the boy's death in the hallways of a distant university, students inevitably felt the mixture of shock, anger, fear, and confusion that attended the news of his murder. And they perhaps experienced that intangible sensation of shared solidarity as they witnessed the renewed support of the clergy, and as Leme's death became a topic of conversation around the country, reinforcing an image and feeling of a national student body, collectively aggrieved. The emphasis on his innocence, like that on Edson Luis's, exonerated them all, while his unjust death stood in for the injustices they had all suffered. This solidarity extended to the past, as students who had verbally expressed ties to the generation of 1968 in their previous acts of homage to Edson Luis now forged their own experiential connection with the prior episode. It should therefore come as no surprise that at Leme's funeral, with security forces surrounding the Cathedral, students and clergy broke out into one of the quintessential protest songs of 1968, as the lyrics of Vandré's "Caminhando" lilted out over the police sirens. The multiple strands of mourning and meaning coalesced, and the memory knot on the student body cried out.

....

As 1968 gave way to the years of lead, students in Brazil struggled to make sense of their new surroundings. Gone were the days of peacefully organizing thousands of young people in city streets, as hard-liners within the military regime implemented new measures in their quest to shut down all forms of opposition. Gone too was the political authority university students had long wielded as legitimate and accepted political actors, as the regime intervened so profoundly in students' institutions and organizations that the aboveground student movement disaggregated into small, local pockets of activity (or inactivity), while UNE itself eventually collapsed. Many students nonetheless continued their efforts to organize politically, pursuing new strategies as the situation demanded and looking to the future. As they did so, they rarely made reference to 1968, notwithstanding its potential appeal as a moment of massive mobilization and national debate. Understanding and responding to the political climate of the 1970s demanded flexibility and creativity rather than adherence to prior organizational models.

The year 1968 did serve as a critical mnemonic reference for the state security forces tasked with monitoring students, in the sense that it was a constant point of comparison and concern. As numerous organizations of the clandestine lefts turned to armed struggle in the post-AI-5 climate, regime officials interpreted this move and the participation of some students and former students as confirmation that the massive protests of 1968 had served as a prelude and training ground for these later developments. As a result, dark memories of 1968 colored their interpretations of student activities as they worked to persecute student leaders and shutter the major student organizations, and they were mindful of any signs of a potential repeat performance.

When students in this period did refer to 1968, it was to honor and commemorate their fallen comrades: first, Edson Luis de Lima Souto, and then, after his death in 1973, Alexandre Vannucchi Leme. These ritualistic acts of mourning nonetheless had the effect of linking generations of students to events that preceded them, and doing so in such a way that 1968 began to take on a special meaning even to those who entered the university several years after. Such connections would prove critical to their later efforts to reassert political authority by reconstituting the student movement and reestablishing UNE.

5

REBUILDING THE HOUSE OF MEMORIES, 1974–1985

In October 1973, a few months after the death of Alexandre Vannucchi Leme, security officials detained, tortured, and eventually murdered another important student activist, the president of UNE Honestino Guimarães.[1] Guimarães had a long history of student movement activism and imprisonment. Since 1966 the police had arrested him on at least three separate occasions, even invading the University of Brasilia in August 1968 in search of him.[2] Back then Guimarães, a young geology student, had attracted officials' attention as a notable force of student leadership in the capital city. Guimarães headed the Federação dos Estudantes Universitários de Brasília (FEUB, Federation of University Students of Brasilia) and was becoming nationally influential as well. His prominence was confirmed in early 1969, when he was elected one of the nine vice presidents of UNE under President Jean Marc von der Weid. By June 1969 the U.S. consulate in São Paulo noted Guimarães's presence there and reported that he was central in organizing students to protest the visit of Nelson Rockefeller.[3] According to a statement Guimarães wrote shortly before his arrest in 1973, he was tried in absentia five times and sentenced to a total of twenty-five years' imprisonment, with all but one prosecution resulting from his participation in "the student struggles of 1968."[4] By the time Guimarães served his final, fatal incarceration, however, his connection with the aboveground student movement had been nearly severed. Twenty-six years old and out of school for five years, he had long since gone underground and joined the APML, an organization of the clandestine left that believed in (but did not yet practice) armed struggle. Thus when the security forces apprehended him in 1973 and even when he died in custody sometime later, students did not mobilize as they had in the cases of Edson Luis de Lima Souto and Alexandre Vannucchi Leme. There is no reason to expect that university students in 1973 would have even been aware of his arrest, and definitely no way they could have known about his death at the time. For Guimarães was one of the many political prisoners who was forcibly disappeared by the state security forces. No written records describe or admit to the circumstances of his death, and it is only from the eyewitness reports of fellow political prisoners that his demise was later established. His disappearance thus produced no immediate protest funerals or demonstrations.

Yet just a few short years after Guimarães's final imprisonment and death his figure became a central commemorative focus for students, joining and then quickly surpassing those of Edson Luis and Leme. If in 1968 the death of Edson Luis initiated a long, dialectical cycle of protest and repression and Leme's death in 1973 worked as a "memory knot" to temporarily jolt students and others into protest, in the late seventies and early eighties invocations of Guimarães's disappearance served to connect students to both of these earlier moments and to authenticate a newly reorganizing student movement. For as student activists in this later period sought to rebuild the student movement and reaffirm its importance, they drew heavily on the language of a transgenerational collective student memory of opposition to the dictatorship and the resulting repression: one of militancy and martyrdom. They turned to Guimarães as a uniquely potent symbol for each. Speaking often of students' "memories of struggle" and invoking a shared responsibility to remember the history and traditions of the student movement, they frequently referred to the student activism of the post-1964 period as a collectively remembered heritage, one that demanded specific responses in the present. As they did so they stressed those aspects of the past that most suited their current political struggles and anticipated future. In the context of the late 1970s and early 1980s celebrations of Guimarães as a staunch defender of democracy obscured his efforts at clandestine organizing for revolution. And notwithstanding the disintegrating legitimacy and organizational collapse UNE had undergone when Guimarães assumed the presidency in 1969, references to him symbolized the student union's perseverance as an aboveground organization with indisputable moral authority. Moreover, despite the fact that the heyday of the former UNE building on Praia de Flamengo Street lay in the years prior to 1964, the headquarters soon came to represent a post-1964 fight against the dictatorship and the repression students had consequently suffered.

Students' efforts to rebuild a student movement reflected and contributed to a broad and important shift in Brazilian political life, one that emanated both from above via governmental changes and from below through the renewed energies and shifting strategies of the opposition. Within the military, less hard-line attitudes began to regain the upper hand. When President Médici's term of office expired in March 1974, the junta succeeded in replacing him with one of their own, Gen. Ernesto Geisel. Early in his presidency Geisel declared his intention to shepherd the country through a "slow, gradual and secure" period of *distensão*, or "stretching"—a prolonged political opening designed to lead to a return to democracy.[5] He followed up on his promised shift by reducing censorship, allowing direct elections of state and national congresses, and generally signaling that increased civil activity might be tolerated. As some scholars have noted, Geisel and his military supporters made these decisions not because of pressure from the opposition but from a sense of confidence in the changes the military had wrought.[6] Soldiers had recently annihilated the last major effort of the clandestine armed lefts in a series of brutal battles in rural Araguaia, where the PCdoB had been trying to spark a rural uprising. Influential sectors of the military believed the subversive threat had been mostly defeated. The distensão was indeed slow, lasting ten years and extending beyond the end of Geisel's presidency in 1979 and through that of his successor, Gen. João Baptista Figueiredo. But the process was not gradual, consistent, or secure, as hard-liners within the military and especially within the security forces continued their persecution of suspected opponents of the regime and gave increased license to armed underground groups from the right who sought to disrupt the stretching process. Moreover, both Geisel and Figueiredo repeatedly backtracked on reforms they made when the results were not what they expected. Nonetheless, the discourse of political opening combined with the real instances of top-down liberalization that the government allowed signaled and inspired real, if slow, political change.

If distensão did not translate into either an end to military repression or a definitive return to democracy, it did give rise to increased political organizing and civic activity, a mobilization from below that both resulted from these government-level shifts and encouraged other constituencies to push for change. Numerous groups emerged at this time to force open the military regime and speed up the return to democracy. From an increasingly confrontational MDB political party to the rise of a new workers' movement and of its most famous leader, Luiz Inácio "Lula" da Silva, many diverse groups pushed for the resumption of the right to make demands on and influence government. Even the clandestine lefts shifted their focus. In the first half of the 1970s numerous leftist organizations had folded in the face of the regime's assaults. Those that survived engaged in fierce self-criticism about an armed struggle that led to the deaths of so many militants. Maria Paula Araujo has written, "The wound of armed struggle opened space for a visceral rejection of violence in the last half of the 1970s that, in contrast with the previous decade, left its mark on the left in Brazil and in the world."[7] In the new context of distensão, the clandestine lefts ceased promoting armed resistance to the regime and instead advocated the return of democracy and increasingly used public, legal means to do so.[8] When, in 1979, the government allowed the formation of multiple opposition parties under certain strict guidelines, several of these organizations participated in a broad front party called the Partido Movimento Democrático Brasileiro (PMDB, Brazilian Democratic Movement Party), while many individual members of the lefts joined the newly formed Partido dos Trabalhadores (PT, Workers' Party) or the Partido Democrática Trabalhista (PDT, Democratic Labor Party). And after a newly democratic civilian government reauthorized the founding of multiple political parties in 1985, some of these groups successfully applied to become fully legal political parties.

As students took advantage of the new possibilities generated in this period of political opening, they did so as members of a student population that had changed profoundly since 1968, the height of student political mobilization. As we have seen, national- and state-level student organizations had been banned for five years, many other student organizations had long been shuttered, and those that remained open were ordered to refrain from engaging in political activity. Most university students therefore had no personal experience with political activism. With each passing year, fewer and fewer of them would have been able to recall a period when open participation in student politics was a normal aspect of university life. Even those who had been active as secondary school students in the pre-AI-5 years were diminishing in number as they completed their university studies and moved on, while the temporal gap between those experiences and the present only widened. The current generation had come of age during an era of intense regime repression, censorship, and propaganda. These youths were consequently presumed to be politically disinterested and were saddled with derogatory nicknames, from the AI-5 generation to the dictatorship's children. Moreover, since 1968 the military government had tried to prevent student unrest and promote economic development by expanding the public universities and authorizing the proliferation of private, for-profit universities. This resulted both in huge increases in the number of university students and in a much more socioeconomically diverse population than that of the 1960s.

Nonetheless, a sizable number of university students continued to be politically involved. Many of them did so through the rise of *tendências políticas* (political tendencies), organized groups of students with common political ideas and close ties to the clandestine lefts. Defined by Araujo as the legal expression of the clandestine lefts within the universities, tendências such as *Unidade* ("Unity," tied to the PCB), *Caminhando* ("Walking," allied with the PCdoB), *Refazendo* ("Redoing," connected to the APML), and *Liberdade e Luta* ("Liberty and Struggle," known by the nickname *Libelu* and aligned with new and influential Trotskyist groups) became the primary forces behind student political mobilization across the country.[9] As noted in the introduction, Aldo Rebelo, then a student at the Federal University of Alagoas and a member of the PCdoB, remembers secretly listening to Vandré's music along with his friends behind closed doors at their CA in 1975.[10] As the PCdoB's tendência was named Caminhando, this act would have had special meaning to him and his PCdoB colleagues. Yet after the politics of the Geisel administration had "'stretched open' [*distensionou*] political life within the universities," they began to listen to it publicly, in the process drawing on the reference to 1968 to appeal to others.[11]

In short, throughout the slow, decade-long stretch toward democracy, student activists sought to unify and mobilize their socially disparate and politically inexperienced classmates by employing a rich mixture of functional and symbolic strategies. By reclaiming or refounding their old institutions, from the CAs to UNE, and by insisting that all students shared a common, collective memory of meaningful political activism, they tried to overcome current apathy and forge a unity of interest. Throughout, their appeals to a shared student memory of militancy and martyrdom became the fundamental mechanism for mobilizing other students, rebuilding student organizations such as UNE, and reasserting the student movement's political authority.

"After the harshest winters, students [in 1974] once again began to mobilize," declared a student newspaper in early 1975. "We can't say that it was a coordinated and satisfactory movement, or that the ME [student movement] finally got up from its deep sleep," but it was a marked increase over the previous year.[12] A few months later another student paper proclaimed, "The year 1975 started off quite agitated in the Brazilian universities, characterized from the start by student dissatisfaction. We believe that from this unhappiness will surge the need for more consequential participation."[13] And by early 1977 student writers announced, "In these last two years we have seen that students have begun to wake up to the need to defend their interests."[14] These multiple references to slowly rousing students point less to any sudden mass mobilization on the part of university students in the mid-1970s than to the enthusiasm of their authors—whether in honest reflection, suggestive promotion, or wishful thinking. For as the regime gave signals (albeit mixed) of tolerating more political activity, and as other civil groups began to press for change, pockets of students across the country found the moment invigorating and actively sought to join in the process. Arguing that a broad-based student movement should contribute to the dictatorship's demise and to the reconstruction of society afterward, many student activists worked through political tendências affiliated with the clandestine lefts, where they found confirmation of and support for their ideas. Meanwhile the reemergence of an active student movement helped further the goals of the lefts as they shifted their focus away from armed struggle and toward a resumption of democratic rights.

One method students employed to rouse their university colleagues was simply to participate in their department- or faculty-level CAs and DAs and in the university-level DCEs.[15] Universities and faculties varied widely as to whether their student organizations remained open and the degree to which those that did were able to function as centers of discussion and advocacy. As we have seen, at PUC in Rio de Janeiro several DAs operated throughout the early 1970s and even continued to provide a platform for students from the lefts (see chapter 4). At the Universidade Estadual de Campinas (UNICAMP, State University of Campinas, São Paulo), however, many student centers were closed, and others existed in name only. When candidates for leadership of four CAs at UNICAMP spoke to a student newspaper in November 1974, one group lamented that "most [of our classmates] see the Centro Acadêmico as a ghost. There are students who are even afraid of it, as they identify it with subversion, etc." When another slate was asked how students viewed their CA, they answered, "Apathetically." All the interviewees, in fact, mentioned a deep concern with the apathy, confusion, and disinformation that characterized their fellow students. Four of the five slates ran unopposed, while in the one contested pairing the second slate claimed to have entered merely to encourage participation by offering voters the semblance of choice. Yet as one group of candidates explained, "The [Academic] Center doesn't blame students themselves for this situation but rather the whole structure that surrounds us and conditions us."[16] By working to revitalize their CAs and in the process change accepted images of student politics, students like these interviewees hoped to transform other students and the organizations themselves.

In other places students worked to restore previously closed organizations or to render current ones more authentic. A growing leftist press celebrated and publicized these accomplishments. *Movimento*, for example, a newspaper initiated in 1975 by various activists of the lefts that later advocated theoretical positions of the PCdoB, reported enthusiastically on student developments throughout this period.[17] In 1976 it paid tribute to students at the University of Brasilia for finally reestablishing their university-level organization after three years of efforts. Similarly, it praised the rector of the Federal University of Minas Gerais for allowing students to choose DCE officers through direct rather than indirect elections.[18] The following year *Movimento* published numerous reports applauding students for reopening faculty-level and university-level organizations across the country.[19] The local efforts of student activists who worked to reinstate these centers and the broader resonance given them by publications such as *Movimento* created the sense of a burgeoning student mobilization.

If some students worked to restore official CAs, DAs, and DCEs in order to forge an institutional and attitudinal basis for wider political reorganization, others opted to create or re-create unofficial or banned organizations, a tactic advocated by more confrontational tendencies such as Libelu. At USP students had experienced resurgent bursts of political activity ever since the demonstrations in 1973 over the death of Leme, an USP student, including participation in protests over two additional murders: those of the journalist and USP professor Vladimir Herzog in October 1975 and of the metalworker Manoel Fiel Filho in January 1976. In the wake of these events, student activists formed a DCE-Livre in 1976. The modifier *livre*, meaning "free," signaled that the organization was not an official DCE and therefore not subject to the federal restrictions that limited its activities and established its authority via government approval. Instead the students who supported it explicitly eschewed such a status, claiming that an independent DCE was more authentic than one approved by an illegitimate dictatorship. They also implicitly rooted the organization's authority in the past. The very idea of a free DCE harkened back to 1964 and 1965, when the military regime first began to interfere with student organizations via the Suplicy Law, and students in some schools created parallel, unofficial organizations that used exactly this modifier.[20] Even more symbolic, the full name USP students gave to their organization was the Alexandre Vannucchi Leme DCE-Livre, a designation that referred to both the state-sponsored murder of an USP student and the protests that ensued. Through their choice of names USP students in 1976 connected themselves to the beginning of antiregime student protest in 1964–65 and to its last major eruption in 1973. Soon students at other universities formed free organizations as well, from the University of Brasilia to the University of Federal Rural Rio de Janeiro.[21] And much to the discomfort of security agents, who lamented "the transformation of subversives into gods," some followed the USP students' lead and bestowed the names of other former activists on their student centers.[22]

This context of difficult mobilization led to new opportunities for politically minded female students. We have seen that women students participated actively in student movement activities and organizations ever since women first enrolled in universities. Yet, as we have also seen, they faced distinct challenges in doing so and only infrequently rose to leadership positions. The waning of the aboveground student movement in the 1970s, however, opened space for new political actors, especially those who could conceivably attract others like them and thereby help the student movement grow. At the same time, the massive increase in the number of women university students meant that they represented a large resource for any political movement; by 1980 women students outnumbered their male colleagues.[23] Hence women students who demonstrated strong political convictions and the desire to act on them attracted special attention from other activists and were heavily recruited. Maria Francisca Alves de Souza, a student in Rio de Janeiro in the late 1970s, recalled her sense that when she spoke out at student gatherings people listened to her more attentively than they did to her male colleagues, as there was still a degree of novelty about a female political speaker.[24] Women activists who were enrolled in women-dominated faculties were even more especially sought after, as it was thought they could involve their classmates in the student movement. Maria Graça Berman, a student at PUC in São Paulo in 1975, remembers attending university assemblies to debate a proposed fee hike. As a first-year student in the female-dominated Faculty of Philosophy and Letters, she says, "I attracted attention from all the clandestine groups that had tendências in the student movement. They all wanted to win me over."[25] Yet at the same time female students were assumed to be even more politically alienated than their male colleagues. Berman described the Faculty of Letters as a place that "only had women; and women were really alienated then, they really were," though she added that her whole generation was alienated. Nonetheless, when some of Berman's male colleagues wanted to simplify their political message before presenting it to her supposedly alienated colleagues, the gesture infuriated her. Forming an all-female slate of candidates to run for election of their DA, she campaigned by telling her classmates, "They think we're a bunch of fools, behind the times, . . . and that we don't care about Brazilian society."[26] According to her, her strategy worked, and her slate won the election. Women like Berman both reflected and contested the idea that women students were uninterested in politics, and they contributed to the mid-1970s drive to mobilize other students.

In order to truly rebuild a student movement, however, students needed to be able to forge connections not only within each university and urban center but also through state- and national-level organizations. They began this process by taking advantage of intellectual and pre-professional conferences that had long been permitted and even encouraged by the regime, who saw them as apolitical spaces for students to build on their training. For example, since 1969 the minister of education and culture had financially supported the Encontro Científico de Estudantes de Medicina (ECEM, Scientific Meeting for Medical Students), an annual meeting of medical students where attendees presented academic papers and discussed intellectual and professional questions related to medicine.[27] Beginning in the mid-1970s, however, student activists tried to use these gatherings for political organizing. They worked for two years to change the structure of the ECEM conference to allow for round-table discussions, a forum that might facilitate political debate.[28] Once they succeeded in this, they were able to introduce discussions of public health as a way of linking medical concerns with broader social and economic problems, a step that eventually cost them the financial support of the ministry.[29] Meanwhile student activists used similar gatherings to forge important national relationships. Rebelo told interviewers that even as a law school student he attended annual entomology meetings in an effort to establish contacts with agronomy students, a group with a reputation for political activism.[30] Through this process, student activists were eventually able to begin hosting national student meetings with the express goal of rebuilding a national student movement. Called Encontros Nacionais de Estudantes (ENEs, National Gatherings of Students), the first such meeting, held in January 1976, was relatively small and characterized by numerous disagreements among student factions. But students persisted and held a second ENE in October 1976 and, after many efforts to prevent it, a third one in September 1977, each one successively larger than the one that preceded it. More important, participants increasingly agreed about the need to advocate for democratic reforms, amnesty for political prisoners, and the end of the dictatorship.[31] And at the third ENE they formed an association of DCEs, the Pro-UNE Commission, with the specific task of re-creating UNE. One of the commission's first tasks was to educate students about UNE's history.[32]

If the above examples all point to some of the tactical initiatives student activists undertook to reconstruct the student movement, many of them also indicate the way students combined these functional efforts with symbolic appeals to the past. From the name Alexandre Vannucchi Leme DCE-Livre to the fact that students sought not to establish new student organizations but to rebuild old ones, invocations of a presumably shared collective memory became more and more important. Indeed, much like the concerns about student apathy noted earlier, some at the time worried that students had no memory whatsoever of the student movement past. Berman recalls this amnesia as being especially acute among women students, who were seen, and sometimes saw themselves, as disengaged politically. After her all-female slate of candidates won the leadership of their DA, she says, they spent the summer studying the history of the student movement, reading Artur Poerner's laudatory *O Poder Jovem* (Youth power) and looking through past issues of *Veja* magazine.[33] At times students revealed their concern about a lack of memory through dark humor, such as the cartoon in a secondary school publication labeled "Political Memories of Brazilian Youth" that depicted a figure with empty thought bubbles over its head.[34] At other times educating students about the student movement past became a specific project for organizers, as was the case for the Pro-UNE Commission. Once students began campaigning to re-create UNE and the UEEs, they organized multiple events designed to teach others about the history of these institutions and of the student movement in general, including holding symposia with former student activists and displaying murals on school walls depicting UNE's history.[35] And they frequently added detailed accounts of student movement history to flyers and publications. After listing a series of national political campaigns in which students took part, one such poster announced, "The importance of [UNE and the Rio de Janeiro UEE] can be measured by the struggles they have set in motion." Connecting that past to current efforts to reestablish UNE, it stated further, "The closing of our entities in 1968, and the period of intense repression between 69 and 73 that followed, were not enough to extinguish in students their tradition of struggle and combativeness."[36]

Sometimes students indirectly suggested that they should make memory political. This was the case with a student newspaper at PUC in Rio de Janeiro called Síntese (Synthesis) that consisted, appropriately enough, of a synthesis of carefully chosen news stories from other Brazilian sources. Because an early strategy students employed to promote political engagement among others was to divulge provocative news, Síntese built on loosening censorship rules by thoughtfully selecting material from national newspapers that was especially meaningful to students. They reprinted a Jornal do Brasil article about Mexican university students at the famous Universidad Autónoma de Mexico who had recently pelted Mexican President Luis Echeverría with bottles and rocks during a speech he gave on campus. The first Mexican chief of state to visit the university since 1968, Echeverría had been the secretary of the interior in that year, and many blamed him for the massacre of demonstrating students in Tlatelolco Square in October 1968. In addition to throwing rocks and bottles, students in 1975 protested his visit with placards declaring that they would "never forget" the events of 1968.[37] If not all of Síntese's reprinted stories had such direct parallels to Brazilian students' own history of repression in 1968 or such specific references to the political uses of memory, they nonetheless regularly emphasized examples of activism.

Sometimes the political actions of students drew such a clear line to the past that participants could not fail to experience them as forging a connection to that past. This was especially true of street protests led by students in São Paulo in May 1977 and the multiple comparisons with 1968 they generated.[38] On April 28, 1977, eight members of the clandestine leftist organization Liga Operária (Workers' League) were arrested for distributing pamphlets about a demonstration to be held on May 1, International Workers' Day. Among the eight were two proletarionized university students—student activists who had chosen to take on industrial jobs and live in working-class neighborhoods in order to better understand blue-collar communities and thereby be better able to advocate for and participate in an eventual worker-led revolution.[39] In the analysis of the historian Natan Zeichner, students in São Paulo were moved to respond to these arrests by the direct appeal of two metalworkers who visited the USP campus requesting help from the student movement and who referred to all eight activists as "fellow workers," "inspir[ing] the hope that it was possible for student activists to make a successful transition from student to worker."[40] For activist students eager to contribute to the workers' struggle and to the redemocratization of the country, this affirmation of the student movement's importance and call to serve was compelling and resulted in rapid mobilization. On May 5 they defied long-standing bans on public assemblies and marched in downtown São Paulo to protest the incarcerations, drawing upward of ten thousand people. Student marchers were keenly aware that no student protests of this size had occurred since 1968. Media sources that mentioned the event later could not avoid comparisons with 1968 and called it the largest student demonstration since then. Yet students in 1977 adopted expressly different tactics from those of 1968, such as avoiding confrontation with the police and declining to use makeshift weapons or ether to combat the tear gas. And they eschewed the practice of having individual student leaders address the crowd from a podium. Instead, they all sat together on the ground and repeated in call-and-response style an open letter that student leaders had written, proclaiming, "We don't want any more dead or mutilated heroes."[41] Nonetheless, their attempts at differentiating themselves reaffirmed their position as students who had learned from the past and hence as the heirs of 1968.

Most important, students made direct appeals to memory through commemorative events, such as their continued observance of the anniversary of Edson Luis's murder. Since 1974 some had expanded the commemoration to include homage to Leme, continuing the process of linking students and student martyrs across generations.[42] And in 1978, on the tenth anniversary of Edson Luis's death, the Pro-UNE Commission organized even larger events, further solidifying the tie between these two figures while also pointing out other abuses for which students held the regime responsible.[43] In Recife, for example, students added to these two names that of Father Antônio Henrique Pereira Neto, a Catholic priest and one of the impassioned speakers at Recife's mass for Edson Luis in 1968, whose own death by torture the year after had led to further funeral protests. And in Porto Alegre students used the occasion to ask the crowds to remember the local journalist Flavio Koutzii, exiled from Brazil for political organizing only to be imprisoned by the military regime of Argentina.[44] Reporting on the protests across the country, *Movimento* described them as being "in memory not just of Edson Luis and Alexandre Vannucchi Leme . . . but also of all the dead and disappeared since 1964."[45] Meanwhile *Em Tempo*, another publication to arise from the clandestine lefts, proclaimed, "Ten years since the death of Edson Luis . . . and five since that of Alexandre Vannucchi . . . , ten thousand university and secondary school students recovered the memory of 200 Brazilians assassinated by the police throughout these last, long 14 years."[46]

While these accounts describe students as natural memory bearers for martyred figures, assembling each March 28 in order to transmit their remembrances to others, in fact students used these events to construct memory as part of their remobilization efforts. At the commemorations in São Paulo on March 28 students involved other attendees in multiple acts of remembrance, ritualistic gestures that would soon be replicated at similar events elsewhere in Brazil. They invited family members of the dead, who offered a material connection to those being commemorated both through their physical presence and at times through mementos they shared with the crowd. At the São Paulo commemoration Leme's mother read aloud the last letter her son had written to his father, sent just a few days before his imprisonment and death. Student organizers also ceremoniously pronounced the names of forty people killed by the regime while those in attendance responded to each with a cry of "Presente!," an act that both educated the participants about those who had died while also encouraging communal identification with them.[47] In addition, they included some of the first memorialistic references to Guimarães, reading aloud a political document he had written shortly before his disappearance in which he detailed the multiple forms of persecution he faced.[48]

At a separate commemoration in São Paulo in March 1978 students recreated one of the defining moments of the street protests the year before by using call-and-response to collectively recite a poem honoring Leme, a performance that implies the extent to which student ideals had changed and how, consequently, memories of Leme had also been transformed. No longer portrayed as a pure victim of the military regime, a geology student uninvolved in politics, in 1978 Leme was recalled as someone killed by the dictatorship precisely because of his commitment to political expression. Having lived through a decade of censorship and propaganda in which even potentially political events like forming movie clubs required official sanction, current students were in many ways fighting for the right to engage in political discourse. They paid close attention to the practice of free speech: an oft-repeated slogan in marches in São Paulo in 1977 was, "Those who are quiet, consent" (*quem cala consente*).[49] The poem they read emphasized this idea by making silencing and voicing the central themes, beginning, "Alexandre, they silenced your voice, *companheiro*." This focus does not mean, however, that Leme's affiliation with the ALN was celebrated. In a moment when even the lefts rejected armed struggle, few glorified what was seen as a tragic misdirection of the lefts. Nonetheless, the combativeness and masculinity that so characterized both the armed struggle and the violence of student–police conflicts in 1968 were emphasized in other ways, as speaking out was portrayed as akin to withstanding torture: "They silenced you, *companheiro*, who in life knew how to talk like a man. And in death, like a man you stayed silent." The poem also presented current readers as, until recently, being temporarily silenced themselves, stating, "We were left with the shame of living your eloquent absence in silence." But the poem ends by suggesting that Leme's death was not in vain, for after stating that no new oppressors "can silence the shout of your muteness," it switches from Leme to the present generation, speaking of the "promise in us" that he will not be forgotten and of "our shouts" of resistance.[50] The collective reading aloud of these lines advanced the message of resistance and made the poem's performance itself an act of mnemonic transmission.

In designing events rooted in student memory, real or constructed, the organizing students hoped the occasions would educate and inspire their colleagues. One student paper made this hope explicit, declaring that the demonstrations "effectively contributed in reviving political debate in the university, sensitizing a larger number of students to the need to fight for democracy." The authors went on to say that their next challenge would be "publicizing for students all over Brazil the need to construct UNE, including encouraging them to remember the fighting traditions of UNE as well as the repression to which it was subject."[51]

UNE Is Us, Our Force and Our Voice

As efforts to restore UNE got under way, students continued and even intensified their appeals to memory. Reforming a national student union posed a unique challenge, in terms both of the organizational strategies required for planning such a venture and of the opposition it generated from the regime. Yet reconstructing UNE offered students vital opportunities for securing outside support, as the growing wave of opposition activity allowed for forming alliances with other groups and helped build national visibility for the incipient student movement. Students tried to cultivate this kind of external backing and internal support from their colleagues by making appeals to memory integral to their reconstruction efforts. More specifically, they worked to ensure that the organization they were creating would not simply be a national student union that assumed the name UNE, but that it would incarnate the old União Nacional dos Estudantes, as if the newly re-created union ensured a continuity of student mobilization across the years of the dictatorship. By encouraging students to consider the re-creation of UNE as the resumption of a temporarily immobilized organization or as a phoenix-like resurrection, they worked to reaffirm continuities between the past and present. In so doing they drew heavily on the language of memory and employed collective acts of remembrance, emphasizing the union's own militancy and martyrdom. In the process, students articulated new sources of authority for UNE, importing the past into the present in a mix of purported continuity and re-creation.

The reconstruction of the student union was understood as a major contribution to the oppositional upsurge that marked the period of political opening in the late seventies. As one student magazine emphasized, "UNE is reborn at a moment in which, throughout the country, antidictatorial manifestations multiply. Workers, peasants, labor, intellectuals: they all rise up against misery and in defense of freedom of expression and of organization. The UNE which is being reconstructed has this movement as its base: it will be a step forward not just for students, but for all of those who have identified with their antidictatorial struggle."[52]

Indeed, students were now able to openly court external support for their efforts, particularly among opposition politicians. When they began preparations for the fourth ENE, at which they planned to make the reconstruction of UNE the major topic of discussion, they first announced their intention at the Chamber of Deputies in Brasilia during a congressional hearing onto the state of higher education.[53] Soon thereafter Rep. Airton Soares, an MDB politician from São Paulo, lobbied the minister of education to meet with representatives from the Pro-UNE Commission. Perhaps owing to his efforts, Education Minister Eduardo Portella received the students in his office—even accepting a Pro-UNE T-shirt—while simultaneously declaring that UNE was illegal and thus could not be reconstituted.[54] Sen. Henrique Santillo, an MDB leader from the state of Goias, spoke openly of his support for the re-creation of UNE in a public address. Soon several MDB politicians were advocating straight from the floor of the Chamber of Deputies that UNE be reestablished[55] As the Pro-UNE Commission grew to include some thirty student organizations and held ever-larger, more detailed planning meetings, by early 1979 various other MDB politicians as well as representatives from the Brazilian Committee for Amnesty were participating. Indeed, all federal congresspersons were invited to attend the ninth ENE meeting's opening ceremonies at the University of Brasilia, although the rector there asked them to turn down the invitation.[56] By the tenth and final meeting held in early May 1979, Sen. Leite Chaves addressed a crowd of six hundred to promise his full support, while Soares detailed his efforts to establish a legal basis for UNE's continued existence.[57] Students managed to secure guarantees of support from the governor of the state of Bahia, Antônio Carlos Magalhães, who said they could hold an UNE Congress there without police intervention. They thus began preparations for a formal event to reconstitute the union in Salvador, Bahia, in late May 1979.

This garnering of external support mattered in both material and symbolic ways. Notwithstanding the expanding opportunities for political organization that marked the late 1970s, students faced severe restrictions. Although President Geisel finally revoked AI-5 in November 1978, the regime maintained broad powers to convene states of emergency without congressional approval. In addition, the modified National Security Law merely adjusted the period of incommunicability for those accused of national security crimes from ten days to eight.[58] Thus the threat of arrest and mistreatment continued as a real possibility for student activists.

When students in Rio de Janeiro protested the inauguration of President Figueiredo in March 1979 and police tried to arrest some of the demonstrators, two local political leaders intervened to prevent them, one even going so far as to kick closed a squad car door.[59] And although, as we have seen, the minister of education met with members of the Pro-UNE Commission, he and the president co-signed a new decree in October 1979 barring all DAs and DCEs from participating in any state or national association.[60] Meanwhile the security forces continued to closely monitor student activities and curtail public demonstrations, while Decree-Law No. 477, which stipulated harsh punishments for students who engaged in political activities, remained in effect. Hence the Bahian governor's supportive promise of a space to hold the UNE gathering was a critical form of assistance and a visible expression of approval.

Students solicited and received symbolic approval from several former UNE leaders as well. The participation of these former leaders at the Pro-UNE Commission meeting highlights some of the ritualistic ways in which later students sought to authenticate the new UNE by connecting it to a specific past. Their presence implied a passing of the torch to current students as well as a stamp of approval by the formal UNE stalwarts. Yet they also resurrected a masculinist ideal of UNE leadership, as all of the former leaders were men, a fact that jarred with the increasing numbers of women activists. Moreover, the language employed often echoed earlier visions of UNE's authority as relying on a gendered militancy. The former UNE leader José Genuino Neto, a member of Guimarães's final directorate and one of the few survivors of the PCdoB's guerrilla faction in Araguaia, told the crowd that while it was true that UNE had fallen, "it fell standing up. It fell fighting in the streets. You are going to reconstruct an organization that has a historical role."[61] Even the absence of two former UNE presidents then incarcerated signified the union's continuing political importance and stoic militancy, as their imprisonment for political activities affirmed the oppositional stance of the union itself. This connection was strengthened through the imprisoned leaders' letters of support, letters that were ceremoniously read aloud at the gathering.

When students invoked the history of UNE, they emphasized its early opposition to the dictatorship. A Pro-UNE magazine rallying support for UNE's reconstruction declared, "From the first moments, it [UNE] fought against the military regime implanted after the coup of April 1, 1964, placing itself on the side of the people in their struggle for freedom against the minority and against injustice.[62] This idea became further rooted in references to the former UNE building on Praia de Flamengo Street. At the same Pro-UNE meeting, the former UNE president, José Serra, said, "When on the first of April the UNE building, which symbolized the whole student movement, was burned, my colleagues and I were sure of one thing: that repressive fire washed over the student movement because it was always in the vanguard of the fight for democracy."[63] Representations of the attack on and burning of the UNE building characterized the organization as an original force of resistance to the military regime in the defense of society at large.

If students in São Paulo had begun to refer to Guimarães at the commemorations of Edson Luis and Leme in 1978, by 1979 his name became closely linked to their efforts to rebuild UNE. In March 1979 the Pro-UNE Commission inaugurated a campaign they called Where is Honestino? in the hope of finding out what had happened to the young man.[64] At the Pro-UNE Commission that same month they resolved to visit the ministers of justice and education in order to request information about him.[65] Although the inquiries produced little information, and the circumstances of his disappearance continued to go unexplained even years later, they nonetheless worked to inform current students and the public of Guimarães's position as the final UNE president and a disappeared prisoner. By the next commission meeting two months later, the nationally known newspaper the Folha de São Paulo took special note of Guimarães. In recounting the formality of the event that now counted on the presence of over 600 people, including many specially invited guests, the paper pointed out that, while other former UNE presidents attended, the disappeared Guimarães had to be represented by a member of his directorate.[66]

All of these efforts ultimately led to the UNE Reconstruction Congress in May 1979, a symbolic event rich with references to the past. Picking up the numbering system students had used since 1938 for their annual meetings, it was called the 31st National Congress, the first since the disastrous mass arrests at Ibiúna in 1968 and the first nonclandestine UNE Congress since 1966. As the date approached, the Pro-UNE Commission intensified its efforts to educate students and others about UNE's history, presenting films and plays about the union, distributing posters, and even installing billboards in the host city of Salvador.[67]

Acts of memory permeated the resulting three-day UNE Congress that drew ten thousand participants. For example, students performed a play they had written that depicted the last seventeen years of the student movement. Others read aloud letters from two former leaders then in jail and one letter from nine others in exile and prohibited from returning to Brazil. After praising the current students for their efforts, the letter writers included a list of names to be pronounced at the congress, reminding their listeners, "When UNE is organized, we cannot fail to remember the names . . . [of those] student leaders who fell in the fight against the dictatorship."[68] On the dais students placed a vacant chair at the head table for Guimarães, and when his name was called out, everyone enthusiastically responded, "Presente!" And during the ceremony to inaugurate the newly created union the students, with some difficulty, sang aloud the old UNE hymn. Reading the lyrics from photocopied sheets, unfamiliar with the tune, they chimed in vociferously at the last refrain, a popular slogan and banner message, and one with added meaning for this generation: "UNE is us, our power and our voice" (A UNE somos nós, nossa força e nossa voz). In acts like these students explicitly harnessed the power of memory to reinforce the reestablishment of a civic political organization.

The most dramatic moment came when an immense illuminated photograph of Guimarães was guided across wires above the main table to grace the meeting hall. Speeches that day made repeated reference to Guimarães and specifically to the prodemocratic aspects of his legacy. One speaker, for example, declared, "The memory of those who fell will continue to be present. Disappeared or dead, Honestino Guimarães will continue being our daily companion, reminding us of the necessity of restoring and deepening democracy." Indeed, the speaker dedicated the UNE Congress itself to "the names of students who were killed, companheiros of the democratic ideal who have left us all the legacy of their mutilated bodies' mute and generous protest."[69] In the context of a much-anticipated return to democracy, students understood Guimarães's revolutionary agenda as complementary to their own struggles for democracy.

In the planning stages of the congress, during the congress itself, and at the later swearing-in ceremony of the new leaders of UNE, memories of the long-suppressed student movement were repeatedly invoked.[70] Through symbolic acts of memory and representation like the participation of former leaders, the reinvention of old traditions, and, most important, current students' own commemorations of UNE's past, they worked to resurrect the union. At the same time, however, these memories revolved around masculine militants and martyrs, suggesting the limits to memory as a force of political renovation.

"The Memory of the People Will Not Be Destroyed"

The invasion and burning of 132 Praia de Flamengo Street on April 2, 1964, not only targeted UNE as an organization but also physically marked the building itself as a crucial symbol. As noted earlier, in the days leading up to the coup in 1964, UNE members draped the building with banners opposing military intervention, converting what many already saw as a center of leftist activity into a physical symbol of resistance. Located on a major avenue and visible to traffic, the decorated building undoubtedly served as a provocation to those who supported a military overthrow of President Goulart. Once the coup was official, its supporters took matters into their own hands and attacked UNE's center and symbol, the building itself. As the historian Antônio Mendes Junior described it, "The old German Club building suffered in its own body the bestiality and ferocity of the new fascists who took power."[71]

Although the building itself was not an important focus of protest for students in 1964–68, it did become a space of considerable symbolic significance. Though physically occupied only occasionally, it continued to represent UNE as an idea. During the era of UNE's reconstruction in the late 1970s both the physical site of the building as well as representations of the attack on it and its burning became notable themes in the later students' actions, publications, and speeches.

In this later period several public demonstrations took place at 132 Praia de Flamengo Street. Shortly after the Reconstruction Congress, for example, the new directorate of the freshly re-formed (and officially illegal) Rio de Janeiro UEE defiantly held their swearing-in ceremony in the building's theater. Slogans chanted at the ceremony demonstrate the mixing of past and present. UEE members responded to the current problem of their organization's illegality and of their own struggle to reconstruct it by repeating, "The UEE is standing up; long live the UEE" (A UEE está de pé; viva a UEE).And they resurrected traditional slogans such as "The people united will never be divided" (O povo unido jamais sera vencido).[72]

A few months later students returned to Praia de Flamengo Street to protest a decree issued by the military president, Gen. João Baptista Figue-

FIGURE 5.1. Students returned to the former UNE building in 1980 to repudiate an anti-UNE law. Agência JB

reido. The new law specified the punishment for university leaders who maintained any relationship with UNE or the UEEs. As in years past they ascended to the second-story balcony whence they hung a huge banner, this one reading, "Students Repudiate the Decree of the Dictatorship! UNE is Us! UNE is our Voice!" (*Os estudantes repudiam o decreto da ditadura. A UNE somos nós! A UNE é nossa voz!*) and waved the UNE flag and the Brazilian national flag. Students proudly posed for journalists' photographs, images that were published in the *Jornal do Brasil* the next day (figure 5.1).

To understand the significance of 132 Praia de Flamengo Street for the students, one must look not just at the moments when they occupied the structure but also at how they represented the burning of the building. In their writings and speeches they often repeated certain aspects of this story while frequently ignoring others. Those involved in the reconstruction in 1979, for example, regularly invoked the fact that the building was burned the day after the military coup. In fact, some student publications that year describe the attack as having taken place on April 1, rather than April 2.[73]

Not a deliberate rewriting of history, this slip is best understood as an error that reveals how closely students associated the coup d'état with the UNE attack, as if they were one and the same.[74] The misremembered date validated UNE's importance prior to the coup, as an entity that merited immediate attention, and also confirmed UNE's oppositional and popular role during the dictatorship that followed. Even when they did not refer to a specific date, students regularly correlated the coup and the attack on the UNE building. A Pro-UNE magazine portrayed the attack's timing and target as follows: "Fifteen years ago, one of the first acts of the dictatorship was to make UNE, along with the CGT [workers' union], the Peasant Leagues, and so many other popular organizations, illegal. Its headquarters were invaded and burned. It was clear that we students would feel the same savage repression that reached all the people, with the closure of unions, organizations, persecution of leaders, prisons, tortures, exiles, assassinations."[75] Cast in this light, the invasion and burning of the building foreshadowed the widespread repression that later came to define the regime. The attack also presaged the targeting of students, thereby confirming their status as opponents to and victims of the regime. A magazine article by Ferdy Varneiro, an artist who had been involved with the CPC in 1964, also reflects this sentiment. He describes his memories of the attack on the building as follows: "Between dusk and the first hours of that night, hordes of terrorists invaded and ignited the headquarters of UNE. The flames devoured the building and the life that flourished in that house: The Popular Cultural Center, the New Theatre, the Popular Theatre, a seedbed of ideas of graphic and creative arts, of vanguard experiences in song and poetry. There died a little bit of the Brazilian intelligentsia, sacrificed in those flames and ashes of UNE, marking the date of the long night of darkness into which Brazil plunged, from April 1, 1964 on."[76] Merging the coup against the nation and the attack on the UNE building he portrays both as a brutal blow that plunged Brazil into a "long night of darkness." In referring to April 1, 1964, as the point of departure for the ruinous path on which the nation embarked, Varneiro not only insinuates that the attack on the UNE building took place on April 1, but, more importantly, sets up a sharp dichotomy between the creativity, hope, and order of the period before that date and the violence, repression, and destruction that came after it.

Students also represented the building through photographs, images that helped impart a sense of ownership of the building's history to the current generation of students. One photo of the UNE building appeared numerous times: a little grainy and dark and taken from a slightly awkward angle, it was nevertheless recognizable as the UNE headquarters on the night of the fire, littered with fallen wires and the broken remains of a barricade, flames lighting up the dark scene.[77] "Camera images, whether photographs, films, or television footage . . . are central to the interpretation of the past," writes the media scholar Marita Sturken. "Photographs are often perceived to embody memory. . . . Just as memory is often thought of as an image, it is also produced by and through images."[78] If students from the late 1970s did not experience the sacking of the UNE building themselves, they nonetheless witnessed it through photography and could draw on this mental picture when thinking about the history of the union and their own relationship to this. And when they reproduced such images they both demonstrated and perpetuated their understanding of the attack on the building as a defining moment. This was the case with posters advertising the Reconstruction Congress that consisted of two large photographs that split the page into upper and lower halves. The top picture was the aforementioned image of the UNE building on the night of the fire. The lower photo showed students sitting formally around a conference table and was a picture taken during a pro-UNE planning meeting in 1978 (see figure 5.2). Above the top photograph was the caption, "1964 the dictatorship invades UNE," while below the lower image it said, "1979 year of UNE's reconstruction." The juxtaposition of these two photographs did not simply highlight the rupture between the attack on UNE and its building and the current context of relatively open student organizing. It also proclaimed to students that both moments were part of their shared past, a past that helped authorize their political activism in the present.

Shortly after the UNE Reconstruction Congress some local news made its way into the Rio newspapers: new buildings were being constructed for the theater and music faculties that had occupied 132 Praia de Flamengo since 1966, and the building would soon be vacant. The UNE directorate decided they needed to act quickly to save the building from destruction. Property values on the beachfront Praia de Flamengo Street had soared in recent years, and it was now filled with high-rise buildings. Once the schools left, the new UNE leaders feared, the regime could sell the lot to developers for a hefty sum, thereby ending hopes of recovering the space in the future.[79]

UNE's plans to repossess the building were published in the *Jornal do*

FIGURE 5.2. This poster announcing the UNE Congress in 1979 reminded viewers that the UNE building was attacked right after the coup d'état in 1964. Arquivo Público do Estado do Rio de Janeiro

Brasil, news that caught the attention of DOPS officials.[80] The stories claimed that students were planning to occupy the building on April 2, 1980, the anniversary of its burning. Following this publication, the DOPS agents went into action. On March 13, with art classes in session, a squadron of civil and military police armed with billy clubs, rifles, machine guns, tear gas, and small bombs stormed the school, forcing everyone inside to quickly evacuate.

The building was declared condemned that same day, and plans were made for its immediate destruction. The wrecking crews entered soon thereafter, just as students began mobilizing to prevent them. They filed several lawsuits seeking to block the condemnation, arranged for an official request that the building be preserved as a monument of national heritage, and held increasingly large demonstrations in front of the structure. Meanwhile the state ignored judicial orders to halt the destruction, secretly ferried workers to and from the site at night and on weekends and holidays, and essentially blocked off the entire Flamengo neighborhood in order to finish tearing the building down (see figure 5.3). Despite student action and even the efforts of a pistol-wielding judge who took matters into his own hands when he learned that his orders to suspend the demolition were not being obeyed, by June 1980 the building was reduced to rubble (see figure 5.4). In this last symbolic battle between UNE and the military state, UNE lost.

But did they really lose? Throughout the process UNE students held vigils and erected signs. They painted the trees, the crumbling walls, the sidewalk, and the street out front with slogans. They climbed on buses and visited theaters to ask for money and expressions of solidarity. They appeared in newspapers and on television. They held gradually larger and larger protest demonstrations in front of the building and—when the police forced them away with smoke bombs and water hoses—moved downtown to Cinelândia Plaza. They attracted the support of politicians and professors, journalists and artists. Members of UNE referred to the building not just as a site of student memory but also as one of national memory, calling it the "patrimony of the people" and "the memory of Brazilian students" and painting graffiti on the building, one of which read, "The Memory of the People will not be Destroyed." In defense of its building UNE, though still officially illegal in 1980, conjured a huge wave of positive publicity and popular support for its actions.

Moreover, the heavy-handed behavior of the police served to illustrate the dichotomy UNE members had earlier emphasized in their Reconstruction Congress posters: an aggressive, authoritarian state which destroyed buildings versus the reasonable nature of their civic organization. Maria Francisca de Souza Alves, an UNE representative who arrived at Praia de Flamengo Street just before police evacuated the building, augmented this disparity in her statements to the press: "I don't understand why they need so much repression. I am the only UNE representative here. I don't know karate and I'm not armed. I didn't come here to take over the building or to expel the students." Her teasing comments about not knowing karate and being unarmed combined with her gender (for women, as we have seen, were considered unlikely participants in armed militancy notwithstanding their repeated participation) combined to juxtapose a new, democratic, peaceful UNE with the old, authoritarian, violent state. She went on to say, "I came precisely to study with the Centro Acadêmico, the Departmental Director and the authorities, a peaceable way for UNE to symbolically occupy the building on April 2, the day on which, 16 years ago, it was burned. This building is a monument to student struggles."[81] The charac-

FIGURE 5.3. Police guard the former UNE building as students and others seek to halt its destruction. Agência JB

FIGURE 5.4. The nearly destroyed former UNE building in 1980. Agência JB.

terization was apt. While students filed petitions in court, the police refused to obey the judge's orders. While students painted signs and sang the national anthem, police blocked off larger and larger areas of the Flamengo neighborhood, creating the visual effect of a state of siege. And while students appealed for the support of various politicians, the police brutalized them, sending three Rio de Janeiro aldermen to the hospital even though this action brought them official condemnation from the Senate floor.[82] As a measure of the broad-based denunciation of the regime's behavior, it is notable that the *Jornal do Brasil* for June 12, 1980, published an editorial and six letters to the editor criticizing as hypocritical police explanations of their activities at the building.[83]

Most important, however, the fight to preserve this site of memory served to unify the student movement itself. Newspapers noted the daily growth of student mobilizations, from a few indignant UNE members to larger groups of protesters to, finally, huge demonstrations with students from all over the country. DOPS officials recorded rumors of busloads of students planning to come from all areas of Brazil (although it is unclear if these plans ever materialized). For a newly re-created organization battling years of student demobilization, struggling to make itself felt on the national oppositional scene, and striving for a sense of legitimacy, the battle for the UNE building provided an ideal scenario. David Lowenthal writes, "Communal identity is often secured, honor satisfied, simply by fervent reiteration of a claim. It may better serve Greek pride to go on demanding the Elgin Marbles' return than actually to get them back. Nothing rouses popular feeling more than a grievance unrectified."[84] Indeed, in an UNE seminar held shortly after the building was destroyed, the organization's president noted the effect the campaign had had on them, saying, "UNE didn't lower its head with the arbitrary demolition of its building, and that act united even more the student masses and the people against the repressive apparatus."[85]

In early June 1980, when federal judges denied the students' first request to halt the demolition of the building, they noted in their decision, "Once the building has disappeared, there will be nothing left to try to fix up."[86] They were mistaken. For, like so many people who were disappeared by the military regime, the nonexistent building continued to play a central role in the reconstruction of shared memories of civil society. Students continued to refer to the former building, to write about it and print pictures of it, both when it was intact and in various stages of destruction.

They briefly proposed building a new UNE headquarters in São Paulo in 1981 and 1982 and even secured the support of Brazil's most famous architect, Oscar Niemeyer, who agreed to design the building, but they soon dropped the idea of a move away from Rio.[87] Notwithstanding the celebrity that would have been generated by a Niemeyer-designed Palace of Youth, as some called the proposal, the mnemonic appeal of Rio de Janeiro and 132 Praia de Flamengo Street were greater.[88] It was UNE's first woman president, Clara Araujo, who secured another building in Rio for the union in 1983, a demonstration of the union's growing political clout and of her importance as president. For although at her election in 1982 opponents of her candidacy had disparaged her with nicknames like Clarinha Bonitinha (Pretty Little Clara), infantilizing suggestions that her gender and her attractiveness made her unfit for political leadership, her election had been well received in the press and by many people.[89] She and the union alike received an important sign of approval from the governor of Rio de Janeiro, Leonel Brizola, when he granted them a building in Rio to use, and after this UNE once again operated publicly in the seaside city.[90] But as soon as the country resumed democratic rule with the inauguration of the civilian president José Sarney in 1985, UNE petitioned for and secured legal status and began to lobby the new government to return the Praia de Flamengo Street site. They even returned to it occasionally, as in 1987, with the building long gone and a barren parking lot in its place, when they commemorated its fiftieth anniversary with a concert there. Thirty years after the fire that dislodged students and ushered in the military dictatorship then-President Itamar Franco "return[ed] a piece of history to the country" when, in 1994, he granted UNE legal rights to the lot.[91]

....

If commemorative events had helped to ensure some degree of continuity and collective political identity among students in the early 1970s, in the second half of the decade invocations of a shared student memory became a fundamental mechanism by which they mobilized their fellow students and rebuilt student organizations such as UNE.

The students who re-created UNE in 1979 did so by dialoguing with the nation's recent history. Coming of age in the late 1970s, during a period when the country as a whole was attempting to come to terms with fifteen years of military dictatorship, students reconstructed their union, in part to remember and join its history of opposition. In this process, the story and image of the former UNE headquarters, invaded and burned at the time of the military coup, provided symbolic power and a material link to the past. Through references to 132 Praia de Flamengo Street they were able to emphasize UNE's immediate opposition to the regime and hence the difference of their response from that of other sectors of society. They could also draw attention to the new era opening in front of them, one of civil liberties and peace instead of violence and confusion, and use that same image to appeal both to other students and to the greater public for support. Moreover, they could point to the injustice of the attack and the ultimate responsibility of the military regime in order to later press the state for retribution. While the students did not succeed in recovering their beloved building, the process was not in vain, as the re-creation of memory it triggered served to unify and strengthen the organization in the new, present moment.

Forty-seven years after supporters of the Brazilian military regime set fire to the UNE building, a democratically elected Brazilian president and former regime opponent joined current and former student activists at 132 Praia de Flamengo Street in Rio de Janeiro for an important rite of remembrance and renewal. As one of his last acts before leaving office, then-President Luiz Inácio "Lula" da Silva stood at the famous address to speak about the history of the former UNE building and to lay a cornerstone for its reconstruction. As we have seen, the building was burned in April 1964 by celebrants of the coup d'état that ushered in the dictatorship, transferred in its charred state in 1966 to the music and drama schools of a metropolitan university, and then razed in 1980 as a dubiously declared safety hazard. The structure's symbolic presence endured, however, and for thirty years the beachfront lot in the prominent Flamengo neighborhood sat mostly empty as students first struggled to reclaim rights to the space and then lobbied to secure funds for a reconstruction.

At President Lula's historic visit one particularly poignant image of 1968 predominated. On an enormous poster, spreading across the length of the empty lot and reaching several feet over the participants' heads, was an enormous black-and-white photograph of a smoky street protest filled with exuberant young people, fists in the air. One bearded young man is closer to the camera than the others, apparently leaping for joy, a rock in his right fist. It is a striking image, snapped at one of the many student demonstrations in Rio de Janeiro in 1968 and capturing in a flash the exuberance of youth, of popular political participation, of the potential strength in collective action. Most important, the leaping figure is widely believed to be Honestino Guimarães, and his towering presence at the site suggested the parallels between the martyrdom and militancy of UNE's disappeared president and that of its disappeared building.[1] Emphasizing still further present-day understandings of the power of that disappeared building, the sign alongside Guimarães's enlarged photo read, "It has been known as the 'House of Youth Power,' and the 'House of Democratic Resistance.' It was burned and demolished by the military dictatorship. From students' struggles and Oscar Niemeyer's drawing board, the dream of reconstruction is born. With an eye to the future we return to this space. Thank you Rio de Janeiro. For UNE, it will be an honor to return home."[2]

Students' long-standing efforts to recuperate their building and, by extension, the union's material authority finally paid off when, a few days before this ceremony in 2010, the Lula government deposited into UNE's coffers the first installment of a R$4.6-million (US$ 26.7-million) indemnity payment, reparations for the students' loss during the dictatorship. Subsequent installments were to be made by the incoming president, Dilma Rousseff. In explaining the government's decision, Paulo Abrão, the president of the Amnesty Commission that authorized the indemnity, labeled it a "moral reparation," explaining that the current government "recognizes student politics as one of the central mechanisms of civic democratic life."[3] It was just the kind of official and symbolic recognition students had long sought.

The political transformation in Brazil between 1964 and 2010 has been remarkable, especially the ascendancy of the Partido dos Trabalhadores (PT), a party that was born out of the labor union movement of the late 1970s and that quickly came to count on a sizable portion of the intellectual sectors as its supporters. Both Presidents da Silva and Rousseff hail from the PT, and their administrations as well as the leadership of the PT more generally have been filled with important figures from the student movement of 1968, including some of the figures discussed here, such as Vladimir Palmeira, José Dirceu, Franklin Martins, and José Genoino. But the PT does not have a monopoly on student activists or on claims to 1968. Former president Fernando Henrique Cardoso has asserted that "more of 1968 remained" in his presidency than in Lula's, and the presidential candidate who has most often run against the PT, José Serra, was the president of UNE at the time of the coup in 1964.[4]

Indeed, memories of 1968 continued to impact the Brazilian political scene long after the return to democracy. By 1998, the thirty-year anniversary of 1968, yet another generation of university students came to evoke that pivotal year. On June 26 they commemorated the March of the 100,000 with a repeat performance, marching the historic route from Candelária Cathedral to Cinelândia. Past and present, however, were impossible to disentangle. For while they marched that day to remember 1968, they also did so to call attention to 1998 and an ongoing strike by faculty and staff at fifty-two federal universities. When some of the marchers decided to call on the minister of education and were blocked by military police, they protested with cries of "Dictators" and "Military sons of bitches." Many participants enthusiastically compared the repression to that which they had read about under the regime, while handbills passed out in the streets unequivocally stated, "The end of the dictatorship is the right to education; the dictatorship has not ended." That Cardoso, a formerly left-leaning academic who had been forcefully retired by the military regime, came to implement neoliberal economic policies as president was seen by the students as an ideological betrayal. And in May 2000 students were outraged by the response of Serra, then minister of health, to an egg-throwing student protester: he threatened to resurrect the Law of National Security. This repressive legislation had not been applied since the end of military rule, and students bitterly criticized the irony of Serra's response.[5] Meanwhile throughout his presidency in 2003–10 Lula was berated for not sufficiently facilitating the search for information on the disappeared. As a former opposition leader, he was presumed to be more sympathetic to this issue than his predecessors had been.

Now, nearly fifty years after the coup d'état that ushered in the military regime, there is no sign that the intense fascination with (and often celebration of) the idea of young people bravely organizing against a repressive dictatorship is waning. Such interest speaks to Brazilian society's mnemonic response to the military period as a whole. As Daniel Aarão Reis Filho has written, "Almost no one today wants to identify with the military dictatorship in Brazil."[6] Few recall the considerable popular support offered to coup organizers in 1964 or the overwhelming popularity of such figures as the military president Emílio Garrastazu Médici. Reis notes that at the thirtieth anniversary of 1968 "Brazilian society, through the media and academia, consecrated a hostile position to the dictatorship" by celebrating the vanquished and condemning the victors.[7] The continued production and consumption of cultural and literary texts devoted to anti-regime activists should similarly be seen as evidence of a willed collective memory of unfaltering opposition to the regime. Every page offers the writer and the reader a chance to live the period anew, repositioning themselves in the face of new understandings. While accounts of the clandestine armed lefts elicit a complex mixture of admiration for their sacrifice and general disapproval of their decision to use force, the massive street demonstrations of 1968 offer a less complicated image of dissent, one that, through its very size and nature, represents the latent disagreement of society at large. The ambivalence with which many observers in 1968 viewed both the military regime and its seemingly unruly student opponents has gradually faded, covered over by layers of new recollections, revelations, and reinterpretations. What is clear is that 1968 lives on in Brazilian national memory. Not only are specific figures such as Serra read through the lens of this earlier period, but cultural, political, and personal references to that year have pervaded student politics and identity in the decades after. Since 1968 people have continued to speak of flowers in ever-changing ways, and, as future generations of student leaders make their impact, they will carry with them these layers of meaning.

Notes

Introduction

1. Dunn, *Brutality Garden*, 137.
2. Octávio Costa, in D'Araujo et al., *Os anos de chumbo: A Repressão*, 264.
3. Dunn, *Brutality Garden*, 148.
4. Dunn, *Brutality Garden*, 137.
5. Here I follow the lead of the many Brazilian historians of this period who initiated this terminology. As one example, see Daniel Aarão Reis Filho's argument in favor of this usage in *Ditadura militar, esquerdas e sociedade*.
6. "Secundarista oferece uma rosa amarela à PM," *Jornal do Brasil*, October 11, 1968.
7. "DOPS prende quem mostra entusiasmo pela canção de Vandré defronte às lojas," *Jornal do Brasil*, October 12, 1968.
8. The expression "the years of lead" (*os anos de chumbo*) emerged in the 1980s and is a Portuguese paraphrase of *Die Bleierne Zeit*, the original title of a film from 1981 by Margarethe von Trotta. The film is a fictionalized version of the real story of two sisters, one of whom is a member of the Red Army Faction in the 1970s and dies in prison, while the other sees her life destroyed by the repression and disruption of the period. For English-language audiences the release title was *Marianne and Juliane*.
9. Aldo Rebelo interview, Projeto Memória do Movimento Estudantil (hereafter PMME).
10. Acronyms in Brazilian Portuguese, when feasible, are typically spoken as words, not spelled out as they are in U.S. English. Therefore, rather than "the U.N.E.," UNE is pronounced as a single word, "oo-nay" and is treated as a proper noun.
11. The literature on student activism in the 1960s around the world is too vast to note in its entirety, but see, for example, the following comparative histories: Boren, *Student Resistance*; Caute, *The Year of the Barricades*; Fraser, *1968: A Student Generation in Revolt*; Klimke, *The Other Alliance*; Suri, *Power and Protest*.

12. Journalist and cultural commentator Inimá Ferreira Simões wrote of film-makers in the first year after the coup who used this kind of dark (and, I would add, gendered) humor to label the military regime a *ditabranda*, or "soft dictatorship." Some have occasionally employed the term to contrast it with the undeniably "hard" *ditadura* that followed. But when in February 2009 a columnist in the *Folha de São Paulo* newspaper referenced the entire 1964–1985 period with the *ditabranda* label in an attempt to cast the Brazilian dictatorship as milder than those of its Southern Cone neighbors, the event elicited outraged letters to the editor, an online petition signed by well-known academic and activist figures, and physical protests in front of the newspaper headquarters. The controversy demonstrates that the repression wrought by the regime is, for many, its defining characteristic and that denying this human and ethical failing is today an offensive act. See Simões, *Roteiro da Intolerância*, 78.

13. See Araujo, *Memórias estudantis*; Ribeiro do Valle, *1968: O diálogo é a violência*; Fávero, *A UNE em tempos de autoritarismo*; Martins Filho, *Movimento estudantil e ditadura militar*; Sanfelice, *Movimento estudantil: A UNE na Resitência ao golpe de 64*; Albuquerque, *Movimento estudantil e consciência social*; Lerche Vieira, *O (Dis)curso da (Re)forma Universitária*; and Saldanha de Oliveira, *A Mitologia Estudantil*.

14. Some older scholarship does indeed posit events in Europe as a catalyst for those in Brazil, but this idea is no longer accepted. See Mendes Junior, *Movimento estudantil no Brasil*, from 1981.

15. The collection of interviews and photographs about 1968 assembled by Daniel Aarão Reis Filho and Pedro de Moraes is one such example of an important book that notes the context of 1968 but does not integrate it into the main part of the text. They include a detailed chronology of the year, listing Brazilian and international events side by side but without explanation. Other examples come from volumes that include articles or chapters on student movements from multiple national locations, presumably in the hopes that readers could forge their own comparative understandings of the international dimensions of 1968. See Aarão Reis Filho and Moraes, *68: a paixão de uma utopia*; Garcia and Vieira, eds., *Rebeldes e Contestadores 1968: Brasil, França e Alemanha*; Scherer, Nussbaumer and di Fanti, eds., *Utopias e distopias: 30 anos de maio de 68, Santa Maria*; and Martins Filho, *A Rebelião Estudantil*.

16. "Why those students are protesting," *Time Magazine*, May 3, 1968.

17. Suri, *Power and Protest*.

18. Wallerstein, "1968, Revolution in the World-System."

19. See Klimke, *The Other Alliance*, and Varon, *Bringing the War Home*.

20. Carey, *Plaza of Sacrifices*, 3, 5.

21. Mark Barry Schwartz dates the start of "the great wave of collective memory research" with the English-language publication in 1980 of Maurice Halbwachs's *Collective Memory* (published in France thirty years earlier). Whatever the beginning moment, since the 1980s the literature has expanded enormously. See especially

Portelli, *The Order has been Carried Out*; Sturken, *Tangled Memories*; Gillis, *Commemorations*; Pollak, "Memória, esquecimento, silêncio."

22. See Steve Stern's three-volume study, *Remembering Pinochet's Chile*; Allier Montaña, *Batallas por la memoria*; Achugar, "El lugar de la memoria."

23. Jelin, *State Repression and the Labors of Memory*.

24. While the large quantity of memoirs and published interviews makes them too numerous to list here, two examples deserve mention. First, the extensive series of interviews with military officials undertaken by Maria Celina d'Aruajo and Celso Castro at Centro de Pesquisas e Documentação Contemporánea (CPDOC) at the Fundação Getúlio Vargas led to the publication of five books, as well as to the availability of many of the interviews through CPDOC's physical or digital archive. Second, the four-volume history of the military regime written by Elio Gaspari and based on military documents released only to him has had enormous popular success in Brazil.

25. See, for example, Comissão de Familiares de Mortos e Desaparecidos Políticos, Instituto de Estudo da Violência do Estado et. al., *Dossiê dos Mortos e Desaparecidos Políticos a Partir de 1964* and Miranda and Tibúrcio, *Dos filhos deste solo*.

26. Among others, and notwithstanding long-standing public campaigns to open them, archives with documents relating to the conflict in Araguaia remain firmly closed.

27. While Thomas Skidmore's book *The Politics of Military Rule in Brazil, 1954–85* (1988) became a much-heralded, early history of the military regime, a long interlude followed in which political scientists paid greater attention to the regime than historians. That is now changing. On the question of the role of the United States, see, for example, Fico, *O Grande Irmão*; Green, *We Cannot Remain Silent*; and Leacock, *Requiem for Revolution*.

28. Kenneth Serbin uncovered previously unknown documents in his writing of *Secret Dialogues*. Meanwhile Maria Paula Araujo helped to assemble a collection of publications from the alternative press, now housed at the Laboratório de Estudos do Tempo Presente of the Universidade Federal do Rio de Janeiro. She used these to write *A Utopia fragementada*. Many of the numerous books about the clandestine lefts that have been published are similarly based on documents carefully preserved by former activists.

29. On the coup of 1964 and the role of individual military figures see Dreifus, *1964, a Conquista do estado*, Fico, *Além do Golpe*, and Elio Gaspari's four-volume study, *As Ilusões Armadas*.

30. Possibly the most well known and widely read book on the history of the student movement in Brazil, Artur Poerner's *O Poder Jovem*, narrates the history of student activism since the early 1700s. As remarkable as this book is for its wealth of detail and gripping descriptions of student struggles, it adopts an uncritical view of students, casting them as ceaseless defenders of democracy, the people, and the nation. Originally written in 1968 when the author was twenty-five years old, and

now in its fifth, revised edition, *O Poder Jovem* is best understood as an important cultural force that has influenced generations of student activists. See also the excellent analysis of the myths engendered by this book in Saldanha de Oliveira, *A UNE e o mito do poder jovem*. Most other books about the student movement in Brazil begin at or shortly before 1968. Additionally, Maria Paula Araujo added important historical contextualization and interpretation to her volume on interviews with student activists from the 1930s to the present. See *Memórias estudantis*. The most notable scholarly studies of the national student movement focus mostly on 1968 itself, but at least one recently completed dissertation promises to help remedy this by looking at the period 1955–1990. See Snider, "Complicated Campuses."

31. An important new dissertation suggests that similarly heated debates about the proper role of youth in general animated military and civilian debates as well. See Cowan, "The Secret History of Subversion."

32. O'Donnell, "Tensions in the Bureaucratic-Authoritarian State and the Question of Democracy."

1. Authority in Student Politics

1. "O Rio para o Universitário: Roteiro Turístico, Cultural e Informativo, XIV Congresso Nacional dos Estudantes," box 171, Register of the United States National Student Association, International Commission Records, 1946–68, Hoover Institution Archives, Stanford University (hereafter USNSA, Hoover). Unless otherwise noted, all translations from Portuguese are mine.

2. Although universities were prohibited, some degree of higher education did take place via the Jesuits and a few isolated programs. The basis for Brazil's university system, however, lies in the period after 1808.

3. In a magazine interview the renowned scholar of Brazilian education, Luis Antônio Cunha, jokingly remarked on the fact that in Bahia in 1808 "they studied surgery without anatomy." He went on to explain, however, that at that time anatomy and surgery were seen as very different professions, the latter having a much higher social status. Cited in Pinheiro et al., "Era uma vez um rei chamado D. João VI . . ." In 1813 the independent *cátedras* of anatomy and surgery were combined into the more inclusive study of medicine, both in Rio and in Bahia.

4. Cunha, "Ensino Superior e Universidade no Brasil."

5. Schwarcz's definition of a *bacharel* (the singular of *bachareis*) is as follows: "The Brazilian bacharel degree is the rough equivalent of a highly specialized bachelor's degree in the United States. Areas of study include either traditional undergraduate disciplines, such as history, economics and biology, or professional studies, such as law and pharmacy." Schwarcz, *The Spectacle of the Races*, 169.

6. Ibid.

7. Cited in Kirkendall, *Class Mates*, 173.

8. Ibid., 163.

9. Since 1837 graduates of the prestigious Cólegio Pedro II in Rio and, after 1891, graduates of all accredited secondary schools had the right to enroll in any faculty or university in the country without taking an entrance exam. This right was revoked in 1911 by the Lei Organica do Ensino Superior e do Fundamental/Decreto 8659. The name *vestibular* for this entrance exam appeared in 1915 through Decreto 11530 of March 18, 1915.

10. Beltrão and Diniz Alves, "Reversal of the Gender Gap in Brazilian Education in the 20th Century."

11. Andrew Kirkendall asserts that the first women to graduate from the Recife Law School did so in 1888. Kirkendall, *Class Mates*, 149.

12. This is from the first issue of the student publication "O Onze de Agosto," cited in Dulles, *The São Paulo Law School and the Anti-Vargas Resistance (1938–1945)*, 10.

13. Ibid., chap. 1.

14. Myhr, "The University Student Tradition in Brazil," 133.

15. Telegram from Euclides da Cunha, published in *O Estado de São Paulo*, October 26, 1897.

16. Myhr, "The University Student Tradition in Brazil," 133.

17. Dulles, *The São Paulo Law School and the Anti-Vargas Resistance (1938–1945)*, 10.

18. See van Aken, "University Reform before Córdoba," and Altbach, "The International Student Movement."

19. Van Aken, "University Reform before Córdoba," 459.

20. Ibid.

21. Milanesio, "Gender and Generation."

22. Manifiesto de Córdoba, 1918. http://www.fmmeducacion.com (November 30, 2009).

23. Ibid.

24. Milanesio, "Gender and Generation," 509.

25. Ibid.

26. Love, *Rio Grande do Sul and Brazilian Regionalism, 1882–1930*, 118

27. Ibid.

28. Of the thirty million inhabitants in Brazil in 1930, twenty-three million, or roughly 77 percent, were illiterate. Instituto Brasileiro de Geografia e Estatística, *Sinopse Estatística do Brasil*, 1946 (Rio de Janeiro: Serviço Gráfico do Instituto Brasileiro de Geografia e Estatística), 19. Of those aged fifteen or older, 70 percent were illiterate. Lourenço Filho, *Evolução da Taxa de Analfabetismo de 1900 a 1960*. R.B.E.P. no. 100. Fundação I.B.G.E. *Brasil: Séries Estatísticas Retrospectivas*, 1970; cited in Romanelli, *História da Educação no Brasil*.

29. Originally called the University of Rio de Janeiro, officials changed the name in 1937 to the University of Brazil to reflect its important status and location in the nation's capital. After Brasilia became the capital in 1960, the name changed again in 1966—to its current one, the Federal University of Rio de Janeiro (Universidade Federal do Rio de Janeiro, UFRJ).

30. Prior to this grouping of individual faculties into federal universities, three fully formed private universities had been created in Manaus (1909), São Paulo (1911), and Paraná (1912). For various reasons these three attempts to found private universities failed (although some individual faculties within them survived and were later incorporated into federal universities).

31. Cunha, "A gratuidade no ensino superior público: da proibição à garantia constitucional."

32. See, for example, French, *The Brazilian Workers' ABC*, and Wolfe, *Working Women, Working Men*.

33. This definition of corporatism comes from Collier and Collier, "Inducements versus Constraints: Disaggregating 'Corporatism,'" 968.

34. Article 93 and Article 103, Section 2 of Decreto No. 19.851 de 11 de abril de 1931. Républica dos Estados Unidos do Brasil. *Coleção das Leis: Atos do Govêrno Provisorio Volume 1, 1931 (Janeiro a Abril)* (Rio de Janeiro: Imprensa Nacional, 1932), 414–17.

35. Ibid., article 104, 418.

36. Because of the long, diverse history of student organizing that predated this law, there are a variety of names for the official student associations at this level. Besides CAs, the name used at the São Paulo Law School, some faculties created Gremios, and a few came up with other names. In addition, in many places students named their centers, again like the Centro Acadêmico 11 de Agosto.

37. Albuquerque, "Movimento Estudantil e Classe Média no Brasil: Estudo comparativo," 122.

38. Article 107 of Decreto No. 19.851 de 11 de abril de 1931, 418–19. Robert O. Myhr states that these changes came about after a group of students and professors, "moved by the Argentine experience," requested student participation on faculty and university governing councils. Although he presents no specific evidence for this influence, the interconnectedness of students in this period suggests that Brazilian students may indeed have been inspired by these earlier movements. Myhr, "The University Student Tradition in Brazil," 135.

39. Like the acronym UNE, UEE is treated as a proper noun and is pronounced "oo-ay." As DA would be confusing as a spoken word and DCE simply unpronounceable, they are spelled out: D-A and D-C-E.

40. See the explanation of the Casa's activities in Casa do Estudante do Brasil, *Relatório 1939*.

41. Student-sponsored pageants were typical of the 1930s. Student organizations like CAs nominated prominent young women to positions, whether or not they were students. For example, in that same year in Ceará the elected Queen of the Students was Rachel Queiroz, a substitute teacher at a normal school who had just published her first novel to much acclaim. On the election of Queiroz, see her autobiography, *Tantos Anos*. On the election of Ana Amélia Queirós, see the interview of José Gomes Talarico, PMME.

42. Dulles, *Carlos Lacerda, Brazilian Crusader*, 1:26–27.

43. Sussekind de Mendonça, *Sensacionalismo*.

44. Altbach, "The International Student Movement," 159.

45. "Congresso Nacional de Estudantes, Circular 1," letter from Clothilde Calvacanti, 1938. Arquivo Gustavo Capanema, Centro de Pesquisa e Documentação de Historia Contemporanea do Brasil (hereafter CPDOC), Fundação Getúlio Vargas (hereafter FGV), CPDOC/GC g 1938.04.18.

46. Altbach, "The International Student Movement," 159.

47. The council instead became a subsection of UNE. Made up of two representatives from each affiliate student organization—which at this point meant a mixture of UEEs, DCEs, and CAs, because not all states had all kinds of organizations—the council elected and advised the UNE leadership.

48. UNE Statutes, 1938. This meeting in December 1938 became known as the 2nd Congress of the National Union of Students, not because all UNE members considered the meeting of August 1937 to be the first but because there had been a short-lived UNE in 1910 that held the first congress of this name. Its members told one participant, Irum Sant'Anna, "The first is ours; you can only be second." Nonetheless, there is still a passionate debate about whether August 1937 or December 1938 should be the date of origin of UNE. Santa'Anna vigorously defends December 1938, but the UNE statutes written at that very meeting state that the union was founded on August 11, 1937. Curiously, when, in 1939, UNE requested official status from President Vargas, its formal typed letter gives the founding date as 1938, but the number "8" is written in by hand on top of the typed letter "7" below. It is unclear if they were simply fixing a typographical error or if it represented, even then, some confusion about the appropriate foundation date. See Irum Sant'Anna interview, PMME, and the UNE statutes.

49. Skidmore, "Failure in Brazil," 142.

50. See Levine, *Father of the Poor?*, and Dulles, *Anarchists and Communist in Brazil 1900–1935*.

51. Prestes became famous for his role as the leader of a revolt of junior army officers in the 1920s.

52. Gomes Vianna, "O PCB: 1929–43."

53. José Gomes Talarico interview, PMME.

54. *Relatórios da União Nacional dos Estudantes*, 1939, 1940, 109–12, cited in Dulles, *The São Paulo Law School*, 57.

55. Altbach, "The International Student Movement," 160.

56. Casa do Estudante do Brasil, *Relatorio 1939*.

57. Dulles, *The São Paulo Law School*, 57.

58. Genival Barbosa, the president of UNE in 1948, told an interviewer that at the UNE Congress in 1948 all the women who attended were from schools of nursing or philosophy (the main discipline for teachers in training). Whether or

not this was true for every single woman, his memories reflect the commonsense view (and often practice) that women pursued higher education in order to follow one of these two careers. Genival Barbosa Guimarães interview, PMME.

59. The other issues included cultural concerns, such as foreign exchange programs, difficulties in acquiring books, and the possibility of creating a student theater; economic questions relating to tuition and fees, housing opportunities, and the potential for paid internships; health issues like physical education and hygiene; and plans to organize intra-university sporting competitions. "Congresso Nacional de Estudantes, Circular 1," letter from Clothilde Calvacanti, 1938. Arquivo Gustavo Capanema, CPDOC, FGV, CPDOC/GC g 1938.04.18.

60. In lists of UNE directorates, the first female name I have come across, after Clothilde Cavalcanti, is Raimunda Ramalho, elected to 3rd Secretary in 1949.

61. José Gomes Talarico interview, PMME, and Irum Sant'Anna interview, PMME.

62. Irum Sant'Anna interview, PMME.

63. José Gomes Talarico interview, PMME.

64. Relatório da UNE, July 1940, cited in Poerner, O Poder Jovem, 143–46.

65. Poerner, O Poder Jovem, 157.

66. Caulfield, "The Birth of Mangue," 89.

67. Irum Sant'Anna recalls that "Paes Leme took UNE home with him." Irum Sant'Anna interview, PMME.

68. For more information on the campaign for women's suffrage and ideas about women generally in this period, see Besse, Restructuring Patriarchy.

69. Jacob Gorender interview, PMME.

70. José Gomes Talarico interview, PMME.

71. Erickson, The Brazilian Corporative State and Working-Class Politics, 2.

72. UNE, "Resoluções da Assembléa do Conselho Nacional de Estudantes, Programa para o periodo 1939–1940."

73. Decreto-Lei No. 4.105 of February 11, 1942.

74. Hilton, "Brazilian Diplomacy and the Washington–Rio de Janeiro 'Axis' during the World War II Era." See also Hilton's Brazil and the Great Powers, 1930–1939.

75. Sterns, "Three Decades of Student Leadership in Brazil, 1933–1965," 22.

76. José Gomes Talarico interview, PMME.

77. See, for example, the Correio da Manhã's coverage, "Unidos em vibrante demonstração de civisimo, os estudantes levaram a efeito ontem um desfile em que significaram sua condenação à politica do eixo," July 5, 1942, reprinted in Araujo, Memórias estudantis, 36.

78. José Gomes Talarico interview, PMME.

79. Curiously, in current Brazilian slang, a galinha is a man who dates many women at one time, perhaps in metaphorical reference to the flocks of women who supposedly flutter around him.

80. I am grateful to Paulina Alberto for suggesting this interpretation of their insults, among her many other helpful comments.

81. Poerner, *O Poder Jovem*, 158.

82. Ibid.

83. The exact story of just how UNE acquired the property is one that would make a fascinating study in itself. Various participants interviewed about this event all remember it differently. José Gomes Talarico said that when a petition requesting the building was delivered to Vargas's office, the president himself came out and immediately signed it. The bearers of the decree, together with a small group of around twenty people, went to the building and occupied it symbolically, calling officials to come and take a complete inventory of the state's new furnishings (furniture, chandeliers, etc.). But João Saldanha, another contemporary, recalls a triumphant group of students who attacked other German-owned property in the area and was about to set fire to the Sociedade Germania too when they suddenly decided to take it over instead. And in *O Poder Jovem* Artur Poerner provides yet another account (though he was not a participant and does not cite his source), declaring that the students first occupied the building, then sent President Vargas a message saying they would not leave until he granted the building to them. It is outside the scope of this book to delve into each story, but the competing memories suggest the lingering power of both the physical space of the UNE headquarters and the symbolic significance of its origins in the divisions brought on by the World War II. See José Gomes Talarico interview, PMME; Máximo, *João Saldanha*, 20; and Poerner, *O Poder Jovem*.

84. Decreto-Lei No. 4.696 de 16 de Setembro de 1942 in Républica dos Estados Unidos do Brasil. *Coleção das Leis. Atos do Poder Executivo Volume V, 1942 (Decretos-Leis de Julho a Setembro)* (Rio de Janeiro: Imprensa Nacional, 1942), 275.

85. Noted in Dulles, *Sobral Pinto*, 235.

86. *Manifesto da Resistência Democrática aos Brasileiros* (Rio de Janeiro: Resistência Democrática, 1945), 3–4, 6; cited in Dulles, *Sobral Pinto*, 233.

87. Letter from Paulo Silveira to Gustavo Capanema, March 5, 1945, reproduced in Fávero, *A UNE em Tempos de Autoritarismo*, 21–22.

88. José Frejat interview, PMME.

89. Note by the president of UNE Roberto Gusmão and read at the Congresso Nacional, October 3, 1947.

90. Letter from Robert S. Smith, vice president of USNSA to UNE, August 5, 1948, box 171, USNSA, Hoover.

91. Letter from Sylvio Wanick Rebeiro, general secretary of the Uniao Nacional dos Estudantes to the USNSA, July 6, 1948, box 171, USNSA, Hover.

92. Letter from Rebeiro to USNSA, July 6, 1948.

93. Genival Barbosa Guimarães, interview, PMME.

94. Publications of UNE list Raimunda Ramalho and Maria de Lourdes Palmeira Florencio as 3rd Secretary for the terms 1949–50 and 1950–51, respectively. See those found in box 171 of the USNSA Collection, Hoover.

95. Genival Barbosa Guimarães interview, PMME.

96. Ibid.

97. Dulles, *Carlos Lacerda, Brazilian Crusader*, 103.

98. Ibid.

99. Araujo, *Memórias estudantis*, 81. This history would go on to inspire Petrobrás's financial support of many UNE activities, a relationship that continues to the present. The image of nationalistic students fortuitously demanding that the state preserve the nation's oil appeals to both the student union and the oil company.

100. Skidmore, *Politics in Brazil*, 98.

101. I say possible CIA funding because it is unclear if the CIA funded this particular trip. By 1952 the CIA was supplying the USNSA with considerable financial support, a relationship that came to light in February 1967 in *Ramparts* magazine and was then widely reported in the rest of the U.S. media. And while State Department officials confirmed CIA funding since 1952, evidence suggests that it had begun even earlier. See, for example, "Ex-Student Describes Intrigue in Getting CIA Loan in '50," *New York Times*, February 16, 1967. That CIA support would have made possible Eisenberg's and Rogers's visit to Brazil to advocate against the IUS would also make sense given the CIS's financial ties to the anti-Communist IUS replacement, the International Student Conference (founded in 1950). When news of this relationship also came to light in 1967, several student unions dropped out of the organization, and in early 1969 it disbanded.

102. Herbert Eisenberg, handwritten notes and typed speech, box 171, USNSA, Hoover.

103. Skidmore, *Politics in Brazil*, 81–142.

104. Ibid, 75.

105. "A mocidade estudantil contra a onda de escandalos no país," *O Povo*, April 1954, reproduced in Araujo, *Memórias estudantis*, 81.

106. José Gregori interview, PMME.

107. See the excellent analysis of his death and the response it provoked (at the time and years later) in Williams and Weinstein, "Vargas Morto: The Death and Life of a Brazilian Statesman."

108. Almino Alfonso interview, PMME.

109. *Movimento: Órgão da União Nacional dos Estudantes*, 1956, box 171, USNSA, Hoover.

2. Students and Political Polarization

1. On the decision to decorate Guevara, see the biography of the Brazilian foreign minister at the time, Arinos Filho, *Diplomacia Independente*, 173–98. Arinos additionally suggests that Guevara's sympathetic assistance in communicating to Fidel Castro the concerns of the Brazilian bishop Armando Lombardi about the recent persecution of Catholic priests contributed to the decision to decorate him. On the pomp and circumstance surrounding Guevara's visit, see "Quadros Honors Guevara," *New York Times*, August 20, 1961.

2. "Recife," *O Estado de São Paulo*, June 9, 1961.

3. As we have seen, the definition of *bacharel* that refers to law school students

implies undergraduates, as in Brazil training in law was and is a specialized undergraduate program rather than a post-bachelor program, as in some other places.

4. "Palestra proibida provoca reação dos estudantes," *O Estado de São Paulo*, June 4, 1961; *Hispanic American Report* 14, no. 6, 555.

5. "Tropas do IV Excercito Enviadas a Recife," *O Estado de São Paulo*, June 8, 1961; "Recife: ocupadas mais 3 faculdades; chegam novos reforços militares," *O Estado de São Paulo*, June 10, 1961; "Enviados para Recife o cruzador Tamandaré e 2 contratorpedeiros," *O Estado de São Paulo*, June 11, 1961; "Jânio Investe Contra as Liberdades Para Defender Professôres Corruptos," *Novos Rumos*, June 16–22, 1961; "Brazil Students Fight Troops: New Army Units Fly to Recife," *New York Times*, June 11, 1961; *Hispanic American Report* 14, no. 6, 555.

6. "Che's Red Mother," *Time*, July 14, 1961.

7. Pereira, "God, the Devil, and Development in Northeast Brazil."

8. "Senadores advertem: Ligas Camponesas representam perigo," *O Estado de São Paulo*, June 3, 1961.

9. Ernest S. Guaderrama, "Operations Memorandum: Request for Additional Personnel," May 4, 1961, 4, in National Archives II, Record Group 84 Lot 66 F 121 Acc. No. 67A 1450, cited in Kirkendall, "Entering History."

10. "Exploração da juventude academica," *O Estado de São Paulo*, June 10, 1961.

11. Ridenti, *Em busca do povo*, 25.

12. Skidmore, *Politics in Brazil*, 174–82.

13. *Movimento: Órgão da União Nacional dos Estudantes*, 1956, box 171, USNSA, Hoover.

14. *Hispanic American Report* 9, no. 6, 309.

15. Tad Szulc, "Dulles Is in Rio for 2-Day Talks," *New York Times*, August 5, 1958.

16. Skidmore, *Politics in Brazil*, 188.

17. Ridenti, *Em busca do povo*, 34.

18. Ibid.

19. See the photograph in Ridenti, *Em busca do povo*.

20. José Carlos Brandão, "Punta del Este: Derrota do Imperialismo" *A Época*, May 1962, no. 203, 13–14.

21. The phrase *liberation theology* emerged in 1971, following the publication of Gustavo Gutierrez's influential book, *A Theology of Liberation: History, Politics, Salvation*, in which he described and furthered this then-developing trajectory of Christian thought.

22. Like UNE, the acronym for JUC is typically treated as a proper noun, and pronounced "Joo-key." The AP acronym, however, is spelled out as A-P.

23. Lima and Arantes, *História da Ação Popular*, 28.

24. This is the sense behind the title of his book, *Educação como prática da liberdade* (1967).

25. Freire, *Education for Critical Consciousness*, 43.

26. Murgel Starling, *Os Senhores das Gerais*, 35.

27. Graham, "The Growth, Change and Reform of Higher Education in Brazil."

28. Álvaro Vieira Pinto, "O que é a universidade?" 1962. Document 10 from Jean Marc von der Weid Collection (hereafter JMV), Série Análisis do Movimento Estudantil, Arquivo Público do Estado do Rio de Janeiro (hereafter APERJ).

29. Documents from the first two of these, the Declaração da Bahia and the Carta do Paraná, were reproduced in their entirety as Anexo 1 and 2, in Fávero, A UNE em Tempos de Autoritarismo. The third seminar took place in Minas Gerais.

30. Carta do Paraná, Anexo 2, in Fávero, A UNE em Tempos de Autoritarismo.

31. Ibid.

32. Buarque de Holanda, Impressões de Viagem, 15.

33. Camila Ribeiro, "Novos caminhos do teatro universitario," Revista Brasiliense, September–October 1962, cited in Kadt, Catholic Radicals in Brazil, 105–6.

34. Genival Barbosa Guimarães interview, PMME.

35. Joe Love, "Report on the 24th UNEB Congress," box 171, folder 3, USNSA, Hoover.

36. Bob Aragon, "Supplementary Comments," box 171, folder 3, USNSA, Hoover.

37. Ibid.

38. Ibid.

39. Ibid.

40. Reis Filho, A revolução faltou ao encontro, 34.

41. Ibid., 38.

42. Ibid., 35.

43. Ibid., 38. He cites text from Manuel Ferreira, "Unidade e defesa dos princípios," in Classe Operária, no. 426, September 1–15, 1963.

44. Antônio Serra interview, PMME.

45. Ibid.

46. Franklin Martins interview, PMME.

47. For the role of IPÊS on education, see Salgado de Souza, Os empresários e a educação. For the role of IPÊS in encouraging the coup d'etat of 1964, see Dreifus, 1964, a Conquista do estado.

48. Deixam o Estudante Estudar (date unknown, made sometime between 1962 and 1964), Arquivo Nacional do Brasil, Seção de Gravação, Som e Imagem, Caixa 8. A summary of this film can be found in Assis, Propaganda e Cinema a Serviço do Golpe, 1962/1964.

49. Pensado, "Political Violence and Student Culture in Mexico," chaps, 2, 4.

50. Bureau of International Cultural Relations, "An Evaluation of Latin American Student Leader Seminars, 1959"; Decimal File 1955–60; Bureau of Educational and Cultural Affairs; Records of the Plans and Development Staff, Evaluation Branch, 1955–60; State Department Central File (hereafter SDCF); Record Group 59 (hereafter RG); National Archives at College Park, Md. (hereafter NACP).

51. Raymundo Eirado interview, PMME.

52. Seganfreddo, UNE Instrumento de subversão, 10.

53. Cowan, "Sex and the Security State." For more information on the Escola Superior de Guerra, see also Cowan, "The Secret History of Subversion."

54. Leacock, *Requiem for Revolution*, 112.

55. Carlos Fico demonstrates that in 1962 and most of 1963 these efforts were limited to destabilization campaigns and would develop into full-blown conspiracies to unseat Goulart only in early 1964. Fico, *O Grande Irmão*, 76–79.

56. Alvarez, *Engendering Democracy in Brazil*, 6.

57. *Hispanic American Report* 15, no. 7, 659.

58. Brasil, "As ações do Comando de Caça aos Comunistas (1968–1969)."

59. *Hispanic American Report* 15, no. 1, 75.

60. Daniel Aarão Reis Filho interview, PMME.

61. "Evitado ontem novo conflito entre estudantes," *O Estado de São Paulo*, June 9, 1961.

62. Martins Filho, *Movimento Estudantil e Ditadura Militar*, 68.

63. Reis Filho, *A revolução faltou ao encontro*, 31; Fico, *O Grande Irmão*, 75–86.

64. Ibid., 88–91.

65. Skidmore, *The Politics of Military Rule in Brazil*, 14.

66. For information on UNE's radio announcements, see Gaspari, *A Ditadura Envergonhada*, 85.

67. We now know that the coup was planned for a few days later, but was initiated early because of the impatience of Gen. Olympio Mourão Filho. See Fico, *Além do Golpe*, 16.

68. For an insightful discussion of this linguistic invention of a revolutionary tradition, see Catela and Carvalho, "31 de marzo de 1964."

69. "Incêndio destruiu UNE parcialmente," *Correio da Manhã*, April 2, 1964, Primer Caderno.

70. Vianna, *Companheiros de Viagem*, 166.

71. The position Gertzel and her colleagues held as "nurses" for the male members of the group and their forced early evacuation speak to the ways in which gender norms circumscribed the behavior of these young activists.

72. Vianna, *Companheiros de Viagem*, 169.

73. Ibid., 171.

74. Martins Filho, *Movimento Estudantil*, 82.

75. Roberto Amaral interview, PMME.

76. With the creation of the new capital of Brasilia in 1960, the former Federal District that encompassed the city of Rio de Janeiro was made into a state called Guanabara. In 1974 Guanabara and the adjoining state of Rio de Janeiro were combined under the name Rio de Janeiro.

77. See the recollections of Alfredo Sirkis in this regard. Sirkis, *Os Carbonários*, 32.

78. Antônio Carlos Silveira Alves, a philosophy student at what is today the UFRJ, died when his gun mistakenly fired as he and others students tried to organize resistance to the coup. In Miranda and Tibúrcio, *Dos filhos deste solo*, 547.

79. Vladmir Palmeira, interview by the author.

80. Jonas José de Albuquerque Barros and Ivan Rocha Aguiar, high school students, were shot in Recife. Miranda, and Tibúrcio, *Dos filhos deste solo*, 547, and Fávero, *A UNE em Tempos de Autoritarismo*, 48.

81. Skidmore, *The Politics of Military Rule*, 19.

82. Institutional Act No. 1, originally published in *Diario Oficial da União*, April 9, 1964, selections reprinted in Alves, *State and Opposition in Military Brazil*, 32. A copy is also available on line at http://pt.wikisource.org.

83. Skidmore, *The Politics of Military Rule*, 19–21.

84. For an excellent analysis of what constituted subversion to the military throughout the 1960s and 1970s, see Cowan, "Sex and the Security State."

85. Alves, *State and Opposition in Military Brazil*, 37–38.

86. Gaspari, *A Ditadura Envergonhada*, 131.

87. Ibid., 134–35.

88. Skidmore, *The Politics of Military Rule*, 24.

89. Gaspari, *A Ditadura Envergonhada*, 145–49.

90. Gaspari notes that there were 204 official complaints of torture in 1964, 84 in 1965, and 66 in 1966. *A Ditadura Envergonhada*, 150.

91. Ibid., 153–58.

92. Cunha, *A Universidade Reformanda*, 56.

93. Ultra-Secreto; Inquérito—Policial—Militar—IPM—UNE-UBES; Relatório, October 21, 1965; Fotocópia in Departamento de Ordem Política e Social (hereafter DOPS); Setor Estudantil, Pasta No. 68; APERJ.

94. "A geração de 64, quarentona," *Istoé*, April 4, 1984, 28–31.

95. Daniel Aarão Reis Filho interview, PMME.

96. José Serra, *História da UNE: depoimentos de ex-dirigentes*, volume 1, 29.

97. Article 14, Lei No. 4.464 of November 9, 1964.

98. Articles 2, 3, 10 and 20, Lei No. 4.464 of November 9, 1964.

99. Article 5, Lei No. 4.464 of November 9, 1964.

100. Article 12, Section 3, Lei No. 4.464 of November 9, 1964.

101. "Suplicy debate restauração dos grêmios," *O Estado de São Paulo*, October 21, 1964; cited in Martins Filho, *Movimento Estudantil*, 87.

102. *Documenta*, no. 29, September 1964; cited in Cunha, *A Universidade Reformanda*, 59.

103. News of Suplicy de Lacerda's plans appeared in "Suplicy pede extinção da UNE e de todas as organizações estudantis nos Estados," *Jornal do Brasil*, June 5, 1964. Both excerpts from this article and the text of UME's telegram of June 7, 1964, are published in Fávero, *A UNE em Tempos de Autoritarismo*, 59–60.

104. Telegram from USNSA to President of Brasil Castelo Branco, June 19, 1964, box 172, USNSA, Hoover.

105. Telegram from União Metropolitana dos Estudantes Brasil to USNSA, June 26, 1964, box 172, USNSA, Hoover.

106. Memorandum, box 172, USNSA, Hoover.

107. Poerner, O Poder Jovem, 256.

108. Diretoria da UNE, "Aos Estudantes e Ao Povo Brasileiro," pamphlet, Guanabara, July 1964; in DOPS; Setor Secreto, Pasta No. 4, APERJ. It is impossible to know if this memo was actually written or approved by many of the outgoing UNE leaders, most of whom had gone into exile. As UNE directorates could encompass numerous individuals who held a variety of posts, it is very likely that a few had a hand in it. It is also conceivable that the memo was written by militants of the clandestine lefts who opposed the possibility of a moderate UNE.

109. Artur Poerner spells the student's last name Abissâmara (O Poder Jovem, 257). The U.S. embassy refers to him as Alberto Abraão Abissamara. Confidential Airgram from American Embassy, Rio de Janeiro, to Department of State. Subject: New Position of the National Student Union; View of UNE President Alberto Abraão Abissamara, February 5, 1965, SNF 1964–66, P&D, PA&R, Brazil 13–2, SDCF, RG 59, NACP.

110. The U.S. embassy maintained a close watch on Brazilian students, a vigilance begun in the late 1950s when signs of supposed anti-Americanism among Brazil's future leaders first seemed to erupt and which only intensified throughout the 1960s.

111. Confidential Airgram from American Embassy, Rio de Janeiro, to Department of State. Subject: New Position of the National Student Union; View of UNE President Alberto Abraão Abissamara, February 5, 1965, SNF 1964–1966, P&D, PA&R, Brazil 13–2, SDCF, RG 59, NACP.

112. Ultra-Secreto; Inquérito—Policial—Militar—IPM—UNE-UBES; Relatório, October 21, 1965; Fotocópia in DOPS; Setor Estudantil, Pasta No. 68; APERJ.

113. Summary of Remarks by Minister Roberto Campos Concerning Students Made during a Speech Delivered at the Graduation Exercises of the Faculty of Economics of the University of Bahia on December 11, 1965, enclosed in Confidential Airgram from American Embassy, Rio de Janeiro, to Department of State, December 21, 1965; Subject-Numeric File 1964–66, Political and Defense, Political Affairs and Relations, Brazil, 13–2; SDCF; RG 59; NACP.

114. Cunha, A Universidade Reformanda, 40–41.

115. Alves, State and Opposition, 44.

116. Two good case studies shed light on the commissions (Comissão Especial de Investigação Súmaria, CEIS) and the climate of distrust they produced within the universities: Associacão dos docentes da Universidade de São Paulo, O livro negro da USP and Associacão dos docentes da Universidade Federal do Rio Grande do Sul, Universidade e Repressão. These books were written without the help of official CEIS documents, which were presumed to have been destroyed at the time. But in January 2010 CEIS papers from the UFRGS were found among the private papers of one of the CEIS members at that university, the sociologist Laudelino Texeira de Medeiros. See Mário Magalhães, "Reaparecem em Instuição de Ensino papeis 'perdidos' da ditadura," Aolha de São Paulo, January 17.

117. Cited in Alves, *State and Opposition*, 45.

118. Jean Marc von der Weid, *Brazil: 1964 to the Present: A Political Analysis: An Interview with Jean Marc von der Weid*. Montreal: Editions Latin America, 1972.

119. Secret Airgram from American Embassy Rio de Janeiro to Department of State, Subject: Communist Influence on Brazilian Youth and Related US Programs, July 23, 1965; SNF 1964–1966; Culture and Information (C&I), Education and Culture (E&C), Brazil, 13–2; SDCF; RG 59; NACP.

120. Confidential Airgram from Frank C. Carlucci, First Secretary American Embassy, Rio de Janeiro, to Department of State, Subject: GOB Initiates Effort to Improve Relations with Students, December 21, 1965; SNF 1964–66, Political and Defense (hereafter P&D), Political Affairs and Relations (hereafter PA&R), Brazil, 13–2; SDCF; RG 59; NACP.

121. President of the National Union of Students (UNE) Statement in Reply to Juracy Magalhães' Offer to Establish an 'open dialogue' with Students, enclosed in Confidential Airgram from American Embassy, Rio de Janeiro, to Department of State, December 21, 1965; SNF 1964–66; P&D, PA&R, Brazil, 13–2; SDCF; RG 59; NACP.

122. Decreto 57.634 of January 14, 1966.

123. Martins Filho, *Movimento Estudantil*, 69.

124. The recollections are from João Bettancourt, cited in Ricardo Ventura, "O Instituto Villa-Lobos e a Música Popular," www.brazilianmusic.com (September 4, 2010).

125. The U.S. embassy reported that the unopposed slate of candidates was elected in January 1966. Unclassified Airgram from American Embassy, Brasilia, to Department of State, Subject: National Students' Directorate Elects Officers, January 14, 1966; Subject-Numeric File 1964–66, P&D, PA&R, Brazil, 13–2; SDCF; RG 59; NACP.

126. Confidential Airgram from Philip Raine, American Embassy, Rio de Janeiro, to Department of State, Subject: Youth Activities—The National Student Directorate (DNE), June 17, 1966; SNF 1964–66, P&D, PA&R, Brazil 13–2; SDCF; RG 59; NACP.

127. Decreto-Lei 228/667 de 28 de fevereiro de 1967.

128. Antônio Serra interview, PMME.

129. See the table of student strikes in Martins Filho, *Movimento Estudantil*, 105.

130. Sales, "A Ação Libertadora Nacional, a revolução Cubana e a luta armada no Brasil," 212.

131. Reis Filho, *A revolução faltou ao encontro*, 13, 47–51.

132. José Gradel, interview with the author.

133. Ibid.

134. José Genoíno interview, PMME.

135. Daniel, *Passagem para o proximo sonho*, 26.

136. Antônio Serra interview, PMME.

137. Ibid.

138. Skidmore, *The Politics of Military Rule*, 31.

139. Alves, *State and Opposition*, 60.

140. Ato Institucional No. 2, de 27 de outubro de 1965.

141. Skidmore, *The Politics of Military Rule*, 44–49.

142. Confidential Airgram from W. Price, American Consulate, Belo Horizonte to Department of State, Subject: XXVIII Congress of National Union of Students, July 19, 1966; SNF 1964–66, P&D, PA&R, Brazil, 13–2; SDCF; RG 59; NACP.

143. Informação No. 826 SNI-ARJ, 19 de julho de 1966, Assunto: XXVIII Congresso Nacional de Estudantes; Servico Nacional de Informacoes (SNI); DOPS; Setor Estudantil, Pasta No. 1; APERJ.

144. Two of these letters can be found in the USNSA archives and were received on July 25 and August 8, 1966. There is no earlier letter in 1966, but the letter of July 26 begins by noting that it was the second contact UNE had established with students from other countries in 1966. Ironically, as the USNSA was by this point heavily subsidized by the CIS, this meant that UNE was inviting representatives of a CIS-funded organization to participate in their congress, something they would have vigorously opposed had they known this. Box 172, USNSA, Hoover.

145. The police estimates of 1966 come from Confidential Airgram from W. Price, American Consulate, Belo Horizonte, to Department of State, Subject: XXVIII Congress of National Union of Students, August 3, 1966; SNF 1964–66; P&D, PA&R, Brazil, 13–2; SDCF; RG 59; NACP.

146. Released in 1966, the book is called *Torturas e torturados*.

147. Informe, Secretaria de Seguranca Publica, Estado de Guanabara, Superintendencia Executiva, Departamento de Ordem Politica e Social, 4 de outubro de 1966; DOPS; Setor Estudantil, Pasta No. 4; APERJ.

148. Telegram from American Embassy, Rio de Janeiro, to Secretary of State, April 28, 1967, Subject: Student Unrest; SNF 1967–69; P&D, PA&R, Brazil, 13–2; SDCF; RG 59; NACP.

149. Cited in Cavalari, *Os Limites do movimento estudantil*, 83.

150. Airgram from American Embassy, Rio de Janeiro, to Department of State, January 16, 1968, Subject: Presidential Decree Established Special Commission on Higher Education; SNF 1967–69; C&I, E&C, Brazil, 1; SDCF; RG 59; NACP.

3. From Martyrdom to Memory

1. As student and media publications regularly refer to Edson Luis de Lima Souto by his first name only, I do the same thing here in order to avoid confusion when citing from them. Maintaining this nomenclature also helps to convey the ways in which references to him often suggest a kind of familiar camaraderie, a long-familiar practice in Brazil by which one refers to politicians with whom one identifies by a first name or nickname, e.g., Lula, Dilma, Jango, and so forth.

2. "Armas festejarão Revolução," *O Estado de São Paulo*, March 28, 1968.

3. Escobar, "The Dialectics of Repression." Many thanks to Michael Cohen for directing me to this insightful essay.

4. For information on the Calabouço, see Diniz, *Calabouço 1968: o cerco das trevas*.

5. Bernardo Joffily interview, PMME.

6. Ibid.

7. Telegram from American Embassy, Rio de Janeiro, to Secretary of State, October 23, 1968, Subject: Student-Police Clashes of October 22; Subject-Numeric File 1967–69; P&D, PA&R, Brazil, 13–2; SDCF; RG 59; NACP.

8. The *Correio de Manhã* reported that students first took the body to the Santa Casa on Rua da Misericórdia, where Dr. Luis Carlos Sá Fortes Pinheiro pronounced him dead. "PM mata estudante durante Invasão" *Correio da Manhã*, March 29, 1968.

9. "Polícia mata estudante em choque no calabouço," *Jornal do Brasil*, March 29, 1968.

10. Published interview with Elinor Brito, in Reis Filho and Moraes, *68: a paixão de uma utopia*, 162.

11. The dispute over the autopsy is recounted by Elinor Brito in his interview, ibid., 163. News of the autopsy, conducted at 1:50 A.M., was reported in "PM mata estudante durante Invasão" *Correio da Manhã*, March 29, 1968.

12. Palmeira writes of rushing to the scene in his (cowritten) memoir on page 85. See the photograph of him holding Edson Luis's shirt on page 73. Dirceu and Palmeira, *Abaixo a Ditadura*. Other reports and images of students using Edson Luis's bloodied shirt can be seen in "PM mata estudante durante Invasão" *Correio da Manhã*, March 29, 1968.

13. "Estudante promete passeata na 2ª," *Correio da Manhã*, March 30, 1968.

14. Although in 1968 newspapers experienced some encroachments on their freedom, they were still able to report on the opposition's activities. For an insightful essay into one example of how this was accomplished, see Vaz Oliveira, "Foto-jornalismo Subversivo: 1968 revisto pelas lentes do *Correio da Manhã*."

15. Scheper-Hughes, *Death without Weeping*.

16. "Milhares de Pessoas no Funeral do Estudante," *O Dia*, March 30, 1968.

17. According to the anthropologist Simone Dubeux, although his death certificate reads Nelson, and indeed he liked to be called by that name, his legal name was Edson. Dubeux, "Narrativas de um acontecimento: a morte do estudante Edson Luis no Calabouço em 1968," 151.

18. Ribeiro do Valle, *1968: O Diálogo é a violência*, 66.

19. Both comments were by the director of DOPS, Gen. Lucídio Arruda. "Negrão proibe concentração," *O Estado de São Paulo*, March 31, 1968. "DOPS diz que sabia dos planos," *O Estado de São Paulo*, March 30, 1968.

20. Informação, 1 de abril de 1968; in DOPS; Setor Estudantil, Pasta No. 37; APERJ.

21. "Milhares de Lenços no Adeus de Edson," *Correio da Manhã*, March 30, 1968.

22. The *Correio da Manhã* reported that his father was dead and his mother lived in Belém ("Milhares de Lenços no Adeus de Edson," March 30, 1968), and that it was his cousin Cléa Vasconcelos who attended the funeral and officially identified

the body ("Estudante promete passeata na 2ª," March 30, 1968). Yet the collection of photos from this same newspaper, now housed at the National Archives in Rio, contains one image of a grieving woman at his wake who is listed as being his mother. I have read extensive media coverage of the death and have never seen any mention that his mother attended these events. Moreover, given how far away she lived and how quickly the wake took place, I suspect the notation was an erroneous assumption added later.

23. Not to be confused with middle-class suburbs in the United States, in Brazil the outlying areas of a city are generally poor and far removed from accessible forms of public transportation.

24. Informação, 1 de abril de 1968; in DOPS; Setor Estudantil, Pasta No. 37; APERJ.

25. "Persiste a tensão depois do entêrro," O Estado de São Paulo, March 30, 1968.

26. "Crise Estudantil Alastra-se às Principais Cidades do País," Correio da Manhã, March 30, 1968.

27. "Milhares de Lenços do Adeus a Edson," Correio da Manhã, March 30, 1968.

28. "Estudante promete passeata na segunda," Correio da Manhã, March 30, 1968.

29. "Brasilia assiste a Novas Violências," Correio da Manhã, April 2, 1968.

30. "Estudante promete passeata na segunda," Correio da Manhã, March 30, 1968.

31. Telegram from American Embassy, Rio de Janeiro, to Secretary of State, March 29, 1968, Subject: Student Incident Having National Repercussion; Subject-Numeric File 1967–69; P&D, PA&R, Brazil, 13–2; SDCF; RG 59; NACP.

32. José Roberto, "Lacerda: protesto deve ser de todos," O Estado de São Paulo, March 30, 1968; telegram from American Embassy, Rio de Janeiro, to Secretary of State, March 29, 1968, Subject: Sitrep on Student Incident; Subject-Numeric File 1967–69; P&D, PA&R, Brazil, 13–2; SDCF; RG 59; NACP.

33. Rose notes the flower petals and confetti in The Unpast: Elite Violence and Social Control in Brazil, 1954–2000, 152.

34. Antônio Serra interview, PMME.

35. "Negrão proibe concentração," O Estado de São Paulo, March 31, 1968.

36. Ibid.

37. "Persiste a tensão depois do entêrro." O Estado de São Paulo, March 30 1968.

38. "Milhares de Pessoas no Funeral do Estudante," O Dia, March 30, 1968. The two were not unknown to the state security forces, however. Files in DOPS make multiple references to Palmeira starting in 1966 and to Brito starting in 1968.

39. Vladimir Palmeira, interview with author. The spontaneousness of their decision is further suggested by the fact that students did not originally want the funeral procession to go via the Flamengo neighborhood and had instead requested another route. "Milhares de Lenços no Adeus de Edson," Correio da Manhã, March 30, 1968.

40. "Haverá passeata em São Paulo," O Estado de São Paulo, March 31, 1968.

41. "Escolas gaúchas fecham de 1 a 6," *O Estado de São Paulo*, March 31, 1968.

42. "Conflitos repetem-se em Brasilia," *O Estado de São Paulo*, March 30, 1968, and "Ordem voltará a qualquer preço," *O Estado de São Paulo*, April 3, 1968.

43. "Govêrno assegura que há infiltração," *O Estado de São Paulo*, April 2, 1968.

44. Escobar, "The Dialectics of Repression."

45. The two in Rio de Janeiro were David Souza Meira and Jorge Aprígio de Paula, both bystanders. In the city of Goiânia, police shot the high school student Oralino Cândido da Silva at close range, in what turned out to be a case of mistaken identity. See also Miranda and Tibúrcio, *Dos filhos deste solo*, 552–55.

46. Telegram from American Embassy, Rio de Janeiro, to Secretary of State, April 4, 1968, Subject: Student Demonstrations; Subject-Numeric File 1967–69; P&D, PA&R, Brazil, 13–2; SDCF; RG 59; NACP.

47. Airgram from American Embassy Brasilia to Department of State, April 19, 1968, Subject: Student Demonstrations Wrap Up; Subject-Numeric File 1967–69; P&D, PA&R, Brazil, 13–2; SDCF; RG 59; NACP.

48. In making this argument I am departing from Maria Ribeiro do Valle's provocative look at violence as a form of "dialogue" between students and the military, wherein the gradual turn among some students toward advocating revolutionary violence coincided with the ascension of hard-liners within the government, and the two groups "argued" out their different interpretations in the streets. Instead, I see the experience of violence as part of the mobilizing dynamic that moved large numbers of students (not just those committed to revolutionary violence) to participate in public protest and that consequently helped reassert the centrality of university students as legitimate political actors. See Ribeiro do Valle, *1968: O Diálogo é a violência*.

49. "Ação policial evitou passeata no DF," *O Estado de São Paulo*, April 3, 1968.

50. "A ordem era para agir com energia," *O Estado de São Paulo*, April 3, 1968.

51. "Gás dissolve passeata," *O Estado de São Paulo*, April 2, 1968.

52. "Três bailes quebram luto," *O Estado de São Paulo*, April 2, 1968.

53. "A Rebelião Universal dos Jovens," *Manchete*, April 13, 1968, 16–23.

54. "Luta atinge a Sorbonne," *O Estado de São Paulo*, May 4, 1968. This article and others like it derived from international news sources like Agence France Presse (in this case) and Reuters or from foreign articles translated into Portuguese (such as from *The New York Times*). Nonetheless, the resulting effect was a steady stream of information proposing an interconnected surge of student activity.

55. "A Rebelião Universal dos Jovens," *Manchete*, April 13, 1968.

56. Mário Busch, "Do Quartier Latin à América Latina," *O Estado de São Paulo*, June 2, 1968, 5 Caderno.

57. Ernani Amaral Peixoto, April 9, 1968, speech and interview in 1968. FGV, CPDOC, Arquivo Ernani do Amaral Peixoto (hereafter EAP), EAP 63,12,04, Série Deputado Federal II, Pasta II.

58. "Bispo pede ponderação," *O Estado de São Paulo*, March 30, 1968.

59. "Entusiasmo da juventude impressionou pe. Arrupe," *O Estado de São Paulo*, May 16, 1968.

60. "Luta atinge a Sorbonne," *O Estado de São Paulo*, May 4, 1968.

61. "DOPS diz que sabia do planos," *O Estado de São Paulo*, March 30, 1968.

62. "DOPS prende 14 estudantes que iam falar com Aragão," *Jornal do Brasil*, April 19, 1968.

63. "Volta a calma à capital do Paraná," *O Estado de São Paulo*, May 15, 1968.

64. "A Culpa da Violência," *Veja e Leia*, September 11, 1968.

65. Estado de Guanabara, Secretaria de Segurança Pública, DOPS, Divisão de Operações, Serviço de Buscas, Seção de Buscas Especiais, Informe No. 192, Assunto: Movimento Estudantil, 28 de junho de 1968; in DOPS; Setor Estudantil, Pasta No. 38; APERJ.

66. "Agitação viria do estrangeiro," *O Estado de São Paulo*, May 18, 1968.

67. "A Culpa da Violência," *Veja*, September 11, 1968.

68. Luís Travassos and Luís Raul Machado, interviewed in José Carlos Marão, "Para êles UNE não representa estudante," *Realidade*, July 1968, 38.

69. Telegram from American Embassy, Rio de Janeiro, to Secretary of State, June 4, 1968, No Subject; Subject-Numeric File 1967–69; C&I, E&C, Brazil, 9–3; SDCF; RG 59; NACP.

70. Luiz Raul Machado, quoted in José Carlos Marão, "Para êles UNE não representa estudante," *Realidade*, July 1968, 38.

71. Telegram from American Embassy, Rio de Janeiro, to Secretary of State, April 17, 1968, Subject: Torture Accusations in Wake of Student Demonstrations; Subject-Numeric File 1967–69; P&D, PA&R, Brazil, 13–2; SDCF; RG 59; NACP.

72. "Lacerda critica violência," *O Estado de São Paulo*, April 3, 1968.

73. Ribeiro do Valle, *1968: O diálogo é a violência*, 53.

74. Olga D'Arc Pimentel, in Reis Filho and de Moraes, *68: a paixão de uma utopia*, 153.

75. GB-Secretaria de Segurança Pública, DOPS, Divisão de Operações, Serviço de Buscas, Seção de Buscas Ostensivas, Informe, Movimento Estudantil, 2 de julho de 1968, in DOPS, Setor Estudantil, Pasta No. 38, APERJ. The officer's name was Nélson de Barros, and he died on June 21, 1968. This incident was widely reported in the newspapers at the time.

76. See Huggins, *Political Policing*, 142. Many memoirs and published interviews with student activists also note these tactics.

77. "A passeata, antes dos tiros," *Correio da Manhã*, October 24, 1968.

78. "Polícia pode ir ao Crusp," *O Estado de São Paulo*, May 11, 1968.

79. "Nota dos Estudantes ao Povo de Guanabara," June 1968, in DOPS, Setur Estudantil; Pasta No. 38; APERJ.

80. Confidential Airgram from W. Price, American Consulate, Belo Horizonte to Department of State, Subject: XXVIII Congress of National Union of Students, July 19, 1966; Subject-Numeric File 1964–66, P&D, PA&R, Brazil, 13–2; SDCF; RG 59; NACP.

81. União Metropolitana dos Estudantes, "Introdução ao 'Relatorio Meira Matos' e às 'Resoluções do Grupo de Trabalho da R.U.'" in DOPS; Setor Estudantil, Pasta No. 32; APERJ, folhas 28–30.

82. "Volta a calma à capital do Paraná," *O Estado de São Paulo*, May 15, 1968.

83. "DOPS prende 14 estudantes que iam falar com Aragão," *Jornal do Brasil*, April 19, 1968.

84. Table 5.1.3.5.4, "Alunos matriculados no início do ano, transferidos de outras escolas, bolsistas e estrangeiros, e conclusões no ano anterior, segundo o sexo— 1971"; Serviço de Estatística da Educação e Cultura. Tabela extraída de: Anuário estatístico do Brasil 1972, vol. 33 (Rio de Janeiro: IBGE, 1972).

85. This is not necessarily the best indicator of female student participation, since women students were probably less able than their male counterparts to travel away from home to a secret location for many days, unsupervised, and among colleagues of both sexes, as participation in the UNE Congress of 1968 required. If anything, I would expect higher percentages of women in the other UNE-related activities, ones in which overnight travel was not required. An explanation of the congress comes later in this chapter but suffice to say here that these attendance figures come from police files, as practically all of the students who were there were arrested when the police raided the gathering. The figures from 1966 come from Poerner, *O Poder Jovem*, 270.

86. "Conflitos repetem-se em Brasilia," *O Estado de São Paulo*, March 30, 1968.

87. The three accounts are Fernando Gabeira's memoir of 1979, *O que é isso companheiro?*, the journalistic account first published by Zuenir Ventura in 1989, *1968: O ano que não terminou*, and José Dirceu's and Vladimir Palmeira's cowritten memoir of 1998, *Abaixo a Ditadura: O movimento de 68 contado por seus líderes*. The three accounts vary in terms of what month this event occurred, whether or not the Brucutu was being used for the first time or for one of the last, and whether Pellegrino made the joke or Elinor Brito did. Nonetheless, they all quote the line exactly and concur that it elicited roars of laughter (*gargalhadas*) from everyone nearby.

88. Gabeira, *O que é isso companheiro?*, 47.

89. GB-Secretaria de Segurança Pública, DOPS, Divisão de Operações, Serviço de Buscas, Seção de Buscas Ostensivas, Informe, Movimento Estudantil, 2 de julho de 1968; in DOPS; Setor Estudantil, Pasta No. 38; APERJ.

90. Telegram from American Embassy, Rio de Janeiro, to Secretary of State, June 19, 1968, Subject: Student Demonstrations; Subject-Numeric File 1967–69; P&D, PA&R, Brazil, 13–2; SDCF; RG 59; NACP.

91. See, for example, "O líder foragido e sua mulher," *Veja e Leia*, September 25, 1968.

92. Throughout much of 1968 the UEE-SP experienced severe internal divisions as student factions disputed the results of the presidential elections, some claiming that Catarina Meloni had won and others proclaiming José Dirceu the victor. This split was politically entrenched in that Meloni hailed from the AP and Dirceu from the DI-SP.

On the subject of UNE vice presidents, it was standard practice to elect multiple vice presidents, each in charge of a different area, hence Resende's position as one of several was not unique.

93. Tavares de Almeida and Weis, "Carro-zero e pau-de-arara," 399.

94. Maria Augusta Carneiro Ribeiro interview, PMME.

95. José Gradel, interview with author.

96. Ventura, 1968: O ano que não terminou, 36.

97. Ibid., 37.

98. "Excedentes só esperam," O Estado de São Paulo, March 21, 1968.

99. Vladmir Palmeira, interviewed in the documentary film Sol, Caminhando contra o Vento (2006).

100. Cited in Tavares de Almeida and Weis, "Carro-zero e pau-de-arara," 370.

101. See, for example, "Agente Policial Agia na Filosofia," Diário de São Paulo, July 6, 1968.

102. "Nudismo e sexo: Os jovems estão implantando uma noval moral?," Manchete, December 14, 1968, 146.

103. Cowan, "Sex and the Security State," 465.

104. "Fala o Presidente," O Estado de São Paulo, March 22, 1968.

105. "Prepara o Partido para grandes lutas: Resolução do C.C." Maio, 1968; Coleção Daniel Aarão Reis Filho, Série MR-8, Documentos de Discussão Interna, in APERJ.

106. "Reflexões sobre o Movimento Estudantil," O Estado de São Paulo, June 21, 1968.

107. Cited in "Polícia e estudantes enfrentam-se no Rio," O Estado de São Paulo, June 20, 1968.

108. Cited in "Dois mortos no Rio: União promete rigor," O Estado de São Paulo, June 22, 1968.

109. GB-Secretaria de Segurança Pública, DOPS, Divisão de Operações, Serviço de Buscas, Seção de Buscas Ostensivas, Informe, Movimento Estudantil, 2 de julho de 1968; in DOPS; Setor Estudantil, Pasta No. 38; APERJ.

110. Ibid.

111. The Correio da Manhã, generally supportive of students, reported the figure of 500 but says official counts were only 286 arrests, of which 65 were women. "A Guerra contra os estudantes," Correio da Manhã, June 21, 1968.

112. Vladimir Palmeira recalls that at the time students found it hard to get a firm figure on the number of dead but believed it to be "at least ten." Dirceu and Palmeira, Abaixo a Ditadura, 132. The figure of three comes from Miranda and Tibúrcio, Dos filhos deste solo, 543.

113. GB-Secretaria de Segurança Pública, DOPS, Divisão de Operações, Serviço de Buscas, Seção de Buscas Ostensivas, Informe, Movimento Estudantil, 2 de julho de 1968; in DOPS; Setor Estudantil, Pasta No. 38; APERJ.

114. Specifically, protests occurred in Recife, Salvador, Brasilia, São Paulo, Porto

Alegre, and São Luís. "Tiros, pedras e fogo contra 'Estado,'" *O Estado de São Paulo,* June 25, 1968.

115. GB-Secretaria de Segurança Pública, DOPS, Divisão de Operações, Serviço de Buscas, Seção de Buscas Ostensivas, Informe, Movimento Estudantil, 2 de julho de 1968; in DOPS; Setor Estudantil, Pasta No. 38; APERJ.

116. For a detailed description of the 100,000 March, see the appropriately named chapter "E Todos se Sentaram" in Ventura, *1968: O Ano que Não Terminou.*

117. GB-Secretaria de Segurança Pública, DOPS, Divisão de Operações, Serviço de Buscas, Seção de Buscas Ostensivas, Informe, Movimento Estudantil, 2 de julho de 1968; in DOPS; Setor Estudantil, Pasta No. 38; APERJ.

118. The text of the official note was published in "Conselho de Segurança acusa estado contra-revolucionário," *Jornal do Brasil,* July 17, 1968.

119. The cited philosopher was Edgar Morin. "MEC-USAID termina hoje sem renovação," *O Jornal do Brasil,* July 1, 1968.

120. "Exército garantiu a ordem e a vida normal da cidade," *Jornal do Brasil,* August 7, 1968.

121. "Luta em Salvador teve baleados," *O Jornal do Brasil,* August 9, 1968.

122. See the chronology of these events in Reis Filho and de Moraes, *68: a paixão de uma utopia,* 209–10.

123. "Justiça liberta dois estudantes do DOPS," *O Jornal do Brasil,* July 5, 1968.

124. Ridenti, *O Fantasma da Revolução Brasileira,* 115.

125. In fact, the controversies at this song festival extended well beyond the outcry over the final awards. During the second round of the contest, the most politicized sector of students vociferously booed Caetano Veloso's performance, leading him to chastise them as the "youth that says its wants to take power in Brazil" but that nonetheless had very limited ideas about political and aesthetic authenticity. I discuss this incident further in "*Il est Interdite d'Interdire*: The Transnational Experience of 1968 in Brazil."

126. José Gradel, interview with author.

127. "Da União Metropolitana dos Estudantes ao Povo da Guanabara," in DOPS; Setor Estudantil, Pasta No. 32; APERJ.

128. See, for example, "Isto é um assalto (político?)" *Veja,* October 23, 1968.

129. Reis Filho and de Moraes, *68: a paixão de uma utopia,* 201.

130. Brasil, "As ações do Comando de Caça aos Comunistas (1968–1969)."

131. See the chronology of these events in Reis Filho and de Moraes, *68: a paixão de uma utopia,* 208–213.

132. "Morrem dois jovens nas ruas de São Paulo," *Correio da Manhã,* October 4, 1968; and Dirceu and Palmeira, *Abaixo a Ditadura,* 155. Despite the headline, the newspaper later confirmed that only one person died.

133. Miranda and Tibúrcio, *Dos filhos deste solo,* 557.

134. Dirceu and Palmeira, *Abaixo a Ditadura,* 156.

135. Loschiavo dos Santos, *Maria antônia: uma rua na contramão.*

136. The two other major proposals had been either to openly defy the law by holding an open conference somewhere else in the state, which then-Governor Abreu Sodré had hinted at allowing, or to scale back the meeting to many fewer delegates. This would have made secrecy easier to maintain but would have left the organization open to criticism of its undemocratic process, a difficult position for them as they defined themselves against the undemocratic military government. I do not agree with Elio Gaspari's suggestion in *A ditadura envergonhada* that student leaders chose the Ibiúna site with the deliberate intention of having everyone arrested and thus radicalizing their colleagues for clandestine struggle. Students had been using security systems similar to the one they adopted at Ibiúna for several years to great effect, successfully organizing prohibited street demonstrations and holding two clandestine congresses. I believe the congress was detected because of the increased commitment of the state security forces to shut it down and the increased divisions among students, which left them unable to adequately recognize and respond to the threats against them. Moreover, the student security detail may have been more taxed than usual, given the many events they had recently been involved in, leading to less than adequate preparation. Indeed, part of the Rio de Janeiro security detail went to São Paulo earlier in the month to help organize the congress and instead spent much of their time trying to defuse the Maria Antonia–USP confrontation.

137. Eduardo Pinto, "Futuro do movimento estudantil é incerto," *Jornal do Brasil*, October 16, 1968.

138. Dirceu and Palmeira, *Abaixo a Ditadura*, 165.

139. See, for example, "Polícia prende Vladimir e mais 1239 no Congresso da ex-UNE," *Jornal do Brasil*, October 13, 1968.

140. "Polícia paulista liga Congresso da ex-UNE a terrorismo e assassinato," *Jornal do Brasil*, October 16, 1968.

141. Maria Augusta Carneiro Ribeiro interview, PMME.

142. "Fotografias das Mulhers que participaram do XXX Congresso da Extinta UNE em Ibiúna." In Arquivo Público do Estado de São Paulo, Coleção DEOPS, Ordem Social, OS-0036.

143. I discuss the uses and meanings of police displays of birth control pills in "Birth Control Pills and Molotov Cocktails."

144. Jean Marc von der Weid, in Reis Filho and de Moraes, *68: a paixão de uma utopia*, 129.

145. On the bus from Ibiúna to São Paulo, Vladimir Palmeira tried to flee out the rear emergency exit, running barefoot down the street before soldiers apprehended him, pulling off his shirt in the process. Grainy photos of the partially disrobed student, surrounded by uniformed officers, appeared in several newspapers the following day. See, for example, the photograph by Carlos Namba in *Veja*, October 16, 1968. Unphotographed but more successful was Jean Marc von der Weid's escape, in which he eluded initial detection by claiming to be someone else and a

few days later also slipped out the back door of a transport bus. He recounts this story in his interview in Reis Filho and de Moraes, 68: a paixão de uma utopia. Finally, José Arantes, then vice president of UNE, despite having been hauled in with the others at Ibiúna, suddenly reappeared mysteriously in Rio de Janeiro a few days later. Keeping the media in suspense, he promised a collective interview to explain how he managed this feat, but only after a week had passed. See "Arantes marca entrevista e vai contar como fugiu," Jornal do Brasil, October 20, 1968.

146. For a good example of one of these dramatic, almost diary-like descriptions of the congress (including the complicated system of secret passwords and meeting places used en route to the clandestine location), see Eduardo Pinto, "Um congresso misterioso que a polícia descobriu," Jornal do Brasil, October 15, 1968. In addition to Pinto, the journalists hauled to São Paulo by DOPS worked for some of the country's major publications, including Manchete, A Folha da Tarde, O Paiz, Última Hora, and Jornal do Comercio. See "DOPS só viu Vladimir quando chegou a São Paulo," Jornal do Brasil, October 14, 1968.

147. "Em Brasilia a passeata é hoje," O Estado de São Paulo, October 15, 1968.

148. Telegram from American Embassy, Rio de Janeiro, to Secretary of State, October 16, 1968, Subject: Reaction to São Paulo Student Arrests; Subject-Numeric File 1967–69; P&D, PA&R, Brazil, 13–2; SDCF; RG 59; NACP.

149. Saldanha de Oliveira, A Mitologia Estudantil, 85–86.

150. "Polícia paulista liga Congresso da ex-UNE a terrorismo e assassinato," Jornal do Brasil, October 16, 1968.

151. "O nôvo bandido," Veja, November 6, 1968.

152. "Polícia confirma Marighela no assalto à carro do IPEG," Jornal do Brasil, November 12, 1968.

153. "Paulistas esperam as pistas de Paulo César," Jornal do Brasil, November 13, 1968.

154. "A Caçada," Veja, November 20, 1968.

155. "Morte de estudantes poderá esclarecer plano subversivo," Jornal do Brasil, November 19, 1968.

156. Ibid.

157. Marighella did have a hand in both the robbery of the armored car and the death of Charles Chandler, but in memoirs of the Chandler assassination the students, Abib and Ferreira, are never mentioned. See Caso, A esquerda armada no Brasil, 1967–1971.

158. Anais da Câmara dos Deputados (Brasilia, 1968), 23:159–65, 432–33.

159. Cited in Flamarion Mossri, "Comissão concede dia 10 liçenca contra Márcio" Jornal do Brasil. December 18, 1968.

160. Alves, State and Opposition in Military Brazil, 95.

161. "Discurso do Marechal cala fundo na ARENA," Jornal do Brasil, December 3, 1968.

162. "Govêrno repele rumôres sôbre medida de exceção," *Jornal do Brasil*, December 5, 1968.

163. "Garrastzau Médici fala em revoluções," *Jornal do Brasil*, December 5, 1958.

164. "Bel Canto," *Jornal do Brasil*, December 5, 1968.

165. In yet another ironic temporal coincidence, this report, entitled "Student Movement Limbers Up," reached the State Department on that same day, December 13. Written three days earlier, the report also mentioned the sixty-day imprisonment of Vladimir Palmeira and others but optimistically noted "a softening of attitude [about students] which would tend to reinforce rumors that President Costa e Silva might grant amnesty to all students still being held at Christmas." Unfortunately for the students in question, he was sorely mistaken. Telegram from American Embassy, Rio de Janeiro, to Secretary of State, December 10, 1968, Subject: Student Movement Limbers Up; Subject-Numeric File 1967–69; P&D, PA&R, Brazil, 13–2; SDCF; RG 59; NACP.

166. Not all of the students in jail had been arrested in Ibiúna. The campaign sought to focus attention on all incarcerated students, of whom about half came from the UNE Congress. The rest had been imprisoned throughout the year for a variety of reasons.

167. "Estudantes lançam campanha para libertar antes do Natal 202 colegas presos," *Jornal do Brasil*, December 3, 1968.

168. "Câmara nega a licença e canta Hino Nacional," *Jornal do Brasil*, December 13, 1968.

169. Alves, *A Grain of Mustard Seed*, 24.

170. Gaspari, *A Ditadura envergonhada*, 331–32.

171. "Militares prevêem para hoje edição de Ato Institucional," *Jornal do Brasil*, December 13, 1968.

172. The meeting was officially recorded via two microphones on the table. The quotation comes from Elio Gaspari's consultation of the tapes. *A Ditadura envergonhada*, 334.

173. Article 10, Institutional Act No. 5.

174. Preamble to Institutional Act No. 5.

175. The photograph is from the Acervo do Arquivo Geral da Cidade do Rio de Janeiro and was published in *Um Rio em 68*. Biblioteca Carioca. Rio de Janeiro: Departamento de Documentação e Informação Cultural, Prefeitura da Cidade do Rio de Janeiro, Secretaria Municipal de Cultura, 1988.

176. Ana Maria Müller, interview for Fundação Perseu Abramo, "Trinta Anos do AI-5—Não Vamos Esquecer," www.fpabramo.org (September 12, 2005).

1. Ventura, 1968: O ano que não terminou; Fico, "1968: O ano que terminou mal."

2. "STF mantém presos Vladimir e Travassos e liberta mais 33," Jornal do Brasil, December 12, 1968.

3. "STF manda soltar Vladimir e Travassos em nôvo julgamento," Jornal do Brasil, December 13, 1968.

4. Ribas was left out of that trade because of political divisions among the clandestine lefts. Gorender, Combate nas trevas, 149.

5. Dirceu and Palmeira, Abaixo a Ditadura, 175.

6. Although this phrase is practically de rigueur today for describing AI-5, I have yet to see an explanation of its origins. The earliest reference I have found comes from the writings of Carlos Marighella, specifically his "O papel da ação revolucionária na organização" (May 1969). He wrote, "Taking refuge in the tactic of a coup with a coup, [the military] unleashed a new fascist coup on the 13th of December of 1968 and decreed Institutional Act Number 5." If indeed Marighella coined the now-ubiquitous phrase, it suggests a fascinating example of "mainstreaming" Brazil's revolutionary past (a theme I return to in chapter 5). The above text by Marighella is found in his collection of writings, La guerra revolucionaria.

7. For example, in April 1969 a student leader from Pernambuco, Cândido Pinto de Mello, was shot by a group of vigilante police officers as he waited at a bus stop. See Gorender, Combate nas trevas, 150.

8. See note 8 of the introduction for the origins of this phrase.

9. Alvarez, Engendering Democracy in Brazil, 7.

10. Pollak, "Memória, esquecimento, silêncio" (emphasis added).

11. Jelin, Los trabajos de la memoria, 70.

12. Ministério do Exército, I Exército—11ª RM, Quartel General, 2ª SEC/EWR 11, Informação No. 310/69, Assunto: Movimento Estudantil da França, em Mai 68, Brasilia DF, 27 de fevereiro de 1969; in DOPS; Setor Secreto, Pasta No. 42; APERJ.

13. Recent new scholarship on the transnational dimensions of 1968 is replete with works that look at the interconnectedness of social movements. But scholars have yet to really explore transnational efforts to disrupt and discredit these movements.

14. Decreto-Lei 477 de 26 de fevereiro de 1969.

15. Telegram from American Embassy, Rio de Janeiro, to Secretary of State, April 25, 1969, Subject: Implementing Regulations to Decree Expulsion of Students; Subject-Numeric File 1967–69; C&I, E&C, Brazil, 9; SDCF; RG 59; NACP.

16. Airgram from American Embassy, Rio de Janeiro, to Department of State, March 18, 1969, Subject: Blacklisting of Students; Subject-Numeric File 1967–69; C&I, E&C, Brazil, 9; SDCF; RG 59; NACP.

17. Airgram from American Embassy, Brasilia, to Department of State, April 23, 1969, Subject: Situation at the University of Brasilia; Subject-Numeric File 1967–69;

P&D, PA&R, Brazil, 13–2; SDCF; RG 59; NACP; Brito, "UFBA. Movimento Estudantil em Salvador e o AI-5."

18. Airgram from American Embassy Rio de Janeiro to Department of State, March 18, 1969, Subject: Blacklisting of Students; Subject-Numeric File 1967–69; C&I, E&C, Brazil, 9; SDCF; RG 59; NACP.

19. Letter from João Moniz de Aragão, Chefe de Gabinete do Reitor da Universidade Federal do Rio de Janeiro to Delegado de Órdem Política e Social, 14 de maio de 1969 and Letter from Jayme Florêncio da Silva, Agente Auxiliar de Polícia Federal to Chefe da Seção de Buscas Ostensivas, 23 de outubro de 1969; both in DOPS; Setor Estudantil, Pasta No. 35; APERJ.

20. Confidential Informe No. 0208 from CENIMAR, Ministério da Marinha, 13 de maio de 1969; in DOPS; Setor Estudantil, Pasta No. 35; APERJ.

21. Delegacia de Ordem Política e Social, Inquérito No. 48/68, by Manoel Villarinho, Delegado, 18 de março de 1969; in DOPS; Setor Secreto, Pasta N° 42; APERJ.

22. *Correio da Manha*, April 30, 1969; cited in Telegram from American Embassy, Rio de Janeiro, to Secretary of State, May 2, 1969, Subject: Student Prosecuted for Subversion; Subject-Numeric File 1967–69; P&D, PA&R, Brazil, 13–2; SDCF; RG 59; NACP.

23. "Many times the beginning of these . . . proceedings was after December 13, as if the declaration of AI-5 had functioned as a signal to attack," Arquidiocese de São Paulo, *Brasil Nunca Mais*, 137.

24. Estado de Guanabara, Secretaria de Segurança Pública, DOPS Divisão de Operações, Informe No. 016, Assunto: Movimento Estudantil, 5 de maio de 1971; DOPS; Setor Estudantil, Pasta No. 38; APERJ.

25. Decreto No. 69.053 de 11 de Agosto de 1971.

26. Aviso Reservado No. 873/73 from Ministro de Educação e Cultura Jarbas G. Passarinho to Reitores das Universidades Federais, 31 de julho de 1973; in DOPS; Setor Estudantil, Pasta No. 39; APERJ.

27. See Marconi, *A Censura Política na Imprensa Brasileira, 1968–1978*.

28. Skidmore, *The Politics of Military Rule*, 82.

29. Cowan, "The Secret History of Subversion," 179.

30. For the major study on these talks, as well as a fascinating biography of Muricy, see Serbin, *Secret Dialogues*.

31. Telegram from Boonstra, American Embassy, Rio de Janeiro, to Secretary of State, Washington, D.C., Subject: Political Prisoners, July 22, 1970; Subject-Numeric File 1970–73; P&D, PA&R, Brazil, 29; SDCF; RG 59; NACP.

32. Ministério do Exército, I Exército, 2a Seção, DOPS/GB–Arq. Rio 30 de abril de 1970, Assunto: Prof Pimenta da Faculdade de Serviço Social do Rio de Janeiro; in DOPS; Setor Estudantil, Pasta No. 36; APERJ.

33. Confidential Informe No. 0208 from CENIMAR, Ministério da Marinha, 13 de maio de 1969; in DOPS; Setor Estudantil, Pasta No. 35; APERJ.

34. Associacão dos docentes da Universidade de São Paulo, *O livro negro da USP*, 38–40.

35. So many people lost their elected offices due to AI-9 and AI-10 that the regime soon issued AI-11 setting out new elections. For another detailed case of academic purges, see Associação dos docentes da Universidade Federal do Rio Grande do Sul, *Universidade e Repressão*.

36. Green, *We Cannot Remain Silent*, 117. See chapter 4 of Green for a fascinating account of the response of U.S. American academics to these purges and to later attacks on Brazilian intellectuals.

37. Article 33, Decreto-Lei 314 de 13 de março de 1967. This law would be updated in September 1969 with a new Law of National Security to which students would be subject.

38. Airgram from American Consulate, Recife, to Department of State, August 8, 1969, Subject: Punitive Actions Against Northwest Students: A Summary and Analysis; Subject-Numeric File 1967–69; P&D, PA&R, Brazil, 13–2; SDCF; RG 59; NACP.

39. Telegram from Boonstra, American Embassy, Rio de Janeiro, to Secretary of State, Washington, D.C., Subject: Political Prisoners, July 22, 1970; Subject-Numeric File 1970–73; P&D, PA&R, Brazil, 29; SDCF; RG 59; NACP. This was not the only instance in which General Muricy made this claim. See a statement of his from 1971 unearthed by Benjamin Cowan in which he reported on the "moral degradation of youth, especially young women" and spoke of a letter from a medical student who claimed to have seen "young ladies being seduced and carried off, by the desperation of their situation, to become part of terrorist groups." Cowan, "The Secret History of Subversion," 298.

40. Secretária da Segurança Pública, Departamento Estadual de Ordem Política e Social, Serviço de Informações, Carta Mensal, São Paulo, CDPP—Comite de Defesa dos Presos Políticos," 30 de setembro de 1974; in DOPS; Setor Comunismo, Pasta No. 136; APERJ.

41. Hermínio Affonso Friede, "Reflexões em tôrno dos problemas da juventude de hoje," in *Projeto Rondon*, Serviço Gráfico do Senado Federal, 1970, Biblioteca Nacional, Rio de Janeiro.

42. Ministerio do Interior, Gabinete do Ministro, Coordenação de Cominicação Social. "A Fundação Rondon ja é uma realidade." Publicação 10/76. Biblioteca Nacional, Rio de Janeiro.

43. "Para o Ministro, Rondon é a solução" *Folha de São Paulo*, July 30, 1977.

44. Such a step was not unprecedented in Brazil, as previous governments had mandated other moral and civic education requirements. In 1925 moral and civic instruction was established for secondary school students, while the Constitution of 1937 made moral and political instruction mandatory for all levels. See Rodrigues da Cruz, *Antecedentes e Perspectivas da Educação moral e cívica no Brasil*, and Nava, "Future Citizens in Public Schools, 1937–1945."

45. Decreto-Lei 869 de 12 de setembro de 1969. In this case the Decree-Law was

issued by a military junta (made up of the ministers of the navy, army, and air force) that officially took over the presidency during September and October 1969.

46. Cowan, "The Secret History of Subversion," 364–65. For a full treatment of the ways in which the program in civic and moral education reflected the "moral panic" of sectors of the Brazilian security establishment, and, most intriguingly, how textbooks aimed at schoolchildren sought to warn them against the dangers of political and sexual subversion, see his chapter 6, "'Brazil Counts on Its Sons for Redemption': Moral, Civic, and Countersubversive Education."

47. Decreto-Lei 869 de 12 de setembro de 1969.

48. Emílio Garrastazu Médici, discurso na Escola Superior de Guerra, 10 de março de 1970; in Ministério de Educação e Cultura, Commissão Nacional de Moral e Civismo, *Educação Moral e Cívica como disciplina obrigatória nos três níveis de ensino*, Março de 1970, Biblioteca Nacional, Rio de Janeiro.

49. Circular No. 1/71 do AESI, Universidade Federal do Rio de Janeiro, to Diretor da Faculdade de Direito 10 de agosto de 1971; in DOPS; Setor Estudantil, Pasta No. 38; APERJ.

50. In May 1969 the rector of the UFRJ reported to DOPS that the president of the DA of chemistry was Walmir Andrade Oliveira. Letter from João Moniz de Aragão, Chefe de Gabinete do Reitor da Universidade Federal do Rio de Janeiro to Delegado de Órdem Política e Social, 14 de maio de 1969; in DOPS; Setor Estudantil, Pasta No. 35; APERJ.

51. Telegram from American Embassy, Rio de Janeiro, to Secretary of State, June 9, 1969, Subject: Growing Apprehension Among Students; Subject-Numeric File 1967–69; P&D, PA&R, Brazil, 13–2; SDCF; RG 59; NACP.

52. For an examination of the ways the military states of Latin America deliberately used fear as a method of social control, see the essays in Corradi et al., eds., *Fear at the Edge*.

53. Telegram from American Consulate, São Paulo, to Secretary of State, June 9, 1969, Subject: Security Rockefeller Mission; Subject-Numeric File 1967–69; P&D, PA&R, Brazil, 13–2; SDCF; RG 59; NACP; and *Contestação: Jornal do movimento universidade crítica*, no. 1, 1969; in Arquivo Edgard Leurenroth, UNICAMP, Instituto de Filosofia e Ciências Humanas (hereafter IFCS).

54. Green, *We Cannot Remain Silent*, 104.

55. Telegram from American Consulate, São Paulo, to Secretary of State, June 9, 1969, Subject: Security Rockefeller Mission; Subject-Numeric File 1967–69; P&D, PA&R, Brazil, 13–2; SDCF; RG 59; NACP.

56. Green, *We Cannot Remain Silent*, 105.

57. Telegram from American Consulate, São Paulo, to Secretary of State, June 9, 1969, Subject: Security Rockefeller Mission; Subject-Numeric File 1967–69; P&D, PA&R, Brazil, 13–2; SDCF; RG 59; NACP.

58. Telegram from American Embassy, Rio de Janeiro, to Secretary of State, June 13, 1969, Subject: Assessment of Student Situation; Subject-Numeric File 1967–69; P&D, PA&R, Brazil, 13–2; SDCF; RG 59; NACP.

59. These figures were documented by the Projeto Brasil Nunca Mais collection and summarized in Gaspari, *A Ditadura Escancarada*, 159.

60. Ibid., 60–64.

61. Ibid., 175–79.

62. Corradi et al., *Fear at the Edge*.

63. There are multiple descriptions of this event, though the most well known is that found in the memoir of Fernando Gabeira, *O que é isso companheiro?*. This was the basis for the Academy Award–nominated film version of these events, *Four Days in September* (1997). See also Elio Gaspari's account, which includes the closed-door responses of military officials, in *A Ditadura Escancarada*, 87–104.

64. The reasons for choosing these fifteen people varied. Gregório Bezerra, for example, then sixty-nine years old, was a well-known member of the PCB, a group that had nothing to do with the kidnapping and opposed armed actions. But Bezerra had been imprisoned since April 1964 (as well as having been imprisoned multiple times before 1964 for his political activism) and was known to have undergone grueling treatment. Hence, according to Gaspari, the ALN chose to include him as a courtesy to the PCB. Luis Travassos was a member of the AP, but as the AP and the MR-8 had a close relationship, he too was included on the list of prisoners to be released. Gaspari, *A Ditadura Escancarada*, 145.

65. Jean Marc von der Weid interview, PMME.

66. "Em Salvador, a primeira condenação à pena de morte no brasil," *Folha de São Paulo*, March 19, 1971.

67. Gaspari, *A Ditadura Escancarada*, 159.

68. Declarações de Vera Sílvia Araújo Magalhães to DOPS, 12 de março de 1970; in DOPS; Setor Estudantil, Pasta No. 35; APERJ. See also other statements in Pastas 35 and 37.

69. Estado de Guanabara, Secretaria de Segurança Pública, Departamento de Ordem Política e Social, Divisão de Operações, Serviço de Buscas, Seção de Buscas Especiais, Informe No. 0133—08 de setembro de 1970; in DOPS; Setor Estudantil, Pasta No. 37; APERJ.

70. From Ministério do Exército, I Exército, 2ª Seção, to CIE—DOPS/GB—ARQ, Assunto: Movimento Estudantil, 7 de janeiro de 1971; in DOPS; Setor Estudantil, Pasta No. 37; APERJ.

71. *Arauta* technically means "arrowroot," but as it is clearly not employed here for its metaphorically herbal qualities I have taken some liberties in its translation.

72. Estado de Guanabara, Secretaria de Segurança Pública, Departamento Geral de Ordem Política e Social, Divisão de Operações, Serviço de Buscas, Seção de Buscas Ostensivas, Assunto: Relatório de Passeata Estudantil (Faz), 14 de novembro de 1973; in DOPS; Setor Estudantil, Pasta No. 39; APERJ; folha 280.

73. Gabeira, *O que é isso companheiro?*, 80.

74. Airgram from American Embassy, Rio de Janeiro, to Department of State, February 14, 1969, No Subject; Subject-Numeric File 1967–69; P&D, PA&R, Brazil, 13–2; SDCF; RG 59; NACP.

75. According to the navy agents who reported on these publications, *Resistência* was initially put out by a coalition of leftist journalists, bankers, professors, artists, and UME members, but when intellectual disagreements arose UME began producing *Combate* on its own. Ministério da Marinha, CENIMAR, Informe 0101, 17 de Março de 1969; in DOPS; Setor Secreto, Pasta No. 42; APERJ.

76. "O fechamento da sala do Diretório," flyer made by Escola de Engenharia da UFRJ, Março 1969; in DOPS; Setor Estudantil, Pasta No. 35; APERJ; and reports of "highly subversive bulletins calling students to strike" reported in Estado do Rio de Janeiro, Secretaria de Segurança Pública, Deparamento de Polícia Política e Social, Serviço de Cadastro e Documentação, Informe No. 24/DPPS/RJ, 21 de março de 1969; in DOPS; Setor Secreto, Pasta No. 42; APERJ.

77. Telegram from American Embassy, Rio de Janeiro, to Secretary of State, April 14, 1969, Subject: Rio Students Clash with Police; Subject-Numeric File 1967–69; P&D, PA&R, Brazil, 13–2; SDCF; RG 59; NACP.

78. Telegram from American Embassy, Rio de Janeiro, to Secretary of State, June 5, 1969, Subject: Student Strike at Rio's Catholic University; Subject-Numeric File 1967–69; P&D, PA&R, Brazil, 13–2; SDCF; RG 59; NACP.

79. Telegram from American Embassy, Rio de Janeiro, to Secretary of State, May 17, 1969, Subject: Students Demonstrate in Streets; Subject-Numeric File 1967–69; P&D, PA&R, Brazil, 13–2; SDCF; RG 59; NACP.

80. Taking place early, the São Paulo meeting was the only one that was not clandestine. But at one of the later ones, the meeting in Paraná, the event was raided, and all the participants were arrested. Feiteiro Cavalari, "Os Limites do Movimento Estudantil, 1964–1980," 145–46.

81. The figure of one hundred comes from Jean Marc von der Weid interview, PMME.

82. Feiteiro Cavalari, "Os Limites do Movimento Estudantil, 1964–1980," 147.

83. Jean Marc von der Weid interview, PMME.

84. Ibid.

85. Ibid.

86. Ridenti, *O Fantasma da Revolução Brasileira*, 125.

87. Ricardo Salles, interview by author.

88. Geraldo Siqueira Filho interview, PMME.

89. Airgram from American Consulate General, Rio de Janeiro, to Department of State, May 11, 1973, Ref: Rio's A-90 of April 18, 1973; Rio's A-80 of March 21, 1973; Subject-Numeric File 1970–73; C&I, E&C, Brazil, 9–3; SDCF; RG 59; NACP.

90. Geraldo Siqueira Filho interview, PMME.

91. Alvarez, *Engendering Democracy*, 51.

92. Estado de Guanabara, Secretaria de Segurança Pública, Departamento Geral de Ordem Política e Social, Divisão de Operações, Seção de Buscas Especiais, Comunicação em 21 de agosto de 1973; in DOPS; Setor Estudantil, Pasta No. 39; APERJ.

93. Estado de Guanabara, Secretaria de Segurança Pública, Departamento de Ordem Política e Social, Serviço de Buscas, Seção de Buscas Especiais, Informação

No. 026 de 27 de junho de 1972, Assunto: Movimento Estudantil; in DOPS; Setor Estudantil, Pasta No. 38; APERJ.

94. From Ministério da Marinha, CENIMAR, to SNI/ARJ—CIE—SISA/RJ—DOPS/GB—DSI/MEC—CENIMAR, No. 1030, 11 de maio de 1970; in DOPS; Setor Estudantil, Pasta No. 36; APERJ.

95. Humanazoutras, Orgão do CACH, Unicamp, 1971; in Arquivo Edgard Leurenroth, UNICAMP, IFCH.

96. "Onde ficamos nós, estudantes," Humanazoutras, Orgão do CACH, UNICAMP, 1971; in Arquivo Edgard Leurenroth, UNICAMP, IFCH.

97. Boletim I, UFF, 1971; in DOPS; Setor Estudantil, Pasta No. 38; APERJ.

98. See the wide range of student newspapers housed in the Arquivo Edgard Leuenroth at the Universdade Estadual de Campinas.

99. Estado do Rio de Janeiro, Secretaria de Segurança, Departamento Autônomo de Ordem Político e Social, Informação por Agente UFF2, 12 de abril de 1973; in DOPS; Setor Estudantil, Pasta No. 39; APERJ; folhas 94–98.

100. Carlos Drummond de Andrade, "Congresso Internacional do Mêdo," first published in Sentimento do Mundo, 1940; my translation.

101. Estado do Rio de Janeiro, Secretaria de Segurança, Departamento Autônomo de Ordem Político e Social, Informação por Agente UFF2, 12 de abril de 1973; in DOPS; Setor Estudantil, Pasta N° 39; APERJ; folhas 94–98.

102. Doralina Rodrigues interview in História da UNE: Volume 1: Depoimentos de ex-dirigentes, 94.

103. "Dos Estudantes da FNM à Opinião Pública," Pamphlet, May 1971; in DOPS; Setor Estudantil, Pasta No. 37, folha 154; APERJ.

104. "Aos Estudantes e à Opinião Pública," nota à imprensa tirada pelos alunos da Escola em 19/4/71; in DOPS; Setor Estudantil, Pasta No. 37, folha 150; APERJ.

105. Ricardo Salles and Sandra Mayrink, interview with author.

106. The deceased student was Ary Abreu Lima da Rosa, listed in Miranda and Tibúrcio Dos filhos deste solo, 517.

107. "O Movimento Universitário," student pamphlet, 1973; in DOPS; Setor Estudantil, Pasta No. 39; APERJ.

108. For example, see the following flyer from 1969: "O fechamento da sala do Diretório," written by Escola de Engenharia da UFRJ, Março 1969; in DOPS; Setor Estudantil, Pasta No. 35; APERJ.

109. Estado de Guanabara, Secretaria de Segurança Pública, Departamento de Ordem Política e Social, Divisão de Operações, Seção de Buscas Espciais; Informe No 0079, 2 de abril de 1970; in DOPS; Setor Estudantil, Pasta No. 35; APERJ.

110. "Denuncia 7" student flyer, 1 de maio de 1971; in DOPS; Setor Estudantil, Pasta No. 38; APERJ.

111. Estado do Rio de Janeiro, Secretaria de Segurança Pública, Deparamento de Polícia Política e Social, Serviço de Cadastro e Documentação, Informe No. 24/DPPS/RJ, 21 de março de 1969; in DOPS; Setor Secreto, Pasta No. 42; APERJ.

112. Ministério do Exército, I Exército—2a Seção, Informe No. 260 CH/69, Assunto: Terrorismo e Sabotagem, 8 de abril de 1969; in DOPS; Setor Secreto, Pasta No. 42; APERJ.

113. DOPS-PR, Pasta 164 (1969) and Pasta 419 (1971); cited in Hagemeyer, "1968: ano da derrubada do ensino pago no Paraná."

114. Serbin, "The Anatomy of a Death."

115. This case was thoroughly investigated and expertly rendered by Kenneth Serbin, and my descriptions draw heavily from his article "The Anatomy of a Death" and his book *Secret Dialogues.*

116. Serbin, "The Anatomy of a Death," 13.

117. Testimony of Neide Richopo to the 1ª Auditoria Militar de São Paulo, 1973; in *Brasil Nunca Mais,* 256. Her description of multiple suicide stories coincides with the fact that another witness testified that DOI-CODI officials said Leme slit his wrists, whereas Serbin discovered that officials cut his throat.

118. Serbin, "The Anatomy of a Death," 13.

119. Telegram from American Consulate, São Paulo, to Secretary of State, April 2, 1973, Subject: Death of Student Provokes Reaction; Subject-Numeric File 1970–73; P&D, PA&R, Brazil, 23–8; SDCF; RG 59; NACP.

120. Serbin, *Secret Dialogues,* 214–215. In 1983 the Leme family was allowed to exhume their son's remains, positively identify him through dental records, and bury him in the family plot (216).

121. Telegram from American Consulate, São Paulo, to Secretary of State, April 2, 1973, Subject: Death of Student Provokes Reaction; Subject-Numeric File 1970–73; P&D, PA&R, Brazil, 23–8; SDCF; RG 59; NACP; and Serbin, *Secret Dialogues,* 208–9.

122. Serbin, "The Anatomy of a Death," 17.

123. See, for example, Secretária da Segurança Pública, Departamento Estadual de Ordem Política e Social, Serviço de Informações, Carta Mensal, São Paulo, "CDPP—Comite de Defesa dos Presos Políticos," 30 de setembro de 1974; in DOPS; Setor Comunismo, Pasta No. 136; APERJ.

124. Serbin, *Secret Dialogues,* 207, and Telegram from American Consulate, São Paulo, to Secretary of State, April 2, 1973, Subject: Death of Student Provokes Reaction; Subject-Numeric File 1970–73; P&D, PA&R, Brazil, 23–8; SDCF; RG 59; NACP.

125. Geraldo Siqueira Filho, quoted in Romagnoli and Gonçalves, *A Volta da UNE,* 19.

126. Stern, *Remembering Pinochet's Chile,* 120–21.

5. Rebuilding the House of Memories

1. Although no documentary proof established exactly when and how Guimarães was killed, the Brazilian government tacitly accepted responsibility for his death by including him on the official list of those disappeared by the military regime for their political activities (Law No. 9140 of December 4, 1995).

2. Maria Rosa Monteiro, Guimarães's mother, says he was arrested three or four times before 1973 and describes his detention in August 1968 as "one of the most terrible imprisonments, as he was locked up a long time." Maria Rosa Monteiro interview, PMME.

3. Telegram from American Consulate, São Paulo, to Secretary of State, June 9, 1969, Subject: Security Rockefeller Mission; Subject-Numeric File 1967–69; P&D, PA&R, Brazil, 13–2; SDCF; RG 59; NACP.

4. Honestino Guimarães, "Mandado de Segurança Popular," reproduced in Romagnoli and Gonçalves, A Volta da UNE.

5. Geisel, Discursos, 1:122.

6. Sader, O anjo torto.

7. Araujo, A Utopia Fragmentada, 98.

8. Ibid., 118.

9. Ibid., 119; and Araujo, Memórias Estudantis, 217.

10. After the PCdoB became a legal political party, Aldo Rebelo would go on to be elected federal deputy throughout the 1990s and 2000s. Between 2005 and 2007 he served as the majority leader of the House of Deputies and even briefly occupied the presidency when then-President Lula was undergoing surgery.

11. Aldo Rebelo interview, PMME.

12. Tendencias, Ano I, No. 1, Abril de 1975; in Departamento de Ordem Política e Social; Setor Estudantil, Pasta No. 39; APERJ.

13. Quilombo dos Palmares, Ano 1, No 1, Setembro, 1975; in Arquivo Edgard Leuenroth, UNICAMP, IFCH.

14. Quilombo dos Palmares, Comissão de Imprensa dos Alunos da PUC/RJ, Ano III, No 6, Março de 1977; in Arquivo Edgard Leuenroth, UNICAMP, IFCH.

15. In some places, both CAs and DAs were generally permitted as long as they followed the strict guidelines established in 1967. While the law regulating this (Decree-Law No. 228 of February 28, 1967, noted in chapter 2) originally permitted only DAs and DCEs, in practice the considerable overlap between CAs and DAs meant that both kinds of organizations continued to operate. DAs were supposed to represent all students from within a certain faculty, such as the Faculty of Philosophy and Social Science. CAs supposedly represented all students from a certain curso (in the United States this would be considered a student's major), such as political science. Hence in some places, such as the example above, there might be several CAs within the same faculty. But in others, such as Faculties of Law or Medicine, the CA and the DA would amount to the same thing, as all students in a Faculty of Law major in law. Adding to this confusion is the fact that individual rectors showed differing degrees of tolerance for student organization. Hence in some places CAs or DAs that followed the strict regulations set out in Decreto-Lei No. 228 were generally both allowed to function, while in other places only DAs were tolerated, and in some schools neither were permitted.

16. Estaca Zero, No. 2, Dezembro 1974 (DCE Unicamp); in Arquivo Edgard Leurenroth, UNICAMP, IFCH.

17. Araujo, *A Utopia Fragmentada*, 25.

18. "Eleições na Universidade de Brasilia," *Movimento*, 15 de novembro de 1976; Flaminio Fantini, "Universidade Federal de Minas Gerais: Um Reitor Paciente," *Movimento*, 28 de junho de 1976, No. 52, 6. Decree-Law No. 228 of February 28, 1967 mandated that DCEs be elected by DA-chosen representatives in an electoral college. Students got around this by holding campuswide "preliminary elections" first and then having the electoral college vote accordingly.

19. See, for example, the issues of June 6, June 20, October 10, November 7, November 21, and November 28, 1977.

20. Ironically, many of those who created *livre* organizations later deemed the tactic a poor one, as once the left-leaning students essentially boycotted the elections for the official groups, their political opponents easily won leadership of them. See José Dirceu's critiques, Dirceu and Palmeira, *Abaixo a Ditadura*, 56.

21. Antonio Carlos, "UnBgate,"*Movimento*, 29 de maio de 1978, 7; Letter from Diretor do Instituto de Veterinária, Prof. Aloysio Ferrari da Silva to Magnífico Reitor da UFRRJ, 14 de agosto de 1980; in DOPS; Setor Estudantil, Pasta No. 73; APERJ.

22. Informação No. 1005-H/79, Ministério do Exército, I Exército, 3 de maio de 1979, to CIE-ARJ/SNI—DPPS/RJ- ARQ, Assunto: Panfletagem; in DOPS; Setor Estudantil, Pasta No. 70; APERJ.

23. Alvarez, *Engendering Democracy*, 51.

24. Maria Francisca "Kika" Alves de Souza, interview with author.

25. Maria Graça Berman, interview with author, April 18, 2000.

26. Ibid.

27. Escorel, *Reviravolta na saúde*.

28. "O encontro estudantil apoiado pelo MEC, Até Quando?" *Movimento*, 1 de agosto de 1977, 8.

29. Escorel, *Reviravolta na saúde*, 71.

30. Aldo Rebelo interview, PMME.

31. Feiteiro Cavalari, "Os Limites do Movimento Estudantil, 1964–1980," 210.

32. Ibid., 217.

33. Maria Graça Berman, interview with author.

34. *Transição Especial: Um Jornal da Tendência Estudantil Secundarista Alternativa*, Rio de Janeiro; DOPS; Setor Estudantil, Pasta No. 75; APERJ.

35. Files in DOPS reported on a poster advertising a symposium on the history of the student movement at the Architecture Faculty of the UFRJ in Resenha Diária No. 072/79—19 Abril 79; in DOPS e Social; Setor Estudantil, Pasta No. 70; APERJ. And they noted a large mural depicting the history of UNE at the Pavilhão Tecnológico at UFRJ in Resenha Diária, 23 de Maio de 1979 in DOPS; Setor Estudantil, Pasta No. 70; APERJ.

36. Diretório Academico Barros Terra (diretoria), Faculdade de Medicina da Universidade Federal Fluminense, "Contribuição para as Discussões sobre a reorganização do Movimento Estudantil no Rio de Janeiro," 18 de abril de 1979 in DOPS; Setor Estudantil, Pasta No. 70; APERJ.

37. *Sintese,* Ano I, No. 21, 18/03/75, Pontífica Universidade Católica do Rio de Janeiro, Diretório Acadêmico Adhemar Fonseca, Diretório Acadêmico Galileu Galilei, Associação de Pós-Graduação da PUC/RJ; in DOPS; Setor Estudantil, Pasta No. 39; APERJ.

38. Students in São Paulo had held a previous public protest demonstration on March 30, 1977, when they walked toward the Ministry of Education and Culture to submit a complaint about recent cuts in education spending, eventually desisting in order to avoid altercations with the police. This event did not have the wide repercussions of their later demonstrations but nonetheless represented an important breaking of barriers for USP students who feared the consequences of a public march. For a description of this event, see Geraldo Siqueira Filho interview, PMME.

39. Zeichner, "Representing the Vanguard."

40. Ibid.

41. Geraldo Siqueira Filho interview, PMME.

42. A DEOPS report stated that in several faculties students marked the first anniversary of the "death by car accident of the terrorist Alexandre Vannucchi Leme." Secretaria de Segurança Pública, Departamento Estadual de Ordem Politica e Social, Serviço de Informações, DOPS, São Paulo, "Carta Mensal," 1 de julho de 1974; in DOPS; Setor DOPS, Pasta No. 193; APERJ.

43. The journalist Igor Fusor reported that the events were directed by the Pro-UNE Commission; see "Estudantes: O dia de protesto," *Movimento,* 27 de marco de 1978, 2.

44. *Em Tempo,* No. 6, 31/3 a 6/4 de 1978, in EPESP, Coleção DEOPS, Ordem Social, OS-0036. For the political makeup of *Em Tempo,* see Araujo, *A utopia fragmentada.* See also the coverage in the *Folha de São Paulo* and the *Estado de São Paulo* on March 29, 1978.

45. "Anistia! Anistia! O dia dos estudantes e a anistia," *Movimento,* 3 de abril de 1978, 6.

46. *Em Tempo,* No. 6, 31/3 a 6/4 de 1978, In APESP, Coleção DEOPS, Ordem Social, OS-0036. For the political makeup of *Em Tempo,* see Araujo, *A utopia fragmentada.*

47. Ibid.

48. "Anistia! Anistia! O dia dos estudantes e a anistia," *Movimento,* 3 de abril de 1978, 6. The document was his "Mandado de Segurança Popular."

49. Maria Graça Berman, interview with author.

50. "No Pasaran," *Movimento,* 3 de abril de 1978, 10.

51. *Manifesto, Um Jornal de Centelha,* Belo Horizonte, Ano 1, No. 0 (April 1978); in Arquivo Edgard Leurenroth, UNICAMP, IFCH.

52. "Agora UNE" magazine. Maio de 1979, in DOPS; Setor Estudantil, Pasta No. 70; APERJ.

53. Seizing the opportunity of a congressional investigation into the state of higher education in the country, representatives from several reconstructed student

organizations in São Paulo attended the event, where they criticized the prohibitions on their student organizations and declared that the fourth ENE would be held in August 1978. "UNE Ressurgirá," *Movimento*, 5 de junho de 1978, 2.

54. "A UNE vai ao ministro e marca reunião," *Istoé*, April 4, 1979, 13.

55. SSP-RJ-DGIE-DPPS, Divisão de Operações, Relatório/DO, 24 de maio de 1979; Assunto: Movimento Estudantil, Referencia: Reorganização da Extinta União Nacional dos Estudantes; in DOPS; Setor Estudantil, Pasta No. 71; APERJ.

56. "A UNE vai ao ministro e marca reunião," *Istoé*, April 4, 1979, 14.

57. "Estudantes vão recriar a UNE e recebem apoio," *Folha de São Paulo*, May 6, 1979; in Arquivo Edgard Leuenroth, UNICAMP, IFCH, Coleção Movimento Estudantil, Pasta 10.

58. Skidmore, *The Politics of Military Rule in Brazil*, 203.

59. Serviço Público Estadual, DGIE, DPPS—DO, Serviço de Buscas, Seção de Buscas Especiais, Assunto: Manifestação Pública na Cinelândia—"Dia Nacional de Luto [sic]" in DOPS; Setor Estudantil, Pasta No. 67; APERJ.

60. Decreto No. 84.035 de 1° de outubro de 1979, *Diario Oficial*, October 1, 1979; clipping in DOPS; Setor Estudantil, Pasta No. 71; APERJ.

61. Ibid.

62. Jornal Pró-UNE, Orgão da Comissão Pró-União Nacional dos Estudantes (editado em São Paulo pela União Estadual dos Estudantes), abril de 1979; in DOPS; Setor Estudantil, Pasta No. 70; APERJ.

63. "Estudantes vão recriar a UNE e recebem apoio," *Folha de São Paulo*, May 6, 1979; in Arquivo Edgard Leuenroth, UNICAMP, IFCH, Coleção Movimento Estudantil, Pasta No. 10.

64. Sérgio Buarque de Gusmão, "No passado, o triunfalismo e a tragédia," *Istoé* May 30, 1979, 9–10. It appears that the Comitê Brasileiro de Anistia may have also joined in the "Where is Honestino?" campaign, for I have seen Internet references to an article by that name in a magazine called *Anistia* (No. 4, March/April 1979, 8), but I have not seen the magazine itself to be able to confirm its sponsorship or existence.

65. SSP-RJ-DGIE-DPPS, Divisão de Operações, Relatório/DO, 24 de maio de 1979; Assunto: Movimento Estudantil, Referencia: Reorganização da Extinta União Nacional dos Estudantes; in DOPS; Setor Estudantil, Pasta No. 71; APERJ.

66. "Estudantes vão recriar a UNE e recebem apoio," *Folha de São Paulo*, May 6, 1979; in Arquivo Edgard Leuenroth, UNICAMP, IFCH, Coleção Movimento Estudantil, Pasta No. 10.

67. "Sérgio Buarque de Gusmão, "Salvador, dia 29: a UNE está de volta," *Istoé*, May 9, 1979, 32–33.

68. José Luis Guedes, José Renato Rabelo, Humberto Mazzini, Daniel Aarão Reis, Luis Travassos, Nilton Santos, Vladimir Palmeira, Jean Marc Van der Weid, and João de Paula Ferreira, Letter to Companheiros do XXXI Congresso da UNE, 1979 in *História da UNE*, 1:125–27.

69. José Serra in Romangnoli and Gonçalves, *A Volta da* UNE, 47.

70. Contrary to the prior format of voting for the UNE directorate at the congress itself, in 1979 students decided to hold direct elections. Thus the swearing-in ceremony took place five months after the Reconstruction Congress.

71. Mendes Junior, *Movimento Estudantil no Brasil, tudo é história*, 74.

72. LDA No. 19.482/80, Serviço Público Estadual, Secretaria de Estado de Segurança Pública, 15 de agosto de 1980; in DOPS; Setor Estudantil, Pasta No. 73; APERJ.

73. See the caption beneath a photo of the building in *Transição Especial: Um Jornal da Tendência Estudantil Secundarista Alternativa*, Rio de Janeiro; DOPS; Setor Estudantil, Pasta No. 75; APERJ.

74. It may also be related to confusion about the date of the coup itself, a day Maria Hermínia Tavares de Almeida and Luiz Weis call "the interminable First of April, 1964": "Interminable because it began on March 30, when General Carlos Luís Guedes prepared to march from Belo Horizonte to Brasília; it continued into the early morning hours of the 31st, when General Olympio Mourão Filho left [the town of] Juiz de Fora on the road to Rio de Janeiro, and it extended into the 2nd when showers of confetti covered the main cities as the latest news went over the radios." Tavares de Almeida and Weis, "Carro-zero e pau-de-arara," 323.

75. *Jornal Pró*-UNE, Orgão da Comissão Pró-União Nacional dos Estudantes (editado em São Paulo pela União Estadual dos Estudantes), abril de 1979; in DOPS; Setor Estudantil, Pasta No. 70; APERJ.

76. Ferdy Varneiro, "A Última Noite da UNE," in *O Pasquim*, Ano XI—No. 554, February 1980, 8–14.

77. See, for example, "Jornal 'Pró-UNE' tem 300 mil exemplares," *Jornal do Brasil*, May 1, 1979; in Arquivo Edgard Leuenroth, UNICAMP, IFCH, Coleção Movimento Estudantil, Pasta No. 10.

78. Sturken, *Tangled Memories*, 11.

79. According to reports in the *Folha de São Paulo*, lawyers for UNE were planning to submit a formal request for the return of their building in January 1979. This was to be part of a larger drive to reestablish the union's legality, in order to legalize the organization itself but also as a means of defending those students arrested for earlier efforts to reorganize it. Obviously the request, if submitted, was unsuccessful.

80. "Diretoria da UNE pretende retomar 'democraticamente' sede da Praia do Flamengo," *Jornal do Brasil*, March 7 1980; in DOPS; Setor Estudantil, Pasta No. 72; APERJ.

81. "Antiga sede da UNE é ocupada pela polícia," 1980, newspaper not listed; DOPS; Setor Estudantil, Pasta No. 72; APERJ.

82. "Vereadores apresentam queixa contra Comando," *Jornal do Brasil*, June 11, 1980. "Violência repercute no Congresso," *Jornal do Brasil*, June 11, 1980.

83. "O Sono da Lei," *Jornal do Brasil*, editorial, June 12, 1980.

84. Lowenthal, "Identity, Heritage and History," 52.

85. Serviço Público Estadual, 1980, Assunto: "Seminário Nacional Sobre a Universidade," 07 de junho; DOPS; Setor Estudantil, Pasta No. 73; APERJ.

86. "TFR cassa liminar do juiz e autoriza a demolição do prédio da UNE no Flamengo," *Jornal do Brasil*, June 4, 1980.

87. *União Nacional dos Estudantes, Boletim Informativo No. 2*, Janeiro 1981; in Arquivo Edgard Leuenroth, UNICAMP, IFCH.

88. "Vamos Construir o Palácio da Juventude," *Jornal da UBES*, Ano 1, No. 0, março 1982; DOPS; Setor Estudantil, Pasta No. 75; APERJ.

89. Clara Araújo interview, PMME with Ana Paula Goulart and Tatiana di Sabatto, PMME, October 25, 2005.

90. "UNE intensifica campanha para obter a legalização," *Folha de São Paulo*, May 19, 1983; in Arquivo Edgard Leuenroth, UNICAMP, IFCH, Coleção Movimento Estudantil, Pasta No. 10.

91. Alexandre Medeiros, "Um pedaço resgatado da história," *Jornal do Brasil*, May 17, 1994.

Epilogue

1. Although several publications that have printed this photo label it as a picture of Guimarães, and although it is now widely recognized as his image, no direct evidence has ever definitively confirmed that the picture is indeed of him. Vladimir Sachetta, archivist at Acervo Iconografia, personal communication, August 8, 2001.

2. This text can be seen in the multiple photographs of the site that appeared in print and online media in the days following the ceremony.

3. "UNE vai receber R$44,6 milhões do governo por reparação da perda da sede durante a Ditadura Militar," *O Globo*, December 17, 2010.

4. Ventura, *1968: O que fizemos de nós*, 177.

5. "Depois do ovo, o arrependimento," *Jornal do Brasil*, May 22, 2000.

6. Reis Filho, *Ditadura militar, esquerdas e sociedade*, 7.

7. Ibid.

Bibliography

Archives and Collections

Arquivo Edgard Leuenroth, Universidade Estadual de Campinas (UNICAMP)
    Instituto de Filosofia e Ciências Humanas
    Coleção Brasil Nunca Mais
    Coleção Movimento Estudantil
Arquivo Nacional do Brasil, Rio de Janeiro
Arquivo Público do Estado do Rio de Janeiro
    Coleção Departamento de Ordem Político e Social
    Arquivo Ângela Borba
    Arquivo Jean Marc von der Weid
Arquivo Público do Estado de São Paulo
    Coleção Departamento de Ordem Político e Social
Coleção do Projeto Memória do Movimento Estudantil, Fundação Roberto
    Marinho
Fundação Getúlio Vargas
    Centro de Pesquisa e Documentação de Historia Contemporanea do Brasil
        (CPDOC)
    Arquivo Ernani do Amaral Peixoto
    Arquivo Gustavo Capanema
Hoover Institution Archives, Stanford University
    Register of the United States National Student Association
Laboratorio de Estudo do Tempo Presente, Instituto de Filosofia e Ciencias
    Humanas, Universidade Federal do Rio de Janeiro
    Coleção Imprensa Alternativa
United States National Archives
    State Department Central Files

Magazines and Newspapers

Correio da Manhã
Em Tempo
O Estado de São Paulo

Folha de São Paulo
Hispanic American Report
Istoé
Jornal do Brasil
Manchete
Movimento
New York Times
Opinião
Realidade
Time Magazine
Veja

Interviews with Author

Maria Francisca Alves de Souza, Rio de Janeiro, May 30 and June 20, 1999
Maria Graça Berman, Rio de Janeiro, April 18, 2000
Pedro Claudio Bocayuva, Rio de Janeiro, April 28, 2000
José Gradel, Rio de Janeiro, June 18, 2009
Fernando Gusmão, Rio de Janeiro, October 20, 1999
Percival Maricato, São Paulo, July 15, 2009
Sandra Mayrink, Rio de Janeiro, April 12 and May 8, 2000
Vladimir Palmeira, Rio de Janeiro, January 20, 2000
Ricardo Salles, Rio de Janeiro, April 12, 2000

Memoirs and Published Interviews

História da UNE: Volume 1: depoimentos de ex-dirigentes. Coleção Historia Presente. São Paulo: Editorial Livramento, 1980.
Aarão Reis Filho, Daniel, and Pedro de Moraes. 68: a paixão de uma utopia. 2d ed. Rio de Janeiro: Fundação Getulio Vargas, 1998.
Daniel, Herbert. Passagem para o proximo sonho. Rio de Janeiro: CODECRI, 1982.
D'Araujo, Maria Celina, Gláucio Ary Dillon Soares, and Celso Castro, eds. Visões do golpe: a memória militar sobre 1964. Rio de Janeiro: Relume-Dumará, 1994.
——, eds. Os anos de chumbo: a memória militar sobre a repressão. Rio de Janeiro: Relume-Dumará, 1994.
——, eds. A volta aos quartéis: a memória militar sobre a abertura. Rio de Janeiro: Relume-Dumará, 1995.
Diniz, Josue Alves. Calabouço 1968: O Cerco das Trevas. Rio de Janeiro: Livraria Editora Catedra, 1986.
Dirceu, José, and Vladimir Palmeira. Abaixo a Ditadura: O Movimento de 68 contado por seus líderes. Rio de Janeiro: Garamond Espaço e Tempo, 1998.
Fundação Perseu Abramo, Interviews for website "Trinta Anos do AI-5—Não Vamos Esquecer." http:www.fpabramo.org.

Gabeira, Fernando. *O que é isso companheiro?* Rio de Janeiro: CODECRI, 1979.

Maklouf Carvalho, Luiz. *Mulheres que foram à luta armada.* São Paulo: Editora Globo, 1998.

Oliveira Costa, Albertina de, Maria Teresa Porciuncula Moraes, Norma Marzola, and Valentina da Rocha Lima, eds. *Memórias das Mulheres do Exílio.* Rio de Janeiro: Paz e Terra, 1980.

Projeto Memória do Movimento Estudantil, Fundação Roberto Marinho Interviews:

Alfonso, Almino. Interview by Angélica Muller, June 17, 2005.

Amaral, Roberto. Interview by Angélica Muller and Carla Siqueira, May 17, 2005.

Araújo, Clara. Interview by Ana Paula Goulart and Tatiana di Sabatto, October 25, 2005.

Barbosa Guimarães, Genival. Interview by Angélica Müller, January 2, 2007.

Carneiro Ribeiro, Maria Augusta. Interview by Carla Siqueira, June 25, 2005.

Eirado, Raymundo. Interview by Angélica Muller and Carla Siqueira, October 14, 2004.

Frejat, José. Interview by Angélica Muller and Carla Siqueira, October 7, 2004.

Genoíno, José. Interview by Caio Túlio Costa, September 9, 2005.

Gorender, Jacob. Interview by Ana Paula Goulart and Angélica Muller, June 15, 2005.

Gregori, José. Interview by Ana Paula Goulart, June 17, 2005.

Joffily, Bernardo. Interview by Ana Paula Goulart and Angélica Muller, November 8, 2004.

Rebelo, Aldo. Interview by Angélica Müller, Ana Paula Goulart, and Paulo Markun, December 4, 2004.

Reis Filho, Daniel Aarão. Interview by Angélica Müller and Ana Paula Goulart, July 5, 2005.

Sant'Anna, Irum. Interview by Angélica Muller and Carla Siqueira, October 14, 2004.

Serra, Antônio. Interview by Ana Paula Goulart, July 22, 2005.

Talarico, José Gomes. Interview by Angélica Muller and Tatiana Di Sabbato, October 19, 2004.

von der Weid, Jean Marc. Interview by Carla Siqueira and Ana Paula Goulart, October 7, 2004.

Rocha, Dora. "Entrevista com Maria Yedda Linhares." *Estudos Históricos* 5, no. 10 (1992): 216–36.

Sirkis, Alfredo. *Os Carbonários: Memórias da guerrilha perdida.* 8th ed. São Paulo: Global, 1983.

Published Documents

Brasil. Congresso. *Anais da Câmara dos Deputados: 2ª Sessão Legislativa Ordinária da 6ª Legislatura.* Brasilia, 1968.

Casa do Estudante do Brasil. *Relatório 1939.* Jornal do Commercio. Rio de Janeiro, 1940, Seely G. Mudd Library, Yale University.

Centro Brasileiro de Pesquisas Educacionais, Instituto Nacional de Estudos Pedagógicos, Ministério da Educação e Cultura. *Caracterização Sócio-Econômica do Estudante Universitário.* Rio de Janeiro: Instituto Nacional de Estudos Pedagógicos, Ministério da Educação e Cultura, 1968.

Colegio Pedro II. *A revolução de 1964 julgada pelos estudantes de 1970.* Rio de Janeiro: Grafica do Colegio Pedro II, 1970.

Comissão de Familiares de Mortos e Desaparecidos Políticos, Instituto de Estudo da Violência do Estado, and Grupo Tortura Nunca Mais—RJ e PE. *Dossiê dos Mortos e Desaparecidos Políticos a Partir de 1964.* Recife, Pernambuco: Companhia Editora de Pernambuco, 1995.

Instituto Brasileiro de Geografia e Estatística. *Sinopse Estatística do Brasil, 1946.* Rio de Janeiro: Serviço Gráfico do Instituto Brasileiro de Geografia e Estatística.

Manifiesto de Córdoba, 1918, www.fmmeducacion.com.ar/Historia (November 30, 2009).

Ministério da Educação e Cultura, Diretoria do Ensino Superior. "Relatório da Equipe de Assessoria ao Planejamento do Ensino Superior—EAPES (Acôrdo MEC-USAID)." Rio de Janeiro, 1968.

——, Secretaria Geral. *Analise do Ensino no Brasil: Estudo Preliminar.* May 1968.

——. "Educação Moral e Cívico: Como Disciplina Obrigatória nos Três Níveis de Ensino." Comissão Nacional de Moral e Civismo, 1970.

Miranda, Nilmário, and Carlos Tibúrcio. *Dos filhos deste solo: Mortos e desaparecidos políticos durante a ditadura militar: a responsabilidade do Estado.* São Paulo: Fundação Perseu Abramo, 1999.

Mita Arquidiocesena de São Paulo. *Perfil dos Atingidos.* Volume 3, Projeto 'Brasil: Nunca Mais.' Petrópolis: Vozes, 1988.

República dos Estados Unidos do Brasil. *Coleção das Leis.*

Books, Articles, and Theses

Achugar, Hugo. "El lugar de la memoria, a propósito de monumentos (Motivos y paréntesis)." Paper presented at the Social Science Research Council workshop on Memory and Repression. Montevideo, Uruguay, 1999.

Albuquerque Favero, Maria de Lourdes de. *Da Universidade "Modernizada" à Universidade "Disciplinada": Atcon e Meira Mattos, Coleção Educação Contemporanea.* São Paulo: Cortez, 1991.

Albuquerque, J. A. Guilhon, ed. *Classes Médias e Política no Brasil.* Rio de Janeiro: Paz e Terra, 1977.

——. *Movimento estudantil e consciência social*. Rio de Janeiro: Paz e Terra, 1977.

Altbach, Philip G. "The International Student Movement." *Journal of Contemporary History* 5, no. 1 (1970): 156–74.

Alvarez, Sonia E. *Engendering Democracy in Brazil: Women's Movements in Transition Politics*. Princeton, NJ: Princeton University Press, 1990.

Alves, Maria Helena Moreira. *State and Opposition in Military Brazil*. Austin: University of Texas Press, 1985.

——. "Dilemmas of the Consolidation of Democracy from the Top in Brazil: A Political Analysis." *Latin American Perspectives* 15, no. 58 (1988): 47–63.

Alves, Márcio Moreira. *Beabá dos MEC-USAID*. Rio de Janeiro: Edições Gernasa, 1968.

——. *A Grain of Mustard Seed: The Awakening of the Brazilian Revolution*. Garden City, NY: Doubleday Anchor Press, 1973.

——. *Torturas e torturados*. Rio de Janeiro: Editora Idade Nova, 1966.

Arapiraca, José Oliveira. *A USAID e a Educação Brasileira: um estudo a partir de uma abordagem crítica da teoria do capital humano*. São Paulo: Cortez Editora, 1982.

Araujo, Maria Paula. *Memórias estudantis: da fundação da UNE aos nossos dias*. Rio de Janeiro: Relume Dumará, Fundação Roberto Marinho, 2007.

——. *A Utopia fragmentada: As novas esquerdas no Brasil e no mundo na década de 1970*. Rio de Janeiro: Fundação Getúlio Vargas, 2002.

Arinos Filho, Afonso. *Diplomacia Independente: um legado de Afonso Arinos*, São Paulo: Paz e Terra, 2001.

Arquidiocese de São Paulo. *Brasil Nunca Mais: Um relato para a história*. 3d ed. São Paulo: Editora Vozes, 1985.

Assis, Denise. *Propaganda e Cinema a Serviço do Golpe, 1962/1964*. Rio de Janeiro: Mauad, FAPERJ, 2001.

Associacão dos docentes da Universidade de São Paulo. *O livro negro da USP: O controle ideológico na universidade*. São Paulo: ADUSP, 1978.

Associacão dos docentes da Universidade Federal do Rio Grande do Sul. *Universidade e Repressão: Os expurgos na UFRGS*. Porto Alegre: L&PM, 1979.

Barcellos, Jalusa. *CPC da UNE: uma historia de paixão e consciência*. Rio de Janeiro: Nova Fronteira, 1994.

Beltrão, Kaizô Iwakami, and José Eustáquio Diniz Alves. "Reversal of the Gender Gap in Brazilian Education in the 20th Century." *Cadernos de Pesquisa* 39 (2009): 125–56.

Besse, Susan K. *Restructuring Patriarchy: The Modernization of Gender Inequality in Brazil, 1914–1940*. Chapel Hill: University of North Carolina Press, 1996.

Brasil, Clarissa. "As ações do Comando de Caça aos Comunistas (1968–1969)." Paper delivered at the IX Encontro Estadual de História, Associação Nacional de História, Seção Rio Grande do Sul.

Brito, Antonio Maurício. "UFBA: Movimento Estudantil em Salvador e o AI-5." Conference presentation at Seminário Internacional 40 anos do AI-5, Universidade Federal do Recôncavo da Bahia, November 12, 2008.

Buarque de Holanda, Heloisa. *Impressões de Viagem:* CPC, *Vanguarda e Desbunde:* 1960/79. São Paulo: Brasiliense, 1981.

———, and Marcos Augusto Gonçalves. *Cultura e Participação nos Anos 60, tudo é história.* São Paulo: Editora Brasiliense, 1982.

Cardoso, Irene. "Memória de 68: Terror e interdição do passado." *Tempo Social— Revista de Sociologia da* USP 2, no. 2 (1990): 101–12.

———. "A dimensão trágica de 68." *Teoria e Debate* 22 (1993): 59–64.

———. "68: A Comemoração Impossível." *Tempo Social—Revista de Sociologia da* USP 10, no. 2 (1998): 1–12.

Carey, Elaine. *Plaza of Sacrifices: Gender, Power and Terror in 1968 Mexico.* In Diálogos Series edited by Lyman L. Johnson. Albuquerque: University of New Mexico Press, 2005.

Caso, Antonio. *A esquerda armada no Brasil, 1967–1971.* Lisbon: Morães, 1976.

Catela, Ludmila da Silva, and Alessandra Carvalho. "31 de marzo de 1964: Una memoria deshilachada." *Las conmemoraciones: Las disputas en las fechas "in-felices,"* ed. Elizabeth Jelin, 195–242. Madrid: Siglo XXI, 2002.

Caulfield, Sueann. "The Birth of Mangue: Race, Nation and the Politics of Prostitution in Rio de Janeiro, 1850–1942." *Sex and Sexuality in Latin America,* ed. Daniel Balderstorm and Donna J. Guy, 86–100. New York: New York University Press, 1997.

Cavalari, Rosa Maria Feiteiro. "Os Limites do movimento estudantil, 1964–1980." MA thesis, UNICAMP Department of Education, 1987.

Centro Cultural Banco do Brasil. *Trinta Anos de 68.* Rio de Janeiro: Centro Cultural Banco do Brasil, 1998.

Collier, Ruth Berins, and David Collier. "Inducements versus Constraints: Disaggregating 'Corporatism.'" *American Political Science Review* 73, no. 4 (December 1979): 967–86.

Colling, Ana Maria. *A Resistênica da mulher à ditadura militar no brasil.* Rio de Janeiro: Rosa dos Tempos, 1997.

Corradi, Juan E., et al., eds. *Fear at the Edge: State Terror and Resistance in Latin America.* Berkeley: University of California Press, 1992.

Cowan, Benjamin A. "Sex and the Security State: Gender, Sexuality and 'Subversion' at Brazil's Escola Superior de Guerra, 1964–1985." *Journal of the History of Sexuality* 16, no. 3 (July 2007): 459–81.

———. "The Secret History of Subversion: Sex, Modernity and the Brazilian National Security State." PhD diss., UCLA, 2010.

Cruz, Sebastião C. Velasco E., and Carlos Estevam Martins. "De Castello a Figueiredo: uma incursão na pré-história da 'abertura.'" *Sociedade Política no Brasil Pós-64,* ed. Bernardo Sorj and Maria Hermínia Tavares de Almeida, 13–61. São Paulo: Brasiliense, 1983.

Cunha, Luiz Antônio. *A Universidade Crítica: O ensino superior na república populista.* Rio de Janeiro: Francisco Alves, 1982.

——. *A Universidade Reformanda: O golpe de 1964 e a modernização do ensino superior.* Rio de Janeiro: Francisco Alves, 1988.

——. "A gratuidade no ensino superior público: da proibição à garantia constitucional." *Magisterio: Formação e Trabalho Pedagógico*, ed. Ilma P. Alencastro Veiga, 31–56. Campinas: Papirus, 1991.

——. "Ensino Superior e Universidade no Brasil." *500 anos de educação no Brasil*, ed. Eliane Marta Teixeira Lopes, Luciano Mendes Faria Filho, and Cynthia Greine Veiga, 151–204. Belo Horizonte: Autêntica, 2000.

Cunha, Luiz Antônio, and Moacyr de Góes. *O Golpe na Educação. Brasil: os anos de autoritarismo.* 2d ed. Rio de Janeiro: Jorge Zahar Editor, 1985.

Departamento de Documentação e Informação Cultural, Prefeitura da Cidade do Rio de Janeiro. *Um Rio em 68: Biblioteca Carioca.* Rio de Janeiro: Secretaria Municipal de Cultura, 1988.

Diniz, Josué Alves. *Calabouço 1968: o cerco das trevas.* Rio de Janeiro: Editora Cátedra, 1986.

Dreifus, René Armand. *1964, a Conquista do estado.* Petrópolis: Vozes, 1981.

Duarte, Teresinha. "Entre a realidade e a utopia: Goiânia em 1968." *1968 Faz 30 Anos*, ed. João Roberto Martins Filho, 129–44. Campinas: Editora da Universidade Federal de São Carlos, 1998.

Dubeux Berardo Carneiro da Cunha, Simone. "Narrativas de um acontecimento: a morte do estudante Edson Luis no Calabouço em 1968." *Antropologia e comunicação*, ed. Isabel Travancas and Patrícia Farias, 149–67. Rio de Janeiro: Garamond, 2003.

Dulles, John W. F. *Carlos Lacerda, Brazilian Crusader.* Volume 1: *The Years 1914–1960.* Austin: University of Texas Press, 1991.

——. *The São Paulo Law School and the Anti-Vargas Resistance (1938–1945).* Austin: University of Texas Press, 1986.

——. *Anarchists and Communist in Brazil 1900–1935.* Austin: University of Texas Press, 1973.

——. *Sobral Pinto: The Conscience of Brazil, Leading the Attack against Vargas (1930–1945).* Austin: University of Texas Press, 2002.

Dunn, Christopher. *Brutality Garden: Tropicália and the Emergence of a Brazilian Counterculture.* Chapel Hill: University of North Carolina Press, 2001.

Erickson, Kenneth Paul. *The Brazilian Corporative State and Working-Class Politics.* Berkeley: University of California Press, 1977.

Escobar, Edward J. "The Dialectics of Repression: The Los Angeles Police Department and the Chicano Movement, 1968–1971." *Journal of American History*, 79, no.4 (March 1993): 1483–1514.

Escorel, Sarah. *Reviravolta na saúde: origem e articulação do movimento sanitário.* Rio de Janeiro: Editora Fiocruz, 1999.

Fávero, Maria de Lourdes de A. *A UNE em Tempos de Autoritarismo.* Rio de Janeiro: Editora UFRJ, 1995.

Feiteiro Cavalari, Rosa Maria. "Os Limites do Movimento Estudantil, 1964–1980," MA thesis, Universidade Estadual de Campinas, 1987.

Ferreira, Jorge, and Daniel Aarão Reis Filho, eds. *A formação das tradições 1889–1945*. Coleção As Esquerdas no Brasil. Rio de Janeiro: Civilização Brasileira, 2007.

Fico, Carlos. *O Grande Irmão, da operação brother sam aos anos de chumbo: O governo dos estados unidos e a ditadura militar brasileira*. Rio de Janeiro: Civilização Brasileira, 2008.

———. "1968: O ano que terminou mal: a escalada da violência da ditadura militar brasileira." Conference presentation at Seminário Internacional 40 anos do AI-5, Universidade Federal do Recôncavo da Bahia, November 12, 2008.

———. *Além do Golpe: Versões e controvérsias sobre 1964 e a Ditadura Militar*. Rio de Janeiro: Editora Record, 2004.

Fonseca Sobrinho, Délcio da. *Estado e População: Uma História do Planejamento Familiar no Brasil*. Rio de Janeiro: Rosa dos Tempos, 1993.

Franco, Jean. "Gender, Death, and Resistance: Facing the Ethical Vacuum." *Fear at the Edge: State Terror and Resistance in Latin America*, ed. Juan E. Corradi, Patricia Weiss Fagen, and Manuel Antonio Garreton, 102–18. Berkeley: University of California Press, 1992.

Freire, Paulo. *Education for Critical Consciousness*. Translated by Myra Bergman Ramos. New York: Seabury Press, 1973.

French, John D. *The Brazilian Workers' ABC: Class Conflict and Alliances in Modern São Paulo*. Chapel Hill: University of North Carolina Press, 1992.

———. "From the Shop Floor to the Praça da Sé: University Students and São Paulo's Industrial Working Class in 1968." Paper presented at the conference The Cultures of Dictatorship: Historical Reflections on the Brazilian Golpe of 1964, University of Maryland, October 14–16, 2004.

Garcia, Marco Aurélio, and Maria Alice Vieira, eds. *Rebeldes e Contestadores 1968: Brasil, França e Alemanha*. São Paulo: Editora Fundação Perseu Abramo, 1999.

Garcia, Nelson Jahr. *Sadismo, sedução e silencio: propaganda e controle ideológico no Brasil, 1964–1980*. São Paulo: Edições Loyola, 1990.

Gaspari, Elio. *A Ditadura Envergonhada*. São Paulo: Companhia das Letras, 2002.

———. *A Ditadura Escancarada*. São Paulo: Compania das Letras, 2002.

———. *A Ditadura Derrotada*. São Paulo: Compania das Letras, 2003.

———. *A Ditadura Encurralada*. São Paulo: Compania das Letras, 2004.

Geisel, Ernesto. *Discursos*. Brasilia: Assessoria de Imprensa e Relações Públicas da Presidência da República, 1975.

Gomes Vianna, Marly de Almeida. "O PCB: 1929–43." *A formação das tradições 1889–1945*, ed. Jorge Ferreira and Daniel Aarão Reis Filho. Coleção As Esquerdas no Brasil. Rio de Janeiro: Civilização Brasileira, 2007.

Gorender, Jacob. *Combate nas trevas: a esquerda brasileira, das ilusões perdidas à luta armada*. São Paulo: Editora Atica, 1987.

Graham, Douglas Hume. "The Growth, Change and Reform of Higher Education in Brazil: A Review and Commentary on Selected Problems and Issues." *Brazil in the Sixties*, ed. Riordan Roett, 275–324. Nashville: Vanderbilt University Press, 1972.

Green, James N. *We Cannot Remain Silent: Opposition to the Brazilian Military Regime in the United States*. Durham, NC: Duke University Press, 2010.

Habert, Nadine. *A Década de 70: Apogeu e Crise da Ditadura Militar Brasileira*. Princípio series edited by Nelson do Reis. São Paulo: Editora Ática, 1992.

Hagemeyer, Rafael Rosa. "1968: ano da derrubada do ensino pago no Paraná." *1968 Faz 30 Anos*, ed. João Roberto Martins Filho, 95–128. Campinas: Editora da Universidade Federal de São Carlos, 1998.

Haussman, Fay, and Jerry Haar. *Education in Brazil, World Education Series*. Hamden, CT: Archon Books, 1978.

Hilton, Stanley E. "Brazilian Diplomacy and the Washington–Rio de Janeiro 'Axis' during the World War II Era." *Hispanic American Historical Review* 59, no. 2 (1979): 201–31.

———. *Brazil and the Great Powers, 1930–1939: The Politics of Trade Rivalry*. Austin: University of Texas Press, 1975.

Huggins, Martha K. *Political Policing: The United States and Latin America*. Durham, NC: Duke University Press, 1998.

———. "Legacies of Authoritarianism: Brazilian Torturers' and Murderers' Reformulation of Memory." *Latin American Perspectives* 27, no. 111 (2000): 57–78.

Jelin, Elizabeth. "The Politics of Memory: The Human Rights Movement and the Construction of Democracy in Argentina." *Latin American Perspectives* 21, no. 2 (1994): 38–58.

———, *Los Trabajos de la Memoria*. Madrid: Siglo XXI, 2002.

———. *State Repression and the Labors of Memory*. Translated by Marcial Godoy-Anativia and Judy Rein. Minneapolis: University of Minnesota Press, 2003.

Kadt, Emanuel de. *Catholic Radicals in Brazil*, London: Oxford University Press, 1970.

Kirkendall, Andrew J. *Class Mates: Male Student Culture and the Making of a Political Class in Nineteenth-Century Brazil*. Lincoln: University of Nebraska Press, 2002.

———. "Entering History: Paulo Freire and the Politics of the Brazilian Northeast, 1958–1964." *Luso-Brazilian Review* 41, no. 1 (2004): 168–89.

Klimke, Martin. *The Other Alliance: Student Protest in West Germany and the United States in the Global Sixties*. Princeton, NJ: Princeton University Press, 2010.

Langland, Victoria. "Il est Interdite d'Interdire: The Transnational Experience of 1968 in Brazil." *Estudios Interdisciplinarios de América Latina y el Caribe* 17, no. 1 (2006): 61–81.

———. "Birth Control Pills and Molotov Cocktails: Reading Sex and Revolution in 1968 Brazil." *In from the Cold: Latin America's New Encounter with the Cold War*, ed. Gilbert M. Joseph and Daniela Spenser, 308–49. Durham, NC: Duke University Press, 2008.

Leacock, Ruth. *Requiem for Revolution: The United States and Brazil, 1961–1969*. Kent, OH: Kent State University Press, 1990.

Lerche Vieira, Sofia. *O (Dis)curso da (Re)forma Universitaria*. Fortaleza: Edições Universidade Federal do Ceara/PROED, 1982.

Levine, Robert M. *Father of the Poor?: Vargas and His Era*. Cambridge: Cambridge University Press, 1988.

Lima, Haroldo, and Aldo Arantes. *História da Acão Popular: Da JUC ao PCdoB*. São Paulo: Editora Alfa-Omega, 1984.

Loschiavo dos Santos, Maria Cecília, ed. *Maria antônia: uma rua na contramão*. São Paulo: Nobel, 1988.

Love, Joseph L. *Rio Grande do Sul and Brazilian Regionalism, 1882–1930*. Stanford, CA: Stanford University Press, 1971.

Lowenthal, David. "Identity, Heritage and History." *Commemorations: The Politics of National Identity*, ed. John R. Gillis, 41–60. Princeton, NJ: Princeton University Press, 1994.

Machado, Ana Maria. *Tropical Sol da Liberdade: A história dos anos de repressão e da juventude brasileira pós-64 na visão de uma mulher*. Rio de Janeiro: Editora Nova Fronteira, 1988.

Marconi, Paolo. *A Censura Política na Imprensa Brasileira, 1968–1978*. São Paulo: Editora Global, 1980.

Marighela, Carlos. *La Guerra Revolucionaria*. Mexico City: Editorial Diógenes, 1970.

Martins Filho, João Roberto. *Movimento Estudantil e Ditadura Militar 1964–1968*. Campinas: Papirus, 1987.

——, *A Rebelião Estudantil*. Campinas: Mercado de Letras, 1996.

——, ed. *1968 Faz 30 Anos*. Campinas: Editora da Universidade Federal de São Carlos, 1998.

Máximo, João. *João Saldanha: sobre nuvens de fantasia*. Rio de Janeiro: Relame, 2005.

McClintock, Anne. *Imperial Leather: Race, Gender and Sexuality in the Imperial Contest*. New York: Routledge, 1995.

Medina, Cremilda, ed. *1968–1988: nos passos da rebeldia, São Paulo de Perfil*. São Paulo: CJE/ECA/USP, 1989.

Mendes Junior, Antonio. *Movimento Estudantil no Brasil, tudo é história*. São Paulo: Editora Brasiliense, 1981.

Menezes, Paulo. "Heranças de 68: cinema e sexualidade." *Tempo Social* 10, no. 2 (1998): 51–62.

Milanesio, Natalia. "Gender and Generation: The University Reform Movement in Argentina, 1918." *Journal of Social History* 39, no. 2 (2005): 505–29.

Moraes, Dênis de. *A Esquerda e o Golpe de 64: Vinte e cinco anos depois, as forças populares repensam seus mitos, sonhos e ilusoes*. Rio de Janeiro: Espaço e Tempo, 1989.

Murgel Starling, Heloisa Maria. *Os Senhores das Gerais: Os Novos Inconfidentes e o Golpe de 1964*. Petrópolis: Vozes, 1986.

Myhr, Robert O. "The University Student Tradition in Brazil." *Journal of Interamerican and World Affairs* 12, no. 1 (January 1970): 126–40.

Nava, Carmen. "Future Citizens in Public Schools, 1937–1945." *Brazil in the Making: Facets of National Identity*, ed. Carmen Nava and Ludwig Laurehass Jr., 95–118. New York: Rowman and Littlefield, 2006.

Niskier, Arnaldo. *Educação no Brasil: 500 anos de Historia, 1500–2000*. São Paulo: Melhoramentos, 1989.

Nova, Cristiane, and Jorge Nóvoa, eds. *Carlos Marighella: O homem por trás do mito*. São Paulo: UNESP, 1999.

O'Donnell, Guillermo. "Tensions in the Bureaucratic-Authoritarian State and the Question of Democracy." *The New Authoritarianism in Latin America*, ed. David Collier, 285–318. Princeton, NJ: Princeton University Press, 1979.

Oliven, Ruben George. "A Relação Estado e Cultura no Brazil: Cortes ou Continuidade?" *Estado e Cultura no Brasil*, ed. Sergio Miceli, 240. São Paulo: Difel, 1984.

Patarra, Judith Lieblich. *Iara: Reportagem Biográfica*. Rio de Janeiro: Editora Rosa dos Tempos, 1992.

Pauland, Jean-Jacques, and Laurence Wolff. "The Economics of Higher Education." *Opportunity Forgone: Education in Brazil*, ed. Nancy Birdsell and Richard H. Sabot, 532–54. Washington, DC: Inter-American Development Bank, 1996.

Pellicciotta, Mirza Maria Baffi. "Uma aventura política: As movimentações estudantis dos anos 70." MA thesis, Instituto de Filosofia e Ciências Humanas da Universdade Estadual de Campinas, 1997.

Pensado, Jaime. "Political Violence and Student Culture in Mexico: The Consolidation of *Porrismo* during the 1950s and 1960s." PhD diss., University of Chicago, 2008.

Pereira, Anthony W. "Persecution and Farce: The Origins and Transformations of Brazil's Political Trials, 1964–1979." *Latin American Research Review* 33, no. 1 (1998): 43–66.

——. "God, the Devil, and Development in Northeast Brazil." *Praxis: The Fletcher Journal of Development Studies* 15 (1999): 113–36.

Pereira, Isabel. "Rompendo a Reprodução: Educação e movimento estudantil secundarista no Rio de Janeiro 1976–1990." MA thesis, Universidade Estadual do Rio de Janeiro, 1991.

Pinheiro, Dalila, Dimitri Pinheiro, and Eduardo Amaral. "Era uma vez um rei chamado D. João VI . . ." *Caros Amigos* (November 2001): 5–7.

Plank, D. N. *The Means of Our Salvation: Public Education in Brazil, 1930–1995*. Boulder, CO: Westview Press, 1996.

Poerner, Artur José. *O Poder Jovem: Historia da participação política dos estudantes brasileiros*. 2d ed. Rio de Janeiro: Civilização Brasileira, 1979.

Pollak, Michael. "Memória, esquecimento, silêncio." *Estudos Históricos* 2, no. 3 (1989): 3–15.

Portelli, Alessandro. *The Order Has Been Carried Out: History, Memory and Meaning of a Nazi Massacre in Rome*. New York: Palgrave, 2003.

Queiroz, Rachel. *Tantos Anos*. São Paulo: Siciliano, 1998.

Reis Filho, Daniel Aarão. *A Revolução Faltou ao Encontro: Os comunistas no Brasil*. São Paulo: Editora Brasiliense, 1990.

——. "1968: O curto ano de todos os desejos." *Tempo Social* 10, no. 2 (1998): 25–35.

——. *Ditadura militar, esquerdas e sociedade*. Descobrindo o Brasil series edited by Celso Castro. Rio de Janeiro: Jorge Zahar, 2000.

——. "Amnesty, the Reconstruction of Memory and the Art of Forgetting." Paper presented at After the Quincentennial: History, Memory and Nation in Brazil, University of Maryland, March 7 2001.

Reis Filho, Daniel Aarão, and Jair Ferreira de Sá. *Imagens da Revolução: Documentos políticos das organizações clandestinas de esquerda dos anos 1961–1971*. Socialismo Hoje series edited by Maria José Silveira, Felipe Lindoso, and Márcio Souza. Rio de Janeiro: Editora Marco Zero, 1985.

Reis Filho, Daniel Aarão, and Pedro de Moraes. *68: a paixão de uma utopia*. Rio de Janeiro: Fundação Getulio Vargas, 1988.

Ribeiro do Valle, Maria. *1968: O diálogo é a violência: Movimento estudantil e ditadura militar no Brasil*. Campinas: Editora da Unicamp, 1999.

Richardson, John M., Jr. *Partners in Development: An Analysis of AID-University Relations, 1950–1966*. East Lansing: Michigan State University Press, 1969.

Ridenti, Marcelo Siqueira. "As mulheres na política brasileira: Os anos de chumbo." *Tempo Social* 2, no. 2 (1990): 113–28.

——. *O fantasma da revolução brasileira*. São Paulo: Editora da Universidade Estadual Paulista, 1993.

——. "O romantismo revolucionario da Ação Popular: do cristiansimo ao maoismo." Paper presented at the Latin American Studies Association, Chicago, September 24–26, 1998.

——. *Em busca do povo Brasileiro: artistas da revolução, do CPC à era da tv*. Rio de Janeiro: Editora Record, 2000.

Rodrigues da Cruz, Maury. *Antecedentes e Perspectivas da Educação moral e cívica no Brasil*. Curitiba: Editora da Universidade Federal do Paraná, 1982.

Romagnoli, Luiz Henrique, and Tânia Gonçalves. *A Volta da UNE: de Ibiúna a Salvador*. Volume 5 of Coleção História Imediata. São Paulo: Editora Alfa-Ômega, 1979.

Romanelli, Otaíza de Oliveira. *História da Educação no Brasil*. Petrópolis: Editora Vozes, 1978.

Rosas, Clemente. *Praia de Flamengo, 132: Crônica do Movimento Estudantil nos Anos 1961–1962*. Recife: FUNDARPE, 1992.

Rose, R. S. *The Unpast: Elite Violence and Social Control in Brazil, 1954–2000*. Athens: Ohio University Press, 2005.

Sader, Emir. *O anjo torto: esquerda (e direita) no Brasil*. São Paulo: Brasiliense, 1995.

Saldanha de Oliveira, José Alberto. *A Mitologia Estudantil: Uma abordagem sobre o* movimento estudantil Alagoano. Maceió, Sergasa: Secretaria de Comunicação Social do Governo do Estado de Alagoas, 1994.

——. A UNE e o mito do poder jovem. Maceió: EDUFAL, 2005.

Sales, Jean Rodrigues. "A Ação Libertadora Nacional, a revolução Cubana e a luta armada no Brasil." Tempo 14, no. 27 (2008): 199–217.

Salgado de Souza, Maria Inês. Os empresários e a educação: O IPÊS e a política educacional após 1964. Petrópolis: Vozes, 1981.

Sanfelice, José Luis. Movimento Estudantil—A UNE na resistencia ao golpe de 64. São Paulo: Cortez, 1986.

Scheper-Hughes, Nancy. Death without Weeping: The Violence of Everyday Life in Brazil. Berkeley: University of California Press, 1993.

Scherer, Amanda Eloina, Gisele Marchioni Nussbaumer, and Maria da Gloria di Fanti, eds. Utopias e distopias: 30 anos de maio de 68. Santa Maria: Universidade Federal de Santa Maria, 1999.

Schmitter, Phillipe C. "The Persecution of Political and Social Scientists in Brazil." PS, 3, no. 2 (spring 1970): 123–28.

Schwarcz, Lilia Moritz. The Spectacle of the Races: Scientists, Institutions and the Race Question in Brazil, 1870–1930. Toronto: Douglas and McIntyre, 1999.

——, ed. História da Vida Privada no Brasil: Contrastes da intimidade contemporânea, Historia da vida privada no Brasil. São Paulo: Companhia das Letras, 1998.

Scott, James C. Domination and the Arts of Resistance: Hidden Transcripts. New Haven, CT: Yale University Press, 1990.

Seganfreddo, Sonia. UNE: Instrumento de subversão. Rio de Janeiro: Edições GRD, 1963.

Serbin, Kenneth P. "The Anatomy of a Death: Repression, Human Rights and the Case of Alexandre Vannucchi Leme in Authoritarian Brazil." Journal of Latin American Studies 30, no. 1 (1998): 1–33.

——. Secret Dialogues: Church–State Relations, Torture, and Social Justice in Authoritarian Brazil. Pittsburgh: University of Pittsburgh Press, 2000.

Skidmore, Thomas E. The Politics of Military Rule in Brazil, 1954–85. New York: Oxford University Press, 1988.

——. "Failure in Brazil: From Popular Front to Armed Revolt." Journal of Contemporary History 5, no. 3, Popular Fronts (1970): 137–57.

Simões, Inimá. Roteiro da Intolerância: A Censura Cinematográfica no Brasil. São Paulo: Editora SENAC, 1999.

Simões, Solange de Deus. Deus Pátria e Família: As Mulheres no Golpe de 1964. Petrópolis: Vozes, 1985.

Soares, Glaucio Ary Dillon. "Brazil." In Student Political Activism: An International Reference Handbook, ed. Philip G. Altbach, 351–58. New York: Greenwood Press, 1989.

Souza, Maria Inês Salgado de. Os Empresários e a Educação: O IPÊS e a Política Educacional Após 1964. Petrópolis: Vozes, 1981.

Stern, Steve. *Remembering Pinochet's Chile: On the Eve of London, 1998*. Durham: Duke University Press, 2004.

———. *Battling for Hearts and Minds: Memory Struggles in Pinochet's Chile, 1973–1988*. Durham, NC: Duke University Press, 2006.

———. *Reckoning with Pinochet: The Memory Question in Democratic Chile, 1989–2006*. Durham, NC: Duke University Press, 2010.

Sterns, Maurice. "Three Decades of Student Leadership in Brazil, 1933–1965: A Study of the Career Lives of Former Student Leaders." PhD diss., University of Chicago, 1974.

Sturken, Marita. *Tangled Memories: The Vietnam War, the AIDS Epidemic, and the Politics of Remembering*. Berkeley: University of California Press, 1997.

Suri, Jeremi. *Power and Protest: Global Revolution and the Rise of Detente*. Cambridge, MA: Harvard University Press, 2003.

Sussekind de Mendonça, Carlos, ed. *Sensacionalismo*. Rio de Janeiro: Casa do Estudante do Brasil, 1933.

Tavares de Almeida, Maria Hermínia, and Luiz Weis. "Carro-zero e pau-de-arara: o cotidiano da oposição de classe média ao regime militar." *História da Vida Privada no Brasil: Contrastes da intimidade contemporânea*, ed. Lilia Moritz Schwarcz, 319–410. São Paulo: Companhia das Letras, 1998.

União Nacional dos Estudantes. *UNE Histórico: 60 anos a favor do Brasil*. Rio de Janeiro: ANC Comunicação and Marketing, 1997.

Van Aken, Mark J. "University Reform before Córdoba." *Hispanic American Historical Review* 51, no. 3 (August 1971): 447–62.

Varon, Jeremy. *Bringing the War Home: The Weather Underground, the Red Army Faction, and the Revolutionary Violence of the 1960s and 1970s*. Berkeley: University of California Press, 2004.

Vasconcelos, José Gerardo. *Memórias do Silêncio: Militantes de esquerda no Brasil autoritário*. Fortaleza: Edições Universidade Federal do Ceará, 1998.

Vaz Oliveira, Gil Vicente. "Fotojornalismo Subversivo: 1968 revisto pelas lentes do *Correio da Manhã*." *Acervo: Revista do Arquivo Nacional* 11, no. 1/2 (1998): 117–26.

Veiga, Ilma P. Alencastro. *Magisterio: Formação e Trabalho Pedagógico*. Campinas: Papirus, 1991.

Velloso, J., ed. *Universidade pública: Política, desempenho, perspectivas*. Magisterio: Formaçáo e Trabalho Pedagogico. Campinas: SP, Papirus, 1991.

Ventura, Ricardo. "O Instituto Villa-Lobos e a Música Popular." www.brazilianmusic.com (September 4, 2010).

Ventura, Zuenir. *1968, O ano que não terminou: A aventura de uma geração*. Rio de Janeiro: Editora Nova Fronteira, 1988.

———. *1968: O que fizemos de nós*. São Paulo: Editora Planeta, 2008.

Vianna, Deocélia. *Companheiros de Viagem*. São Paulo: Brasiliense, 1984.

Von der Weid, Jean Marc. *Brazil: 1964 to the Present: A Political Analysis: An Interview with Jean Marc von der Weid*. Montreal: Editions Latin America, 1972.

Wallerstein, Immanuel. "1968, Revolution in the World-System." *Geopolitics and Geoculture: Essays on the Changing World-System*, ed. Immanuel Wallerstein, 65–83. Studies in Modern Capitalism. Cambridge: Cambridge University Press.

Williams, Darlye, and Barbara Weinstein. "Vargas Morto: The Death and Life of a Brazilian Statesman." *Body Politics: Death, Dismemberment and Memory in Latin America*, ed. Lyman L. Johnson, 217–316. Albuquerque: University of New Mexico Press, 1994.

Wolfe, Joel. *Working Women, Working Men: São Paulo and the Rise of Brazil's Industrial Working Class, 1900–1955*. Durham, NC: Duke University Press, 1993.

Xavier Ferreira, Elizabeth F. *Mulheres, Militância e Memória*. Rio de Janeiro: Editora Fundação Getulio Vargas, 1996.

——. "O Autoritarismo, a Guerrilha Urbana e a Violência." *Tempo* 1, no. 1 (1996): 142–65.

Zeichner, Natan. "Representing the Vanguard." *Brown Journal of History*, no. 1 (spring 2007): 7–23.

Zerubavel, Eviatar. "Social Memories: Steps to a Sociology of the Past." *Qualitative Sociology* 19, no. 3 (1996): 283–99.

Index

Page numbers in italics indicate illustrations.

Alliance for Progress, 64

ALN. *See* Ação Libertadora Nacional

Alvarez, Sonia E., 84, 169

Alves de Souza, Maria Francisca "Kika," 222–23, 239, 241

Amaral, Roberto, 89

Amaral Peixoto, Ernani do, 128

amnesty, 230, 246, 275n165, 287n64

Andrade de Oliveira, Walmir, 183–84, 185

ANL. *See* Aliança Nacional Libertadora

AP. *See* Ação Popular

APML. *See* Ação Popular Marxista-Leninista

Aprígio de Paula, Jorge, 268n45

Aragon, Bob, 78–79

Araguaia, 217, 231

Aranha, Euclides, 42

Aranha, Oswaldo, 42

Arantes, Aldo, 70–71

Arantes, José, 274n145

Araujo, Clara, 242

Araujo, Maria Paula, 54, 218, 219, 251n28, 252n30

Araújo, Serfim Fernandes de, 128–29

ARENA. *See* Aliança de Renovação Nacional

Argentina: military regime of, 227; university reform movement in (1918), 28–30, 42

Arinos Filho, Afonso, 258n1

armed struggle. *See* clandestine lefts

armed forces. *See* military dictatorship; military forces

Arns, Paulo Evaristo, 209, 210–11

Arruda, Lucidio, 129

Atos Institucionais (AIs): definition, 90; AI-1, 90; AI-2 and AI-3, 103; AI-4, 103; AI-6, AI-7, and AI-8, 174; AI-9 and AI-10, 178; AI-11, 278n35; AI-12, 189; AI-13 and AI-14, 188; AI-15, AI-16, and AI-17, 189

Ato Institucional Número 5 (AI-5): additional restrictive legislation passed under, 173–74; approval of, 162–63, 165; immediate effects of, 167–69, 188–89; as launching coup within a coup, 169, 276n6; political and moral orders linked in, 176–77; revocation of, 230–31; students' activist possibilities closed off by, 16–17, 197–201; students' response to, 194–97; students' understanding of implications, 170–72; subversive activities defined in, 175–77; supplement to (No. 38), 163, 168; torture institutionalized after, 185–86; writing of, 159–60. *See also* laws and decrees

Bahian Law School, 27

Barbosa Guimarães, Genival, 51, 52, 53, 77, 255–56n58

Barros, Nélson, 269n75

Berman, Maria Graça, 223, 224

Bezerra, Gregório, 280n64

Boal, Augusto, 77

Borrul, Estevão Leão, 24, 31

Brasilia: armored tanks in, 162; Che Guevara trip to, 61; construction and inauguration as capital, 67, 253n29, 261n76; fictionalized weather report for, 168, 170; student protests in, 90, 123, 125. *See also* University of Brasilia

Brazilian Congress: closure of, 106, 163, 168, 194; condemnation of police violence from, 241; elections of (1962), 84; diminished powers under AI-1, 91; indirect election of president by, 90, 91, 102–3; Moreira Alves's parliamentary immunity considered in, 159–60, 161–62, 167, 175; president's right to suspend, 162–

coup commemorated by, 107–8

coup d'état of 1964: anniversaries of, 107, 205–7; disputes over date of 88, 261n68; evolution of, 86–91, 261n67; impact on UNE building, 87–89, 234–36, 238; as turning point, 89, 100, 106, 231–32

Couto e Silva, Golbery do, 84, 92

Cowan, Benjamin A., 141, 177, 182, 278n39, 279n46

Cresta, Isolda, 88

Cuba: agrarian reforms in, 63, 65; Revolution in (1959), 64, 68–70. *See also* Castro, Fidel; Guevara, Che

Daniel, Herbert, 101

d'Araujo, Maria Celina, 251n24

D'Arc Pimentel, Olga, 132

DAs. *See* Diretórios Acadêmicos

DCE-Livre, 222, 224, 285n20

DCEs. *See* Diretórios Centrais dos Estudantes

Débray, Regis, 127

democracy: call for restoration of, 162; Guimarães commemorated as defender of, 216–17, 232–33; potential for return to, 217–19; questions about student activism and, 67–68; reflections on return to, 245–48; UNE commitment to, 48–51, 54–55, 56, 58

Departamento de Ordem Política e Social (DOPS, Department of Political and Social Order): alleged undercover agent of, 140; Edson Luis's killing and, 116; fake student associations set up by, 182–83; on international student protests, 129; on March of 100,000, 145–46; student cultural events followed by, 200–202; student identifications by, 174–76; student interrogations and

reports in, 15, 190–92, 267n38; students' fears of, 148; on students' links to clandestine lefts, 155, 157–59, 189–91; torture by, 183–85; UNE building demolition and, 238–39, 240; UNE Congress raided by (1968), 153, 154, 155. *See also* military forces; police; security forces; violence of government

Destacamento de Operação de Informações–Centros de Operações de Defesa Interna (DOI–CODI, Information Operation Detachment–Internal Defense Operations Centers), 186, 208–9, 283n117

O Dia (newspaper), 121

Dirceu, José, 140, 150, 167–68, 187, 246, 270–71n92

Diretório Nacional de Estudantes (DNE, National Student Directorate), 94, 98, 108

Diretórios Acadêmicos (DAs, Academic Directorates), 122, 183–84, 185, 220–21, 284n15

Diretórios Centrais dos Estudantes (DCEs, Central Student Directorates): acronym for, 254n39; attempts to revitalize, 220–21; DCE-Livre as unofficial, 222, 224, 285n20; elections for, 48; leadership of, 138; military regime efforts to circumscribe, 93–94, 98–99, 198, 231; official status of, 34, 37; place within student movement hierarchy, 37; protests of, 118, 130–31, 198; sharing UNE building 45. *See also* Pro-UNE Commission

disappearances, 194, 199, 216–17, 247, 283n1

Dissidências (DI-GB and DI-RJ, Dissidents), 101, 187

distensão, 217–18, 219

Federal Fluminense University (UFF, Universidade Federal Fluminense), 197, 198

Federal Rural University of Pernambuco (Recife), 62

Federal University of Minas Gerais, 30, 96, 221

Federal University of Paraná, 118, 129, 134

Federal University of Pernambuco (Recife), 61–64, 66, 82, 106

Federal University of Rio de Janeiro (Universidade Federal do Rio de Janeiro, UFRJ [earlier University of Rio de Janeiro, 1920–37, then University of Brazil, 1937–65]): attempt to purge faculty at, 178–79; blacklist of, 174; campaign to free incarcerated students and, 161; Castelo Branco booed at, 97; DOPS torture of student of, 183–84, 185; flower offered to police at, 3–4; founding and name changes of, 30–31, 253n29; March 28 commemorations and, 205, 206, 207; student event request from, 200; students arrested at, 129, 134, 195, 203; UNE building space for DCE of, 45

Federal University of Rio Grande do Sul, 203

Feiteiro Cavalari, Rosa Maria, 196

female students: as alleged DOPS agent, 140; arrests of, 153, 154, 155, 271n111; clothing of, 51, 52, 78, 141; coup against Goulart and, 88, 261n71; educating themselves about movement's past, 224; enrollments of, 27, 28, 134–35, 135, 136, 222; home tutoring of, 23; limitations on, 270n85; as movement leaders, 138, 242, 270–71n92; others' response to participation of, 78–79, 137–38;

political opportunities for (1980s), 222–23; as protesters (1968), 132, 133, 134–35, 270n85; in secondary schools, 25–26, 26; sexuality of, 138–41; as UNE Congress attendees, 77–78, 255–56n58; UNE participation of, 22, 52, 257n91; wartime roles delegated to, 45

Ferreira, Catarina Helena, 158–59, 274n157

FEUB. See Federação dos Estudantes Universitários de Brasília

Fico, Carlos, 86, 167, 261n55

Fiel Filho, Manoel, 221–22

Figueira, Antonio, 95

Figueiredo, João Baptista, 217, 231, 234–35

film and movies, 76, 82, 96, 176, 250n12, 280n63

flowers, 3–4, 113–14, 115, 117, 120, 151, 202, 203

Flying UNE, 77

Folha de São Paulo (newspaper), 232, 250n12, 288n79

Ford Motor Company, 186

foreign investment, 67, 186, 198

Forum of University Rectors, 94

Franca, Antonio, 42

France: Brazilian security discussions with, 172–73; student protests in, 127–28, 129, 131, 142, 143, 147

Franco, Itamar, 242

Freire, Paulo, 71–72, 74, 75

Frejat, José, 49

Frente Ampla (Broad front), 103

Frente Unida de Estudantes do Calabouço (FUEC, United Front of Calabouço Students), 111–13, 116, 121

Friede, Hermínio Affonso, 180–81

FUEC. See Frente Unida de Estudantes do Calabouço

100,000, 144–45; on police attacks and student responses, 124–26, 132, 134, 137; on potential resurgence of student actions, 160–61; prohibitions on, 162; right-wing attacks on, 149; on sexual revolution, 141; on Sílvia, 158; on student prosecutions, 175; students' mobilization of, 104–5, 130–31; on UNE Congress (1968), 153, 155; on worldwide student activism, 127–29, 142, 147. *See also* censorship

Médici, Emílio Garrastazu, 160, 182, 188, 189, 198, 204, 217, 247

Meira Mattos, Carlos de, 106

Meira Mattos Commission, 105–6, 134

Meireles, Heli Lopes, 153, 155, 157

Meloni, Catarina, 138, 140, 270–71n92

Melo Franco, Afrânio de, 38

memory: approaches to studying, 5, 10–11, 14, 17, 171–72, 250–51n21; Edson Luis as touchpoint in, 118, 120, 171, 205–8, 212–13, 214, 226–27; of "1968," 109, 170–72, 246–48; "knots" of, 212; of militancy and martyrdom, 216–17; of military officials, 169, 190–93, 202, 213–14; student activists' appeals to, 13, 97–98, 206, 221–22, 224–29. *See also* Guimarães, Honestino; Leme, Alexandre Vannucchi; Lima Souto, Edson Luis de; UNE building

Mendes, Antônio, Jr., 234

Mexico: oil production nationalized in, 49; student protests in, 9, 28, 225

Milanesio, Natalia, 30

military forces: campaign in Canudos (Bahia, 1890s), 26–27; Vargas removed by, 47, 48, 90. *See also* Departamento de Ordem Política e Social; military dictatorship; police; security forces; violence of government

military police inquiries. *See* inquéritos policiais militares

military regime (1964–85): approach to studying, 11–12; crackdown on students and universities, 91–99; *distensão* period of, 217–19; economic failings of, 102–3; Edson Luis's death as opportunity to criticize, 120–21, 123; faculty purges of, 96–97, 178–79; hard-liner ascendance within, 7, 159–63, 165, 217, 250n12; on international student protests, 129–30; junta takeover of, 188–89, 278n45; March 28 commemorations as highlighting, 205–8; paternalistic rhetoric of, 179–83; political divides preceding and during, 6, 109; protest song in context of, 1–5, 148, 149; public relations campaigns of, 198; scholarship on, 12, 251n24, 251n27; students' labeling as dictatorship, 95, 103–4, 114, 195, 206; UNE building's burning merged with beginning of, 235–36, 288n74. *See also* AI-5; coup d'état of 1964; police; repression; security forces; Supreme Revolutionary Command; torture; violence of government

Minas Gerais: Federal University of, 30–31, 96, 221; protests of Edson Luis's death in, 123; UNE Congress held in, 103–4

Ministério de Educação (MEC, Ministry of Education), 31–32, 43, 99–100, 174, 223–24, 230, 231

Moniz de Aragão, Raymundo Augusto de Castro, 178

Monteiro Bezerra, Paulo César, 157–58

Moreira Alves, Márcio: exile of, 168; parliamentary immunity questioned, 159–60, 161–62, 167, 175; torture exposé of, 104–5

Popular Action (*cont.*)
sages advanced in, 200–202; student activists' uses of, 75–77; World Cup win and, 198. *See also* "Caminhando"; theater
Popular Revolutionary Vanguard. *See* Vanguarda Popular Revolucionaria
Portella, Eduardo, 230
O Povo Canta (The people sing, album), 77
Praia de Flamengo, 132. *See also* UNE building
Prestes, Luis Carlos, 37–38, 46, 255n51
Projeto Rondon, 180–82
Pro-UNE Commission, 224, 225, 226–27, 230–32, 233
PSB. *See* Partido Socialista Brasileiro
PSD. *See* Partido Social Democrático
PTB. *See* Partido Trabalhista Brasileiro
PUC. *See* Pontifical Catholic University

Quadros, Jânio, 61, 63, 68
Queirós Carneiro de Mendonça, Ana Amélia, 34, 39–40, 41
Queiroz, Rachel, 254n41

racial inequalities, 25–26, 30
racial privilege, 31, 41
Rademaker Grunewald, Augusto, 90
Ramalho, Raimunda, 256n60, 257n91
Rebelo, Aldo, 5, 219, 224, 284n10
Recife: Celia Guevara's speech in, 61–63, 64, 66, 82, 106; commemorations in, 227; coup against Goulart and killings in, 90, 262n80; student killed at anti-Vargas rally in, 47–48; student protests resumed in, 155
Recife Law School (earlier in Olinda), 24, 253n11
Reis, Rangel, 181
Reis Filho, Daniel Aarão, 15, 80, 93, 104, 247, 250n15

Remy Gillet, Nelson, 191
repression: dialectics of, 109–10, 131–32, 143, 164–65; military's collective memory of 1968 and, 169, 190–93; military's heightened use of, 172–87; student mobilization in face of, 123–26, 148–49. *See also* AI-5; censorship; military regime; violence of government
Resende, Helenira, 138, 271n92
Resistência (magazine), 195, 280–81n75
Resistência Democrática, 46–47
Revista Brasiliense (magazine), 77
Ribas, Antônio Guilherme Ribeiro, 167–68, 276n4
Ribeiro, Maria Augusta Carneiro, 139, 153, 168, 187
Ribeiro, Sylvio Wanick, 51
Ribeiro do Valle, Maria, 116, 131–32, 268n48
Richopo, Neide, 208, 283n117
Ridenti, Marcelo Siqueira, 65, 68, 148, 197
right-wing groups: goals of, 82–85; during *distensão*, 217; Mackenzie students' alleged link to, 149–50; public acts of violence, 149. *See also* military regime; *and specific organizations*
Rio de Janeiro: army troops occupying streets of, 149; bank robberies in, 157–59, 274n157; Candelária Cathedral of, 124, 124; March of 50,000 in, 146, 146–47; March of 100,000 in, 144–46, 145, 148; new building for UNE in, 242; Portuguese royal court in, 23; student guide to, 19; student protests in (1979), 231; student protests resumed in, 155, 156, 157; student-public-police skirmishes in, 143–44, 144; tram fare increases protested, 53, 67. *See also* Calabouço

(restaurant); Federal University of Rio de Janeiro; UNE building
Rio de Janeiro Law School, 35, 90, 102, 261n78
Rockefeller, Nelson, 183–85, 215
Roda Viva (play), 149
Rodrigues, Humberto, 95
Rogers, Helen Jean, 54–55, 258n98
Romeiro dos Santos, Teodomiro, 188
Rondon, Cândido, 180
Roosevelt, Franklin D., 44, 54
Rousseff, Dilma, 246
rumo (magazine), 35
rural and urban workers, 32, 66, 71, 77, 207, 218, 226. See also peasant leagues

Sáenz Peña law (Argentina), 29, 30
Salles, Ricardo, 197, 198
Salvador da Bahia: cátedra in surgery in, 23; student blacklists in, 174; student protests of bus fare increases in, 147–48
Sant'Anna, Irum, 40, 255n48, 256n67
Santillo, Henrique, 230
São Paulo: automobile industry in, 67; bank robberies in, 158; confrontation between universities in, 149–50, 151; student protests and commemorations in (1977), 225–28, 286n38. See also São Paulo Law School, University of São Paulo
São Paulo Law School, 24, 26–27
Sarney, José, 242
Sarno, José Fidelis, 102, 103
Schwarcz, Lilia Moritz, 24, 252n5
Schwartz, Mark Barry, 250–51n21
Scientific Meeting for Medical Students. See Encontro Científico de Estudantes de Medicina
secondary schooling: enrollments in, 25–26, 26, 72, 72, in Argentina, 29;

scarcity of, 25, 117–18; two-track system eliminated, 31–32; for women, 25, 26
secondary students: attrition from student activism, 218; and the Calabouço, 107, 111; joining clandestine lefts, 101; and memory, 224, 227; union of (UBES), 69. See also Brito, Elinor; Gradel, José; Joffily, Bernardo; Lima Souto, Edson Luis de; Ribeiro Ribas, Antônio Guilherme
security forces: assumptions about clandestine lefts and student groups, 110; attempts to discredit student protests, 123; collective memories of, 169, 190–93; discussions with other countries, 172–73; intelligence divisions in, 92; interviews of officials, 251n24; March 28 concerns of, 207–8; moral panic of, 177; nicknamed gorillas, 206; response to protest after Celia Guevara's speech, 62, 63–64; undercover agents of, 177–78, 206–7. See also Departamento de Ordem Política e Social; military regime; police; violence of government
Serbin, Kenneth P., 208, 210, 251n28, 283n117
Serra, Antônio Amaral, 80–81, 99, 102, 120
Serra, José, 92–93, 232, 246, 247, 248
Serviço Nacional de Informações (SNI, National Information Service), 92
Setembrada (events), 105
sexual behavior: experimentations with premarital sex, 4; foreign influences alleged in, 140–41; military's paternalistic rhetoric about, 179–80, 278n39; relationships and double standards of, 138–40; subversion linked to, 176–77, 179, 182, 279n46

and, 208–13; media mobilized in, 104–5; military monitoring of, 177–78; *tendências* and, 219, 220, 223. *See also* Ação Popular; Juventude Universitária Católica; União Nacional dos Estudantes

student organizations: abolishment of, 98–99; AI-5's effects on, 194–201; connections to clandestine lefts, 197; constraints on, 175–76, 198; early facilities provided for, 27; fake, created by military, 182–83; hierarchical structure of, 36–37; leadership of, 190; mandated by Vargas, 32–34; official recognition of, 43–44; recreation of, 201, 221–24, 224–29 political authority of, 194, 196, 213. *See also* União Nacional dos Estudantes; *specific groups*

Sturken, Marita, 237

subversion, 175–79, 207, 279n46. *See also* repression; violence of government

suffrage, 25, 30, 41, 71

Suplicy de Lacerda, Flávio, 93–97, 129

Suplicy Law, 93–99, 222

Supreme Court, 167, 174

Supreme Revolutionary Command, 90–92, 103

Suri, Jeremi, 9

Talarico, José Gomes de, 40, 41–42, 257n83

Tavares de Almeida, Maria Hermínia, 139, 288n74

Távora, Fernandes, 63

Teatro de Arena (São Paulo), 76

tendências políticas, 219, 220, 223

Tenentes Revolt (1920s), 37–38

theater, 76, 77, 149, 201–2

Time magazine, 8–9, 63

Tinoco, Brígido, 62, 63

torture: efforts to halt, 203; protests against, 202, 206; of students, 208, 215

transnational dimensions of 1968, 10, 127, 173, 276n13

Travassos, Luís, 105, 130, 138, 167–68, 187–88, 280n64

Tribuna da Imprensa (newspaper), 53, 55

UDN. *See* União Democrática Nacional

UEE. *See* União Estadual de Estudantes

UFF. *See* Universidade Federal Fluminense

UFRJ. *See* Universidade Federal do Rio de Janeiro

Ultragás (company), 186

UME. *See* União Metropolitana de Estudantes

UNE. *See* União Nacional dos Estudantes

UNE building: as antidictatorship symbol, 216–17, 232, 234; attacks on and burning of, 85, 88–89, 89, 235–36, 288n74; commemoration at site of, 242, 245–46; demolition of, 237–39, 240; formality of, 47; given to students, 45–46, 257n83; hopes to reclaim, 95; indemnity payment and reconstruction of, 246; Edson Luis's funeral and, 121–22, 122, 267n39; original use of, 20–21; Resistência Democrática meeting at, 46–47; shared with other organizations, 98; as site of memory, 235–37, 238, 239, 241–42; students' occupations of, 155, 157, 175, 234; students' return to (1980), 234–35, 235, 237–38; as symbol of authority of, 19–20, 20, 52–53, 56, 57, 58; theater in, 77, 87

UNE congresses: of 1938, 39–42, 255n48, 256n59; of 1942, 45–46; of 1948, 52, 255–56n58; of 1951, 19–

Vanguarda Popular Revolucionaria (VPR, Popular Revolutionary Vanguard), 141–42

Vargas, Getúlio: building given to UNE, 45–46, 257n83; military's removal of, 47, 48, 90; opposition to, 46–51, 54, 55–56; political disarray after death of, 67–68; relationship to students and universities, 21, 31–32; return to presidency (1951), 54; student movement tolerated by, 41–42; student organizing mandated by, 32–34; suicide of, 55; on UNE, 36–38, 43–44. See also Estado Novo

Varneiro, Ferdy, 236

Vasconcelos, Cléa, 266–67n22

Vaz, Rubens Florentino, 55

Veja (magazine), 129, 130

Veloso, Caetano, 272n125

Ventura, Zuenir, 139, 167

Vereza, Carlos, 88

Vianna, Luis Werneck, 88

Vieira Pinto, Álvaro, 74

Vietnam War, 127

violence of government: AI-5 as license for, 168–69; arrests, torture, and killings after military takeover, 91–92, 104–5, 131, 183–84, 185, 262n90; continued centrality of torture and murder, 185–87, 189, 190, 193, 199, 203, 206, 208–11, 215–16, 221–22, 227; as dialectical force, 7; increased, after ban on protests, 147–48; March 28 commemorations as highlighting, 205–8; as mobilizing dynamic (collective self-sacrifice), 125–26, 268n48; plan for, 172–73;

students' sworn statements gathered via, 190–92; threats of, 146–47, 230–31; in UNE attacks, 85. See also Departamento de Ordem Política e Social; police; repression; security forces

violence of students: debates about, 2–4, 142, 148–49, 164–65; emergence of, 126–27, 131–32, 134; objects thrown in, 132, 133

von der Weid, Jean Marc: in absentia conviction of, 175; arrest and torture of, 187–88, 199, 206; escape from police, 273–74n145; hunt for, 183; personal collection of, 15; prisoner exchange for, 189; as UNE leader, 196, 215

voting, 25, 30, 41, 71

VPR. See Vanguarda Popular Revolucionaria

Wallerstein, Immanuel, 9

Weis, Luiz, 139, 288n74

West Germany, student protests in, 127

women: "boycott of militarism" suggested to, 159; as faculty members, 138; right-wing organization of, 84; UNE's abandonment of issues related to, 39–40. See also female students; gender

Women's Campaign for Democracy. See Campanha da Mulher pela Democracia

World War I, 35

World War II, 21, 22, 37, 38, 43, 44

Zeichner, Natan, 226